JOINING TOGETHER
Group Theory
and Group Skills

DAVID W. JOHNSON
University of Minnesota

FRANK P. JOHNSON
University of Maryland

PRENTICE-HALL, INC., *Englewood Cliffs, New Jersey*

Library of Congress Cataloging in Publication Data

Johnson, David W.
    Joining together.

    1. Social groups. 2. Leadership. 3. Group
relations training. I. Johnson, Frank P.,
joint author. II. Title.
HM131.J613   301.18'5   74-23698
ISBN 0-13-510388-6
ISBN 0-13-510370-3 pbk.

● 1975 by Prentice-Hall, Inc.,
Englewood Cliffs, New Jersey

Printed in the United States of America

10 9 8 7 6 5

Prentice-Hall, International, Inc., *London*
Prentice-Hall of Australia, Pty. Ltd., *Sidney*
Prentice-Hall of Canada, Ltd., *Toronto*
Prentice-Hall of India Private Limited, *New Delhi*
Prentice-Hall of Japan, Inc., *Tokyo*

This book is dedicated to our parents,
who created the basic group
to which we first belonged.

Contents

PREFACE   *ix*

1   INTRODUCTION   *1*

Importance of Groups   Effective Groups and Effective Group Skills
Learning Group Skills   Experiential Learning and Motivation   Role Playing
Process Observation   Yourself as a Group Member   Learning Contract

2   LEADERSHIP   *17*

Understanding Your Leadership Behavior   Approaches to Leadership
Distributed Functions Theory of Leadership   Your Leadership Behavior   Matching Exercise 1
Matching Exercise 2   Selecting a Color Exercise   Survival at Sea Exercise
Hollow Square Exercise   Vietnam Negotiation Exercise   Tower Building Exercise
Encouraging Participation Exercise   Importance of Maintenance Functions   Process Observer
Assumptions about Group Members Exercise   Leader Attitudes Survey
Theory X and Theory Y   Interpersonal Patterns Exercise   Other Leadership Exercises
Situational Theory of Leadership   Interaction Process Analysis   Your Leadership Behavior
Your Leadership Philosophy   Checklist of Skills   Answers

3   DECISION MAKING   *55*

Introduction   Your Decision-Making Behavior   Effective Decision   Methods of Decision Making
Method and Effectiveness   Survival in the Winter Exercise
Other Similar Decision-Making Exercises   Wrecked on the Moon   Grievances of Black Citizens
Hazard Potentials of Some Common Drugs   Bean Jar Exercise
Individual Versus Group Decision Making   Involvement in Decision Making

Strengths and Limitations of Decision-Making Methods   Time and Decision Method
Feelings, Conflict, and Decisions
Summary Table, Advantages and Disadvantages of Decision-Making Methods
Questionnaire on Decision Making   Implementing Your Decision Exercise
My Decision-Making Behavior   Checklist of Skills   Answers

4   GROUP GOALS   *87*

The What and Why of Group Goals   Your Goal-Related Behavior   Hidden Agendas Exercise
Individual Members' Goals and Group Goals   Broken Squares Exercises
The Million Dollar Gift Exercise   Goal Structure
Summary Tables: Effects of Cooperation and Competition on Problem-Solving Groups
Clear and Unclear Goals Exercise   Operational and Clear Goals
Aspects of Effective Group Goals   Helping Groups Set Effective Goals   Identifying Group Goals
Your Goal-Related Behavior   Checklist of Skills   Answers

5   COMMUNICATION WITHIN GROUPS   *109*

Introduction and Definitions   Your Communication Behavior
Interpersonal Versus Group Communication   Sending Messages Effectively
Receiving Messages Effectively   Bewise College Exercise   Energy International Exercise
Distributed Information Exercise   Murder Mystery Exercise
Communicating Information for Problem Solving
Patterns of Communication among Group Members   Effects of Competition on Communication
Physical Barriers to Communication   Transmission of Information Exercise
Communication Within an Authority Hierarchy
Informal Communication Networks and Opinion Leaders
Effects on the Message of a One-Way Procedure   Group Observation
Norms and Communication Exercise   Circle Exercise   Taking a Survey
Improving Communication among Group Members   Your Communication Behavior
Checklist of Skills   Answers

6   CONTROVERSY AND CREATIVITY   *139*

Introduction   Nature of Controversy   Your Behavior in Controversies
Stranded in the Desert Exercise   Constructive Controversy Checklist   Discussion Questions
Faculty Meeting Exercise   Things I Value Exercise   Value of Controversy
"Win-Lose" Versus Problem-Solving Orientation   Values and Beliefs   Norms and Rules
Avoiding Controversies Exercise   Constructive and Destructive Controversy   Creativity
Brainstorming   Brainstorming Exercises   Methods of Generating New Ideas   Creativity Problem
The Joe Doddlebug Problem   Open and Closed Mindedness   Baseball Team Exercise
Creativity Warm-Ups   Your Behavior in Controversies   Checklist of Skills   Answers

7 CONFLICTS OF INTEREST *171*

What Are Conflicts of Interest? Interpersonal Conflict Skills Your Conflict Behavior
Group Member Excellence Exercise Negotiation Exercise Definition of Negotiation
Goals of Negotiation The Negotiation Relationship Strategies of Negotiation
The Use of Role Reversal Feelings of Rejection Exercise Feelings of Distrust Exercise
Breaking Balloons Exercise Intergroup Conflict Exercise Battleship Exercise
Other Intergroup Conflict Exercises Intergroup Conflict
Intergroup Confrontation: Blake and Mouton Union Management Exercise
Intergroup Confrontation: Beckhard Constructive Management of Conflict of Interests
Your Conflict Behavior Checklist of Skills Answers

8 THE USE OF POWER *203*

Your Power-Oriented Behavior Personal Power and Personal Goal Accomplishment
Determining Your Personal Goals Determining Your Personal Resources
Determining Your Needed Coalitions Contracting Help with Your Goals
Discussion of Personal Power and Personal Goal Accomplishment Bases of Power
Unequal Resources Exercise Power Politics Exercise Power and Problem Solving
Power to the Animals Exercise Unequal Power The Seventeen Girls Exercise
Campus Development Exercise Group Power Exercise
Dominance and Submissiveness Exercise Power Fantasy Low Power Fantasy Picture Exercise
Power and Conflict Your Power Behavior Checklist of Skills Answers

9 COHESION AND NORMS *233*

Your Cohesion Behavior Member Needs and Group Development Exercise
Inclusion, Control, and Affection Inclusion Exercise 1 Inclusion Exercise 2
Affection Exercises Control Exercise 1 Control Exercise 2 Cohesion Exercise 1
Cohesion Exercise 2 Cohesion Exercise 3 Cohesion Exercise 4 Your Trust-Building Behavior
My Group Behavior Expressing Support Exercise Developing and Maintaining Trust
Group Norms Norm Exercise 1 Norm Exercise 2 Norms and Power
Implementation of Group Norms Your Cohesion Behavior Checklist of Skills Answers

10 PROBLEM SOLVING *275*

Your Problem-Solving Behavior Five Steps in Problem Solving Defining the Problem
Diagnosing the Problem A Problem-Diagnosis Program Formulating Alternative Strategies
Deciding Upon and Implementing a Strategy Evaluating the Sucess of Strategies
Blocks to Problem-Solving Effectiveness Groupthink and ProblemSolving Climate
Group Membership Your Problem-Solving Behavior Checklist of Skills Answers

11   LEADING DISCUSSION GROUPS *277*

Nature of a Discussion Group   Necessity of Group Skills
Basic Procedure for Discussion Groups   Characteristics of Productive Discussion Groups
Required Member Behaviors   Discussion Leader or Coordinator

12   LEADING GROWTH GROUPS *287*

Introduction   Goals   Leading a Growth Group   Becoming a Facilitator
Feelings, Intuition, and Conceptual Frameworks

13   TEAM BUILDING *299*

Feedback Exercise   Feedback Questions   Beginning a New Team Exercise

EPILOGUE

Terminating a Group   Self-Contract

APPENDIX A   CONDUCTING SKILL-TRAINING EXERCISES *309*

APPENDIX B   ETHICS OF EXPERIENTIAL LEARNING *314*

APPENDIX C   HOW TO COMPUTE A GROUP AVERAGE *316*

APPENDIX D   ANSWERS *317*

APPENDIX E   EXERCISE MATERIALS *332*

REFERENCES *467*

Preface

Joining Together seeks to provide the theory and experiences necessary to develop an understanding of group dynamics and effective group skills. It is more than a book reviewing current social psychological knowledge in the area of small groups, and it is more than a book of group exercises. The theory and exercises are integrated into an inquiry or experiential approach to learning about the dynamics of small groups.

The authors wish to thank many people for their help in writing this book and in preparing the manuscript. Our younger sister, Edythe Johnson Holubec, contributed most of the questions the reader will find in the text. Special thanks go to our brother-in-law Buddy Holubec who, at great personal risk, made Edythe get up at 6:30 a.m. every morning so she could do the preliminary editing of the manuscript. We owe much to the social psychologists who have influenced our theorizing and to the colleagues with whom we have conducted various types of laboratory-training experiences. We have tried to acknowledge sources of the exercises included in this book whenever possible. Some of the exercises presented are so commonly used that the originators are not traceable. If we have inadvertently missed giving recognition to anyone, we apologize. Special thanks are extended to our wives, Linda Mulholland Johnson and Jane Johnson, who contributed their support to the development and writing of this book. All photographs were taken by David W. Johnson and Thomas Allen.

D. W. J.
F. P. J.

1

Introduction

IMPORTANCE OF GROUPS

Groups are incalculably important in the life of every human being. And skills in group functioning are vital to all of us. Belonging to groups is the most important aspect of your life. The quality of your life depends upon the effectiveness of the groups to which you belong, and this effectiveness is largely determined by your personal group skills and knowledge of group processes. This book, therefore, has two purposes: to provide you with a systematic analysis of group effectiveness and to describe a variety of exercises in which you can participate to develop competent group skills.

Why are groups so important? As humans we are social animals and have an inherent social nature. It is not in our nature to live alone. We are born into a group called the family and would not survive the first few minutes, the first few weeks, or the first few years of our lives without membership in this group. Our personal survival as well as the survival of our species has always been linked to the interrelationships formed among human beings. It is within the family and peer groups that we are socialized into ways of behaving and thinking, educated, and taught to have a certain outlook on the world and ourselves. Our personal identity is derived from the way in which we are perceived and treated by other members of our groups. Almost all of our time is spent interacting in groups; we are educated in groups, we work in groups, we worship in groups, we play in groups. Our whole life is spent in a variety of group memberships. Even our species identity as a human is developed in our interactions with others within groups. What makes us human is the way in which we interact with other persons, and we learn how to interact within the groups in which we are socialized and educated. At all stages of our lives we *need* to belong to groups.

Many of our goals can be achieved only with the cooperation and coordination of others. The pooling of resources to accomplish common objectives results in advantages for each group member that he or she could never enjoy through individual action. The history of mankind is the history of organized groups created to obtain mutual benefits and to find ways of improving the quality of life and satisfying the needs of members. It is the productivity resulting from effective groups that makes the development of group skills one of the most essential aspects of our education. An efficient and effective group is the best friend you will ever have.

Finally, our psychological health depends upon our group memberships. *Psychological health* is the ability to be aware of and manage effectively our relationships with other people. Psychological illness is reflected in difficulties in interpersonal relationships. It is through socialization into our family and peer groups that the social competencies necessary for psychological health are developed. It is through memberships in productive and cohesive groups that psychological health is maintained throughout our lives.

What is a group? How do you tell when you are a member of a group? If you are interacting with other persons to satisfy some need or to accomplish some goal and there is a mutual recognition of who does and does not belong in the activities, you are a member of a group. A *group* is a collection of persons in face-to-face interaction, each person aware of his own membership, each aware of the membership of others, and each getting some satisfaction from participating in the activities taking place. Under this definition, are you at this moment a member of a group?

In this book we focus on groups that have defined goals and use a problem-solving process to achieve them. Of course these goal-directed, problem-solving groups are not the only collections of persons that fit the concept *group*, but they are probably the most commonly recognized example of a group. Such groups are based upon the cooperative interdependence among members wherein each relies upon the others to help accomplish mutually desired goals. Thus, for our purposes a group can be defined as a collection of persons who are in cooperative, face-to-face interaction, each aware of his or her own membership in the group, each aware of the others who belong in the group, and each getting some satisfaction from participating in the group's activities.

EFFECTIVE GROUPS AND EFFECTIVE GROUP SKILLS

This is not a book that you can read detachedly. This book is written to involve you with its contents. Ideally you will master the theoretical and empirical knowledge now available in the social psychology of group behavior by reading this book. Yet ideally this book will also help you to master the skills necessary to apply this knowledge in practical ways within the groups to which you belong. Our society is presently in a crisis over the failure to teach what we know about interaction among persons in ways that promote the application of this knowledge to everyday situations. Often those who are concerned with teaching others how to behave do not pay close attention to current knowledge, and those concentrating upon validating theory, through research, do not pay close attention to applying their knowledge to practical situations. The knowledge about effective groups and the actual behavior of many people in groups are divided. We shall try in this book to directly apply existing information on the social psychology of groups to the practicing of effective group skills. Through the combined presentation of skill building exercises, diagnostic procedures to assess current skill levels, and discussions of valid knowledge in the areas covered, the bridges between etween and practice are directly drawn.

To be an effective group member, you need a conceptualization, or idea, of group effectiveness and an understanding of how your behavior can contribute to this effectiveness. Any effective group has three core activities: (1) accomplishing its goals, (2) maintaining itself internally, and (3) developing and changing in ways that improve its effectiveness. A successful group has the quality and kind of interaction among members that integrates these three core activities. Group members must have the skills to eliminate barriers to the accomplishment of the group's goals, to solve problems in maintaining high quality interaction among group members, and to overcome obstacles to developing a more effective group.

There are several dimensions, or characteristics, of group effectiveness that pertain to these three core activities, and together they make up a model that can be used to evaluate how well the group is functioning. This model gives a sense of direction to the building of a productive group by stating what, ideally, the group would like to be. By being aware of the difference between the ideal model and the way which the group is functioning, group members are motivated to improve group effectiveness. These dimensions, discussed in detail in later chapters, are as follows:

1. Group goals must be clearly understood, be relevant to the needs of group members, stimulate cooperation, and evoke from every member a high level of commitment to their accomplishment.

2. Group members must communicate their ideas and feelings accurately and clearly. Effective, two-way communication is the basis of all group functioning and the interaction of its members.

3. Participation and leadership must be distributed among members. All should participate, all should be listened to; as leadership needs arise, members should take turns meeting them. Any member should feel free to fulfill a leadership function as he or she sees the need. The equalization of participation and leadership is necessary to make certain that all members are involved in and satisfied with the group, and that all are committed to putting into practice the decisions made by the group. It also assures that the resources of every member are fully used, and it increases the togetherness or cohesiveness of the group.

4. Appropriate decision-making procedures must be used flexibly in order to match them with the needs of the situation. There must be a balance between the availability of time and resources (such as members' skills) and the method of decision making used. Another balance must be struck between the size and seriousness of the decision, the commitment needed to put it into practice, and

the method used for making the decision. The most effective way of making a decision, of course, is by consensus (everyone agrees); consensus promotes distributed participation, the equalization of power, productive controversy, cohesion, involvement, and commitment.

5. Power and influence need to be equal throughout the group and be based on expertise, ability, and access to information, not on authority. Coalitions to help fulfill personal goals should be formed among group members on the basis of mutual influence and interdependence.

6. Conflicts among those with opposing opinions and ideas are to be encouraged; conflicts promote involvement in the group, quality and creativity in decision making, and commitment to putting decisions into practice. Minority opinions should be accepted and used. Conflicts prompted by incompatible needs or goals, by the scarcity of a resource (power or money), and by competitiveness must be negotiated in a manner that is mutually satisfying and does not weaken cooperative interdependence among group members.

7. Group cohesion needs to be at a high level. Cohesion is related to interpersonal attraction among members, each members' desire to continue as part of the group, the members' satisfaction with and liking for their group membership, and the level of acceptance, support, and trust among the members. Group norms supporting psychological safety, individuality, creativeness, conflicts among ideas, and growth and change need to be encouraged.

8. Adequacy in problem solving needs to be high. Problems must be resolved with minimal energy and in a way that eliminates them permanently. Structures and procedures should exist for sensing the existence of problems, inventing and putting into practice possible solutions, and evaluating the effectiveness of the solutions. When problems are dealt with adequately, the problem-solving ability of the group is increased, innovation is encouraged, and the group effectiveness is improved.

9. The interpersonal effectiveness of members needs to be high. Interpersonal effectiveness relates to how well the consequences of your behavior matches your intentions. Johnson (1972) has focused upon this subject, and, therefore, it will not be discussed at length in this book.

The aspects of group effectiveness (Figure 1.1) are covered in the following chapters, each aspect being in a separate chapter. Building effective work groups and leading discussion and growth groups are then briefly covered in later chapters. Specific instructions for people leading skill exercises are included in the appendices.

Because an experiential approach to learning about group theory and to developing group skills is taken in this book it is necessary to explain what is meant by experiential learning, how it relates to skill learning, and what motivates students to learn experientially. The next three sections of this chapter focus on these topics. Role playing and the use of observation procedures are then discussed as two important aspects of experiential learning. The chapter concludes with a procedure for you to reflect on your behavior in groups and with a learning contract for you to sign.

FIGURE 1.1 Comparison Between Effective and Ineffective Groups

Effective groups	*Ineffective groups*
Goals are clarified and changed to give the best possible match between individual goals and the group's goals; goals are cooperatively structured.	Members accept imposed goals; goals are competitively structured.
Communication is two-way and the open and accurate expression of both ideas and feelings is emphasized.	Communication is one-way and only ideas are expressed; feelings are suppressed or ignored.
Participation and leadership are distributed among all group members; goal accomplishment, interval maintenance, and developmental change are underscored.	Leadership is delegated and based upon authority; membership participation is unequal with high-authority members dominating; only goal accomplishment is emphasized.
Ability and information determine influence and power; contracts are built to make sure the individual goals and needs are fulfilled; power is equalized and shared.	Position determines influence and power; power is concentrated in the authority positions; obedience to authority is the rule.
Decision-making procedures are matched with the situation; different methods are used at different times; consensus is sought for important decisions; involvement and group discussions are encouraged.	Decisions are always made by the highest authority with little group discussion; members' involvement is minimal.
Controversy and conflict are seen as positive keys to members' involvement, the quality and originality of decisions, and the continuance of the group in good working condition.	Controversy and conflict are ignored, denied, avoided, or suppressed.
Interpersonal group and intergroup behavior are stressed; cohesion is advanced through high levels of inclusion, affection, acceptance, support, and trust. Individuality is endorsed.	The functions performed by members are emphasized; cohesion is ignored and members are controlled by force. Rigid conformity is promoted.
Problem-solving adequacy is high.	Problem-solving adequacy is low.
Members evaluate the effectiveness of the group and decide how to improve its functioning; goal accomplishment, internal maintenance, and development are all considered important.	The highest authority evaluates the group's effectiveness and decides how goal accomplishment may be improved; internal maintenance and development are ignored as much as possible; stability is affirmed.
Interpersonal effectiveness, self-actualization, and innovation are encouraged.	"Organizational persons" who desire order, stability, and structure are encouraged.

WHAT IS EXPERIENTIAL LEARNING?

We all learn from our experiences. By touching a hot stove we learn to avoid heated objects. By dating we learn about male-female relationships. By being in a family we learn about family life. By giving his younger sister all his used furniture (and having her sell it at exorbitant prices and keeping the money) one of the authors learned about being conned! Everyday we have experiences we learn from. In fact, education is often defined as changes in behavior caused by experience. Certainly many things about relating to other people can only be learned by experience. Reading a book about marriage is not the same as directly experiencing marriage! Hearing a lecture about love is not the same as learning about love through experience! Experiential learning is one of the most pervasive aspects of our lives.

The use of experiential procedures to learn about behavior in groups was greatly influenced by the personal style and theories of the famous social psychologist Kurt Lewin. Lewin's colleagues and students have been the chief promoters of experiential learning in the area of group theory and group skills. One of Lewin's tendencies was to discover valuable concepts and principles from observing his own experiences and the experiences of others. The most trivial experience, the most casual comment, might spark a thought in Lewin's mind that would result in a new theoretical breakthrough in the social psychology of groups and interpersonal relations. Those associating with him never knew when an important discovery would be made and this gave their association with Lewin an excitement rare in a relationship with a professor or teacher. Students and colleagues learned from Lewin how important it is to examine their own experiences for potential principles about the way in which groups develop and work effectively. Thus, Lewin's personal style focused upon experiential learning.

Much of Lewin's research and theorizing focused upon groups and also supported the use of experiential methods for learning about group dynamics. In the late 1930s and the early 1940s Lewin conducted a series of studies on group behavior. The findings of his research emphasize the importance of active participation in groups in order to learn new skills, develop new attitudes, and make behavioral patterns more effective. Thus Lewin's research demonstrates that learning is achieved most productively in groups where people could interact and then reflect upon their mutual experiences. In this way they are able to spark each other's creativity in coming to conclusions relevant to group dynamics and in making commitments to the group to behave in more effective and skillful ways.

Lewin also had a deep commitment to democracy. Through his influence (as well as through the influence of others) democratic procedures pervade the social psychology of groups and underlie the practice of letting students formulate their own learning goals and pursue their own interests in the area of group dynamics. From Lewin, therefore, came the emphasis on studying one's own experiences in order to learn about group dynamics, on discussing mutual experiences with associates in order to increase mutual creativity and learning, and on behaving democratically in structuring learning situations.

How do you tell when you are in an experiential learning situation? When you generate from your own experience a set of concepts, rules, and principles to guide your behavior and then continually modify these concepts, rules, and principles to improve their effectiveness, you are learning experientially. Experiential learning can be conceived of as a four-stage cycle: (1) concrete, personal experiences are followed by (2) observation of, reflection upon, and examination of one's experiences, which leads to (3) the formulation of abstract concepts and generalizations, which leads to (4) hypotheses to be tested in future action in future experiences. This learning cycle (Figure 1.2) results in personal theories about effective behavior and is continuously recurring as you test out and confirm or modify your theories and generalizations.

Figure 1.2   Experiential Learning Cycle

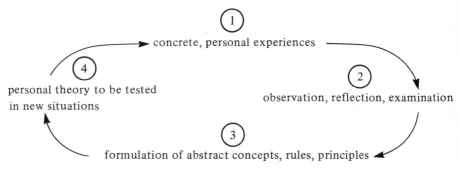

Experiential learning is based upon three assumptions: that you learn best when you are personally involved in the learning experience, that knowledge has to be discovered by yourself if it is to mean anything to you or make a difference in your behavior, and that a commitment to learning is highest when you are free to set your own learning goals and actively pursue them within a given framework. Experiential learning is a process of making generalizations and conclusions about your own direct experiences. It emphasizes directly experiencing what you are studying, building your own commitment to learn, and your being partly responsible for organizing the conclusions drawn from your experiences. If you want to learn experientially about leadership, for example you would take part in an exercise focusing upon leadership and then reflect upon it in order to build conclusions about the nature of leadership and how you may engage in effective leadership behavior.

In experiential learning the responsibility for your learning is upon you—not the teacher or the coordinator of the exercise. In experiential learning you need to become active and aggressive in your learning role and give direction to constructing your conclusions. The experiential situation is structured so that you can experiment with your behavior, try things out, see what works, build skills, and generalize for yourself out of your own experience. Appropriate theory is then presented to help summarize your learning and to help you build frameworks of knowledge that organize what you know. While experiential learning is a stimulating and involving activity, it is important to always remember that experience alone is not beneficial: you learn from the combination of experience and the conceptualization of your experiences.

Finally, in experiential learning feelings are emphasized as important sources of information about you and the learning situation. Open and genuine relationships in which participants are not defensive about their behavior are encouraged. What experiential learning seeks to achieve are the knowledge, values, attitudes, and skills necessary for effective behavior. As you, the reader, proceed through this book experiential learning will be increasingly understood.

The format of this book is based upon the principles of experiential learning presented above. Chapters and exercises are organized to help you learn skills and knowledge through experiential methods, and Appendix A gives specific instructions on how to apply these methods. At the beginning of each chapter, a preliminary conceptual or idea framework is presented to introduce the chapter and to introduce the concepts to be studied within the chapter. A short diagnostic instrument is presented to help you become more aware of your current behavior. A series of exercises is then provided, aimed at developing the skills and understandings in the area of group dynamics discussed in the chapter. Each exercise reviews the objectives, procedures, and discussion questions taken up in the chapter; they also contain necessary materials, observation forms, and questionnaires. As part of the discussion phase of your experiences in the exercises, an analysis of your experiences is encouraged and provided for in ways to help you reach conclusions and conceptualizations about them. The theory in social psychology that has to do with the exercises and the conclusions you have made is then presented. You are asked to integrate this theory into your own ideas and conclusions about the experiences in the exercise. At the end of the chapter, a procedure for looking at your changes in behavior and your current level of skills is also given.

Experiential learning procedures are especially useful when you want to learn skills to apply knowledge. No one wants to ride on an airplane when the pilot has read a book on how to fly but has never actually experienced flying a plane. In the next section we shall review how skills are learned.

LEARNING GROUP SKILLS

How do you learn group skills? What is the best way to proceed in doing so? Everyone passes through several phases in learning a complex skill. Knowing what these phases are will help you successfully develop effective group skills.

Step 1: Understand why the skill is important and how it will be valuable to you. To be motivated to learn a skill you must see the need for the skill.

Step 2: Understand what the skill is, conceptually and behaviorally. To learn a skill you must have an idea about what the skill is and how it is employed. This step includes identifying the behaviors involved in the skill and putting them in close, proper sequence. The learning of a skill is structured by conceptualizing how it is learned, how its parts are performed, and what to expect in learning it. Often it is helpful to have the skill demonstrated by someone proficient at it, have it described step by step, and then have it demonstrated again.

Step 3: Set up practice situations. Once the skill is properly conceptualized, the behavioral patterns that it entails need to be practiced until they are firmly learned. Practicing the skill is the third phase of skill learning. The timing, coordination, and ordering of the behaviors involved in the skill must be developed through practice. Repetition is usually necessary if the skill is to be performed easily and efficiently. Ideally, you should practice the skill a short time each day for several days or weeks in order to learn it completely.

Step 4: Ensure that you receive feedback on how well you are performing the skill. Receiving and digesting feedback on performance is necessary in order to correct errors, to identify problems in learning the skill, to determine your progress in skill mastery, and to compare actual performance with the desired standard of performance. Feedback is the description by others of their perceptions and reactions to your behavior. It may be the single most important factor in acquiring a skill. The more immediate, specific, and descriptive (as opposed to evaluative) the feedback, the more it will help your skill development (see Johnson, 1972, for a full discussion of feedback). Thus you should have someone observe your practice and comment immediately on how well you perform. The better you have conceptualized the skill in advance, the more helpful the feedback will be. You will find not only that feedback on your behavior is interesting but also that it will probably increase your motivation to learn the skill. After a skill is mastered you can often sense if you are behaving skillfully, thus providing feedback to yourself.

Step 5: Persevere in practicing the skill. In learning most skills there is a period of slow beginning, then a period of rapid improvement, followed by a plateau in which performance remains stable, followed by another spurt of learning, then another plateau, and so on. Plateaus are quite common in skill learning, and you just have to stick with it until the next period of rapid improvement begins. To develop your greatest proficiency, you need to be alert to the plateaus in the learning process—where the lack of apparent improvement precedes further progress—and persevere in your practice (Figure 1.3).

FIGURE 1.3   A Typical Learning Curve

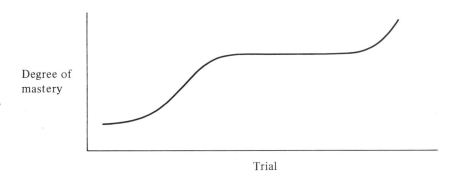

Step 6: Seek out situations in which the skills can be used successfully. You need to experience success in skill development. It is your increasing sense of

mastery that motivates further efforts to learn complex skills. This issue is discussed further in the following section on motivation.

Step 7: Use the skills often enough so that they become integrated into your behavior repertoire. A new skill must be integrated into your behavioral repertoire. It is at this stage that the performance of the skill becomes involuntary, automatic, and natural. When you have engaged in the skill long enough, it will become a natural response in which you engage with little conscious awareness of doing so. While practicing a group skill most people at first feel self-conscious and awkward; practicing the behaviors involved in the skill sometimes seems more like role playing than "real" behavior. You should not let this self-consciousness impede the improvement of your group skills, for it is through such role playing that all skills are developed. If you keep practicing the behaviors, the self-consciousness and awkwardness will pass, and you will become comfortable in using the skill. It is at this point that the skill becomes a part of your natural behavior.

Step 8: Support group norms that promote the use of the skills. Even if you master needed skills, you will not use them unless other group members believe they are appropriate and desirable. Conflict management skills, for example, will never be used if a group suppresses and avoids all conflict! Thus group norms need to be established that encourage the use of the skills you have learned. Setting group norms is discussed in depth in Chapter 9.

A mechanical process is involved in conceptualizing a skill and practicing it. As you do the exercises in this book, at times you may feel the process is somewhat mechanical and unreal. This is true of all skill development. Learning how to play the piano, for example, also involves the mechanical practice of specific behaviors (such as scales) that seem unreal in comparison with playing a beautiful concerto. It is when your new skills are applied to real situations that you will feel a sense of excitement that may sometimes be lacking in the practice of the behavioral parts of the skill.

This book gives you the chance to increase your group skills, and it is up to you to use the material and the exercises for that purpose. The extent of your learning and skill development rests entirely on your commitment to use the book in productive ways.

EXPERIENTIAL LEARNING AND MOTIVATION

What motivates you to learn concepts and skills? If someone offered you the opportunity either to earn a great deal of money or to experience a basic sense of accomplishment and satisfaction for learning a skill, which one would you choose? Some educators seem to believe that students must be forced or persuaded into learning; others seem to believe that learning is fun and enjoyable in its own right. What do you believe? Experiential learning stresses the intrinsic sense of success or accomplishment in learning. Motivation is based upon what you see as desirable learning goals and the method you choose to accomplish them. The goal-directed aspect of motivation places an emphasis upon your feelings of success or failure in the learning situation. What leads to a psychological feeling of success in a learning situation? Kurt Lewin and his associates (1944) came up with four factors; they found evidence that you will experience psychological success (as opposed to psychological failure) if:

1. You are able to define your own goals,
2. The goals are related to your central needs and values,
3. You are able to define the paths to accomplishing the goals,
4. The goals represent a realistic level of aspiration for you—neither too high nor too low, but high enough to challenge and test your capabilities.

Feelings of success will be promoted when you are encouraged to take as much responsibility for your own behavior as you can handle. You must believe that you are in control of (or at least have some influence over) your learning in order to feel psychological success. Experiential learning offers the opportunity for experiencing success by allowing you freedom to decide what aspects of your experience you wish to focus upon, what skills you wish to develop, and how you conceptualize the conclusions drawn from your experience. This is quite different from the traditional lecture approach to learning in which you are a passive listener and the control of the material being presented is in the hands of the instructor. When an instructor decides what material will be presented and how it will be presented without letting learners have any influence over the decision, learners will experience psychological failure no matter how entertaining the presentation is.

Although the primary motivation for learning in experiential situations is psychological success, there are extrinsic factors that will encourage further learning. The approval and support of other learners is an example of extrinsic motivators that facilitate learning without interfering with intrinsic motivators, such as a sense of accomplishment. As you participate in the exercises in this book your learning will accelerate if other participants give you approval and recognition for successful learning. You should consciously try to give approval to other readers who are seriously trying to increase their group skills. Few influences on our behavior are more powerful than the support and approval of a group of friends or acquaintances. Using such group influences to help in learning is one of the most constructive ways of assuring the development of group skills and knowledge.

ROLE PLAYING

In this and the following section two important procedures for experiential learning will be briefly discussed: role playing and observation of the dynamics of a group. *Role playing* is a tool for bringing a specific skill and its consequences into focus and thus is a vital tool for experiential learning. It provides a way in which you can experience concretely the type of interaction under examination. An imaginary life situation is set up in which readers act and react in terms of the assumptions they are asked to adopt, the beliefs they are asked to hold, and the characters they are asked to play. Role playing is intended to give you experience for practicing skills and for discussing and identifying effective and ineffective behavior. The outcome of a role-playing situation is not determined in advance, and the situation is not rehearsed. Initial instructions are given and the actors determine what happens. When participating in a role-playing exercise, remain yourself and act as you would in the situation described. You do not have to be a good actor to play a role; you only need to accept the initial assumptions, beliefs, background, or assigned behaviors and then let your feelings, attitudes, and behavior change as circumstances seem to require. The role-playing instructions describe the point of departure and the beginning frame of reference; you and the situation then take over.

What happens in group role playing may lead you to change behaviors and attitudes, and you may have emotional experiences that were not expected when the role playing began. The more real the role playing and the more effective the exercise, the more emotional involvement you will feel and the more you will learn. That role playing can simulate real-life situations makes it possible to try new ways of handling situations without your suffering any serious consequences if the methods fail.

In role playing, questions may be raised in discussion that are not covered by the instructions given in this book. When this happens role players are free to make up facts or experiences that accord with the circumstances; a role player should avoid making up experiences or facts that do not fit the role. In participating in a role-playing exercise, you should not consult or look at your role instructions; once they are used to start the action, you should be yourself. A role player should not act the way she feels a person described in the instructions should behave; the role player should act as naturally as possible, given the initial instructions of the role.

The coordinator of the exercise should help the role players get into the situation by introducing it in such a way that the players are emotionally involved. Using name tags and asking the players questions to help them get a feeling for the part are helpful. Introduce the scene to the role players and the observers. Always "de-role" after the role playing has ended.

PROCESS OBSERVATION

Within a group a distinction can be made between the *content* the group is discussing and the *process* by which the discussion is being conducted. Group process involves such things as leadership, decision making, communication, and controversy. Content is *what* is being discussed, while process is *how* the group is functioning. To observe the group process is to observe how the group is functioning. A person highly skilled in process observation can both participate in group work and observe group process at the same time, thus becoming a *participant-observer*.

Observation procedures are aimed at describing and recording behavior as it occurs. From the behavior of group members an observer can make inferences about the group process, the way in which the group is functioning. Five steps are usually involved in observation procedures, the first being to decide which aspects of a group process you wish to observe. The model of effective groups presented in a previous section covers the basic aspects of group process that you will be interested in observing. By the time you finish this book you will have a clear understanding of the aspects of group process that are important to observe.

The second step in observation procedures is to find or construct an observation sheet that specifies observable and countable behaviors reflecting the area of group process to be studied. Numerous observation sheets are included in this book. The third step is to observe the group and count the number of members engaged in a specified behavior. When there is more than one observer, you may be able to focus on only part of the group members. The fourth step is to look at the frequency with which group members are engaged in their specified behaviors and then infer how well the group is functioning in that phase of the group process under observation. The final step is to summarize the observations in a manner that is clear and useful to the group members and to present it to the group as feedback. The group can then discuss the observations and revise the group process to make it more effective.

The purpose of process observation is to clarify and improve the ways in which the group is presently functioning through an objective assessment of its group process. Information about group process is collected and then openly discussed so that modifications in group procedures and members' behavior can be made in order to improve the group's effectiveness.

By the time you finish this book you will have developed skills in observing group process. At first the observation tasks specified in the exercises will seem difficult, but gradually you will find them easier and more helpful as your skills develop. As effective future behavior depends upon being aware of the consequences and nature of its current characteristics, there is no substitute for direct observation in skill development and in facilitating group effectiveness. Any effective group member must be able to be aware of group process while participating in the group, and it is through observation practice that such skills are developed.

Before going on, you may want to look at how you currently see yourself behaving in groups. The questionnaire below gives you a chance to start the process of self-evaluation that is essential if you are to learn the skills presented in this book.

YOURSELF AS A GROUP MEMBER

How do you see yourself as a group member? What three adjectives best describe your behavior in most groups? How do others see you as a group member? If you were asked to give a ten-minute lecture on your strengths and weaknesses in functioning effectively in groups, what would you say? These are important questions to consider before beginning the next chapter. In the space below, describe yourself as accurately as you possibly can.

1. How do you see yourself as a group member? What is your style of functioning within groups? _I offer advice and opinions whenever possible. I try to participate always. I am an active listener, also._

2. What are your strengths in functioning in groups? How do they fit into how you see yourself as a group member? _I always talk. Because, the more I talk, the more possibility there is that I will be helping the group to keep things rolling._

3. What situations within groups do you have trouble with and why? How do you feel when faced with them? How do you handle them? How would you like to handle them? _I don't express my feelings about myself in relation to the group or personally._

4. In what group skills do you wish to grow and develop? What changes would you like to make in your present group behavior? What new strengths in group behavior would you care to develop? What new group skills would you like to acquire? _To be able to be more open about me._

_____

_____

_____

_____

As you go through the exercises included in this book you may want to keep a personal diary of what you are learning about yourself and about how you behave in interpersonal and group situations. A diary will be of great interest after you have finished all the areas of study in the book. You may also want to include specific information you have learned about the social psychology of groups and about how to behave effectively in groups as well as a progress report on how well you yourself are developing the skills you want.

LEARNING CONTRACT

Before beginning the next chapter, we would like to propose a learning contract. The contract is as follows:

I understand that I will be taking an experiential approach to learning about the social psychology of groups and to developing the skills needed to function effectively in groups. I willingly commit myself to the statements hereunder:

1. I will use the structured experiences in this book to learn from. This means I am willing to engage in specified behaviors, seek out feedback about the impact of my behavior on others, and analyze my interpersonal interactions with other class members in order to make the most of my learning.
2. I will make the most of my own learning by (a) engaging in specified behaviors and in being open about my feelings and reactions to what is taking place in order that others may have information to react to in giving me feedback and in building conclusions about the area of study, (b) setting personal learning goals that I will work actively to accomplish—which means that I will take responsibility for my own learning and not wait around for someone else to "make me grow," (c) being willing to experiment with new behavior and to practice new skills, (d) seeking out and being receptive to feedback, and (e) building conclusions about the experiences highlighted in the exercises.
3. I will help others make the most of their learning by: (a) providing feedback in constructive ways, (b) helping to build the conditions (such as openness, trust, acceptance, and support) under which others can experiment and take risks with their behavior, and (c) contributing to the formulation of conclusions about the experiences highlighted in the exercises.
4. I will use professional judgment in keeping what happens among group members in the exercises appropriately confidential.

Signed: _Nancy Ranzo_ _____

2

Leadership

INTRODUCTION

Each of us has a theory of leadership. In some groups we think the leadership is good, and in other groups we think the leadership is bad. We all have our ideas as to what we would do if we were in an important leadership position.

What are your ideas about leadership? How do you tell when the leadership of a group is good or bad? Before proceeding further, take a few minutes to write down your impressions of good leadership. You may do this by listing adjectives (like powerful, forceful, kind) or by writing a description. Then read the definitions given below.

At this point, my ideas about good leadership are: initiative to start group, advice & opinion giver, authority in a mild sense

Whenever two or more individuals join together to achieve a goal, a group structure develops. Part of the structure pertains to the way in which members influence one another while trying to reach the desired goals. Within a group, when two or more members who depend on one another to reach the group's goals influence one another, leadership exists. The process of leadership is an influence relationship occurring among mutually dependent group members. Because all group members will at times influence other members, each group member will at times exert leadership. From this definition it may be seen that a difference exists between being a designated leader of a group (such as chairperson) and engaging in leadership behavior within a group (such as influencing other members to make the next meeting a wine-and-cheese-tasting party). *Leadership* implies that one person is influencing other group members; a *designated leader* implies that one person is in charge of the group and has been given the authority to exert influence within it. In any effective group, the designated leader is not the only member to engage in leadership behavior; any other member can be the leader when he influences the others in order to help the group reach its goals.

You can test your understanding of this section by choosing the best answer to the following questions (answers on page 53).

1. When does a group structure develop?
    a. When a person wants other people to help him reach his goals.
    b. When two or more people join together to reach mutual goals.
    c. When two or more people join together.
    d. When your parents chaperon your dates.
2. When does group leadership exist?
    a. When your big brother bosses you around.
    b. When there is a leader and a follower.
    c. When two or more people get together to reach the group's goals.
    d. When two or more people try to influence each other to reach the group's goals.
3. Who is a leader?
    a. A person who runs the group.
    b. The authors.
    c. A person who tries to influence the other members of the group in order to reach the group's goals.
    d. A person who makes the decisions for the group in order to reach the group's goals.

UNDERSTANDING YOUR LEADERSHIP BEHAVIOR

When you are a member of a group, what is your leadership behavior like? In what ways do you try to influence other group members toward accomplishing the group's goals? The purpose of the survey below is to get a description of your behavior in groups in order to introduce a discussion on leadership theories. Circle the letter to the left that most appropriately describes your likely behavior—(A) always, (F) frequently, (O) occasionally, (S) seldom, or (N) never—in connection with the given statement. Each of the items below describes aspects of leadership behavior; respond to each one according to the way in which you would be *most likely* to act if you were part of a problem-solving group. Then read the next two sections, after which the instructions will appear for analyzing your responses to the survey.

When I am a member of a problem-solving group . . .

A:F:O:S:N   1. I offer facts, give my opinions and ideas, provide suggestions and relevant information to help the group discussion.

A:F:O:S:N   2. I warmly encourage all members of the group to participate, giving them recognition for their contributions, demonstrating receptivity and openness to their ideas, and generally being friendly and responsive to them.

A:F:O:S:N   3. I ask for facts, information, opinions, ideas, and feelings from other group members to help the group discussion.

A:F:O:S:N   4. I try to persuade members to analyze constructively their differences in opinions and ideas, searching for common elements in conflicting or opposing ideas or proposals, and trying to reconcile disagreements.

A:F:O:S:N   5. I propose goals and tasks in order to start action within the group.

A:F:O:S:N   6. I try to relieve group tension and increase the enjoyment of group members by joking, suggesting breaks, and proposing fun approaches to group work.

A:F:O:S:N   7. I give direction to the group by developing plans on how to proceed with group work and by focusing members' attention on the tasks to be done.

A:F:O:S:N   8. I help communication among group members by showing good communication skills and by making sure that what each member says is understood by all.

A:F:O:S:N   9. I pull together related ideas or suggestions made by group members and restate and summarize the major points discussed by the group.

A:F:O:S:N   10. I ask members how they are feeling about the way in which the group is working, and about each other, as well as share my own feelings about group work and the way the members interact.

A:F:O:S:N   11. I coordinate group work by showing relationships among various ideas or suggestions, by pulling ideas and suggestions together, and by drawing together activities of various subgroups and members.

A:F:O:S:N   12. I observe the process by which the group is working and use my observations to help in examining the effectiveness of the group.

A:F:O:S:N   13. I determine why the group has difficulty in working effectively and what blocks progress in accomplishing the group's goals.

A:F:O:S:N   14. I express group standards and norms and the group goals in order to make members constantly aware of the direction in which the work is going—the progress being made toward the group goal—and in order to get continued open acceptance of group norms and procedures.

A:F:O:S:N   15. I energize the group by stimulating group members to produce a higher quality of work.

A:F:O:S:N   16. I listen to and serve as an interested audience for other group members, weighing the ideas of others, and going along with the movement of the group when I do not disagree with its action.

A:F:O:S:N   17. I examine how practical and workable the ideas are, evaluate the quality of alternative solutions to group problems, and apply decisions and suggestions to real situations in order to see how they will work.

A:F:O:S:N   18. I accept and support the openness of other group members, reinforcing them for taking risks, and encouraging individuality in group members.

19

A:F:O(S)N   19. I compare group decisions and accomplishments with group standards, measuring accomplishments against goals.

A(F)O:S:N   20. I promote the open discussion of conflicts between group members in order to resolve disagreements and increase group togetherness.

APPROACHES TO LEADERSHIP

There are four major approaches to leadership theory: trait, position, style, and distributed functions. Far back in philosophical thought, the leader was felt to be someone who had unique, inborn leadership *traits*. Aristotle, for example, once remarked, "From the hour of their birth some are marked out for subjugation, and others for command." Some people seem to dominate others through their force of personality and what they stand for. Thus, one approach to the study of leadership is to examine the traits or personal characteristics that may make leaders different from nonleaders. This is the "great woman" or "great man" theory of leadership; it implies that leaders are born, not made and, therefore, that leaders are discovered, not trained. Many studies have compared the characteristics of a leader (defined as an individual holding a position of authority, such as the President of the United States) with the characteristics of a follower (defined as an individual not holding a position of authority, such as a low-level government worker), finding results that are contradictory and nonsignificant. Though being intelligent and well adjusted may have some relationship to leadership; it is evident that many of the most intelligent people never get positions of leadership and that many leaders, like Adolf Hitler, have shown signs of being emotionally maladjusted. In other words, traits found in leaders are also found in followers, and different leadership positions may require different qualities in effective leaders. Perhaps the safest conclusion to make from the trait studies is that people who are highly motivated to become leaders, who have the energy, drive, self-confidence, and determination to succeed, will become leaders, because they work hard to get leadership positions.

A second approach to the question "Who is a leader?" is in terms of high-authority *positions* within organizations. The president of a business might be described as a leader; so, too, might a person holding a lower-echelon position in the organization. Leadership within organizations begins with the formal role system (president, vice-president, manager, supervisor, foreman, worker), which, among other things, defines the authority hierarchy. Authority is legitimate power, power vested in a particular position to ensure that persons in lesser positions meet the requirements of their organizational role. A foreman, for example, is given the authority to make sure that workers are doing their job. Because it is an organizational law that subordinates shall obey their designated supervisors with respect to matters of role performance, a person with authority will influence those under him or her. The trouble with the position approach to a leadership theory is that it is unclear how certain individuals are placed in high-authority positions. All their behavior is certainly not leadership behavior. Furthermore, other group members besides the designated leader influence the behavior of group members, and there is no way to take this fact into account when leadership is defined as a position of authority.

Research on leadership traits was disappointing and unsatisfactory because contradictory results were found by different investigators. So attention shifted to a leadership *style* approach to the theory of leadership. Based upon an experiment by Lewin, Lippitt, and White (1939), three leadership styles were examined: autocratic, democratic, and laissez-faire. In the autocratic style the leader determines all policy and gives orders to the group members. In the democratic style the policies are set through group discussion and decision, with the leader encouraging and helping the group to interact. In the laissez-faire style there is very little participation by the leader. Most of the research indicated that the democratic style is the most effective, but it also became evident that different styles are effective under different conditions. Certain conditions existed, for example, under which autocratic leadership seemed most effective (such as when an urgent decision had to be made). Other conditions suggested that a democratic style would be most effective (when a great deal of membership commitment to the implementation of a decision needed to be built). There were even conditions under which the laissez-faire style seemed best (when the group was committed to a decision, had the resources to implement it, and needed a minimum of interference to work effectively). Because different leadership styles seemed to be required in different situations, even with the same group, the attention of social psychologists moved to the distributed-functions approach to leadership.

We shall take up the fourth approach in the next section, but first test your understanding of this section by choosing the best answer to the following questions (answers on page 53).

(True) False   1. The four major approaches to leadership theory are the trait approach, the style approach, the position approach, and the distributed-functions approach.

True (False)   2. In the trait approach to leadership it is felt that leaders are made, not born.

(True) False   3. Different situations often require different leadership styles if the leader is to be effective.

True (False)   4. The true leader of the group is always the person with the most authority, such as the teacher in the classroom.

Match the following leadership styles with their definition:

5. Laissez-faire. C   a. The group determines policy, aided by the leader.

6. Democratic. A   b. The leader determines policy and gives orders to the rest of the group.

7. Autocratic. B   c. The leader participates very little in the group.

                           d. No one decides anything.

DISTRIBUTED FUNCTIONS THEORY OF LEADERSHIP

Most views of leadership today emphasize that leadership is a matter of abilities and skills that are learned, and they stress that certain functions have to be filled if the group is to solve the problems necessary for it to operate effectively. The functional theory of leadership tries to discover what actions are necessary for a group to achieve its goals under various conditions and how different group members should take part in these group actions. Leadership is defined as the performance of acts that help the group reach its goals, maintain itself in good working order, and adapt to changes in the environment, and these acts are group *functions*. Leadership functions include setting goals, helping the group proceed toward these goals, and providing necessary resources to accomplish the goals. Other functions not directly related to achieving the group's goal, such as improving the group's stability and making sure that individual members are satisfied, are also part of leadership behaviors.

The theory of functional leadership includes two basic ideas: (1) any member of a group may become a leader by taking actions that serve group functions, and (2) any leadership function may be fulfilled by different members performing a variety of relevant behaviors. Leadership, therefore, is specific to a particular group in a particular situation. Under specific circumstances, any given behavior may or may not serve a group function. Under one set of conditions, a particular behavior may be helpful; under another it may impair the functioning of the group. For example, when a group is trying to define a problem, suggesting a possible solution may not be helpful; however, when the group is naming various solutions to a defined problem, suggesting a possible solution may indeed by helpful.

It is useful to look at different group functions and see which function contributes to which type of group objective. Goal achievement and group maintenance are generally considered to be the two basic objectives of a group. Any given behavior in a group may affect both. Both may be served simultaneously by the actions of a group member, or one may be served at the expense of the other. A member who helps the group work cooperatively on a task may at the same time be helping the group reach its goal and increase group solidarity. On the other hand, a member who pushes hard to get the task done may help the group accomplish its goal, but he may do it in a way that creates friction among members, thereby jeopardizing the future existence of the group.

The functional approach to leadership assumes that leadership is a learned set of skills that anyone with certain minimal requirements can acquire. From this theoretical point of view, responsible membership is the same thing as responsible leadership. Effective group membership and leadership both depend upon flexible behavior, the ability to diagnose what behaviors are needed at a particular time for the group to function most efficiently, and the ability to fulfill these behaviors or to get other members to fulfill them. A skilled member or leader, therefore, has to have diagnostic skills in order to be aware that a given function is needed in the group, and he must be sufficiently adaptable to provide the diverse types of behaviors needed for different conditions. In addition, he must be able to use the abilities and receive the cooperation of other group members in order to provide the functions needed by the group.

The functional approach to leadership is, at this time, the most concrete and direct approach available for improving the leadership skills of an individual and for improving the effectiveness of a working group. People can be taught the diagnostic skills and behaviors that help the group accomplish its task and maintain good working relationships.

Most people supporting the functional theory of group leadership emphasize that it is necessary for the behaviors that fulfill group functions to be distributed among the group members. If leadership functions are distributed, the chances are greater that all the relevant expertise and resources in the group will surface and be used. The result will be that all members will feel that they share equally in opportunities for influencing the direction of the group effort, and the inter-personal climate within the group will not be dominated by just a few people.

Sometimes behaviors within a group not only help it to operate, they can also serve the self as well. Sometimes these individually oriented behaviors interfere with group work and sometimes they support it. Much of this self-oriented behavior involves issues of personal identity (Who am I in this group, and where do I fit?), personal goals and needs (What do I want from this group, and are the group goals consistent with my personal goals?), power and control (Who will control what we do, and how much power and influence do I have?), and intimacy (How close will we get to each other, and how much can I trust the other group members?).

Test your understanding of this section by choosing the best answer to the following questions (answers on page 53).

True / False   1. Any group member is a leader if he does things that help the group reach its goals.

True / False   2. In order to be a group function, a behavior must be helpful at the time it is performed in the group.

True / False   3. Under the functional approach to leadership, anyone can learn the skills needed to be a group leader.

4. Leadership functions include which five of the following?
   a. Telling group members what to do and how to do it.
   b. Making sure members are satisfied.
   c. Buying the coffee and donuts.
   d. Setting goals.
   e. Improving group stability.
   f. Showing that you care about the state of the world.
   g. Helping the group proceed toward its goals.
   h. Providing the resources necessary to accomplish the goals.
   i. Reading this book.

5. The two basic objectives for a group are:
   a. Goal achievement.
   b. Group maintenance.

c. Goal maintenance.

d. Group achievement.

6. Effective group membership and leadership depend on which three?

a. Flexible behavior.

b. The ability to diagnose what behaviors are needed at a particular time for the group to function most efficiently.

c. Being the biggest and strongest person in the group.

d. The ability to fulfill the needed behaviors or to get other members to do them.

e. The ability to motivate the group members to do what you want them to.

f. Not offending anyone in the group.

YOUR LEADERSHIP BEHAVIOR

The procedure for analyzing your responses to the survey on page 19 is as follows:

1. If you circled (A) give yourself 5 points, (F) is 4, (O) is 3, (S) is 2, and (N) is 1 point.

2. To get your total score for task functions and maintenance functions, which will be discussed fully in a moment, write the score for each statement in the following table.

Task Functions	*Maintenance Functions*
_5_ 1. Information and opinion giver	_4_ 2. Encourager of participation
_4_ 3. Information and opinion seeker	_3_ 4. Harmonizer and compromiser
_2_ 5. Starter	_3_ 6. Tension reliever
_1_ 7. Direction giver	_2_ 8. Communication helper
_4_ 9. Summarizer	_2_ 10. Evaluator of emotional climate
_1_ 11. Coordinator	_3_ 12. Process observer
_3_ 13. Diagnoser	_1_ 14. Standard setter
_3_ 15. Energizer	_5_ 16. Active listener
_4_ 17. Reality tester	_4_ 18. Trust builder
_2_ 19. Evaluator	_4_ 20. Interpersonal problem solver
_29_ Total for task functions	_31_ Total for maintenance functions

3. Locate yourself on the Task-Maintenance Grid (Figure 2.1) by finding your score for task functions on the bottom, horizontal axis of the grid and move up the column corresponding to your Task score to the point of intersection with

your score for maintenance functions. Place an "X" at the intersection that represents your two scores. Numbers in parentheses correspond to the major styles of task-maintenance leadership behaviors.

FIGURE 2.1   Task-Maintenance Grid

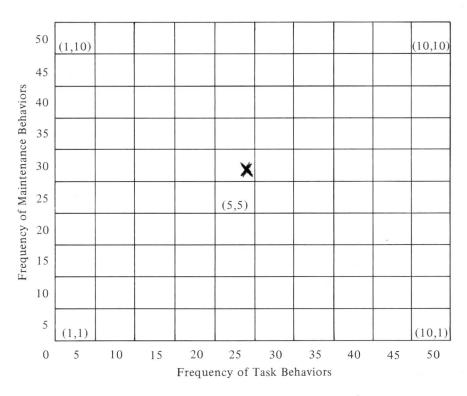

Frequency of Task Behaviors

4. The description of the task-maintenance styles is as follows:

   (1,1):   Only a minimum effort is given in order to get the required work done and general noninvolvement prevails with other group members. This person may well be saying "To hell with it all," or be so inactive in the group as to have no influence whatsoever on other group members.

   (1,10):   High value is placed on keeping good relationships within the group. Thoughtful attention is given to the needs of other members for satisfying relationships in order to help create a comfortable, friendly atmosphere and work tempo. Such a person may be great running a social club or a country club, but the group may never get any work accomplished.

   (10,1):   Accomplishing the task is emphasized in a way that shows minimum concern with group maintenance. Work is seen as important while relationships among group members are ignored. This member would make a splendid army drill master, but the productivity of the group would soon suffer as its morale and cohesiveness deteriorated.

(5,5): The task and maintenance needs of the group are balanced in order to complete work while the morale of members is maintained at a satisfactory level. This person will be continually making compromises between task needs and maintenance needs while neglecting to seek or find the creative integration of these two needs so important for optimal productivity.

(10,10): All members plan and make decisions together, all being committed to getting the task done as they build relationships of trust and respect. A high value is placed on sound, creative decisions that result in understanding and agreement. Ideas are sought out and listened to, even when the ideas, opinions, and attitudes are different from one's own. The group as a whole cooperatively defines the task and works for its completion. Such a member encourages the creative integration of task and maintenance needs and is the ideal leader for a group.

5. Divide into groups of three, and discuss the following:
   a. Your scores on the leadership survey and how you react to them.
   b. The theory underlying the survey and the task-maintenance grid.
   c. Your reactions and feelings to the results of placing yourself on the grid.
   d. Plan how you could get feedback on your behavior in groups to see if other people see you behaving in the same way in which you think you behave.

SUMMARY OF TASK AND MAINTENANCE FUNCTIONS

Task Functions

1. Information and Opinion Giver: Offers facts, opinions, ideas, suggestions, and relevant information to help group discussion.
2. Information and Opinion Seeker: Asks for facts, information, opinions, ideas, and feelings from other members to help group discussion.
3. Starter: Proposes goals and tasks to initiate action within the group.
4. Direction Giver: Develops plans on how to proceed and focuses attention on the task to be done.
5. Summarizer: Pulls together related ideas or suggestions and restates and summarizes major points discussed.
6. Coordinator: Shows relationships among various ideas by pulling them together and harmonizes activities of various subgroups and members.
7. Diagnoser: Figures out sources of difficulties the group has in working effectively and the blocks to progress in accomplishing the group's goals.
8. Energizer: Stimulates a higher quality of work from the group.
9. Reality Tester: Examines the practicality and workability of ideas, evaluates alternative solutions, and applies them to real situations to see how they will work.
10. Evaluator: Compares group decisions and accomplishments with group standards and goals.

Maintenance Functions

11. Encourager of Participation: Warmly encourages everyone to participate, giving recognition for contributions, demonstrating acceptance and openness to ideas of others, is friendly and responsive to group members.

12. Harmonizer and Compromiser: Persuades members to analyze constructively their differences in opinions, searches for common elements in conflicts, and tries to reconcile disagreements.

13. Tension Reliever: Eases tensions and increases the enjoyment of group members by joking, suggesting breaks, and proposing fun approaches to group work.

14. Communication Helper: Shows good communication skills and makes sure that each group member understands what other members are saying.

15. Evaluator of Emotional Climate: Asks members how they feel about the way in which the group is working and about each other, and shares own feelings about both.

16. Process Observer: Watches the process by which the group is working and uses the observations to help examine group effectiveness.

17. Standard Setter: Expresses group standards and goals to make members aware of the direction of the work and the progress being made toward the goal and to get open acceptance of group norms and procedures.

18. Active Listener: Listens and serves as an interested audience for other members, is receptive to others' ideas, goes along with the group when not in disagreement.

19. Trust Builder: Accepts and supports openness of other group members, reinforcing risk taking and encouraging individuality.

20. Interpersonal Problem Solver: Promotes open discussion of conflicts between group members in order to resolve conflicts and increase group togetherness.

MATCHING EXERCISE 1

To help you learn the task and maintenance functions, match the following terms with their definitions (answers on page 53).

Task Functions

____ 1. Information and Opinion Giver
____ 2. Information and Opinion Seeker
____ 3. Starter
____ 4. Direction Giver
____ 5. Summarizer
____ 6. Coordinator
____ 7. Diagnoser
____ 8. Energizer

Definitions

a. Promotes open discussion of conflicts between group members to resolve conflicts and increase group togetherness.

b. Compares group decisions and accomplishments with group standards and goals.

c. Accepts and supports openness of other group members, reinforcing

____ 9. Reality Tester

____ 10. Evaluator

____ *Maintenance Functions*

____ 11. Encourager of Participation

____ 12. Harmonizer and Compromiser

____ 13. Tension Reliever

____ 14. Communication Helper

____ 15. Evaluator of Emotional Climate

____ 16. Process Observer

____ 17. Standard Setter

____ 18. Active Listener

____ 19. Trust Builder

____ 20. Interpersonal Problem Solver

risk taking and encouraging individuality.

d. Examines the practicality and workability of ideas, evaluates alternative solutions, applies them to real situations to see how they will work.

e. Listens and serves as an interested audience for other members, is receptive to others' ideas, goes along with the group when not in disagreement.

f. Stimulates a higher quality of work.

g. Expresses group standards and goals to make members aware of the direction of the work and the progress being made toward the goal and to get open acceptance of group norms and procedures.

h. Figures out sources of difficulties the group has in working effectively and the blocks to progress in accomplishing the group's goals.

i. Watches the process by which the group is working and uses the observations to help examine group effectiveness.

j. Shows relationships among various ideas by pulling them together and harmonizes activities of various subgroups and members.

k. Asks members how they feel about the way in which the group is working and about one another, and shares own feelings about both.

l. Pulls together related ideas or suggestions and restates and summarizes major points discussed.

m. Shows good communication skills and makes sure that each group member understands what other members are saying.

n. Develops plans on how to proceed and focuses attention on the task to be done.

o. Eases tensions and increases the enjoyment of group members by joking, suggesting breaks, and proposing fun approaches to group work.

p. Proposes goals and tasks to initiate action within the group.

q. Persuades members to analyze constructively their differences in opinions, searches for common elements in conflicts, and tries to reconcile disagreements.

r. Asks for facts, information, opinions, ideas, and feelings from other members to help group discussion.

s. Warmly encourages everyone to participate, giving recognition for contributions, demonstrating acceptance and openness to ideas of others, is friendly and responsive to group members.

t. Offers facts, opinions, ideas, suggestions, and relevant information to help group discussion.

MATCHING EXERCISE 2

Match the following statements with the task or maintenance function they best seem to fill (answers on page 53).

Task Functions

C 1. Information and Opinion Giver
H 2. Information and Opinion Seeker
L 3. Starter
O 4. Direction Giver
R 5. Summarizer
I 6. Coordinator
D 7. Diagnoser
P 8. Energizer

Statements

a. "Boy, we've been working hard! Let's take a five-minute break and stretch our legs."

b. "I think that this solution compares very favorably with what we set out to do."

c. "Before we go any further, I'd like to tell you how other groups I've been in have gone about this task."

_K_ 9. Reality Tester

_B_ 10. Evaluator

Maintenance Functions

_Q_ 11. Encourager of Participation

_J_ 12. Harmonizer and Compromiser

_P_ 13. Tension Reliever

_F_ 14. Communication Helper

_M_ 15. Evaluator of Emotional Climate

_S_ 16. Process Observer

_G_ 17. Standard Setter

_N_ 18. Active Listener

_I_ 19. Trust Builder

_E_ 20. Interpersonal Problem Solver

d. "I think our problem is that we've gotten off on a tangent."

e. "I think we should openly discuss the conflict between Dave and Linda to see if we can help resolve it."

f. "Keith, I hear you saying that you're not really satisfied with the solution we've reached, is that right? Is that what other group members heard?"

g. "We seem to have decided that we should attack the problem as a whole rather than dividing it into parts. Is that the way we want it to be?"

h. "Does everyone think we should try to solve the problem in this particular way?"

i. "I think Edye's idea is a lot like Buddy's, and I think they could be put together."

j. "Jane, I don't think your ideas are so different from Frank's. Why don't you see if you can't figure out what you have in common?"

k. "Let's try the solution ourselves to see if it will really work."

l. "Let's get started by figuring out what we need to do first."

m. "I feel pretty good about the solution we've just reached. How does everyone else feel about it?"

n. "I think Dale has a good idea. I'm willing to go along with it."

o. "Let's not get away from our task, which is to solve this particular problem."

p. "I think we're headed for a really good solution, if we just put a little more work into it."

q. "Helen, I'd like to hear what you think about this; you had such a good idea last time."

r. "What we've said this far in the discussion is that we need to have an easy, collective plan that we all agree on."

s. "I noticed that several people seem to be dominating the discussion. I think we would be a more effective group if everyone participated more equally."

t. "I think it's great that you were able to disagree openly with Annette, Roger. You have such a unique way of viewing the task."

SELECTING A COLOR EXERCISE

The objectives of this exercise—the selection of a color by a group—are to develop through role playing an understanding of leadership that is distributed and functional and to give you an opportunity to observe the task and maintenance functions in a decision-making group. Exercise material includes observation sheets for task and maintenance behaviors (see Appendix E) and a large envelope containing specific role-playing instructions for each group member. The exercise is designed for seven to ten participants, although more may be included. The coordinator should allow approximately thirty minutes to conduct it, and proceed as follows:

1. Introduce the exercise by stating the objectives. Then explain the following group functions (see page 26 for definitions):
   a. Information and Opinion Giver
   b. Information and Opinion Seeker
   c. Starter
   d. Diagnoser
   e. Encourager of Participation
   f. Harmonizer and Compromiser
   g. Tension Reliever
   h. Active Listener

2. Select two observers, give them the task-maintenance observation sheets, and tell them how to use them. Observers should be on the lookout for:
   a. The functional behaviors present and absent in the group.
   b. How well participation is distributed in the group.
   c. What specific functional behaviors are being provided by each group member.

3. Place the large envelope (below) containing the role-playing instruction envelopes in the center of the group with no further instructions or information.

4. After the exercise is completed, conduct a general discussion of the experience and include these questions:
   a. What functional behavior was each member supposed to have role played, and how were these carried out?
   b. What functional behaviors were present and absent in the group decision making, and what were the consequences of the behaviors being present and absent?
   c. What were the feelings of the participants and their reactions to the exercise and experience?
   d. What conclusions could be drawn about leadership and group functioning from the exercise?

The instructions given for use in the exercise are as follows:

Instructions written on the large envelope, which contains all other envelopes:

Enclosed you will find three envelopes containing directions for the phases of this group session. You are to open the first one (labeled Envelope I) at once. Later instructions will tell you when to open the second (Envelope II) and third (Envelope III).

Envelope I contains the following directions on a separate sheet:

Directions for Envelope I:

Time allowed: fifteen minutes.

Special instructions: Each member is to take one of the enclosed envelopes and follow the individual role-playing instructions contained in it.

Task: The group is to select a color.

DO NOT LET ANYONE ELSE SEE *YOUR* INSTRUCTIONS!

(After fifteen minutes go on to the next envelope.)

Envelope II contains the following directions on a separate sheet:

Directions for Envelope II:

Time allowed: five minutes

Task: You are to choose a group chairperson.

(After five minutes go on to the next envelope.)

Envelope III contains the following directions on a separate sheet:

Directions for Envelope III:

Time allowed: ten minutes.

Task: You are to evaluate the first phase of this group session.

Special instructions for Phase II: The newly selected chairperson will lead a discussion on the roles and functions of group members in the process of decision making and their feelings and reactions to that process. The discussion should begin with the report of the observers.

(After ten minutes return the directions to their respective envelopes and prepare for a general discussion of the exercise.)

Individual instruction envelopes for Phase I

Each envelope will have instructions for leadership function and position. Two of the instruction envelopes will also include special knowledge. The information will be given on a card in each envelope. The leadership functions, positions, and special information listed below will be assigned in the following order:

a. Leadership function: Information and Opinion Giver. Position: support blue.

b. Leadership function: Encourager of Participation. Position: introduce the idea of a different color—orange.

c. Leadership function: Information and Opinion Seeker. Position: Support red.

d. Leadership function: any. Position: any.
   (You have the special knowledge that the group is going to be asked to select a chairperson later in the exercise; you are to conduct yourself in such a manner that they will select you as chairperson.)

e. Leadership function: Tension reliever. Position: against red.

f. Leadership function: Diagnoser. Position: support green.

g. Leadership function: any. Position: any.
   (You have the special knowledge that the group is going to be asked to select a chairman later in the exercise; you are to conduct yourself in such a manner that they will select you as chairman.)

h. Leadership function: Harmonizer and compromiser. Position: at a point in which there seems to be a clear polarity in the discussion suggest a compromise color such as purple or orange.

i. Leadership function: Starter. Position: against blue.

j. Leadership function: Active Listener. Position: support blue.

If fewer than ten participate in the group, simply eliminate as many of the last three leadership functions and positions as necessary. At least seven people must be in the group. If more than ten participate, just add more leadership functions and positions.

SURVIVAL AT SEA EXERCISE

This exercise extends your leadership behavior by giving you an opportunity to practice leadership functions in which you ordinarily do not engage. Here is the procedure for the coordinator of the exercise:

1. Introduce the exercise by stating the objective. Hand out the briefing sheet (below) and ask each person to read it. Then randomly divide into groups of seven.

2. Ask each participant to review the list of task and maintenance functions on page 26 and select two types of functional behaviors that would be new to the participant. State that during this exercise the person is to practice these behaviors while participating in the group's decision-making process.

3. For each group have two observers. Give them the task-maintenance observation sheets (see Appendix E) and tell them how to use them. Observers should be watching:

   a. Which functional behaviors are present and absent in the group.

   b. How well distributed is participation in the group.

   c. What specific functional behaviors are being provided by each member.

4. Tell the groups to begin and give them twenty minutes to complete the task.

5. Conduct a general discussion of the experience, including such questions as:

   a. What functional behaviors did each member engage in?

   b. What functional behaviors were present and absent in the group decision making, and what were the consequences of the behaviors being present or absent?

   c. What were the feelings and reactions of each participant to the exercise and experience?

   d. What conclusions could be drawn about leadership and group functioning from the exercise?

Survival at Sea Briefing Sheet

Suppose that as a result of a marine disaster the following seven people find themselves in a lifeboat with twenty others, mainly women and children. The lifeboat is a thousand miles from the nearest land and off the shipping lanes and has food and water sufficient in terms of normal consumption to sustain them for five days, two sets of oars, a small sail, and a compass.

Mr. McKay, forty, a self-made man, the owner and director of a million-dollar company that has been built during the past fifteen years.

Mrs. McKay, thirty-two, a social psychologist who is also the president of the League of Women Voters.

Reverend Price, fifty, an ordained minister, a leader in his church, and the pastor of one of the largest churches in New York City.

A Soviet sea captain who cannot understand the others nor be understood verbally by them.

Mr. Pope, sixty, a wizened little man with forty-five years at sea as a deckhand.

Mr. Smith, fifty-five, an official of the Teamsters union who has battled his way up from the picket lines as an organizer.

Mr. Gordon, forty-one, a prominent motion picture star of the Gregory Peck school. A yachtsman and a playboy.

The sea is calm. The immediate emergency is over. The problem now is survival. Which of these seven persons would rise to a position of leadership, and how would it be accomplished?

HOLLOW SQUARE EXERCISE

The Hollow Square Exercise is a problem-solving situation in which you can observe leadership functions. You can see the processes of group planning, the problems of communication between a planning group and an implementing group, and the problems with which an implementing group must cope when carrying out a plan it did not make itself, all of which requires effective leadership behavior. The specific objectives for the exercise are to provide a problem-solving task in which you can observe leadership behavior, to increase your awareness of the problems involved in using a formal hierarchy in group problem solving, and to give you practice in observing groups and in giving the group feedback on your observations.

The exercise is carried out in clusters of ten to twelve persons. Each cluster is divided into three subgroups: four persons are planners, four are implementers, and the rest observers. The planners decide how they will instruct the implementers to do a task, the implementers carry through the task as best they can, and the observers watch the process of both groups in the two phases. Here is the specific procedure for the coordinator of the exercise:

1. Tell the participants the objectives of the exercise and divide them into four-person planning teams, four-person implementing teams, and observers. Each team goes to a separate room or different parts of a large room (out of earshot) to await instructions.

2. Hand out the appropriate instruction sheets (pp. 342, 343, 345, Appendix E) to each team. Give them adequate time to read them, then review them with each team. The observers should be fully briefed first, the planners next, and the implementers last.

3. The planners are given the general diagram sheet (page 344, Appendix E) and the pieces of the puzzle and are instructed to begin Phase I. Each planner is given four pieces of the puzzle. The exact distribution of the pieces is not crucial, but they should not have any labels marked on them. Phase I lasts forty-five minutes. All information the planners need to know is on their briefing sheet. Instructions for making the puzzle are on page 317.

4. At the end of Phase I the planning team gives the implementing team its instructions. The planners are then prohibited from giving any further help; they must remain silent and uninvolved as the implementing team works.

5. Implementers are to finish the task, Phase II, according to their instructions, taking as much time as necessary.

6. When the task is completed a discussion is held involving all the members of each cluster. This discussion is to include reports from the observers, planners, and implementers, and a comparison of similarities between the exercise and other organizational and group experiences of the members. Questions for the discussion should include:

   a. What leadership functions were present and absent in the planning and implementing teams? What were the consequences of the functions being present or absent?

   b. What leadership functions were needed for each type of activity?

   c. How could the functioning of each team have been improved?

   d. Were the leadership functions distributed among all the team members? Was participation and influence fairly evenly distributed throughout the team?

   e. How was communication between the planning and implementing teams handled? How could it have been improved?

   f. What did it feel like to wait for the planners' instructions, and what did it feel like to watch the implementers carry them out?

7. The major points of the discussion should be summarized with an emphasis placed upon the conclusions about the leadership functions being present, absent, and distributed within the teams. Other types of learnings that typically take place during the exercise are:

   a. Planners often place limitations on team behavior that do not appear in the instructions, thereby making their task harder. They could, for example, ask the implementing team to observe their planning meeting.

   b. There is considerable frustration in planning something that others will carry out without yourself being involved. The commitment to implement a plan is usually built through the planning process, and when the planners cannot put the plan into effect they often experience frustration.

   c. Planning is so interesting and absorbing that planners can forget what their implementing team is experiencing. Implementers can become anxious because they do not know what the task will be, though this concern does not usually enter the minds of the planners.

   d. Planners often fail to use all the resources at their disposal to solve the problem, such as getting the silent members of the planning team to participate.

   e. Planners can spend so much time planning the task that they do not allow enough time to communicate their plans adequately to the implementers, which results in wasting much of their effort.

   f. In communicating their plan to the implementing team the planning team often does not take into account the implementers' anxieties, their needs for being physically comfortable, and so on. Their preoccupation with giving information under pressure blinds them to the needs of the members of the implementing team, which reduces the effectiveness of the communication.

   g. Implementers ususally develop some feelings of antagonism or hostility toward their planners while they are waiting for their instructions. This antagonism increases if they are given complex instructions in a short amount of time and left confused as they take responsibility for finishing the task.

VIETNAM NEGOTIATION EXERCISE

This exercise is based on one developed by Bert Brown in 1965. Vietnam is no longer a crucial political issue, and relationships among nations have changed somewhat since then. Even so, the exercise still offers a fascinating role-playing situation in which to diagnose leadership behaviors. Its objectives are to provide an opportunity both to experiment with the fulfillment of various leadership behaviors and to observe some specific leadership behaviors in a concrete negotiating situation. The coordinator's procedure for the exercise is as follows:

1. Introduce the exercise by stating the objectives and reviewing the distributed functions theory of leadership. Review also the various task and maintenance functions in a problem-solving group.
2. Divide the participants into group of seven role players and at least two observers.
3. Meet with the observers and give them copies of the task and maintenance observation sheets (the same as those used in the Hollow Square Exercise). Explain the observers' role as focusing upon such issues as:
   a. What leadership functions are present and absent during the negotiations.
   b. What leadership functions each of the role players contribute.
   c. What kinds of behavior block or help the reaching of an agreement.
   d. What the communication among role players is like.
   e. What process is used to reach a decision.
4. Distribute the role-playing instructions (pp. 347 and 349 in Appendix E) randomly to the group members. Give them several minutes to read the instructions and think about their role.
5. Begin thirty minutes of negotiations. To help the role players become involved in the situation, state that the negotiations are being held in a rear-lines area and that the whole world is waiting for a peace agreement to be reached. Set the stage appropriately.
6. After thirty minutes end the negotiations and conduct a discussion in each group. Questions that can be raised are:
   a. What are the feelings and reactions of the role players to the negotiations?
   b. How would they and the observers describe the negotiation activities?
   c. What leadership functions was each negotiator engaging in? How did the negotiators specifically try to represent their position during the negotiations?
   d. What leadership functions were present and absent and what were the consequences?
   e. What was the process of decision making and problem solving?

TOWER BUILDING EXERCISE

This exercise is offered to give participants a chance to observe leadership behavior in a competitive situation. Several groups are needed for this study, all of which should have at least six members. Under the basic procedure here, groups will build a tower from supplied materials. The towers are to be judged on the basis of certain criteria. A large room is needed to permit the several groups to work separately, but in sight of one another. The time needed to complete the exercise is approximately one and a half hours. The specific procedure for the coordinator of the exercise is as follows:

1. Introduce the exercise by reviewing the task and maintenance functions of leadership. Tell the participants that this exercise will give them a chance to observe leadership behavior in a competitive situation.

2. Divide participants into two or more groups of six or more members. In addition, two observers for each group and at least two judges must be selected.

3. Hand out three-by-five-inch cards and pins and ask each group to choose a name or symbol for each group member and pin the card on the shirt or blouse.

4. While the groups are proceeding under (3), brief the observers. Give each a task-maintenance function observation sheet and explain how the sheets are used. Also, ask the observers to take note of:

    a. How the group organized for work.

    b. How decisions were made by the group. Were alternatives collected and tested? Did the group arrive at a consensus? Did one person railroad his ideas through?

    c. Whether participation and influence was distributed throughout the group or whether a few members dominated.

    d. What task and maintenance functions were needed to improve group functioning but were not provided.

    e. How the group members reacted to winning or losing.

5. Give the building group their instructions:

    a. Distribute a box of supplies to each group. The supplies should include construction paper, newsprint, paper, tape, magazines, crayons, pipe cleaners, scissors, and glue.

    b. Give the criteria upon which each tower will be judged: (1) height, (2) strength, (3) beauty, and (4) cleverness

    c. The groups have one hour to build their tower.

    d. The winning group will receive a box of candy.

6. During the hour the judges meet to decide how they will evaluate the towers on the basis of the four criteria. At the end of the hour the judges are to make a decision on which tower wins.

7. The groups then meet with their observers to discuss the exercise. All

impressions concerning how the group functioned and what the leadership behavior was like should be presented and reviewed.

ENCOURAGING PARTICIPATION EXERCISE

This exercise is based on one that Jay Hall (1969) originated. Its objectives are to show the importance of maintenance functions in a decision-making group, to emphasize the necessity of involving all members in group decision making, and to give further practice in observing leadership behavior in a group. It concentrates upon the maintenance function of encouraging group members to participate and become involved in group activities. Here is the eight-step procedure for the coordinator to follow:

1. Introduce the exercise by reviewing the task and maintenance functions in a group and by telling the participants that this exercise focuses upon leadership behavior in a decision-making group.

2. Form groups of ten to fourteen members; large groups are essential in this exercise. For each group two additional observers should be tapped. Hand out copies of the case study "Overcoming Resistance to Change" (page 351, Appendix E).

3. Meet with the observers and give them copies of the task and maintenance functions observation sheets. Explain that their role is to give their attention to the leadership and decision-making behavior of the group.

4. Give the groups thirty minutes to arrive at a decision on the case study, indicating that their decision should be based upon accurate information and facts.

5. At the end of the thirty minutes, have every group member fill out the individual-reaction form (page 353, Appendix E). On the basis of the response to question number one, divide the reaction forms from all groups into two categories as follows: place in the high-participator category any person who responded "6" or higher on the first question and in the low-participator category anyone who responded "5" or below. For each category determine the mean response to the rest of the questions by totaling the responses for each question and dividing by the number of persons in the category. Enter the mean response in the Results Table (Table 2.1).

6. Present the results to the participants, ask each group to discuss them, and propose a theory concerning both the effects of participation in group decision making on the implementation of a decision and the effects of maintenance functions (especially encouraging participation) on group decision making. Give each group up to thirty minutes to formulate its theory.

7. Share the theories across groups and have a general discussion covering the material presented in the section entitled "Importance of Maintenance Functions." The correct ranking of the alternatives presented in the case study appear on page 317, Appendix D.

8. Have each group analyze the leadership behavior in its group using the information gathered by the observers. Review the leadership behavior of group members in terms of the theories just formulated in Step 6. Of special interest should be information on who encouraged the participation of other members and how often such behavior was engaged in.

TABLE 2.1   Results Table

	High participators		Low participators	
	This exercise	*Research**	*This exercise*	*Research**
Amount of Satisfaction Gotten from Participation		7.4		4.4
Feelings of Responsibility for Making the Decision Work		6.9		5.6
Feelings of Commitment to the Group's Decision		7.6		5.4
Amount of Frustration Felt during Group Meeting		3.4		5.1
Appraisal of Decision Quality		7.5		6.9
Influence Felt on the Group's Decision				
Direct Dealing with Conflict				
Working with the Group in the Future				

*These results are reported in Hall (1969) after 300 persons (260 high participators and 40 low participators) took part in a similar exercise.

IMPORTANCE OF MAINTENANCE FUNCTIONS

Groups, like all human and mechanical systems, require maintenance. Just as a person would not think of driving a car without putting oil in the engine, members of groups should not think of taking part in group activities without trying to keep the group in good working order. Yet though most people are aware of the maintenance needs of mechanical systems, they tend to overlook the vital maintenance needs of groups.

One of the most crucial maintenance functions in problem-solving groups is that of encouraging all members to participate. In the Encouraging Participation Exercise you have just completed, you have two sources of information about the effects of participation on group functioning: the results of the five-alternatives ranking task, which indicates your theory of reducing resistance to change, and the theory your group developed explaining the questionnaire results dealing with the effects of participation in the discussion of the ranking task. Both sources of information should point out that participation by all group members is extremely important if a group is to work effectively. There are at least three reasons why this is so. The first is that distributed participation is a key factor in using the resources (ideas, opinions, information, conclusions) of all group members to arrive at a high-quality decision; if they fail to participate, their resources cannot be utilized by the group. When all group members do contribute their resources, differences will develop that, if fully explored, will lead to creative and effective decisions. Chapter 6 will deal exclusively with this issue. In the exercise you have just completed, were differences of opinion, ideas, and information brought out into the open and resolved? If not, why not? The results of the discussion in Step 8 may help you answer this question.

One noticeable symptom of ineffective groups is that members make little effort to put into practice the decisions made by the group. In many cases—among the Sleep-Eze employees, for example—members of a group may actively or passively resist putting decisions into practice when it requires them to change their behavior and accustomed ways of doing things. A second reason why member participation is so important has been revealed in a number of studies: a person will be committed to implementing a group decision if he has been involved in helping make it. The usual indication of involvement in decision making is how much a person participates in the group discussion and how much influence she has upon the decision. It is at this point that your theory on the effects of participation in decision making on implementing the decision is relevant. The basic conclusion from research on this issue is that people will work to make successful what they have helped to create. The more members participate in decision-making discussions, the more they will believe they have influenced the decision, the more they will be committed to it, and the more responsibility they will take for making the decision work.

The third reason distributed participation is necessary for effective group action is that it generates feelings among members about the group and their membership. The basic conclusion from the research on this issue is that people will value and support what they help create. The more members participate in decision-making discussions, the more they will tend to be satisfied with the decision, to be approving of member interaction, and to believe they could work effectively with the group in the future. Group cohesion, consequently, will be high, and the group will be seen by its members as a source of social and emotional rewards.

In the most productive kind of participation group members actively state their points of view, ideas, rationales, feelings, conclusions, and hunches. When all members put forth their positions, productive controversies result that are important for a well-considered decision. To get widespread participation within a group, some members have to take the responsibility for encouraging the others to participate, by asking them to contribute, and by giving them support when they do. There must be openings and encouragement for less aggressive members to participate. Silence cannot be trusted to mean consent. Encouraging all members to share openly in the group's endeavors is the number one way of ensuring that the group will maintain itself in good working order.

One particularly interesting result of the previous exercise is that usually little difference materializes between high and low participators on the evaluation of the quality of the decision. It is often assumed that if a person agrees with a decision, and believes it to be a good one, she will work to implement it and be a happy member of the group. The results of this exercise clearly show that this is not the case. Though low participators may believe the decision to be sound, they do not become committed to carrying it out nor do they feel good about their group membership. In other words, convincing low-participating members that a decision is of high quality will not help the group maintain itself. Members need to participate *actively* in the group discussions for maintenance needs to be met.

Frequently, two different types of low participators can be discerned within a group. Some are naturally silent, believing that they have nothing to contribute; by sitting quietly, they experience little frustration. Other low participators want to be more active, but they believe they have no influence within the group. They are in disagreement with the discussion, yet they are reluctant to raise a conflicting point of view, feeling that their contributions are not valued. Many of them, therefore, experience a great deal of frustration in their silence. No matter what the reason for silence, however, it still indicates that the group is not using all its resources effectively and is not working on group maintenance.

Any time a group makes a decision, its ability to make effective ones in the future is affected. When maintenance needs are looked after, a group will continually be improving its decision-making effectiveness; when maintenance needs are ignored, a group's decision-making abilities are deteriorating. Careful attention to group maintenance will constantly promote future group effectiveness.

To check your understanding of this section, answer the following questions (answers on page 53).

1. The more a person participates in a group, the more she feels (check three):
   a. Satisfied.
   b. Dumb.
   c. Responsible.
   d. Verbal.
   e. Committed.
   f. Like a leader.

2. People in a group are more frustrated when they:
   a. Take part in the discussion.
   b. Don't take part in the discussion.
   c. Have the authors as discussion leaders.

True   False   3. If a group member convinces the other members that a decision is best, they will feel committed to that decision.

True   False   4. Group members should encourage everyone in the group to participate, if they want everyone to help implement the decision.

PROCESS OBSERVER

Other maintenance functions are fundamental for group effectiveness besides encouraging all members to participate actively. In different chapters of the book different maintenance functions will be emphasized, but one that we shall stress throughout the book is that of process observer. Unless a person develops process-observation skills, he cannot become an effective leader; further, without feedback on its process, a group cannot function effectively for long. Although this topic was discussed in Chapter 1, it may be helpful to review it briefly here. A process observer collects information about how the group is functioning, and presents it to the appropriate members of the group—usually everyone. The group then plans what action needs to be taken to improve its functioning. To maintain itself in good working order, the group must evaluate regularly the processes by which it accomplishes its tasks and take steps to improve them.

Any effective group should plan procedures for process observation and courses of action. Throughout this book various aspects of group process are emphasized, and the skills for observing the process and for intervening in the group to improve it are underscored. When a high level of skill is obtained, you will find yourself able to participate fully in the group while at the same time being aware of its processes.

ASSUMPTIONS ABOUT GROUP MEMBERS EXERCISE

Sometimes a person is appointed or designated to be a leader of a problem-solving group. On such occasions the assumptions she makes about group members and what motivates them will greatly influence her behavior. The following exercise is aimed at providing a discussion about the assumptions a designated leader makes concerning members of a problem-solving group. The coordinator's procedure is:

1. Introduce the exercise as an opportunity to examine one's assumptions regarding group members after being designated chairperson, boss, or supervisor of the group.
2. Hand out copies of the Leader Attitudes Survey. Ask each person to complete it.
3. Lead a group discussion concerning the Theory X and Theory Y style of leadership.
4. In groups of four, discuss everyone's responses to the survey, what the implications are when leaders make assumptions about group members, and how group members are motivated.

LEADER ATTITUDES SURVEY

Here are ten ways in which a designated leader might act in relation to group members. Read each carefully and then put a check mark in one of the columns to indicate what you would do.

If I were the designated leader, I would:	Make a Great Effort to Avoid This	Tend to avoid doing this	Tend to do this	Make a great effort to do this
1. Closely supervise my group members in order to get better work from them.	—	—	✓	—
2. Encourage my group members to set their own goals, objectives, and performance standards.	—	—	—	✓
3. Set up controls to make sure that my group members are getting the job done.	—	✓	—	—
4. Help each group member accept responsibility for his own personal effectiveness, thereby taking the first step in realizing his potential as a person.	—	—	—	✓
5. Make sure that the group members' work is planned out for them.	—	—	✓	—
6. Allow group members to make important decisions.	—	—	—	✓
7. Set the goals and objectives for my group members and sell them on the merits of my plans.	—	—	✓	—
8. Delegate authority to group members on all matters directly affecting their work.	✓	—	—	—
9. Push my group members to meet schedules if necessary.	—	—	✓	✓
10. Judge a group member's performance on the basis of his success in meeting the goals he has set for himself.	✓	—	—	—

THEORY X AND THEORY Y

In writing about management styles in organizations, Douglas McGregor (1960) got people to look at the reasons underlying the way in which they tried to influence those under them. He saw management thinking and behavior as being based on two different sets of assumptions, one set he labeled "Theory X" and the other "Theory Y." He suggested that a manager's effectiveness, or ineffectiveness, lay in the subtle, frequently unconscious, consequences of his assumptions about motivating subordinates and that these assumptions affected his attempts to direct or influence others.

After looking at the structures, policies, procedures, and work rules in traditional organizations, McGregor concluded that job responsibilities are closely spelled out, goals are imposed without individual employee involvement or consideration, rewards are contingent on working within the system, and punishment falls on those who deviate from the established rules. This traditional managerial style McGregor called "Theory X," and he concluded that it was based upon the following set of assumptions:

1. The average human being has an inherent dislike for work and will avoid it if he can.
2. Because of this human characteristic of dislike for work, most people must be forced, controlled, directed, or threatened with punishment to get them to put forth an adequate effort toward the achievement of organizational objectives.
3. The average human being prefers to be directed, wishes to avoid responsibility, has relatively little ambition, and wants security above all.

These assumptions, of course, are not in agreement with what behavioral scientists consider to be effective procedures for influencing, directing, and motivating people.

McGregor proposed another managerial style—not altogether the opposite of "X"—which he labeled "Theory Y." The assumptions on motivating subordinates underlying this approach are:

1. It is natural to use physical and mental effort in work as it is in play or rest.
2. External control and threat of punishment are not the only ways in which to bring about effort toward organizational objectives. Man will exercise self-control in the service of objectives to which he is committed.
3. Commitment to objectives depends on the rewards a person gets when they are achieved. The most important rewards are those that satisfy needs for self-respect and personal improvement.
4. The average human being learns, under proper conditions, not only to accept responsibility, but to seek it.
5. Most people have the ability to show a relatively high degree of imagination, ingenuity, and creativity in solving problems of the organization.
6. Under the conditions of modern industrial life, the intellectual potentialities of the average human being are only partly used.

To give people responsibility can be very demanding, because it automatically sets standards and expects people to work to meet them. To give people responsibility also involves risks on the part of the manager, because he must let those under him experiment with activities for which he may believe they presently lack capability. The learning and growth resulting from such challenges, however, may be a far more effective reward than any amount of money the manager can offer.

The X manager views man as static, incapable of much further development, whereas the Y manager views man as a growing, developing, learning being. The X manager tries to reduce responsibilities to a level where no mistakes will be made; nonetheless, when they do occur he uses them as clubs for forcing submission to prescribed ways of doing things. The Y manager allows people to test the limits of their capabilities; he uses errors for learning better ways of doing things. He structures work so that the person can have a sense of accomplishment and personal growth; the motivation comes from the work itself. The X manager uses external rewards, like money, to get compliance for work that is so structured that it is distasteful or uninteresting.

What are your assumptions about the individual members of a group for which you are the designated leader? Are you more a Theory X or a Theory Y group leader? The Leader-Attitudes Survey that you have just taken will provide some clues to these questions. Statements 1, 3, 5, 7, 9 all reflect Theory X behaviors. Statements 2, 4, 6, 8, 10 all reflect Theory Y behaviors. Giving the most negative response a "1" and the most positive response a "4," add up your responses for the Theory X and the Theory Y styles of leading groups and compare the results. What conclusions can you draw?

INTERPERSONAL PATTERNS EXERCISE

The following exercise focuses upon your behavior toward other group members. It will help you think about how you conduct yourself in a group. The procedure for the exercise is as follows:

1. Divide into groups of three. Each person fills out the form below involving a verb checklist.
2. Turn to the next page and analyze the meaning of the verbs you checked.
3. Share with the other two members of your triad the results of the exercise and ask for their comments on whether they see you similarly or differently.

Here are the instructions: There are twenty verbs listed below that describe some of the ways in which people feel and act from time to time. Think of your behavior in groups. How do you feel and act? Check five verbs below that best describe your behavior in groups as you see it.

In a group, I:

____ Acquiesce.	____ Concur.	____ Lead.
____ Advise.	____ Criticize.	____ Oblige.
____ Agree.	____ Direct.	____ Relinquish.
____ Analyze.	____ Disapprove.	____ Resist.
____ Assist.	____ Evade.	____ Retreat.
____ Concede.	____ Initiate.	____ Withdraw.
____ Coordinate.	____ Judge.	

Two underlying factors or traits are involved in the list of verbs: *dominance* (authority or control) and *sociability* (intimacy or friendliness). Most people tend to like to control things (high dominance) or to let others control things (low dominance). Similarly, most people tend to be warm and personal (high sociability) or to be somewhat cold and impersonal (low sociability). In the box below, circle the five verbs you used to describe yourself in group activity. The set in which three or more verbs are circled out of the five represents your interpersonal pattern tendency in groups.

	HIGH DOMINANCE	LOW DOMINANCE
HIGH SOCIABILITY	advise coordinate direct initiate lead	acquiesce agree assist oblige concur
LOW SOCIABILITY	analyze criticize disapprove judge resist	concede evade relinquish retreat withdraw

OTHER LEADERSHIP EXERCISES

1. An exercise for an ongoing group is to place the task and maintenance functions singly on three-by-five-inch cards, shuffle the cards, and deal each member one or two of them face down. During a meeting of the group, each member then practices the task or maintenance function on the cards dealt to him. Be sure there are at least two observers. After the meeting discuss which functions different members fulfilled and which ones they were trying to fulfill.

2. Form groups of six members, choose a designated leader, and then analyze why you choose that person.

3. Ask members to lie on the floor with their heads toward the center of the group. Begin a group fantasy about what the perfect leader for this group would have to be like. When the fantasy is ended, review the experience.

4. Paint or draw a picture of the perfect leader for your group. Discuss both the process of making the picture and the resulting content.

SITUATIONAL THEORY OF LEADERSHIP

Social psychologist Fred Fiedler did a series of studies on leadership (1964, 1967, 1969) in many different situations and groups. Defining a leader's effectiveness in terms of the group's performance in achieving its goals, Fiedler divided leaders into those that were task oriented and those that were maintenance oriented. He found no consistent relationship between group effectiveness and leadership behaviors, the reason being that maintenance-oriented leaders were more effective in certain situations and task-oriented leaders more effective in other situations.

A task-oriented leader is effective under two sets of conditions. Under the first he is on very good terms with the group members, the task is clearly structured, and he has a position of high authority and power; under such conditions the group is ready to be directed and is willing to be told what to do. Under the second set of conditions he is on poor terms with group members, the task is ambiguous, and he has a position of low authority and power; under these conditions he can also be effective in taking responsibility for making decisions and directing group members. When moderately good or poor relations exist between the leader and the group members, when the leader has a position of moderate authority and power, and when the task is moderately clear, the maintenance-oriented leader who emphasizes member participation in decision making seems to be the most effective.

Fiedler's results imply that the distributed-functions theory of leadership needs to be modified to take into account the situational conditions influencing the impact of leadership styles upon a group. There are some difficulties with Fiedler's theory, however. For example, how can a person tell if the situational conditions of leader-member relations, task-clarity, and leader-power are high, moderate, or low? Almost all group situations fall into the moderate range; in only the most extreme cases are the sets of conditions in the high or low categories. A second difficulty is that though Fiedler's theory is more complex than the outdated leadership-style theory, which held that a leader should always be democratic, it may not be complex enough. A good leader is always paying attention to the situational conditions that influence the group, modifying his behavior to make it effective. Moreover, leader-member relations, task-clarity, and leader-power may be only three of many different situational factors important for group leaders to be aware of.

You may check your understanding of this section by determining what kind of leader would work best in each situation (answers on page 52).

1. Joe has called a group of his friends together to help plan the local rodeo. He has been in charge of the rodeo for the last five years, is well liked, and is felt to have done a good job. In this situation Joe should probably be:
   a. A task-oriented leader.
   b. A maintenance-oriented leader.

2. Ann has been asked to be in charge of a group of fellow professors to study the beautification of the university. She does not know the other faculty members very well, but she is aware that they are not particularly interested in the task. Even as chairwoman, there is little Ann can do if the other group members decide not to attend meetings or work on the task. In this situation Ann should probably be:
   a. A task-oriented leader.
   b. A maintenance-oriented leader.

3. A group of interested high-school students are meeting together to find ways in which to get girls more involved in sports at the school, and to get boys' and girls' sports more integrated. Buddy, the student body president, has been asked to lead the group and make recommendations for changes to the principal. Buddy knows the other students, but has never worked on a project with them before. As student body president, he can influence whether any of these

students are selected for such desired positions as yearbook staffer, planner for the senior trip, and graduation-dance official. In this situation Buddy should probably be:

a. A task-oriented leader.

b. A maintenance-oriented leader.

INTERACTION PROCESS ANALYSIS

The task- and maintenance-observation sheets used for most of the exercises in this chapter are not the only formats for observing leadership behavior in a group. Bales (1950, 1952, 1955) did a series of studies from which he developed an instrument to check task behaviors and social-emotional behaviors (which are the same as maintenance behaviors in most cases). His set of categories are designed to give a systematic classification for each act of participation in a group. As shown in Figure 2.2, the categories are polarized dimensions: 1 is the opposite of 12, 2 the opposite of 11, and so on. The first three categories are positive emotions, the last three express negative feelings. Categories 7, 8, and 9 ask for aid, while categories 4, 5, and 6 offer it.

Bales' research shows that positive emotions (1, 2, 3) are usually expressed more than twice as often as negative emotions (10, 11, 12). Opinions and information are much more often volunteered (46 percent) than asked for (7 percent). His research also indicates that problem-solving groups move through three stages: (1) orientation (What is the problem?), (2) evaluation (How do we feel about it?), and (3) control (What shall we do about it). As the discussion moves from the intellectual examination of the problem in the first phase (orientation), to evaluation and decision (control), emotions are expressed more often.

In conjunction with Figure 2.2 on the Bales system of categories, an observation form (Figure 2.3, p. 52) is provided for use in observing member inter-action in a group. Why not try experimenting with the Bales system in future exercises?

YOUR LEADERSHIP BEHAVIOR

Now that you have completed some or all of the exercises in this chapter and read some or all of the information presented, it may be helpful for you to again take stock of your leadership behavior. Here is a suggested procedure for doing so:

1. Describe the task and maintenance activities you usally take part in.

2. Describe the task and maintenance activities you would like to practice and become better at.

3. Ask other members of your group to describe your usual task and maintenance behaviors and help you decide which ones would be helpful for you to practice.

4. Plan how you can practice being a process observer in order to determine which task and maintenance behaviors would be most helpful for the group to focus upon.

FIGURE 2.2 Bales's System of Categories Used in Observation

Social-Emotional Area: Positive

1. Shows solidarity, raises others' status, gives help, rewards

---

2. Shows tension release, jokes, laughs, shows satisfaction

---

3. Agrees, shows passive acceptance, understands, concurs, complies

---

Task Area: Neutral

4. Gives suggestions, direction, implying autonomy for others

---

5. Gives opinions, evaluation, analysis, expresses feeling, wishes

---

6. Gives orientation, information, repeats, clarifies, confirms

---

Task Area: Neutral

7. Asks for orientation, information, repetition, confirmation

---

8. Asks for opinions, evaluation, analysis, expressions of feeling

---

9. Asks for suggestions, direction, possible ways of action

Social-Emotional Area: Negative

10. Disagrees, shows passive rejection, formality, withholds help

---

11. Shows tension, asks for help, withdraws, leaves the field

---

12. Shows antagonism, deflates others' status, defends or asserts self

---

5. Plan how you can encourage other group members to engage in needed task and maintenance behaviors.
6. Respond to the following survey on Your Leadership Philosophy.
7. Complete the Checklist of Skills.

YOUR LEADERSHIP PHILOSOPHY

A variety of task and maintenance goals and needs, both individual and group, operate in the average group situation. In general, how do you weigh their relative importance? Rank the following statements in the order that most accords with your view (1) to least accords with your view (5).

_____ The tasks of the group are dictated primarily by the official goals of the group,

FIGURE 2.3 Cumulative Interaction Form

Date _____ Group _____

Time: _____ to _____ Observer _____

Members

BEHAVIOR											TOTALS
POSITIVE EMOTIONS	Shows solidarity											
	Shows tension release											
	Agrees											
TASK	Gives suggestions											
	Gives opinions											
	Give orientation											
	Asks for orientation											
	Asks for opinions											
	Asks for suggestions											
NEGATIVE EMOTIONS	Disagrees											
	Shows tension											
	Shows antagonism											
	TOTALS											

51

and the individual member of the group, regardless of rank or needs, can do little to change them significantly.

___ A group that functions effectively advances by taking care of the needs of the group members and providing the conditions of high morale.

___ The needs of the group come first, and group members must sacrifice their personal goals when necessary in order to maintain a high quality of performance.

___ Both the needs of individual members and the needs of the group are equally important in determining the quality of group funcitoning; neither can be sacrificed if the best results are to be obtained.

___ Though the needs of both individual members and the group are important, in the final analysis it is the needs of the group that should be met.

These five positions can be placed on the task-maintenance grid presented at the beginning of this chapter. Their grid positions, in order of presentation, are: (1,1), (1,10), (10,1), (10,10), (5,5). How do your responses to this survey compare with the responses to the one at the beginning of this chapter?

CHECKLIST OF SKILLS

Check the knowledge or skills that you feel you have mastered.

___ 1. I know the difference between "leader" and "leadership."

___ 2. I know the task and maintenance functions.

___ 3. I can identify the leadership (task and maintenance) functions when they are used in a group.

___ 4. I can fulfill the leadership functions when they are needed in a group.

___ 5. I know the disadvantages of silent membership.

___ 6. I know when task-oriented leaders are most productive.

___ 7. I know when maintenance-oriented leaders are most productive.

___ 8. I know my own leader style or tendencies.

___ 9. I know my interpersonal pattern as a group member.

___ 10. I know the assumptions behind my leadership style(s).

The skills that I need more work on are: _____

_____

_____

_____

_____

_____

ANSWERS

Page 18: 1: b; 2: d; 3: c.

Page 21: 1: true; 2: false; 3: true; 4: false; 5: c; 6: a; 7: b.

Page 23: 1: true; 2: true; 3: true; 4: b, d, e, g, h; 5: a, b; 6: a, b.

Page 27: 1: t; 2: r; 3: p; 4: n; 5: 1; 6: j; 7: h; 8: f; 9: d; 10: b; 11: s; 12: q; 13: o; 14: m; 15: k; 16: i; 17: g; 18: e; 19: c; 20: a.

Page 29: 1; c; 2: h; 3: 1; 4: o; 5: r; 6: i; 7: d; 8: p; 9: k; 10: b; 11: q; 12: j; 13: a; 14: f; 15: m; 16: s; 17: g; 18: n; 19: t; 20: e.

Page 42: 1: a, c, e; 2: b; 3: false; 4: true.

Page 47: 1: a; 2: a; 3: b.

3

Decision Making

INTRODUCTION

A group that functions effectively is one that can make good, sound decisions. A decision implies that some agreement prevails among group members to do something, and it is almost always a choice among several different possibilities. After a decision is made, of course, it must be put into effect. Groups are continually making decisions—when and where to meet, how to organize, how to divide up time, what procedures to use in discussions, what course of action to take toward accomplishing goals. Not all decisions involve weighty issues. Some are about such trivial matters as how long a coffee break to take. Sometimes a group is not aware of how it is making decisions, and at other times it will spend long hours of intense discussion over what procedure is necessary to make a certain decision. Seldom is the same method used for all decisions because different circumstances usually call for different decision-making processes.

If a situation is complex, a better decision can usually be made by an effective group than by a person working alone. In our society the really important decisions are almost always made by groups; guilt or innocence, for example, is ordinarily decided by a jury, not one person. How good the decisions are depends upon how effective the group is. This chapter will look at the different methods a group can use to arrive at a decision, under what circumstances each method is useful and productive, and what the likely outcomes are for these methods.

YOUR DECISION—MAKING BEHAVIOR

We are about to start a series of exercises and discussions on decision making. But before we do, it may be helpful to look briefly at both the ways in which we like to make decisions and how we act in a group when it is time to make a decision. Think about the groups to which you belong. How do they make decisions? Do different groups use different methods? Does your family use the same procedure you and your friends do? If you had your preference, how would the groups you belong to make decisions?

Listed below are a variety of decision-making procedures. Divide into groups of three. Each person should then quickly choose the method he would prefer to use. Discuss for fifteen minutes why each picked the method he did.

If I had my way, the groups I am a member of would use the following method of making decisions:

_____ 1. Rely on the person in charge of the group because she should have the power to make the decision she believes is best, no matter what the rest of the group members think. The designated leader has the responsibility; she should also have the power to make the decisions.

_____ 2. Postpone making a decision and wait it out. Time takes care of everything and with a little luck a decision will never have to be made if the group waits long enough.

_____ 3. Find out what each member thinks, and then choose the most popular alternative—that is the quickest and best way to make a decision involving everyone in the group.

_____ 4. Let the expert make the decision. Give the person in the group with the most expertise the authority to make whatever decision he thinks best.

_____ 5. Put the decision in the hands of a knowledgeable and qualified committee that would look at the issues and decide what the group should do, telling the group members its decision.

_____ 6. Flip a coin, roll the dice, or pick a number out of a hat.

_____ 7. Take a vote; the only American way to make decisions is by a majority vote. The issues should be presented to the group, discussed, and then a vote held with the majority deciding.

_____ 8. Ask the group next door what it is going to do and then do just the opposite.

_✓__ 9. Obtain a basic agreement as to what the decision should be among everyone in the group. The issues should be thoroughly discussed with each member participating until all agree what the group should do.

Now that you have discussed how you prefer to make a decision, it may help you to look at how you behave in a group that is making a decision. Different people will act in different ways when they are members of groups that are making decisions. Even the same person may act differently, depending upon the group, the decision to be made, and the circumstances. But in general, how would you say you act when a group of which you are a member is making a decision? In the following three statements, choose the description that best characterizes the way in which you behave when your group is making decisions. Be as objective and honest as you can; the results are only for your own use.

1. When my group is making a decision I:

_____ Passively defer to others.

_____ Try to get a decision that satisfies everyone without worrying about how good it is.

_____ Look entirely at the merits of a decision without thinking about how the members of the group feel or how satisfied they are.

___✓___ Look for decisions that work, though I might not personally think they are the best.

_____ Try to get strong, creative decisions with a common basis of understanding among group members.

2. When my group is facing a decision I:

_____ Show little interest in the decision or the other group members.

___✓___ Think mostly about how people in the group get along, without worrying about what the decision will be.

_____ Push for a really good decision, and view the other members as only providing resources for helping make a better decision.

_____ Try to get good relations among the members and a good solution, though willing to sacrifice a little of both to get the job done.

_____ Avoid compromise and work for everyone to agree to and be satisfied with a decision that is based upon looking at the situation in a realistic way.

3. When my group is making a decision I:

_____ Wait for the group to tell me what to do and accept what they recommend for me.

_____ Help others participate by giving moral support to members and by testing to see if members can agree.

_____ Give information, evaluate how well the group is working toward the task, set ground rules for behavior, and see that everyone stays at the task.

___✓___ Summarize periodically what has been discussed, call for things to be made clearer, and encourage people to compromise.

_____ Help the group think of alternatives, discuss how practical they are, and work out ways by which the group can come to an agreement.

You can plot your self-assessment on the task-maintenance grid employed in the previous chapter. Each of the opening statements can be completed in five possible ways. The first alternative for each statement is a (1,1) response; it shows that this person has little or no interest in either maintaining the group or helping it accomplish its task of making a decision. The second alternative is a (1,10) response, showing that this member emphasizes group maintenance while ignoring the task. The third alternative is a (10,1) response; here the person focuses on getting the task done, but ignores group maintenance. The fourth alternative is a (5,5) response, indicating a member who compromises on both task and maintenance in order to reach a decision. The fifth alternative for each question is a (10,10) response; this person tries to get a creative, consensual decision, emphasizing both the task and maintenance functions of the group.

Look at your five responses. Locate each on the task-maintenance grid. Then discuss the results in groups of three, comparing your responses here to those you gave on the leadership surveys in the previous chapters, and to the way you would like to be in groups.

EFFECTIVE DECISIONS

Making a decision is just one step in the more general problem-solving process of goal-directed groups—but it is a crucial one. After defining a problem or issue, thinking over alternative actions, and weighing the advantages and disadvantages of each an effective group will use some method of decision making through which it picks the alternative that it wants to execute. In this problem-solving, decision-making process, however, a group needs to know which decision-making method it will use *before* it starts defining the problem.

The purpose of an effective group decision is to get well-considered, well-understood, realistic action toward goals everyone wants. There are five major characteristics of an *effective decision*: (1) the resources of the group members are well used; (2) time is well used; (3) the decision is correct, or of high quality; (4) the decision is put into effect fully by all the necessary group members; and (5) the problem-solving ability of the group is enhanced. A decision is effective to the extent that these five criteria are met; if all five are *not* met, the decision has *not* been made effectively.

Some groups have a hard time making decisions; they do not agree on what the decision should be. There are several reasons for indecisiveness—fear of the consequences of the decision, membership loyalties to other groups that undermine a commitment for making good decisions, conflicts among group members that destroy their ability to reach decisions cooperatively and put them into effect, rigid methods of decision making that do not fit the immediate situation. To help assure that a group will arrive at effective decisions, members must pay attention to the factors that may block effective decision making, as well as work on the factors that facilitate effective decision making.

To check your reading of the above section, answer the following questions: (answers on page 85).

1. What are the five steps in general problem solving?
   a. Making a decision.
   b. Deciding on a meeting time and place.
   c. Weighing advantages and disadvantages of alternatives.
   d. Thinking about the effectiveness of the leader.
   e. Thinking of alternative actions.
   f. Weighing the advantages and disadvantages of this book.
   g. Defining the problem or issue.
   h. Defining why David Johnson wears a beard.
   i. Deciding on a method of decision making.

2. What are the <u>five</u> major characteristics of an <u>effective decision?</u>
   ⓐ The decision is put into effect by the necessary group members.
   b. The problem solving ability of the group is not increased.
   ⓒ Resources of group members are well used.
   d. The least amount of time is used to make a decision.
   ⓔ Time is used well.
   f. Everyone votes on the final decision.
   ⓖ The decision is correct or of high quality.
   h. Everyone is able to quit the group and go home.
   ⓘ The problem solving ability of the group is not lessened.
3. What <u>four things may keep a group from making decisions?</u>
   ⓐ Conflicts among group members.
   b. Disagreement from higher-ups.
   ⓒ Fear of the effects of the decision.
   ⓓ Rigid methods of decision making.
   e. Fear of the effects of not making a decision.
   ⓕ Loyalties to other groups.
   g. Reading this book.

METHODS OF DECISION MAKING

There are many ways in which a group can make a decision, and we shall take up the major ones below. In going through the exercises in this chapter, the reader is advised not to judge quickly any one method as better than another. Each has its uses and each is appropriate under certain circumstances. Each also has its particular consequences for the group's future operation. An effective group understands the consequences of each decision method well enough to choose the decision-making method that is best for: ① the type of decision it has to make, ② the amount of time and other resources available, ③ the past history of the group, ④ the nature of the task being worked on, ⑤ the kind of climate the group wishes to establish, and ⑥ the type of setting in which the group is working.

Seven methods of decision are to be reviewed. These are decisions made by:

1. Agreement (consensus) of the entire group.
2. Majority vote.
3. A minority of group members.
4. Averaging the individual opinions of group members.
5. The member with the most expertise.
6. The member with the most authority after a group discussion of the issues.
7. The member with the most authority without a group discussion.

What follows is a series of short exercises introducing each type of decision making.

The examination of each method includes a short introductory statement, an exercise, and a questionnaire. For each new method participants are asked to form new groups of six. Obviously, in most situations it will not be possible to have all new groups every time, but the groups should change as much as possible. The coordinator may need to recruit someone to help organize the questionnaire information for the Summary Table (Table 3.1). The basic role of the coordinator is to introduce the exercises, supervise them, collect the questionnaire results, find the mean or average response to each question for each exercise (by totaling the scores for each question and dividing by the number of participants), put the results in the Summary Table, and organize a review of the experience. The questions participants should discuss are included in the section "Method and Effectiveness."

Method 1: Decision by Consensus

The most effective method of group decision making is by consensus, but it also takes the most time. Perfect consensus means that everyone agrees what the decision should be. Unanimity, however, is often impossible to achieve. There are degrees of consensus, all of which bring about a higher quality decision than does majority vote or other methods of decision making. Consensus is more commonly defined as a collective opinion arrived at by a group of people working together under conditions that permit communications to be sufficiently open—and the group climate to be sufficiently supportive—so that everyone in the group feels he has had his fair chance to influence the decision. When a decision is made by consensus, all members understand the decision and are prepared to support it. Operationally, consensus means that all members can rephrase the decision to show that they understand it, that all members have had a chance to tell how they feel about the decision, and that those members who continue to disagree or have doubts will, nevertheless, say publicly that they are willing to give the decision an experimental try for a period of time.

To achieve consensus, time must be allowed for all members to state their views and, in particular, their opposition to other members' views. They should get the feeling that others really do understand them. Group members, therefore, must listen carefully and communicate effectively. Decisions made by consensus are sometimes referred to as synergistic decisions, because the group members working together arrive at a decision of higher quality than they would if each one worked separately. In reaching consensus, differences of opinion need to be seen as a way of (1) gathering additional information, (2) clarifying issues, and (3) forcing the group to seek better alternatives.

The basic guidelines for consensual decision making are:

1. Avoid blindly arguing for your own individual judgments. Present your position as clearly and logically as possible, but listen to other members' reactions and consider them carefully before you press your point.
2. Avoid changing your mind *only* to reach agreement and avoid conflict. Support only solutions with which you are at least somewhat able to agree. Yield only to positions that have objective and logically sound foundations.

60

3. Avoid "conflict-reducing" procedures such as majority vote, tossing a coin, averaging, or bargaining in reaching decisions.

4. Seek out differences of opinion. They are natural and expected. Try to involve everyone in the decision process. Disagreements can help the group's decision because they present a wide range of information and opinions, thereby creating a better chance for the group to hit upon more adequate solutions.

5. Do not assume that someone must win and someone must lose when discussion reaches a stalemate. Instead, look for the next most acceptable alternative for all members.

6. Discuss underlying assumptions, listen carefully to one another, and encourage the participation of *all* members.

The only way to understand a method of decision making is by trying it. Divide into groups of six or seven members and use consensus to arrive at a group ranking of the statements listed below on Parental Control of Older Teen-agers. Do not spend a great deal of time arguing the subtleties of every point, but discuss each alternative until group members clearly understand one another, and arrive at a group ranking that all members can live with and support. In ranking the items, place a "1" before the alternative that is deemed best, a "2" before the alternative that is next best, and so on. After you have completed the ranking exercise, fill out the Post-decision Questionnaire (below) and go on to the next method of decision making. Your experiences will be discussed after all methods of decision making have been covered.

Parental Control for Older Teen-agers

___ Parents should not give much direction and guidance. Kids have to learn many things for themselves and should be left free to do so.

___ The best thing a parent can do for his teen-ager is to give responsibility with freedom as soon as he can handle it.

___ Parents have a right and a duty to keep a firm hand on their children for as long as they are financially supporting them.

___ Parental direction and responsibility are necessary if we are to have a healthy society. Giving teen-agers too much freedom is like giving a child matches to play with.

___ Parents should give their children the freedom and encouragement to live their own lives. Giving direction and control will stunt creative self-expression.

Post-decision Questionnaire ✓  Part II

Record your answers to this questionnaire in the following manner: take a sheet of notebook paper and write "Consensus" at the top. Record your answers to the questions and hand them into the coordinator.

1. How understood and listened to did you feel in the group?

    Not at all 1 : 2 : 3 : 4 : 5 : 6 : 7 : 8 : 9 Completely

2. How much influence to you feel you had on the group's decision?

None   1 : 2 : 3 : 4 : 5 : 6 : 7 : 8 : 9   A great deal

3. How committed do you feel to the decision your group made?

Very uncommitted 1 : 2 : 3 : 4 : 5 : 6 : 7 : 8 : 9   Very committed

4. How much responsibility for making the decision work do you feel?

None   1 : 2 : 3 : 4 : 5 : 6 : 7 : 8 : 9   A great deal

5. How satisfied do you feel with the amount and quality of your participation in reaching the group decision?

Very dissatisfied   1 : 2 : 3 : 4 : 5 : 6 : 7 : 8 : 9   Very satisfied

6. Write one adjective that describes the group's atmosphere during the decision making. _____

Method 2: Decision by Majority Vote

Majority vote is the method of group decision making used most often. Its procedure is to discuss an issue only as long as it takes at least 51 percent of the members to decide on an alternative. This method is so common in our society that it is often taken for granted as the natural way for any group to make decisions.

To experience briefly this method of decision making, form a new group of six members and by majority vote decide the best ranking of the statements listed below about religion. First read the statements, then vote as to which one should be ranked "1", "2", and so on. After finishing this exercise, answer the questions in the Post-decision questionnaire, this time marking a sheet of notebook paper with "Majority Vote" and then listing your answers. Turn the answer sheets into the coordinator.

Religion

___ Religion is good for meeting individual needs. It gives some people security and a code to live by.

___ We are children of God and we must obey His laws.

___ Religion is a crutch that we do not need today. We can love and help each other because it is right, not because some god tells us to or because we are afraid of going to hell if we don't.

___ Religion is an out-of-date and ineffective way of trying to understand what life is all about.

___ Religion and faith in God are what made this country great; if we lose this we lose everything.

Method 3: Decision by Minority

Minorities—members constituting less than 50 percent of the group—can make the group's decisions in several ways, some legitimate and some rather illegitimate. One legitimate method is to have an executive committee, composed of only a few members, make all but the most major decisions for the group. Another is to create temporary committees to consider special problems and decide what action the group should take. The illegitimate methods involve subgrouping and railroading. For instance, sometimes two or more members will come to a quick agreement on a course of action, challenge the group with a sudden "Does anyone object?" and, if no one replies fast enough, proceed with a "Let's go ahead, then." Decisions are often railroaded through a group by a small minority forcibly recommending a course of action—implying that anyone who disagrees is in for a fight—then moving ahead before other members can carefully consider the issue. We shall focus upon the legitimate methods of minority decision making, but group members should be able to tell when they are being railroaded.

Form a new group of six and draw straws (or some other procedure, such as drawing slips of paper out of a hat) to determine which two members will be the executive committee. This committee will then meet and determine the group's ranking of the items listed below concerning the sex standards of young people. The executive will announce its decision to the group and then *all* group members will fill out the Post-decision Questionnaire. Mark "Minority Decision" on the top of the page of notebook paper being used for an answer sheet and hand it in to the coordinator.

Sex Standards for Young People

___ Sex is an expression of love and belongs in a close enduring relationship; marriage is not necessary.

___ Sex is simply a biological function; there is every reason to experiment with it. Sex can be for showing affection, for fun, for kicks, or simply for learning how to handle it.

___ Sex is a natural extension of friendship.

___ Sex outside of marriage violates the Seventh Commandment. We believe in virgin brides and grooms and faithful mates.

___ Sex for young people is not bad in and of itself, but it can lead to influences and situations a young person cannot be ready for and cannot handle.

Method 4: Decision by Averaging Individual Opinions

Another method of making decisions is by separately asking each group member his opinion and then averaging them. When a chairperson of a group, for example, calls each member on the telephone, asks what the person's opinion is, and then takes the most popular opinion as the group's decision, she is using the averaging method. This procedure is like majority vote, except that the group's decision could be determined by less than 50 percent of the members (simply being the most common opinion does not mean that more than half the members hold it) and no direct discussion is held among members as to what decision the group should take.

For the purpose of experiencing this method of making decisions, divide into new groups of six and randomly choose a designated leader. Each person then moves to a different part of the room so that he cannot hear the opinions of the other group members. Each reads the items below concerning hippies and others

63

who drop out of society. The designated leader then moves from person to person asking his opinion as to what the ranking should be. He takes the most popular ranking to be the group's decision and informs the members. They will then fill out the Post-decision Questionnaire, marking the sheet of notebook paper being used as the answer sheet "Averaging," and hand it in to the coordinator.

Hippies and Others Who Drop Out of Society

____ They are basically parasites; they live off the work the rest of us do.

____ They show the vitality of the American way of life; they are developing a new ethic for future society.

____ We have positive feelings about some hippies and negative feelings about others. It depends on the individual person; there are all kinds of hippies.

____ They are bums who do not want to do their share of the work; they should be put into jail and assigned to road gangs.

____ They are young people who are finding themselves and their place in the world. They need time to figure it all out.

Method 5: Decision by Expert Member

Group decisions can also be made by letting the most expert member in the group decide what the group should do. The procedure for this method is to select the expert, let him consider the issues, and then have him tell the group what the decision is. To experience this method of decision making, divide into new groups of six. Within three minutes decide who is the most expert member on womanhood, and then wait for her decision. The expert should read the items listed below on womanhood and report her ranking to the group. All group members should then complete the Post-decision Questionnaire, marking the notebook sheet "Expert," and hand it into the coordinator.

Womanhood I

____ Women should have the right to abortion on demand.

____ The use of female sex appeal in advertising should be stopped.

____ Women should receive preferential treatment right now to compensate for past discrimination.

____ Women, because of their sensitivity, are superior to men in all work that does not rely primarily on brute strength.

____ A woman should be able to have herself sterilized without her husband's permission.

Method 6: Decision by Authority after a Group Discussion

Many groups have an authority structure that clearly indicates that the designated leader will make the decisions. Groups that function within organizations—businesses, schools, churches, government—usually employ this method of decision making. The group does originate ideas and hold discussions, but it is the designated leader who makes the final decision. Under the procedure for this method, the designated leader calls a meeting of the group, presents the issues, listens to the discussion until she is sure of what she thinks the decision should be, and then announces it to the group. To get a good idea how this method works, divide into new groups of six, randomly pick a designated leader, and read the items listed below about women. The designated leader should then call the meeting to order, explain that she wants the group to discuss the issues before she decides how to rank them, and then listens to the group discussion, joining in if she feels inclined to do so. When the leader has reached a decision, the discussion is ended. All members are to fill out the Post-decision Questionnaire, mark the answer sheet "Authority with Discussion," and hand it into the coordinator.

Womanhood II

___ Employment practices in the United States discriminate against women.
Women should receive equal pay for equal work.

___ Marriage is an institution that benefits males primarily.

___ Free day care for children is a right that all women should be able to demand.

___ Birth-control information and devices should be readily available to any female over fourteen who requests them.

Method 7: Decision by Authority without Group Discussion

The final method of decision making that we shall discuss is the one where the designated leader makes all the decisions without consulting the group members in any way. This method is quite common in organizations. To experience it, again divide into new groups of six, randomly select a designated leader, and sit back and wait for her to take control. The designated leader should exercise control by such activities as telling the group how to sit while waiting for the decision to be made and how to use their time while she is struggling with the issues. The leader should then make the decision on how the items listed below about racism should be ranked—before announcing it to the group. Again, all members should complete the Post-decision Questionnaire, this time marking the answer sheet "Authority without Discussion," and hand it in to the coordinator.

Racism

___ Every person alive in the United States is a racist, whether he or she knows it, because everyone is affected in one way or another by the basically racist culture in which we live.

___ Most whites in the United States are quite accepting of members of other races and would love to see them be educated and find good jobs.

___ It is up to the members of the various races to make sure that they have a good job. No amount of discrimination could keep a good person down if they really wanted to "make it."

_____ The only way the present situation can change is for whites to change. Without whites allowing equal opportunity, minority people cannot possibly make their lives better.

_____ There should be forced integration of all parts of American life, such as housing, schools, occupational organizations, churches, and so on.

Part III *(2 groups, each do main exercisis)*

TABLE 3.1: Summary Table: Methods of Decision Making

Method	Understood	Influence	Committed	Responsible	Satisfied	Atmosphere
Consensus ✔	7.1	7.2	7.3	7.4	7.4	
Majority Vote						
Minority Rule						
Average Member						
Expert Member						
Authority with Discussion ✔	7		5			
Authority without Discussion ✔	7		.			

do these

METHOD AND EFFECTIVENESS

The results of the previous series of exercises should give you some insight into the relationship between the method of decision making used and the effectiveness of the decision. Three aspects of an effective decision are: (1) the extent to which the resources of the members are used, (2) the commitment of the members to put the decision into effect, and (3) the improvement of the problem-solving ability of the group. The six questions in the Post-decision Questionnaire deal specifically with these issues. The extent to which a member feels understood and influential in the group is related to how well his resources were used. The extent to which a member feels committed to the decision and responsible for its implementation relates to the member's commitment to implement the decision. The extent to which a member feels satisfied with his participation and the positiveness of the atmosphere of the group is related to the future problem-solving ability of the group.

Summary table 3.1 explanation

Looking at the results in the Summary Table, in what methods were the resources of the members used most fully? In what methods were the members most committed to implementation? In what methods was the future problem-solving ability of the group improved? Usually it is found that the more group members directly involved in the decision making, the more effective the decision is. Based on the experiences you have just been through and the results in the

Summary Table, what conclusions can you draw about the method of decision making and the effectiveness of the decision made? What were the participants' reactions to and feelings about each method? Answer these questions and summarize your experiences in a group of six members.

Before we look at the relevant theory and research on the different methods of decision making, a number of exercises are presented below that examine the other aspects of decision effectiveness.

SURVIVAL IN THE WINTER EXERCISE

The purpose here is to compare the effectiveness of five different methods of making decisions. Three of the methods call for the decision without a group discussion and two call for the decision after a group discussion. The methods compared are: (1) decision by a designated leader before a discussion, (2) decision by averaging members' opinions, (3) decision by expert member, (4) decision by a designated leader after a discussion, and (5) decision by consensus. Ideally, at least four groups, of eight to twelve members each, should take part in this exercise. Inasmuch as the results are so predictable, however, fewer groups with fewer members may be used if necessary. The exercise takes approximately two hours to complete.

The materials needed for this exercise are:

Winter Survival Situation Description and Decision Form: Appendix E, page 355.

Winter Survival Group Summary Sheet: Appendix E, page 356.

Instructions to Observers: Appendix E, page 357.

Instructions, Decision by Consensus: Appendix E, page 359.

Instructions, Decision by Leader: Appendix E, page 361.

A coordinator for the exercise should use the following procedure.

1. State that the purpose of the exercise is to compare several different methods of decision making. Set the stage by pointing out that group decision making is one of the most significant aspects of group functioning, that most consequential decisions are made by groups rather than individuals, that though many decisions are routine others are extremely crucial, and that participants in this exercise are now in a situation where the decisions they make as a group may determine whether or not they survive.

2. Divide the participants into groups of approximately ten members—eight participants and two observers. Give each group a number or name for purposes of identification; ask the observers to meet at a central place to be briefed; then distribute the description and decision form to the participants. Review the situation with the participants, again emphasizing that their survival depends upon the quality of their decisions. In half the groups designate one person as the "leader"; in the other groups make no mention of leadership. Then instruct the participants to complete the decision form individually,

working quietly and alone so that the results indicate their own personal decisions. They have fifteen minutes to complete the decision form and make a duplicate copy of their ranking. The designated group leaders should write "leader" on their duplicate copy and all participants must write their group number on their duplicate copy. At the end of the fifteen minutes the duplicate copy of their ranking is collected.

3. While the participants are completing their decision forms, brief the observers. Give each a copy of the Instructions to Observers and a copy of the description and decision form (to orient them to the group task). Review the instructions to observers to make sure they understand their task.

4. Distribute one copy of the Group Summary Sheet and the appropriate instructions to each participant. The groups with "leaders" receive the Decision by Leader Instruction sheet and the groups without leaders receive the Decisions by Consensus instruction sheet. Observers should receive a copy of the instructions for their group. The groups should be placed far enough apart so that they cannot hear each other's discussions or be aware that they have different instructions. The groups are given forty-five minutes to decide upon a group ranking of the items on the decision form. They are to make a copy of their group ranking with their group designation clearly written at the top.

5. While the groups are working on their rankings, score the individual worksheets in the following way:

   a. Score the net difference between the participant's answer and the correct answer. For example, if the participant's answer was 9, and the correct answer was 12, the net difference is 3. Disregard all plus or minus signs; find only the net difference for each item. The correct ranking is on page 321, Appendix D.

   b. Total these scores for the participant's score. The lower the score the more accurate the ranking.

   c. To arrive at an average member score, total all individual members' scores for each group and divide by the number of members.

   d. Put the scores in order from best to worst for each group. This ranking will be used to compare how many members, if any, had more accurate scores than the group's score.

   e. In Table 3.2, enter the average member's score for each group and the score for the most accurate group member. Then for the groups with designated leaders enter the score of the designated leader.

6. At the end of forty minutes, give a five-minute warning. After 45 minutes instruct the groups to complete their ranking in the next thirty seconds and, with the group number or name clearly marked on the paper, to turn in their group ranking. Quickly score the groups' rankings and enter them in the appropriate place in Table 3.2. Recruit one or two observers to help if they are needed.

7. In a session with all the participants, give the correct ranking and the rationale for each item. The correct ranking and the rationale appear on pages 318 to 322,

Appendix D. Then explain how the rankings are scored so that each person can determine his own score.

8. Present the data in the Summary Table. Ideally, this table should be drawn on a blackboard or a sheet of newsprint so that everyone can see it. Review the purpose of the exercise (to compare five different methods of making decisions), and then present the data in this order:

   a. State that one way to make a decision is to have the designated leader make it, and that this is a very common practice in most organizations. Write in the leader scores and compare them to see which group had the most accurate leader.

   b. Move on to the next column, which is reserved for another way in which to make a decision: to poll the group and take the average opinion. Enter this data in the table and compare it with the leader scores. Usually the group average will be better than the designated leader scores.

   c. Refer to the third column as a third decision-making method: to let the most expert member make the decision. Enter this data in Table 3.2 and compare with the other two methods. The expert score is usually far superior to the other two. The problem is, however, that it is often hard to identify who the most expert member of the group is; the person with the most power often believes he is the most expert.

   d. Point out that these first three methods represent decision procedures that do not require group interaction, that the next two procedures do involve interaction among group members and discussion as to what the decision should be, and that research on decision making overwhelmingly indicates that, under most conditions, discussion methods are better than nondiscussion methods.

   e. Review the instructions to the "leader" groups. Then state that a fourth way of making decisions is to have a designated leader make the decision after a group discussion. This method is also very common in most organizations. Enter the relevant data and compare it with the first three methods.

   f. Indicate the fifth column as representing another way of making decisions: by group consensus. Review the instructions for "consensus" groups. Enter the appropriate data and compare it with the other four methods. When a group is functioning well, the consensus score should be better than all the other methods.

9. Give the groups twenty minutes to discuss the data presented and the way in which they functioned, using as a basis of their discussions the notations of the observers. Ask each group to write out on newsprint a list of conclusions that can be shared with the other groups. Questions the group might discuss are:

   a. How well did the group use its resources? Was there anyone who had valuable information who could not persuade others to his point of view, and if so why? How were silent members treated by the group—encouraged to participate or left alone?

TABLE 3.2: Summary Table: Accuracy of Decision

Group	Before Group Discussion			After Group Discussion					
	Designated leader score	Average member score	Most accurate member score	Leader group score	Consensus group score	Gain or loss over designated leader score	Gain or loss over average member score	Gain or loss over most accurate member score	Number of members superior to group score
1									
2									
3									
4									

b. What factors caused the group to use its resources well—or not well? Who behaved in what ways to influence group functioning?

c. Was there anyone who forced his opinion on the group? Why was she able to do so?

d. Did the group follow its instructions in making decisions? What influence did the instructions have on the way the group functioned?

e. What were the personal reactions of one particular group member to the group decision making? How did she feel? What was she thinking?

f. How similar were the behaviors during this exercise to those of other group sessions and meetings? What implications does this exercise have for group meetings?

10. Share the conclusions of each group in a general session and discuss the material on decision making included in this chapter.

OTHER SIMILAR DECISION—MAKING EXERCISES

The winter survival situation was developed especially for this book. Several other situations can also be used for the same exercise. The most famous is the Wrecked on the Moon situation developed by Jay Hall for use in an exercise similar to the previous one. Other examples are the Grievances of Black Citizens and Hazard Potentials of some Common Drugs situations. The decision forms are given below. The correct rankings can be found in Appendix D.

WRECKED ON THE MOON 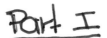 Part I

You are a member of a space crew originally scheduled to rendezvous with a mother ship on the lighted surface of the moon. Due to mechanical difficulties, however, your ship was forced to land at a spot some 200 miles from the rendezvous point. During re-entry and landing, much of the equipment aboard was damaged and, since survival depends on reaching the mother ship, the most critical items available must be chosen for the 200-mile trip. Below are listed the fifteen items left intact and undamaged after landing. Your task is to rank them in terms of their necessity to your crew in reaching the rendezvous point. Place the number 1 by the most crucial item, the number 2 by the second most crucial, and so on through number 15, the least important. (The correct ranking is on page 322, Appendix D).

_15_ Box of matches _15_
_4_ Food concentrate
_6_ Fifty feet of nylon rope
_8_ Parachute silk
_13_ Portable heating unit
_11_ Two .45-caliber pistols

_12_ One case dehydrated Pet milk

_1_ Two 100-pound tanks of oxygen

_3_ Stellar map (of the moon's constellation)

_9_ Life raft

_14_ Magnetic compass

_2_ Five gallons of water

_10_ Signal flares

_7_ First-aid kit containing injection needles

_5_ Solar-powered FM receiver transmitter

GRIEVANCES OF BLACK CITIZENS

During the fall of 1967, the research staff of the National Advisory Commission on Civil Disorders (The Kerner Commission, 1968) studied conditions in twenty cities that had experienced riots during 1967. Nine of the cities had suffered major destruction, six were New Jersey cities surrounding and including Newark, and five had witnessed riots though the degree of violence was less than the other fifteen.

In each city the most-interviewed citizens were the black residents living in or near the disorder area. Also interviewed were persons from the official sector (mayors, city officials, policemen and police officials, judges) and the private sector (businessmen and labor and community leaders). Altogether, more than 1,200 persons were interviewed.

Using the interview material, the research investigators identified and gave special weight to the four grievances that appeared to have the greatest significance to the black community in each city. For each city they made judgments about how severe particular grievances were and then ranked the four most serious. These judgments were based on how often a grievance was mentioned, how intensely it was discussed, how frequently incidents illustrating it were cited, and how severe the people estimated it.

Four points were assigned to the most serious type of grievance in each city, three points to the second most serious, and so on. When the point values were added for all cities, a list of twelve grievances emerged in order of seriousness. The most serious in the most cities was ranked number one, that which seemed least serious was ranked twelfth. The following grievances are the twelve reported by the Kerner commission. You are to guess how they were ranked by the commission staff.

Put a "1" beside the grievance you believe the black citizens in the twenty cities felt to be the most serious to them. Put a "2" beside the second most serious and widespread, and so on down to the twelfth most widespread and serious. (See page 322 in Appendix D for the correct rankings.)

_4_ *Inadequate education:* de facto segregation, poor quality of instruction and facilities; inadequate curriculum.

_7_ *Disrespectful white attitudes:* racism and lack of respect for dignity of Negroes.

_10_ *Inadequate municipal services:* inadequate sanitation in garbage removal, inadequate health care facilities, and so forth.

_1_ *Discriminatory police practices:* physical or verbal abuse, no grievance channels, discrimination in hiring and promoting Negroes.

_3_ *Inadequate housing:* poor housing-code enforcement; discrimination in sales and rentals, overcrowding.

_12_ *Inadequate welfare programs:* unfair qualification regulations, unfair attitude of welfare workers toward recipients.

_5_ *Poor recreational facilities:* inadequate parks, playgrounds; lack of organized programs.

_2_ *Unemployment and underemployment:* discrimination in hiring and placement by organizations or by unions. General lack of full-time jobs.

_8_ *Administration of justice:* discriminatory treatment in the courts, presumption of guilt.

_9_ *Inadequate federal programs:* insufficient participation by the poor, lack of continuity, inadequate funding.

_11_ *Discriminatory consumer and credit practices:* Selling of inferior goods at higher prices, excessive interest rates, deceptive commercial practices.

_6_ *Unresponsive political structure:* inadequate representation of blacks; lack of response to complaints; hidden official grievance channels.

HAZARD POTENTIALS OF SOME COMMON DRUGS

A noted authority* has ranked several drugs by their relative hazard potentials. He based his judgments on such criteria as the drug's overall potential to be used repeatedly or compulsively, be taken intravenously, be used in a self-destructive manner, produce physical dependence, impair judgment, predispose to social deterioration, produce irreversible tissue damage and disease, and cause accidental death from overdose.

Below are listed twelve drugs. Your task is to rank the twelve drugs in the same order of hazard potentials as they were ranked by the authority. Place the number 1 by the drug you think he ranked most potentially hazardous, a 2 by his second choice, and so on through to your estimate of the least potentially hazardous of the twelve in the list. In a few instances, two drugs tie for the same ranking; these should be noted by placing the same ranking number beside the tied drugs. (The correct ranking is on page 323 in Appendix D.)

*Samuel Irwin, professor of psychopharmacology at the University of Oregon Medical School and author of a paper entitled "Drugs of Abuse: An Introduction to Their Action and Potential Hazards."

_3_ Alcohol
_5_ Barbiturates
_4_ Cigarette smoking (tobacco)
_2_ Dexedrine
_1_ Glue sniffing
_6_ Codeine
_6_ Heroin
_5_ Hypnotics
_7_ LSD-25
_8_ Marijuana
_7_ Mescaline
_2_ Methamphetamine

BEAN JAR EXERCISE   Do this?

The purpose of this exercise is to show the involvement of more and more people in the decision-making process affects decision accuracy. The exercise can be done in an hour, and its prime requisite is a large jar full of a known quantity of beans. The procedure for the coordinator to follow is:

1. Introduce the exercise as focusing upon the accuracy of a decision made by different combinations of people. Then set a large jar of beans in front of the participants. You need to know exactly how many beans are in the jar. Tell the participants they will be asked to estimate how many beans the jar contains.
2. Have each person estimate the number of beans, working by himself. Record the estimates.
3. Have the participants pick a partner, have the two-people teams work out a system for estimating how many beans are in the jar, and record their estimates.
4. Have the pairs pick another twosome and the four-people teams estimate the number of beans. Record their estimates.
5. Have the quartets pick another foursome and the eight-member groups estimate the number of beans. Record their estimates.
6. Have the octets pick another group and the sixteen-member groups estimate the number of beans. Record their estimates.
7. The coordinator asks for the final estimates and then tells the participants the number of beans in the jar. In groups of eight the participants should then be asked to discuss their experience, how they felt during the decision making, and the way in which they operated in the groups. Finally, they are to be asked to build a set of conclusions about the effect an increasing number of members has on the accuracy of the decision and why the number of members influenced decision accuracy the way in which it did. The conclusions are then shared among all the participants and discussed.

INDIVIDUAL VERSUS GROUP DECISION MAKING

The following sections offer a brief overview of much of the theory and research on decision making. For those who are interested, a much longer discussion can be found in Watson and Johnson (1972). In this section the issue of individual versus group decision making will be covered. In the next two sections the issue of involvement in decision making and the strengths and limitations of each decision method will be reviewed. Finally, a summary of the discussions will be presented in Summary Table 3.4.

A basic distinction can be made between the decision-making procedures in which group members must interact and those in which they do not. Making decisions by decree of the designated leader (without group discussion), by edict of the expert, and by averaging members' opinions do not require any group interaction. The other methods do. Much research is available comparing the effectiveness of individual and group decision making. The overwhelming conclusion is that group decision making is much better than individual decision making. Even when the decision comes from the expert, who knows more than any other single member in the group, a group decision is usually better.

Watson and Johnson have reviewed the factors that help cause group decision making to be better than individual decision making. First, a number of studies show that a person working around other people acts somewhat differently than he would if he were working at the same task alone. The mere presence of others increases the quality of his work, providing, of course, he knows the information well on which the decision is based. Second, in group interaction the resources of members are pooled. Members usually have distinct contributions to make, and in most situations the information needed to solve a problem is distributed among several people. Only by pooling the resources of its members can the group see all the pertinent difficulties and possible solutions. This complementary knowledge must be coordinated properly; the more the resources of each member are judged correctly, and the more the members are assigned to their areas of expertise, the more likely it is that the group will make a high-quality decision.

A third factor contributing to the superiority of group over individual decision making is, the more people working on a problem—and people have different abilities—the more likely it is that a person with a great deal of ability (either in knowledge or motivation) will be in on the decision making. If the decision is necessary and important, and if it is not known whether any particular member will put forth the necessary effort to make it a good one, having the group make the decision increases the likelihood that at least one conscientious person will see to it that the decision is made properly.

A fourth factor is that errors made by chance will cancel out when more than one person is working on a decision. Some mistakes are due to chance or random influences that act differently on the various members of a group. Mistakes will not only be averaged out in a group, the probability of their being caught and corrected is far greater. A fifth factor in the superiority of group decisions is that blind spots are often corrected in a group. It is easier for us to see other people's mistakes than it is to see our own. Our own will be remedied by other group members, and we can remedy theirs. The sixth factor is that group discussion often stimulates ideas that might not occur to the individual working alone. In a musical jam session, for example, each member continuously responds to the stimulation of others in building a creative product. Finally, there is more security in taking risks in group decision making than in individual decision making.

INVOLVEMENT IN DECISION MAKING

In general, the more people participating in the making of a decision, the more effective it will be. High involvement in decision making increases the use of the members' resources, increases their commitment to implement the decision, and increases their allegiance to the group, all of which affects their future efforts in group work. Whenever possible, therefore, it is best to involve as many people as possible in making a decision. All too often, decisions that could profit from the special knowledge of those who will be carrying them out are made without capitalizing on their knowledge. Most groups can become a lot more effective than they are now if they would just use the resources they already have. They can use them by getting the people who must carry out a decision to help make it. Perhaps the only times decisions should be made by one or a few people are (1) when the decisions are about matters that do not need committed action by most members of a group, (2) when they are so simple that coordination among group members and understanding of what to do is easy, and (3) when the decisions have to be made quickly.

STRENGTHS AND LIMITATIONS OF DECISION-MAKING METHODS

A. Decision by Authority without Group Discussion

This method is efficient in the sense that it can take a short time to execute, but it is not very effective. Even if the designated leader is a good listener who sorts out the correct information upon which to make his decision, it is still the group that has to act on the decision, and under this method the involvement of the other group members is pretty small. Furthermore, when the designated leader makes the decision, all members of the group may not understand what the decision is; they may not, therefore, be able to implement it. And if they disagree with it, they may not want to implement it. Under this method, how well the decision is implemented is particularly crucial.

B. Decision by Expert

There is one major flaw in the method of letting the member with the most expertise make the decision: how to tell which member has the most expertise. On most complex issues, people disagree about the assumptions and approaches, which makes it difficult for them to identify the expert. Personal popularity and the amount of power a person has over group members often get in the way of selecting the most expert member. A classic story illustrating this point involves a consultant watching a general with a high-school education and several captains with Ph.D.'s in engineering discuss how a bridge should be built. Needless to say, it was the general who designed the bridge, simply because he had the most power. People with a lot of power notoriously overestimate their own expertise while underestimating that of others. Unless a clear and effective way exists to determine who the expert is, this method does not work too well. Moreover, it too fails to win the involvement of other group members, which is necessary to implement the decision.

C. Decision by Averaging Individual Opinions

Because individual errors and extreme opinions tend to cancel themselves out under the average-opinion method, it is usually a better procedure to follow than the designated-leader method (without a group discussion). At least, members are consulted in this method. The disadvantage lies in the fact that the opinions of the least knowledgeable members may annul the opinions of the most knowledgeable members. Letting the most expert member make the decision is always better than a group average. Although group members are consulted before the decision is made, there is still little involvement in the decision making; consequently, the commitment to the decision is not very strong. If implementation requires the efforts of all group members, the effectiveness of the decision made by this method will probably be slight.

D. Decision by Authority after Group Discussion

Listening to a group discussion will usually improve the accuracy of a decision made by the group's leader. The greater the designated leader's skill as a listener, the greater will be the advantages of the group discussion. Although members can become involved in the discussion under this method, they have no part in the decision making, which does not help the decision's effectiveness. As a result, a situation tends to develop wherein the group members either compete to impress the leader, or tell the leader what they think she wants to hear.

E. Decision by Minority

The minority members who make the decision under this method may be committed to it, but the majority may not only be uncomitted, they may even want to keep the decision from being implemented. When decisions are railroaded by a few members, furthermore, the assumption seems to be that if people are silent they agree. But often a majority of group members need more time to organize their thoughts against a proposal, or sometimes members keep silent because they are afraid they are the only ones who disagree. When a group has a large number of decisions to be made, and does not have time to deal with them all, setting up decision-making committees may be efficient. Also, when a large number of decisions do not need member involvement to be implemented, this method may be effective. In general, however, decision by minority is not a good method of decision making.

F. Decision by Majority Vote

The method of reaching a decision by majority vote is almost a ritual in our society, and it is certainly one of the methods that is used most often. On the surface it looks like our political system, but there are critical differences between elections and the use of majority vote in most groups. In our political system minority rights are carefully protected through the Bill of Rights and the Constitution; and political minorities always have the right to compete on equal terms in the next election in order to become a majority. In most groups, however, minority opinions are not always safeguarded. Thus, majority voting often splits a group into "winners" and "losers," encourages "either-or" thinking (when there may be other ways of looking at a problem), and fosters blind argument rather than rational discussion. A minority that has often been outvoted is not contributing its resources toward influencing the decision. This circumstance not only reduces the quality of the decision, but often creates coalitions of people who resent losing the vote and who try to regroup, pick up support, and overturn the decision. When a task needs the support of everyone in the group, when the lack of support or sabotage by one or more members could seriously damage the undertaking, a decision by vote can be dangerous. Where commitment by everyone is not essential, of course, a majority vote can serve very well. If voting is to be used, however, the group must be sure that it has created a climate in which members feel they have had their day in court, and where members feel obliged to go along with the majority decision.

G. Decision by Consensus

To produce an innovative, creative, and high-quality decision that all members will be committed to implementing, one that uses the resources of all group members and that increases the future decision-making effectiveness of the group, the best method to use is consensus. Consensus, however, is difficult to achieve. It requires a fairly sophisticated understanding of the dynamics of controversy, conflict, distributed participation and leadership, communication, and all other group and interpersonal skills. All group members must participate actively, and power must be distributed evenly among them. Decisions by consensus take a great deal of time and member motivation, and will often prove frustrating to designated leaders. But in terms of the future ability of the group to make high-quality decisions, consensus productively resolves controversies and conflicts—which majority vote, minority rule, and all other methods of decision making do not. Research shows that the more effective groups tend to have designated leaders who allow greater participation, more differences of opinions to be expressed, and greater acceptance of different decisions (Torrance, 1957). Effective leaders have been shown to encourage minority opinions and conflict to a greater extent than less effective leaders (Maier and Solem, 1952). Groups members with little influence over a decision not only fail to contribute their resources to it, but usually are less likely to carry it out when action is required (Coch and French, 1948). If consensus is to be used effectively, all group members must contribute their views on the issue and their reactions to proposed alternatives for group action; no one should be allowed to remain silent. For a group to achieve consensus, furthermore, time must be allowed for everybody to state their opposition and to state it fully enough to get the feeling that the others understand them—a procedure that requires careful listening and effective communication by the group members.

TIME AND DECISION METHOD

Every method of decision making takes a different amount of time to carry out. Obviously, methods that involve group discussion will take more time than methods that do not. Usually, the more people involved in the decision-making process, the longer the time it will take to reach a decision. Figure 3.1 summarizes the relationship among number of people involved, type of method being used, quality of decision, and time needed to arrive at a decision. If time is considered in terms of both making and implementing a decision, however, the time factor becomes less clear. Often the extra time taken to make a consensual decision will greatly reduce the time needed to implement it. Thus, many group authorities insist that if the whole process of decision and implementation is considered, consensus is the *least* time-consuming method.

FIGURE 3.1 General Types of Group Decisions

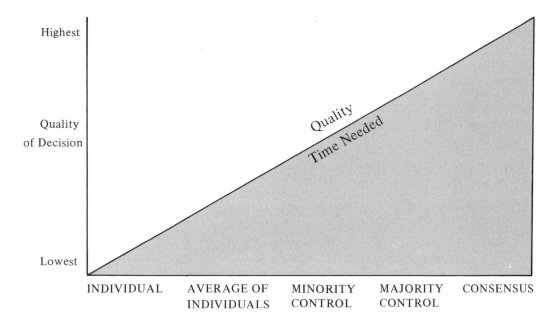

FEELINGS, CONFLICT, AND DECISIONS

Two other factors about group decision making should be mentioned. The first is that it is necessary to have group members express their *feelings*, as well as their ideas and opinions, in a decision-making discussion. The second is that *controversies* and *conflicts* are extremely important when it comes to making high-quality, creative decisions.

Our society has a history of repressing feelings, and there is a general myth that to be "objective" and "rational" is to rule out all emotions from decision making. Nothing is further from the truth. Being "objective" and "rational" means that *all* available information is used in making a decision, and feelings are an important source of information. If a group puts pressure on members not to express their feelings, members will tend to hide them and the chances for creative decisions will be lost. As a defensive reaction to suppressed feelings, members tend to limit themselves to those ideas that are not threatening, that will not violate group norms. Suppressed feelings increase misunderstandings and distortions in perception. In short, the quality of a group's decisions will be seriously impaired if feelings are not expressed.

Two chapters in this book will deal with the importance of conflicts in decision making. Often, group members hide their feelings because they are afraid that controversy or conflict will destroy group maintenance and their personal security in the group. True, as conflict increases, and people become tense and emotionally aroused, greater skill is needed in conducting a productive discussion. But such tensions are at the heart of personal commitment to the decisions being made. A conflict is the major ingredient in creating decisions of exceptionally high quality. A basic rule for any effective decision-making group is to make sure that feelings are expressed and controversies are encouraged.

SUMMARY TABLE 3.3   Advantages and Disadvantages of Decision-Making Methods

Methods of decision making	Disadvantages	Advantages
Authority rule without discussion	One person is not a good resource for every decision; advantages of group interaction are lost; no commitment is developed for implementing the decision by other group members; resentment and disagreement may result in sabotage and deterioration of group effectiveness; resources of other members are not used.	Applies more to administrative needs; useful for simple, routine decisions; should be used when very little time is available to make the decision, when group members expect the designated leader to make the decision, and when there is a lack of skills and information among group members to make the decision any other way.
Expert	It is difficult to determine who the expert is; no commitment is built for implementing the decision; advantages of group interaction are lost; resentment and disagreement may result in sabotage and deterioration of group effectiveness; resources of other members are not used.	Useful when the expertise of one person is so far superior to that of all other group members that little is to be gained by discussion; should be used when the need for membership action in implementing the decision is slight.
Average of members' opinions	There is not enough interaction among group members for them to gain from each others' resources and to get the benefits of group discussion; no commitment is built for implementing the decision; unresolved conflict and controversy may damage future group effectiveness.	Useful in a situation where it is difficult to get group members together to talk, when the decision is so urgent that there is no time for group discussion, when member commitment is not necessary for implementing the decision, and when a lack of skills and information exists among group members to make the decision any other way;

Methods of decision making	Disadvantages	Advantages
		applicable to simple, routine decisions.
Authority rule after discussion	Does not develop commitment for implementing the decision; does not resolve the controversies and conflicts among group members; tends to create situations in which group members either compete to impress the designated leader or tell the leader what they think he wants to hear.	Uses the resources of the group members more than previous methods; gains some of the benefits of group discussion.
Majority control	Usually leaves an alienated minority, which damages future group effectiveness; relevant resources of many group members may be lost; commitment for implementing the decision is not totally present; full benefit of group interaction is not obtained.	Can be used when sufficient time is lacking for decision by consensus or when the decision is not so important that consensus needs to be used, and when complete member commitment is not necessary for implementing the decision; closes discussion on issues that are not highly important for the group.
Minority control	Does not utilize the resources of many group members; does not establish widespread commitment for implementing the decision; unresolved conflict and controversy may damage future group effectiveness; not much benefit from group interaction.	Can be used when everyone cannot meet to make a decision, when the group is under such time pressure that it must delegate responsibility to a committee, when only a few members have any relevant resources, when broad member commitment is not needed to implement the decision; useful for simple, routine decisions.
Consensus	Takes a great deal of time and psychological energy and a high level of member skill. Time pressure must be minimal and no emergency in progress.	Produces an innovative, creative, and high-quality decision; elicits commitment by all members to implement the decision; uses the resources of all members; the future decision-making ability of the group is enhanced; useful in making serious, important, and complex decisions to which all members are to be committed.

QUESTIONNAIRE ON DECISION MAKING

To check your understanding of the previous sections, answer the following questions (answers on page 85):

1. Seven ways in which group decisions are better than individual decisions are:
   - (a.) Group interaction pools the resources of the group.
   - b. Individuals are anxious to make a decision quickly.
   - c. Groups are more pleasant places for decision making.
   - (d.) An expert is likely to be in a group.
   - (e.) Mistakes are likely to be canceled out by other members.
   - (f.) Blind spots are often corrected.
   - g. Feelings will not influence the final decision.
   - (h.) Groups stimulate new ideas.
   - (i.) People working in a group do better work than if they work alone.
   - j. The leader can easily push a decision through.
   - (k.) Groups offer more security in risk taking.

Match the following decision-making methods with their definitions:

_b_ 2. Consensus   a. Leader makes decision.

_c_ 3. Majority Vote   b. Everyone must agree.

_g_ 4. Minority   c. At least 51 percent of the members must agree.

_f_ 5. Averaging

_e_ 6. Expert   d. Leader makes decision after listening to group.

_d_ 7. Authority with Discussion

_a_ 8. Authority without Discussion   e. The one who knows the most makes the decision.

f. Leader polls members; decision is the most popular response.

g. A small subgroup makes the decision.

Check these true-false statements:

(True) False   9. The more people involved in decision making, the longer it takes to reach a decision.

True (False)   10. The fewer people involved in decision making, the higher the quality of the decision.

(True) False   11. The extra time needed to make a consensual decision is offset by the lesser time it takes to implement it.

True (False)   12. Group members should not tell their feelings because to do so holds up effective decision making.

True (False)   13. Controversies and conflicts should be avoided in a group.

14. Feelings are a part of rational decision making.

15. You are a superintendent of a small, traditional, school system. You would like to introduce new methods like individualized teaching into the system. What decision-making method(s) would you use to get the teachers to adopt the new system? Why? What are the risks in the method? What are the advantages?

16. You are a teacher who would like to change your class in order to increase student involvement. What decision-making method(s) for change would you use? Why? What are the risks in the method? What are the advantages?

ORGANIZATIONAL DECISION MAKING

Effective decision making is one of the most significant determinants of organizational success. Almost all organizational decision making occurs in small groups and, therefore, group decision making is the key aspect of how organizations arrive at their decisions. All the material in this chapter applies to organizational decision making. It may be helpful to note, however, that several characteristics of organizations operate to influence the process of making decisions.

The first characteristic is that some decisions within organizations are routine and programmable, based primarily upon technical factors, and apply to highly structured situations. Other decisions apply to problem situations that are less structured, and interpersonal factors greatly influence the decision-making process. As decisions become less routine and programmable, the relationships among group members become more crucial.

A second characteristic is that no single person in an organization can expect to have all the information necessary to make a decision. Most decisions must be handled by groups because each individual member will have only a certain amount of the information necessary to make a valid one. As a result, the accuracy of the information received by the key decision-making group is of utmost importance. Mutual dependence among organizational group members for precise information underscores the importance of communication—the subject of Chapter 5.

Even when group members have all the information needed to make a good decision, group process factors can either help or hurt effective decision making. A high level of interpersonal and group skill is needed by group members in order for decision making to proceed effectively. The resources of all group members must be properly identified and well utilized by the group.

Another important characteristic is that a decision made by one group within an organization often has implications for other parts of the organization. This interdependence creates a need for coordination of organizational decisions. In order to harmonize decisions, an organization must develop a "problem-finding mechanism" that helps it to identify problems, establish priorities, and regulate group decisions made about its problems.

Finally, the decisions made in organizations affect all members of the organization, both directly and indirectly. As a consequence, people's feelings and reactions and relationships with other members are often as important in making a good decision as facts and logic. The effectiveness of a decision depends upon both logical soundness and the level of psychological commitment to it by the members who have to implement the decision. Individuals uninvolved in the decision-making group may withhold information necessary to arrive at a high-quality decision; they may also put forth only a minimum effort to implement it. A logical decision to which people are uncommitted is not an effective decision.

IMPLEMENTING YOUR DECISION EXERCISE

This exercise provides a brief experience in implementing, and not implementing, a personal decision. It is often used as a basis for forming new groups. It is placed here to give you a more personal experience in making and implementing a decision before the chapter is concluded. The exercise can be done in less than a half hour and the procedure is as follows:

1. Look around the room. In your mind select someone with whom you would like to pair up.
2. Now make a second choice.
3. Choose a partner and pair up with that person.
4. Take a moment to think about why the decisions you made did, and did not, get implemented. Are you with your first choice? Your second choice? Are you with neither? What kinds of decisions did you make in order to be with the person of your final choice? As you think about your behavior, is it typical of you in similar situations? Are you usually a "chooser" or a "choosee"? As a pair, which of you, do you think, exerted the most influence to bring the two of you together?
5. Discuss the answers to these questions with your partner.
6. Discuss the experience with others in the room. In the simple act of choosing a partner, people react differently. Many find they feel better being chosen than choosing; for them, being forced to choose one person over others is distasteful. Others feel better making sure whom they are with by searching them out and asking them to be a partner.

MY DECISION—MAKING BEHAVIOR

Before this chapter ends it might be useful to again consider your decision-making behavior. How do you usually behave in a decision-making group? How would you like to behave? As a closing exercise, put yourself into a group of three and do the following:

1. Throw all your loose change into the center of the group. Decide (using consensus) how to use the money. Then look at the group decision in terms of your personal behaviors. How did each one of you behave? What task and maintenance functions did you yourself fulfill? How did you feel about your participation? How did your usual behavior reveal itself in making a group decision?

2. Review as a group the task and maintenance functions listed in the previous chapter. Discuss what other group functions concerning decision making could be added. Examples are:

Clarification or elaboration: interpret or reflect ideas or suggestions; clear up confusion; indicate alternatives and issues before the group; give examples.

Summarization: pull together related ideas; restate suggestions after the group has discussed them.

Consensus testing: check with the group to see how much agreement has been reached; test to see if the group is nearing a decision.

Communication of feeling: express your feelings concerning the issues the group is discussing and the way in which it is functioning.

Verification of feeling: ask other members how they are feeling; check to see if your perception of their feelings is correct.

Pick the task and maintenance functions you usally engage in; pick those you would like to perform better. Give one another feedback about behavior.

3. Review your answers to the questions listed in the beginning of this chapter. Have there been any changes? Have you received any feedback on your behavior that has increased your awareness of how you do behave? How would you now describe your behavior in decision-making situations?

4. Decide as a group when to end this exercise.

CHECKLIST OF SKILLS

I understand when and how to use the following decision-making methods:

✓ Decision by consensus

✓ Decision by majority vote

✓ Decision by minority

✓ Decision by averaging individual opinions

✓ Decision by expert member

✓ Decision by authority after discussion

✓ Decision by authority without discussion

ANSWERS

Page 58: 1: a, c, e, g, i; 2: a, c, e, g, i; 3:a, c, d, f.

Page 82: 1: a, d, e, f, h, i, k; 2: b; 3: c; 4: g; 5: f; 6: e; 7: d; 8: a; 9: true; 10: false; 11: true; 12: false: 13: false; 14: true.

4

Group Goals

THE WHAT AND WHY OF GROUP GOALS

All problem-solving groups have goals. The goal may be to build a better mousetrap, to climb a mountain, to get the most pay for the least amount of work, or to apply the material being presented in this book. But there is a goal if it is a problem-solving group! One of the most important aspects of group effectiveness is the group's ability to define its goals and achieve them successfully. In this chapter we shall focus upon the formation of group goals, the cooperativeness of group goals, and the clarity of group goals.

What is a goal and what is a group goal? The essential idea about a goal is that it is an ideal. It is a desired place or objective toward which people are working, a state of affairs that people value. A *group goal* is a future state of affairs desired by enough members of a group to get the group working toward its achievement: A group goal, for example, might be to learn more about group effectiveness, and if enough members of a group want to learn about it they will behave in ways to achieve their purpose! In discussing a goal, three aspects need to be stressed. The first is the group goal itself, the second, the tasks the group must perform in order to accomplish the goal, and the third, the processes of interaction among members necessary to accomplish the goal. Thus the group's goal may be to plan a camping trip, the tasks may be to gather the information and equipment needed to take such a trip, and the processes of interaction among members may be characterized by a division of labor, sharing ideas and materials, and constructive resolution of conflicts.

Most groups have several goals, some immediate and some long range. It is usually the immediate goals that are of greatest significance; the activities of group members are directly related to short-term goals, and only indirectly related to long-range goals. The immediate goals are stepping stones to the more distant long-range ones. If group members are clear about the immediate objectives that lie along a path toward accomplishing a long-range goal, they can avoid misunderstandings about their final destination. In setting goals it is extremely important to choose immediate ones that can be easily recognized when achieved and that can be reached in a specified, reasonable length of time.

Why are goals important? There are several answers to this question. Goals are guides for action, and it is through group goals that the efforts of group members are planned and coordinated. The efficiency and usefulness of group procedures are evaluated on the basis of how they facilitate goal accomplishment. Conflicts among group members are resolved on the basis of what assists the group in achieving its goals. But the most important answer is that goals are the motivating force in the behavior of group members. Without member motivation the group would take no action to achieve its goals. All group goal accomplishment is based upon the members' commitment to accomplishing the goal. It is the group's goals that direct and motivate members' behavior. As the member commits herself to achieving a certain goal an inner tension system is aroused that continues until the goal has been accomplished or until some sort of psychological closure is achieved concerning the goal. It is this internal tension that motivates the group member to work towards goal accomplishment. Thus when a group member commits herself to the group goal of planning a camping trip, an internal tension system is set up that makes her restless and dissatisfied until the group completes its plans. A member's commitment to accomplishing a group goal depends upon several factors, such as: (1) how attractive or desirable the goal seems, (2) how likely it seems that the group can accomplish the goal, (3) how challenging the goal is (a moderate risk of failure is more challenging than is a high or low risk of failure), (4) being able to tell when the goal has been achieved, (5) the satisfaction or reward the member expects to feel or receive when the goal is achieved, and (6) the ways in which the member will relate to other members in working toward the accomplishment of the goals (some ways of relating to other group members are more fun and involving than others).

The motivation of members to work for their group's goals is heightened by participation in setting the goals. This increase in motivation comes in part from the fact that participation produces (1) a better matching of the group goals to the motives of members, which brings about greater acceptance of the goals, (2) a better understanding of group actions needed to achieve the goals, and (3) a better appreciation of how individual behavior contributes to the necessary group action.

If they are accepted, understood, and desired by group members, group goals direct, channel, motivate, coordinate, energize, and guide the behavior of group members. The goals of a group are, therefore, the beginning point of evaluating a group's effectiveness.

To check quickly your understanding of the preceding section, please answer the following questions (answers on page 107).

1. Pick out the five reasons you should pay attention to group goals:
    a. If you don't pay attention to them, they won't pay attention to you.

b. Goals are guidelines for the group.

c. Members work together better if they agree on group goals.

d. When goals are specified, group effectiveness can be achieved and evaluated.

e. Goals motivate the group members.

f. Specified goals make the group more sociable.

g. Conflicts can be dealt with more easily if goals are specified.

h. Goals keep the group on business, not pleasure.

2. A group goal is:

a. A desired place toward which group members are working.

b. The same as an individual goal.

c. A desired place the leaders want to be and toward which group members are working.

3. A group task is:

a. A job of work to do.

b. What must be done in order for the goals to be achieved.

c. What must be done in order to figure out the goals.

4. How are group goals like individual goals?

a. They arouse or excite individual members until the task is completed or dropped.

b. They bring individual members together in one common purpose.

c. If the leader carries a big stick, he can make individual and group goals the same.

5. The degree to which members are committed and motivated to accomplish a group goal depends on what two things?

a. How attractive the goal is for them.

b. How easy the goal is for them.

c. How much they are paid.

d. Whether they think the group can accomplish the goal.

6. How does participation in setting the goal help motivate members? (Choose three.)

a. They understand the hidden dynamics better.

b. They get paid more for the extra time.

c. The goals fit the members better.

d. The members understand better the group action needed to reach the goal.

e. The members appreciate better how individual behavior contributes to group action.

YOUR GOAL—RELATED BEHAVIOR

When you are a member of a problem-solving group, how do you behave when it comes to group goals? Please answer the following questions as honestly as you can in order to clarify your goal-related behavior to yourself before going on with this chapter. Check as many responses to each question as are characteristic of your usual and regular behavior.

1. When I am a member of a group that does not seem to have a clear awareness of what its goals are or how they are to be achieved, I usually:

   __✓__ Ask that the group stop and discuss its goals until all group members clearly understand what they are and what actions the group needs to take to accomplish them.

   ____ Feel disgusted and refuse to attend meetings.

   ____ State, as specifically as possible, what I consider the goals of the group to be and comment on how present actions of the group relate to goal accomplishment.

   ____ Ask the designated leader to stop messing around and tell the group what it is supposed to be doing.

2. When I am a member of a group that has a clear understanding of its goals, but seems to have little commitment to accomplishing them, I usually:

   ____ Try to shame other group members into being more motivated.

   ____ Blame the designated leader for being incompetent.

   ____ Ask the group members to look at how meaningful, relevant, and acceptable the goals are to them.

   ____ Try to change the group's goals in order to make them more relevant to the members' needs and motives.

   __✓__ Point out the sacrifices other members have made in the past toward goal accomplishment and hope they become more committed.

3. When I am a member of a group that has conflicting opinions on what its goals should be, or that has members with conflicting needs and motives, I usually:

   __✓__ Figure out how much cooperative and competitive behavior exists in the group and give feedback on my observations to the group in an attempt to increase cooperativeness among its members.

   ____ Start a group discussion on the personal goals, needs, and motives of each group member in order to determine the extent to which there are competing goals among them.

   ____ Declare one member of the group to be the winner and ask all other group members to work toward accomplishing that person's goals.

   __✓__ Ask the group to determine how the members' actions can become more coordinated.

   ____ Form a secret coalition with several other group members so that our goals will become dominant in the group.

The three questions above deal with the clearness of group goals as well as the degree of commitment and cooperation they inspire among members. Each of these issues will be examined further in this chapter. At this point divide into groups of three and discuss for fifteen minutes your answers to the questions and why you answered them as you did. Try to develop as much awareness of your behavior in goal-related situations as possible.

HIDDEN AGENDAS EXERCISE

This exercise is designed to create an awareness of the underlying motivations that govern a persons's behavior in a group and affect the establishment and accomplishment of group goals. It requires five role players and several observers, and it can be done within an hour. The specific procedure for the coordinator of the exercise to use is as follows:

1. Introduce the exercise as an experience contrasting individual and group goals.
2. Divide into groups of seven, five role players—who are to be members of a fact-finding committee—and two observers.
3. Distribute the role instructions and the problem sheets to the role players (see pp. 363 and 365, Appendix E). Warn them not to reveal their roles to anyone, including other role players. Give them five minutes to study the problem sheet and their role sheet. They are also to be given the following role-playing instructions: "Read your role sheet carefully and play the part conscientiously; put yourself in the role you have been given; be natural and do not overact—but emphasize the behavior aimed at fulfilling your role."
4. While the role players are studying their sheets, brief the observers. Tell them they are to seek answers to these questions:
   a. What is the basic goal of the group? How did each member contribute to or hinder goal accomplishment?
   b. Toward what goals were the individual members working?
   c. What task and maintenance behaviors were present and absent?
   d. What was the group atmosphere like? Did it change from time to time?
   e. Was participation and influence distributed throughout the group? If not, who dominated?
   f. How far did the group get in attaining its goal?
5. Set the stage for the role players. Review the problem sheet and state that you are the chairman of the Middlebury City Council waiting for the committee report on the poverty-representatives issue and that a decision has to be made by the role players' committee in the next fifteen minutes. Commence the role playing.
6. End the role playing after fifteen minutes, whether the group has completed the agenda or not. Ask the observers to report their findings to the group; the group members and the observers should then discuss for fifteen minutes the interaction among group members.
7. Have the role players read their parts to the group with Jack reading his last. Outline the material on individual versus group goals, and then ask each group participating in the exercise to spend at least fifteen minutes writing out its

conclusions concerning the effect of hidden agendas on the goal functioning of problem-solving groups. Some points to be covered are:

a. How do hidden agendas affect the group; how do they affect each group member?

b. What are some of the indications that hidden agendas are operating?

c. Is the recognition of hidden agendas necessary to understand what is going on in the group?

d. How can hidden agendas be productively handled to help in accomplishing the group's goals?

8. If more than one group is participating in the exercise, see to it that their conclusions are shared. Ensure that the material on individual versus group goals is discussed and integrated into the conclusions made by the groups.

INDIVIDUAL MEMBERS' GOALS AND GROUP GOALS

A group goal is a combination of the individual goals of all group members. It is the individual members who set the goals for the group. People become group members because they have certain personal and subjective goals and motives, for which they look for either expression or fulfillment through group membership. Each person brings to the group a wish to satisfy personal goals. These personal goals are not always clearly known to an individual member; he may be completely aware, partially aware, or totally unaware of his personal goals and motives during a group meeting. As group goals are agreed upon by the group members they must be relevant to the individual needs of the members. Usually a group member is trying to achieve both individual and group goals, and the degree to which both can be accomplished by the same activities determines how effective the group will be in attaining its goals. The situation is further complicated by the fact that different members value different goals at different times; even the same member places different values on the same goal at different times.

The personal goals of the group members can be homogeneous (alike) or heterogeneous (different). Homogeneity of individual members' goals (or consensus about what the group's goals should be) usually helps group functioning, whereas heterogeneity of individual members' goals (or disagreement about what the group's goals should be) usually interferes with group functioning. Individual group members with homogeneous goals are usually happier with the group and its tasks than are members of groups with heterogeneous individual goals. Members with heterogeneous goals easily acquire hidden agendas that interfere with group effectiveness; they establish competitive or opposing forces that destroy the effectiveness of group functioning. A *hidden agenda* is a personal goal that is unknown to all the other group members and is at cross-purposes with the dominant group goals. It is a covert personal goal that is markedly different from the group's goal. Hidden agendas can be destructive to a group and greatly hinder group effectiveness. Yet in almost every group some hidden agendas will be present. A group, therefore, must develop procedures to both increase consensus among group members on what the group's goals should be and decrease disagreement among different members' goals. Some suggestions are:

1. When you first form a group, thoroughly discuss its goals, even when they are prescribed by superiors within an organization or by the constitution of the group. Such a discussion will clarify the members' understanding of the goals and help clear away any misunderstandings concerning the tasks necessary to reach them. During the discussion the group should reword, reorganize, and review the goals until the majority of members feel a sense of "ownership" regarding them.

2. As the group progresses in its activities, remember that it is continuously working on two levels at once: toward the achievement of the group's goals and toward the achievement and satisfaction of the individual members' motives and goals. Look for hidden agendas that may be present. The recognition of a group problem is the first step in diagnosing and solving it.

3. Bear in mind that there are conditions under which hidden agendas should be brought to the surface and rectified, and that there are also conditions under which they should be left undisturbed. A judgment must be made about the consequences of bringing hidden agendas to the attention of the entire group. One way in which to tell how willing other group members are to deal with hidden agendas is to initiate a discussion in the subject, while taking care not to force anyone into admitting their hidden agendas. A statement like the following one may be helpful: "I wonder if we have said all that we feel about the issue. Maybe we should take time to go around the table so that any further thoughts can be opened up."

4. Do not scold or pressure the other group members when hidden agendas are recognized. They are present and legitimate and must be worked on in much the same manner that group tasks are. At different times hidden agendas should be given different amounts of attention, depending upon their influence on the group's effectiveness and on the nature of the group and its members.

5. Spend some time evaluating the ability of the group to problem solve hidden agendas. Each experience should show better ways in which to handle agendas more openly. As groups mature, hidden agendas are reduced.

To check your understanding of this section, please answer the following questions (answers on page 107).

True	False	1. A hidden agenda is bad.
True	False	2. A hidden agenda ruins the group.
True	False	3. A hidden agenda should always be brought up and talked about.
True	False	4. A hidden agenda is a personal goal, unknown to other group members.
True	False	5. A hidden agenda disagrees with the dominant group goals.
True	False	6. People are always aware of their own hidden agendas.

BROKEN SQUARES EXERCISE

The purpose of this exercise is to explore the results of cooperation and competition among group members in solving a group problem. The exercise is done in small groups of five participants and two observers. Individual tables that seat five should be used. At least four groups are recommended, but two may do in a pinch. Place the tables far enough apart so that members of one group cannot observe the activities of the other groups. One set of squares is needed for each group of five. Instructions for making a set of squares are on page 325. The exercise takes approximately one hour to conduct, and the procedures for the coordinator are:

1. Introduce the exercise as one that focuses upon the way in which goals are defined by members of a group. State that it will consist of completing a group task about puzzles.
2. Hand out the observation instructions (page 371, Appendix E) to the observers. Within each group give an instruction sheet (pp. 367 and 369, Appendix E) to each person and an envelope containing the appropriate pieces of the puzzles (see directions for making a set of squares in Appendix D). Half of the groups should receive instructions that are cooperative and half instructions that are competitive. State that the envelopes are not to be opened until the signal is given. Review the instructions with each group so that cooperative groups do not hear the competitive instructions of the other groups and vice versa. Ask if the observers understand their role.
3. Give the signal to begin. The groups are to work until all of them have solved the puzzle. Each group should be carefully timed by the observers. If a group becomes deadlocked for more than twenty-five minutes, this phase of the exercise should be ended.
4. Collect the observation sheets and record the information in Table 4.1. While you are doing so instruct the groups to discuss their experiences by pairing a cooperative group with a competitive group and sharing their instructions and experiences with each other. Group observers are to participate fully in this discussion. At the end of this discussion they should have recorded their

TABLE 4.1: Results Table

	Cooperative	*Competitive*
Number of groups completing the task		
Time for task completion		
Number of times a member gave away a puzzle piece		
Number of times a member took away a puzzle piece		
Number of members who cut themselves off from others		
Cooperative behaviors		
Competitive behaviors		

conclusions about the differences between working in a cooperatively oriented and a competitively oriented problem-solving group.

5. Share the results of the discussions among all groups. Then present the information gathered by the observers. Using the material in the following section on goal structures, define cooperation and competition and discuss the impact of goal structures on group functioning and effectiveness.

6. This exercise may be conducted with only one group by leaving out the instructions about cooperative and competitive orientations and the comparison between cooperative and competitive groups. The issue of goal structure can still be discussed profitably.

THE MILLION DOLLAR GIFT EXERCISE

This exercise focuses on cooperation and competition among three subgroups within a group. The exercise usually takes less than one hour, and the procedure for the coordinator is as follows:

1. Introduce the exercise as an experience concerning decision making, coordination, and group representation.

2. Divide a group into three smaller subgroups of five or more members. Members of each subgroup are told they have fifteen minutes to meet one another and get acquainted and to appoint a representative. They are also told that they will be given a common task to work on with the other subgroups.

3. Seat the three representatives in the center of the room. Members of each subgroup sit together in a position where they can see their representative clearly. The following role-playing situation is then explained. A national foundation wishes to award $1 million to the school system that is made up of the three subgroups—on condition that the entire school system agrees on a project on which the million dollars will be spent. The representatives are then told to go back to their respective subgroups and within fifteen minutes develop a million-dollar, school-project proposal to be presented to the other two subgroups. The representatives will present the proposals.

4. After fifteen minutes have the three represenatives again meet in the center of the room. Tell them that they are to present their proposals and that they must come to an agreement on one that will be acceptable to all three subgroups for presentation to the foundation. After all three proposals have been presented, the representatives should reconfer with their subgroups for five minutes before continuing their meeting.

5. After the five-minute meeting with subgroups, have the representatives continue their discussion. They are to meet for five minutes and then break for another five-minute meeting with their subgroup. During the representatives' meeting the subgroups may communicate with their representative through notes. This sequence is repeated three times or until agreement is reached.

6. Ask the representatives to state what they are feeling, and the members of the

three subgroups how they feel. Hold a summary discussion, paying particular attention to such issues as:

a. Did the group reach agreement on a common proposal? Were they too locked into their own position to compromise even when the prize was $1 million?

b. Did the three subgroups tend to compete rather than cooperate? Did the degree of cooperation within each subgroup differ from one subgroup to another? If so, why?

c. What sorts of group pressures were felt by the representatives? How much power and freedom were given to each representative?

d. What were the goals of the subgroups in the negotiations? How did they affect the behavior of the subgroup and its representatives?

e. How were the decisions made within each subgroup? How were they made among the representatives?

f. Was the participation and leadership behavior distributed among subgroup members? What task and maintenance functions were present and absent?

GOAL STRUCTURE

The personal goals of group members may be structured cooperatively or competitively within any group. Coordinated action, pooling of resources, division of labor, open and accurate communication, trust, cohesion, and many other aspects of effective groups depend upon cooperatively oriented group members and a cooperative goal structure within the group. There is nothing more destructive in both the task and the maintenance areas of group functioning than competition among group members. Yet many groups are made up of highly competitive members and have competitive goal structures.

A *goal structure* specifies the type of interdependence among group members. Two types of goal structures are relevant for groups: cooperative and competitive. A *cooperative goal structure* exists when the individual goals of all members are perceived to be identical, compatible, or complementary. In an extremely cooperative goal structure, if one group member achieves her goal, all members achieve their goals (Deutsch, 1949); for example, if one member of a baseball team wins a ball game, all the members of the team win the ball game. Within a cooperative goal structure group members will coordinate their efforts to achieve their mutual goals. A *competitive goal structure* exists when the individual goals of group members are perceived to be different, incompatible, opposed, or mutually exclusive. In an extremely competitive goal structure a member can achieve his goal only if the other group members fail to obtain their goals (Deutsch, 1949); for example, if one member wins a race all other members lose the race. Within a competitive goal structure, group members will strive for goal accomplishment in a way that blocks all others from obtaining the goal.

Competitive or cooperative efforts on the part of group members are largely determined by the perceived goal structure of the group. What are the effects of cooperation versus competition? There has been a great deal of research on this question. Goal structures have very definite effects on member interaction and the goal accomplishment of a group. These effects are summarized in Table 4.2 (see Johnson and Johnson, 1975, for a more complete discussion of cooperation and competition).

SUMMARY TABLE 4.2.   Effects of Cooperation and Competition on Problem-Solving Groups

Cooperation	*Competition*
High effectiveness in solving complex problems	Low effectiveness in solving complex problems
Builds member skills in problem solving	Does not build problem-solving skills of members
Encourages acceptance of cultural and individual differences	Encourages rejection of cultural and individual differences
Encourages acceptance of differences of opinion and divergent thinking	Encourages rejection of differences of opinion and divergent thinking
Promotes positive attitudes toward the task and the group	Promotes negative attitudes toward the task and the group
Promotes group cohesion and liking among group members	Promotes dislike among group members and reduces group cohesion
Promotes positive self-attitudes	Promotes negative self-attitudes
Promotes cooperative attitudes and values	Promotes competitive attitudes and values
Promotes interpersonal skills	Does not promote interpersonal skills
Promotes group skills	Does not promote group skills
Promotes moderate anxiety about goal accomplishment	Promotes high anxiety about goal accomplishment
Promotes effective communication	Promotes ineffective communication
Promotes trust	Promotes distrust and suspicion
Promotes mutual influence	Decreases mutual influence
Promotes helping and sharing	Decreases helping and sharing
Increases emotional involvement in group goal accomplishment	Increases emotional involvement in individual goal accomplishment
Promotes coordination of effort and division of labor	Decreases coordination of effort and division of labor
Promotes creativity	Decreases creativity

The summary table makes it clear how important it is for group members to build cooperative goal structures and to reduce all competition among themselves. Most cooperative and competitive behavior on the part of group members is a direct reflection of the goal structure of the group. Nonetheless, some individuals adopt a cooperative pattern of behavior toward all situations and some adopt a competitive pattern of behavior toward all situations.

What happens when a competitive person joins a group made up of cooperative members? In terms of protecting group effectiveness, the question is important. Kelley and Stahelski (1970) found that several things happen. First, the cooperative members begin behaving in competitive ways. Second, the competitive person sees the former cooperative members as having *always* been competitive. Third, the cooperative members are aware that their behavior is being determined by the other's competitive behavior, but the competitive person is not aware of his impact upon the cooperators. Deutsch (1958, 1960, 1962) and many other researchers have found that trust, openness of communication, liking for one another, and a problem-solving orientation are all easily destroyed by a competitive person. He uses the openness and trust of others to exploit them and take advantage of them. Without much question, a member who is cooperative with other group members runs the risk of being taken advantage of, and the result of such exploitation is usually anger and equally competitive behavior. Therefore, because competitive behavior dominates in groups, cooperative people will want to make sure that all members of their group are cooperatively oriented. They will also want to intervene when a member's competitive behavior is subverting the cooperative goal structure of the group.

Several ingredients must be present in a group in order to have cooperative interaction among its members. They were necessary in the exercises you took immediately before this section, and they are necessary in most problem-solving situations. They are:

1. Individual members must understand the total problem that has to be solved.
2. Individual members must see how each can contribute toward solving the problem.
3. Individual members must be aware of the potential contributions of the other group members.
4. Individual members must see the other members' problems in order to help them make their best contribution.
5. Individual members must be aware of the cooperative goal structure of the group.

Given the need for cooperative goal structures in effective groups, the question of how to get a cooperative goal structure in a group becomes crucial. The basic procedures, however, are rather simple:

1. Members must interact, give and receive help from one another, and share ideas, information, and resources to help accomplish the group's goals.
2. The group goal of getting the task done at the highest level possible must be accepted by everyone, and members need to develop commitment to the group goal.
3. Because the possibility exists of different group members doing different subtasks, groups may divide the labor in various ways to accomplish their goals.
4. Rewards, if any, must be based upon the quality and quantity of group performance, not individual performance.

The cooperativeness of a group's goal structure is one of the most important aspects of its effectiveness. A book giving specific procedures for putting cooperative goal structures into practice has recently been published (Johnson and Johnson, 1975).

You may wish to test your comprehension of this section by answering the following questions (answers on page 107):

Match the following goal structures of a group with their definition:

<u>a</u> 1. Cooperation
<u>b</u> 2. Competition
<u>c</u> 3. Individualism

a. In order for a person to reach her goals, the group must reach its goals.
b. In order for a person to reach his goals, no one else must reach his goals.
c. The goals of the members are independent of each other.

Match each of the following characteristics with the goal structure it characterizes:

<u>a</u> 4. The actions of the members are interchangeable.
<u>b</u> 5. Members will hinder other members' efforts.
<u>a</u> 6. Members will like other members.
<u>a</u> 7. Members will be influenced positively by other members.
<u>b</u> 8. Members will not be satisfied with other members' actions.
<u>a</u> 9. Everyone is a winner.
<u>a</u> 10. There is not much anxiety among the members.

a. Cooperation
b. Competition

11. What three things happen when a competitive person joins a cooperative group?
    a. The competitive person starts acting cooperatively.
    ⓑ The cooperative people start acting competitively.
    ⓒ The competitive person sees the cooperative persons as being competitive.
    d. The competitive person sees the cooperative persons as being cooperative.
    ⓔ The cooperative persons see that their behavior is being changed by the competitive person.
    f. The competitive person sees that she is changing the behavior of the cooperative persons.

12. What four things must be present for a group to have cooperation?
   a. The total problem must be understood by everyone.
   b. The problem must be a simple one.
   c. Everyone must see how he can help solve the problem.
   d. Members must be aware of other members' problems and potential contributions.
   e. Someone must force the group to act cooperatively, whether they like it or not.
   f. Members must be aware of the group's cooperative goal structure.

CLEAR AND UNCLEAR GOALS EXERCISE

This exercise shows the contrasting behavioral consequences of having clear and unclear goals. Approximately one hour is needed to complete it. Here is the procedure for a coordinator to follow:

1. Seat the participants in groups of six to eight, formed into circles.
2. Introduce the exercise as focusing upon clear and unclear group goals.
3. Have each group select an observer, who reports to a designated place for instructions. While the observers are being briefed, urge the group members to get acquainted with one another.
4. Give each observer a copy of the Observation Guide (Appendix E, page 373) and tell them that the groups will work on two tasks. The first task will be unclear, the second will be clear. Their job is to make careful observations of group behavior on the two tasks. The observers then return to their groups, but sit outside the circle.
5. Brief all groups as follows: "We are going to study group behavior by working on two brief tasks. Your observer will not participate, but will report to you at the end of the second task. Your first task will take about eight minutes. I will give you a warning a minute before the time is up. The task is: list the most appropriate goals to govern the best development group experiences in order to maximize social development in a democratic society."
6. While the groups work on the task, the observers should take notes. After seven minutes give the warning and after eight minutes end the discussion.
7. Give Task 2: "List as many of the formally organized clubs or organizations that exist in a typical community as you can." State that the groups will have six minutes to work on the task. At the end of five minutes give a one-minute warning and after six minutes end the discussion.
8. Copies of the observation form are distributed to all participants. Each group discusses their experience using the information obtained by the observers as their major resource. This discussion should last ten to fifteen minutes.
9. Form clusters by asking one group to pull its chairs in a circle around another group. The inner group becomes Group A and the outer group becomes Group

B. Instruct Group A to produce a list of characteristics of clear and unclear goals with one person recording them on newsprint in two columns. Six minutes is allowed for this task. Group B is to listen to Group A, take notes, and be ready to add to the list. After six minutes Group B is instructed to comment on the list and both groups jointly select the four or five most important characteristics of clear and unclear goals from the list. They are given nine minutes to do so.

10. Groups A and B then change places, with Group B now in the center. Group B is told to list behavioral symptoms of each of the characteristics of clear and unclear goals listed on the newsprint, beginning with the most important characteristics. After nine minutes Group A joins in the discussion, which should take another six minutes.

11. Each cluster presents its work to the other group. A general discussion on the nature of group goals and their consequences in feeling and behavior is held, using the material in the following section on clear and operational goals.

OPERATIONAL AND CLEAR GOALS

For individual members to perform effectively within a group they must know what the group's goals are, understand what actions need to be taken to accomplish them, know the criteria by which the group can tell when they have been reached, and be aware of how their own behavior can contribute to group actions. Goal and task accomplishment depend upon members coordinating and synchronizing their actions. The clarity of the group goal and the clarity of the actions required to achieve it are important if individual members are to accept the group goal, to experience a feeling of group belongingness, to be interested in goal-related behaviors, and to be willing to accept influence from the group. One of the most common practical problems of groups is trying to keep up with precisely where the group is in relation to its goals and what steps need to be taken by group members to reach them. The group and the group's tasks become more attractive as the goal becomes clearer and as the nature of the tasks and the responsibilities of each member within the group is made more tangible. Goals become clarified as they are made more specific, operational (workable), measurable, and observable.

The distinction between operational and nonoperational goals is drawn according to whether a basis exists for relating the goal to possible action by the group. If some way can be figured out as to whether and to what extent the goals will be achieved by a particular sequence of group actions, then the goals are *operational*; otherwise they are not. An example of an operational goal is "Name three qualities of a good group member" and an example of a nonoperational goal is "Make conclusions about the theoretical and empirical findings of qualities of effective actions by a group member." Again, a goal is operational if there is some basis for relating it to group activities that will achieve it; it is nonoperational when there is no basis for relating it to possible courses of action. The distinction between operational and nonoperational goals is also drawn according to whether alternative courses of action can be tested with respect to an objective or goal.

Broad, long-range goals are often nonoperational and can be related to specific actions only through the formation of subgoals. Subgoals are often substituted for the more general goals of a group to gain operational advantages.

A crucial aspect of even a well-stated group goal is being able to tell when it has been accomplished. There is no sense in going somewhere if you do not know when you have arrived. An operational goal has indicators that will make it evident when it has been achieved. The goal "Name three qualities of a good group member" is operational in the sense that when you have listed three items, and if they refer to group membership, you will know the goal has been reached. The goal of "Make conclusions about the theoretical and empirical findings of qualities of effective actions by a group member" is nonoperational in the sense that it may be difficult to tell when such a goal has been achieved. Whatever indicators are used to tell when a group has accomplished its goals, several of them are better than one, and indicators that are observable, countable, and specific are better than those that are nonobservable, noncountable, and ambiguous. Usually a problem-solving group will have indicators that relate to both the accomplishment of a goal (profit, new members gained, problems solved) and to group processes and group maintenance (group cohesion, communication effectiveness, decision-making ability, level of trust among members).

There are several advantages to a group in having operational goals. The main advantage is in helping communication among its members and among other groups. A goal must be stated in such a way that it succeeds in telling what the group intends to accomplish, and this communication is successful when any knowledgeable person can look at the group's behavior or products and decide whether or not the goal has been reached. When the goal has been made workable in terms of behaviors so that others can reliably agree on whether a group's performance or product fulfills the goal, then the goal is sufficiently specific.

The second advantage in having operational goals is that they help guide the group in planning and carrying out its tasks. If a group is not certain what outcomes it is trying to effect, it will have difficulty planning how it will do its work. Operational goals help a group to select and to organize the appropriate resources and methods for working on its tasks. They make it easier for a member to diagnose what leadership behaviors are needed and to accept responsibility for achievement. The more completely group members know what they are trying to accomplish with any specific task, the better they can direct their attention and efforts. And the problems of revision, modification, and change in the group are helped when the overall effort is broken down into smaller operational parts.

The third advantage in operational goals is that they help the group evaluate both the group process and the group outcome or product. By specifying the group's goals and the criteria by which the group will know when they are reached, it becomes possible to evaluate how well the group has accomplished them. Similarly, operational goals facilitate feedback among group members about the accomplishments resulting from their behavior and the effectiveness of current procedural methods.

A fourth advantage is that when goals are operational, conflicts and differences about the course of group action are more likely to be decided by rational, analytic processes. When goals are not operational or when the operational subgoals are not relevant to most group members, differences are less likely to be adjusted through negotiation. If goals are operational, members can more readily see the logic of different courses of action. If goals are nonoperational, there is no logical and testable answer to such differences of judgment, and the likelihood is that not only will a compromise result based upon concessions and trading, but a greater emphasis will be placed upon maintaining harmony within the group than upon accomplishing its goals.

How are clear, operational goals developed? It must be recognized that, for most groups, clear goals cannot always be determined in advance, especially if they are to be acceptable to all or most of the members. The first job of any group, therefore, is to modify any stated goal until all the group members understand it and a consensus exists concerning how it is to be put into practice (operationalized). Through such discussions, commitment to goals is built and the goals become acceptable to the group members. The more time a group spends establishing agreement on clear goals, the less time it needs in achieving them—and the more likely it will be that the members will work effectively for the common outcome.

How do you tell whether a group's goals are sufficiently understood and operationalized? If the reader has done the Clear and Unclear Goals Exercise, he will have a list of both the characteristics of clear and unclear goals and the behavioral symptoms of groups with clear or unclear goals. Remember that some of the symptoms of unclear goals are a high level of group tension, joking or horseplay, the group being distracted by side issues, and the group's failure to use, support, or build on good ideas.

To check your understanding of this section, please answer the following questions (answers on page 107):

1. For individual members to perform effectively within a group, they must (choose four):

   a. Know what the group's goals are.
   b. Understand what actions are needed to accomplish the goals.
   c. Know the other members of the group.
   d. Know how the behavior of other group members can contribute to group actions.
   e. Know the criteria by which goal accomplishment will be identified.
   f. Know what the other members want out of the group.

2. Operational goals (choose two):

   a. Must be related to a course of action.
   b. Are not related to a course of action.
   c. Are general goals.
   d. Must be observable and specific.
   e. Have to do with doctors.

3. You are on a committee to upgrade the medical facilities in your town. The committee is considering the following four goals. Which one is an operational goal?

non-operational
optrational
non
non

   a. To achieve better hospital care.
   b. To raise the $5 million needed for the new hospital.
   c. To upgrade the hospital services.
   d. To get more doctors and nurses in town.

4. What are the four advantages of operational goals?

   a. They are clearly communicated to the group members and to other people.
   b. They help get a variety of responses from the group members.
   c. They guide the group in planning and carrying out its task.
   d. They help get compromises based on concessions and trading.
   e. They help the group evaluate the outcome and the group process.
   f. They put emphasis on group harmony and getting along.
   g. They offer a basis for solving differences of opinion rationally.

5. You are a teacher who wants to develop clear, operational goals for your classes. How would you best do this?

   a. Talk to the principal, discussing and changing them until they are clear.
   b. Consult with the other teachers, discussing and changing the goals until they are clear.
   c. Talk the goals over with the students, discussing and changing them until they are clear.
   d. Sit down and write them yourself, remembering that they must be clear, specific, and observable.

ASPECTS OF EFFECTIVE GROUP GOALS

Several factors regarding group goals have been shown in research studies to have important effects on behavior. These aspects are:

1. The extent to which the goals are operationally defined, countable, and observable.
2. The extent to which group members see the goals as being meaningful, relevant, realistic, acceptable, and attainable.
3. How cooperative the goal structure is and how cooperatively oriented the group members are.
4. The degree to which both group and individual members' goals can be achieved by the same tasks and activities.
5. The degree to which conflict exists among the group members about the group's goals and the tasks the group must complete to achieve the goals.
6. The extent to which the goals are challenging and offer a moderate risk of failure.

7. The degree of coordination achieved among group members.
8. How available the resources are that are needed to effect the group's tasks and goals.
9. How specific the goals are because specific goals indicate what needs to be done next.
10. How easily the goals can be modified and clarified.
11. How long a period of time a group has to attain its goals.

HELPING GROUPS SET EFFECTIVE GOALS

The first job of any group is to clarify and modify stated goals until they are clear and acceptable. The two methods of helping groups set effective goals are survey-feedback and program evaluation and review.

The survey-feedback method begins with the consultant or leader interviewing the individual members of the group about group goals and the priorities of the group as they see them. These interviews are conducted before a periodic meeting of the group (such as annually or semi-annually), and on the basis of the information collected, and working within organizational goals, the consultant conducts a group session in which the group sets its goals and priorities for the next six months or year. During this meeting the group plans its short-term goals, reviews its long-range goals, develops the tasks necessary for accomplishing its short-term goals, defines specific responsibilities for working on the tasks, ranks the tasks and goals in terms of priority to the group, and sets group-development goals for more effective group work. Special attention is paid to specifying the leadership and membership-role relationships necessary not only to work on the tasks, but to develop ways in which to identify and solve group relationship problems that might hinder goal achievement.

Under the Program Evaluation and Review Method, or the Critical Path Method as it is sometimes called, groups are helped in setting effective goals by first specifying the end state or final goal they want to achieve. Working backward from this final goal, the group then details what must happen immediately *before* the final goal is achieved, and the tasks and subgoals needed to accomplish the final goal are all spelled out. The group decides which of the activities and subgoals are most critical for final goal accomplishment and allocates resources accordingly. A timetable is set on when each subgoal is to be accomplished. The whole process is then reviewed and responsibilities assigned.

IDENTIFYING GROUP GOALS

Group goals can usually be identified by observing the activities of group members or by asking them to state the group's goals in an interview or in response to questionnaire items. To determine the group's goals through observation, one needs to watch the group over a period of time and record how much time members spend on each one of their activities; this procedure gives a pretty accurate view of what a group's goals are. If members of the group are to be given a questionnaire or are to be interviewed, the following questions may prove helpful:

1. What are the three most important things you do as a member of this group?
2. Do any of these activities add to the main goals of the group? If yes, which ones?
3. Do you believe that the group is making progress toward its main goals? Can you elaborate on your answer?
4. Are there important things you do in this group that you think would not be considered important by other group members? If yes, what are they?
5. What are some of the goals you would like to see this group working toward that it is not now engaged in pursuing?
6. What are the three most important goals of this group?
7. Would you describe members of this group as working together cooperatively or competitively? What are some of the behaviors of group members that indicate cooperativeness or competitiveness?
8. How committed are the members of this group to achieving the group's goals? How committed are you to achieving the group's goals?
9. What personal goals are met for you by your membership in this group?
10. How are the group's goals established?
11. In this group goals are:

Confused	1 : 2 : 3 : 4 : 5 : 6 : 7	Clear
Diverse, conflicting	1 : 2 : 3 : 4 : 5 : 6 : 7	Similar, congruent
Unaccepted	1 : 2 : 3 : 4 : 5 : 6 : 7	Accepted
Nonoperational	1 : 2 : 3 : 4 : 5 : 6 : 7	Operational
Not shared	1 : 2 : 3 : 4 : 5 : 6 : 7	Shared by all members
Competitive	1 : 2 : 3 : 4 : 5 : 6 : 7	Cooperative

12. In this group members' feelings about the group's goals can be described as:

Uncommitted	1 : 2 : 3 : 4 : 5 : 6 : 7	Committed
Indifferent	1 : 2 : 3 : 4 : 5 : 6 : 7	Caring
Uninvolved	1 : 2 : 3 : 4 : 5 : 6 : 7	Involved
Not responsible	1 : 2 : 3 : 4 : 5 : 6 : 7	Proprietary

13. In a list of the official goals of your group, how does your ranking of them according to their importance compare with the rankings of other group members? Are you more in agreement or disagreement with the others?
14. Indicate the extent of your agreement or disagreement with the following statements:
    a. Members of this group know exactly what they have to get done.
    b. Members of this group have little idea of what the group is trying to accomplish.
    c. The goals of this group are specific.
    d. Each member knows the goals of this group.
    e. Each member has a clear idea of what the group's goals are.

YOUR GOAL—RELATED BEHAVIOR

Describe below how you would act if you were a member of a problem-solving group that did not have clear goals and whose members were not only not committed to them, but had competing personal goals. Use all your experiences in the exercises in this chapter, the content material presented in the chapter, and any other personal experience that is relevant. After thirty minutes, meet with two other group members and discuss what each of you wrote about your behavior.

CHECKLIST OF SKILLS

___ I can initiate discussions of goals that increase the relevance of the group goals to the needs of the group members and increase the commitment of the members toward achieving the goals.

___ I can appropriately initiate discussions about hidden agendas that result in a clearer understanding of every member's needs and goals.

___ I can structure cooperative goals for the group.

___ I can recognize competition among members' goals and initiate a discussion to reduce it.

___ I can state clear, operational goals for the group.

___ I can help a group set effective goals.

I need more work on developing the following skills: _____

_____

_____

_____

_____

ANSWERS

Page 88: 1: b, c, d, e, g; 2: a; 3: b; 4: a; 5: a, d; 6: c, d, e.

Page 93: 1: false; 2: false;, 3: false; 4: true; 5: true; 6: false.

Page 99: 1: a; 2: b; 3: c; 4: a; 5: b; 6: a; 7: a; 8: b; 9: a; 10: a; 11: b, c, e; 12: a, c, d, f.

Page 103: 1: a, b, d, e; 2: a, d; 3: b; 4: a, c, e, g; 5: c.

5

Communication Within Groups

INTRODUCTION AND DEFINITIONS

Communication is the basis for all human interaction and for all group functioning. Every group must take in and use information. The very existence of a group depends upon communication, upon exchanging information and transmitting meaning. All cooperative action is contingent upon effective communication, and our daily lives are filled with one communication experience after another. Through communication members of groups reach some understanding of one another, build trust, coordinate their actions, plan strategies for goal accomplishment, agree upon a division of labor, conduct all group activity—even exchange insults. It is through communication that the members interact, and effective communication is a necessary prerequisite for every aspect of group functioning.

One prime difficulty in discussing communication within groups is that there are so many definitions for the concept of communication and so little agreement about which definition is the most useful. Dance (1970), for example, did a content analysis of ninety-five definitions of communication that he found published in several different academic fields. From his survey he came up with several distinct conceptual parts of communication. He notes that the variety of definitions has taken different theorists and researchers in different and sometimes contradictory directions. Dance concludes that the concept of communication is overburdened and that a family of concepts replacing it needs to be developed. Despite the difficulties in defining communication, however, there are ways in which to view the process of transmitting information that are helpful in discussing interpersonal and group communication skills.

Two people seeing each other will have a continuous effect on each other's perceptions and expectations of what the other is going to do. Interpersonal communication, then, can be defined broadly as any verbal or nonverbal behavior that is perceived by another person (Johnson, 1972, 1973). Communication, in other words, is much more than just the exchange of words; all behavior conveys some message and is, therefore, a form of communication. *Interpersonal communication*, however, is more commonly defined as a message sent by a person to a receiver (or receivers) with a conscious intent of affecting the receiver's behavior. A person sends the message "How are you?" to evoke the response "Fine." A teacher shakes his head to get two students to stop throwing erasers at him. Under this more limited definition, any signal aimed at influencing the receiver's behavior in any way is a communication.

This definition of communication does not mean that a sequence of events in time always exists where a person thinks up a message, sends it, and someone else receives it. Communication among people is a process in which everyone receives, sends, interprets, and infers all at the same time and there is no beginning and no end. All communication involves people sending one another symbols to which certain meanings are attached. These symbols can be either verbal (all words are symbols) or nonverbal (all expressions and gestures are symbols). The exchange of ideas and experiences between two people is possible only when both have adopted the same ways of relating a particular nonverbal, spoken, written, or pictorial symbol to a particular experience.

How do you tell when communication is working effectively and when it is not? What is effective communication? What is ineffective communication? *Effective communication* exists between two people when the receiver interprets the sender's message in the same way the sender intended it. If John tries to communicate to Jane that it is a wonderful day and he is feeling great by saying "Hi" with a warm smile, and if Jane interprets John's "Hi" as meaning John thinks it is a beautiful day and he is feeling well, then effective communication has taken place. If Jane interprets John's "Hi" as meaning he wants to stop and talk with her, then ineffective communication has taken place.

The model of communication presented by Johnson (1972) is typical of the applied approaches to interpersonal communication. In this model (Figure 5.1) the communicator is referred to as the *sender* and the person at whom the message is aimed as the *receiver*. The *message* is any verbal or nonverbal symbol that one person transmits to another; a message refers to information about a subject matter being referred to in a symbolic way (all words are symbols). A *channel* can be defined as the means of sending a message to another person: the sound waves of the voice, the light waves involved in seeing words on a printed page. Because communication is a process, sending and receiving messages often taken place simultaneously; a person can be speaking and at the same time paying close attention to the receiver's nonverbal responses.

Figure 5.1 represents a model of the process of communication between two people. The model has seven basic elements, as follows:

1. The intentions, ideas, feelings of the sender and the way he decides to behave, all of which lead to his sending a message that carries some content.
2. The sender encoding his message by translating his ideas, feelings, and intentions into a message appropriate for sending.

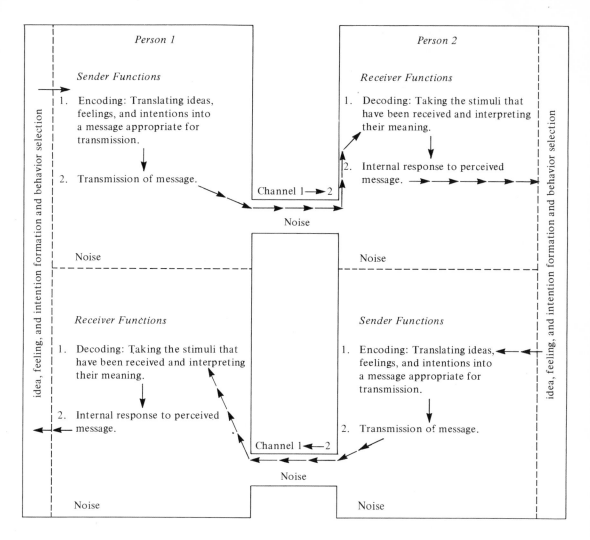

FIGURE 5.1   The Interpersonal Communication Process (Source: David W. Johnson, *Reaching Out.* Englewood Cliffs, N. J.: Prentice-Hall, Inc., 1972, p. 63.)

3. Sending the message to the receiver.

4. The channel through which the message is translated.

5. The receiver decoding the message by taking it and interpreting its meaning. His interpretation depends on how well the receiver understands the content of the message and the intentions of the sender.

6. The receiver responding internally to this interpretation of the message.

7. The amount of *noise* in the above steps. Noise is any element that interferes with the communication process. In the sender, noise refers to such things as the attitudes, prejudices, frame of reference of the sender, and the appropriateness

of his language or other expression of the message. In the receiver, noise refers to such things as his attitudes, background, and experiences that affect the decoding process. In the channel, noise refers to (1) environmental sounds, such as static or traffic, (2) speech problems, such as stammering, (3) annoying or distracting mannerisms, such as a tendency to mumble or other distractions. To a large extent, the success of communication is determined by the degree to which noise is overcome or controlled.

To check your understanding of this section, please answer the following questions (answers on page 137).

(True) False   1. Communication is the basis for all human interaction and all group functioning.

True (False)   2. Interpersonal communication is any verbal or nonverbal behavior that is sent by a person.

(True) False   3. Effective communication takes place when the receiver interprets the sender's message in the way it was intended.

(True) False   4. Noise is any element that interferes with the communication process.

(True) False   5. Prejudice can be a noise in the communication process.

6. Describe the communication model to someone to see if you received it correctly.

YOUR COMMUNICATION BEHAVIOR

What is your communication behavior like in a group? How would you describe your communication actions? Begin a discussion of communication within groups by answering the following questions as honestly as possible:

1. If I as group chairperson were giving a set of instructions and the other group members sat quietly with blank faces, I would:

____ state the instructions clearly and precisely and then move on.

__✓__ encourage members to ask questions until I was sure that everyone understood what they were supposed to do.

2. If the group chairperson gave a set of instructions to the group that I did not understand, I would:

____ keep silent and later ask another group member what she meant.

__✓__ immediately ask the chairperson to repeat the instructions and answer my questions until I was sure I understood what she wanted me to do.

3. How often would you let other group members know when you liked or approved of something they said or did?

Never 1 : 2 : 3 : 4 : 5 : (6) : 7 : 8 : 9 Always

4. How often would you let other group members know when you felt irritated, impatient, embarrassed by, or disagreed with, something they said or did?

Never 1 : 2 : 3 : (4) : 5 : 6 : 7 : 8 : 9 Always

5. How often do you check out what other group members are feeling and how they are reacting rather than assuming that you know?

    Never 1 : 2 : 3 :(4) : 5 : 6 : 7 : 8 : 9 Always

6. How often do you encourage other group members to let you know how they are reacting to your behavior and actions in the group?

    Never 1 : 2 :(3) : 4 : 5 : 6 : 7 : 8 : 9 Always

7. How often do you check to make sure you understand what other group members mean before agreeing or disagreeing?

    Never 1 : 2 : 3 : 4 : 5 : 6 :(7) : 8 :(9) Always

8. How often do you paraphrase or restate what other members have said before responding?

    Never 1 : 2 : 3 : 4 :(5) : 6 : 7 : 8 : 9 Always

9. How often do you keep your thoughts, ideas, feelings, and reactions to yourself in group sessions?

    Never 1 : 2 : 3 : 4 :(5) : 6 : 7 : 8 : 9 Always

10. How often do you make sure that all information you have about the current topic of discussion is known to the rest of the group?

    Never 1 : 2 : 3 : 4 : 5 : 6 : 7 :(8) : 9 Always

The questions above deal with several aspects of communication in groups that will be discussed in this chapter. The first two questions refer to whether communication is one-way (from the chairperson to the rest of the group members) or two-way. The third and fourth questions focus on your willingness to give feedback to other group members on how you are receiving and reacting to their messages. Questions five and six refer to your willingness to ask for feedback about how other group members are receiving and reacting to your messages. Questions seven and eight focus on receiving skills, and the final two questions relate to your willingness to contribute (send) relevant messages on the group's work. Review your answers to these questions and summarize your present communication behavior in a group.

INTERPERSONAL VERSUS GROUP COMMUNICATION

All communication within groups is between individuals and is, therefore, interpersonal communication. There are many discussions of the skills needed for effective interpersonal communication, and one of the authors has published a training program for interpersonal skill development that includes communication skills (Johnson, 1972). The focus in this chapter is on the unique aspects of communication among members of a problem-solving group, including the communication of task-relevant information among group members and the passage of messages through several authority levels. An example of the latter would be the passage of a chairperson's message to a vice-chairperson who sends it to a committee chairperson who sends it to the rest of the group.

SENDING MESSAGES EFFECTIVELY

The first aspect of effective communication is the sending of a message. At this point divide into groups of three. Make a list in the space below of five aspects of sending messages effectively:

1. _____

2. _____

3. _____

4. _____

5. _____

Share your group list with the other groups of three. How does your list compare with theirs? Are there points on their lists that would cause you to change yours? What do you think now are the five most important aspects of sending messages effectively?

What can a group member do to make sure her ideas and feelings are effectively communicated? Research supports the conclusions that the skills of sending messages involve (Johnson, 1972, 1973, 1974a):

1. *Clearly "own" your messages by using personal pronouns such as I and my*; personal ownership includes clearly taking responsibility for the ideas and feelings that are expressed. Group members "disown" their messages when they use terms like "most people," "some members," or "our group." Such terms make it difficult to tell whether the person really thinks and feels what he is saying or whether he is repeating the thoughts and feelings of others.

2. *Make your messages complete and specific.* Include clear statements of all necessary information the receiver needs in order to comprehend the message. Being complete and specific seems so obvious, but often a group member will not communicate the frame of reference he is taking, the assmuptions he is making, the intentions he has in communicating, or the leaps in thinking he is making. Thus while a person may hear the words she will not comprehend the meaning of the message.

3. *Make your verbal and nonverbal messages congruent with each other.* Every face-to-face communication involves both verbal and nonverbal messages. Usually these messages are congruent, so if a person is saying that he has appreciated your help, he is smiling and expressing warmth nonverbally. Communication problems arise when a person's verbal and nonverbal messages are contradictory. If a person says "Here is some information that may be of help to you" with a sneer on his face and a mocking tone of voice, the meaning you receive is confused by the two different messages being simultaneously sent.

4. *Be redundant.* Repeating your messages more than once and using more than one channel of communication (such as pictures and written messages as well as verbal and nonverbal cues) will help the receiver understand your messages.

5. *Ask for feedback concerning the way your messages are being received.* In order to communicate effectively you must be aware of how the receiver is interpreting and processing your messages. The only way to be sure is to continually seek feedback as to what meanings the receiver is attaching to your messages.

6. *Make the message appropriate to the receiver's frame of reference.* The same information will be explained differently to an expert in the field than to a novice, to a child than to an adult, to your boss than to a co-worker.

7. *Describe your feelings by name, action, or figure of speech.* When communicating your feelings it is especially important to be descriptive. You may describe your feelings by name ("I feel happy"), actions ("I feel like dancing my happiness"), or figures of speech ("I feel like I'm floating on a pink cloud"). The description will help communicate your feelings clearly and unambiguously.

8. *Describe other members' behavior without evaluating or interpreting.* When reacting to the behavior of other members be sure to describe their behavior ("you keep interrupting me") rather than evaluating it ("you're a rotten, self-centered, egotist who won't listen to anyone else's ideas").

Effective skills in sending communications are prerequisite to developing the skills covered in this chapter. Sending skills are not examined further, however, because they have been covered in detail in Johnson (1972), which discusses the basic theory behind sending effective verbal and nonverbal messages and includes specific exercises to develop skills in message sending. It is suggested that readers review and learn these skills before (or in combination with) learning the skills in this chapter.

RECEIVING MESSAGES EFFECTIVELY

Developing sending skills meets only half the requirements for communicating effectively; you must also have receiving skills. Again divide into groups of three. Make a list in the space below of the five most important aspects of receiving messages effectively:

1. _____

2. _____

3. _____

4. _____

5. _____

Again compare your list with those made by the other groups of three. Modify your list to make it the best list of aspects of receiving messages you can think of.

The skills involved in receiving messages deal with giving feedback about the reception of the message in ways that clarify and aid continued discussion. Receiving skills have two basic parts: (1) communicating the *intention* of wanting to understand the ideas and feelings of the sender, and (2) understanding and

115

interpreting the sender's ideas and feelings. Of the two parts, many theorists consider the first—communicating the intention to understand correctly, but not evaluate, a message—to be the more important. The principal barrier to building effective communication is the tendency most people have to judge, evaluate, approve, or disapprove of a message they are receiving. For instance, the sender makes a statement and the receiver responds inwardly or openly with "I think you're wrong," "I don't like what you said," "I think you're right," or "That is the greatest (or worst) idea I have ever heard!" Such evaluative receiving will make the sender defensive and cautious, thereby decreasing the openness of the communication. Though the tendency to give evaluative responses is common in almost all conversations, it is accentuated in situations where feelings and emotions are deeply involved. The stronger the feelings, the more likely it is that two group members will evaluate each other's statements from their own point of view only. Thus it is highly important for the receiver to indicate that he wants to fully understand the sender before he makes an evaluation. The specific receiving skills are paraphrasing, perception checking for feelings, and negotiating for meaning.

1. Paraphrase accurately and nonevaluatively the content of the message and the feelings of the sender. The most basic and important skill involved in receiving messages is paraphrasing. Paraphrasing involves restating the words of the sender; it should be done in a way that indicates an understanding of the sender's frame of reference. The basic rule to follow in paraphrasing is: *you can speak up for yourself only after you have first restated the ideas and feelings of the sender accurately and to the sender's satisfaction.* When paraphrasing it is helpful if you restate the sender's expressed ideas and feelings in your own words rather than mimicking or parroting her exact words, avoid any indication of approval or disapproval, do not add or subtract from the sender's message, and place yourself in the sender's shoes and try to understand what she is feeling and what her message means.

2. Describe what you perceive to be the sender's feelings. Sometimes it is difficult to paraphrase the feelings of the sender if they are not described in words in the message. Thus a second receiving skill is the perception check for the sender's feelings simply describing what you perceive as the sender's feelings. This description should tentatively identify those feelings without expressing approval or disapproval and without attempting to interpret them or explain their causes. It is simply saying, "Here is what I understand your feelings to be; am I accurate?"

3. State your interpretation of the sender's message and negotiate with the sender until there is agreement as to the message's meaning. Often the words contained in a message do not carry the actual meaning. A person may ask, "Do you always shout like this?" and mean, "Please quiet down." Thus sometimes paraphrasing the content of a message will do little to communicate your understanding of the message. In such a case, you negotiate the meaning of the message. You may wish to preface your negotiation for meaning response with, "What I think you mean is . . . " If you are accurate, you then make your reply; if you are inaccurate, the sender restates the message until you can state what the essential meaning of the message is. Keep in mind that it is the process that is important in negotiating meaning, not the actual phrasing you use. After the process becomes natural, a variety of introductory phrases will be used. Be tolerant of others who are using the same phrases over and over as they are developing this skill.

These basic receiving skills, so important to effective communication, are not dealt with further in this book. A complete treatment of them, along with specific skill exercises to develop verbal and nonverbal competence in them, can be found in Johnson (1972). These skills should be reviewed and learned by all readers as a prerequisite for the skills discussed in this chapter.

Finally, one of the major influences upon the reception of a message is the usefulness of its content toward the accomplishment of the receiver's goals and tasks. All messages may be evaluated in terms of whether they help or hinder the receiver's task performance within the group, and messages which are seen as helping goal and task accomplishment are comprehended most accurately and easily. Of course, it is quite common for group members to misunderstand the usefulness of certain messages; opposition and disagreement, for example, are seen as being a short-term obstruction instead of the long-term help they might be by generating new and better ways of accomplishing tasks and goals.

To check your understanding of this section, please answer the following questions (answers on page 137).

1. It is a good communication practice when sending messages to (choose three):
    a. Use more than one way of getting the message across.
    b. Ask the receiver to give feedback on the content and intentions of the message.
    c. Make evaluations and inferences when listening to other group members.
    d. Describe your feelings.
    e. Speak for others in the group who are too shy to speak for themselves.
2. The two basic parts of communication receiving skills are (choose two):
    a. Understanding that the sender wants to communicate.
    b. Communicating the message.
    c. Understanding the message.
    d. Communicating that you want to understand the message.
3. The major barrier to building effective communication is the tendency most people have to:
    a. Talk too much.
    b. Talk too little.
    c. Judge and evaluate.
    d. Not listen.
4. Paraphrasing is the receiving skill of:
    a. Changing the phrasing of a message.
    b. Checking on the sender's feelings and negotiating for their meaning.
    c. Being able to reply to the message to the sender's satisfaction.
    d. Being able to restate the message and feelings, without evaluation, to the sender's satisfaction.

BEWISE COLLEGE EXERCISE

In this exercise we will examine the communication patterns within a task-oriented group. Our objectives are to see how task-relevant information is shared within a work group and to explore the effects of collaboration and competition in group problem solving. The materials needed for the exercise are a briefing sheet, a series of data sheets (pp. 375 to 383, Appendix E), a candidate summary sheet (pp. 385 and 386, Appendix E), and an observer frequency chart (page 119). The exercise takes about two hours. Participants are organized into groups of five with two observers. An unlimited number of groups may be directed at the same time. The procedure for the coordinator is as follows:

1. Introduce the exercise as focusing upon communication within a problem-solving situation. Set the stage for the role playing by reviewing in a realistic manner the Bewise College Briefing Sheet (page 376, Appendix E).
2. Divide into groups of seven—five participants plus two observers. Instruct the groups to choose the correct president based upon the data they will receive. Suggest that there is one correct solution to their problem and caution them that they must reach their solution independent of the other groups. Then distribute a Briefing Sheet, the Candidate Summary Sheets, and one Bewise College Data Sheet to each participant. Ensure that all five differently coded data sheets are distributed to different members within each group. Each sheet is coded by the number of dots ranging from one to five following the second sentence in the first paragraph. Each sheet contains data unique to that sheet. Tell the participants not to let other group members read their sheets.
3. While the five role players are studying their sheets, meet with the observers. Distribute copies of the Patterns of Communication Frequency Chart and brief observers on how they are used. A copy of the chart appears below. Each observer will need several copies of the chart, so time should be given for them to make their extra copies.
4. Give the signal to begin the group meeting. An element of competition may be introduced by posting groups' solutions in order of completion and by posting the number of minutes used by each group in solving the problem.
5. After all the groups have submitted their solution to the problem, review the answers and compare them with the right answer. The correct answer appears on page 326, Appendix D. Then ask the group to discuss their experience, using the observations of the observers. Questions relevant for discussion are:
   a. What were the patterns of communication within the group? Who spoke to whom? Who talked, how often, and how long? Who triggered whom in what ways? How did members feel about the amount of their participation? What could be done to gain wider participation?
   b. Was the needed information easily obtained by all the group members? Did group members share their information appropriately, request each other's information, and create the conditions under which the information would be shared?

c. Were the resources of all group members shared and used? Was everyone listened to?

d. How cooperative or competitive were the group members?

e. How did the group make decisions?

f. What problems did the group have in working together?

g. What conclusions about communication can be made from the group's experience?

6. Have all the groups share their conclusions with one another. Review the observation sheets and discuss the nature of communication within goal-oriented groups.

FIGURE 5.2   Observer's Frequency Chart: Patterns of Communication

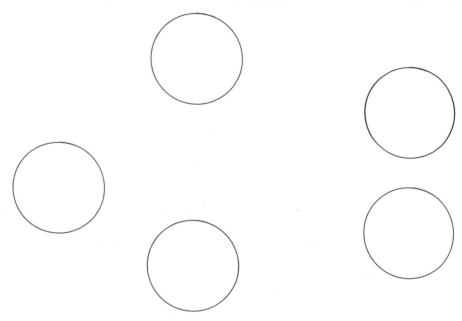

Interval_____(Use one sheet for each five-minute interval) Label the circles with the names of the group members. Indicate a sender to a receiver by an arrow; when someone sends a message to the entire group indicate by an arrow to the center. Indicate frequency of message sending by tally marks (‖‖ ‖); place an "x" in the member's circle every time he interrupts or overrides another group member; place a check " ✓ " in the member's circle every time he encourages another member to participate. An example is given below.

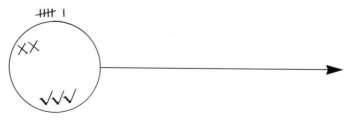

ENERGY INTERNATIONAL EXERCISE

An exercise similar to the Bewise College Exercise is the Energy International Exercise developed by Bob Euritt. This exercise can be used in the same way as the Bewise College Exercise; that is, the identical procedure, observations, and discussion questions can be used. The necessary Briefing Sheet, Data Sheets, and Candidate Summary Sheets appear in Appendix E, pages 387 to 398. The answer appears in Appendix D.

DISTRIBUTED INFORMATION EXERCISE

The following exercise is based upon the same principle as the previous two, but it is somewhat simpler and may be done in forty-five minutes. The same basic procedure, observation patterns, and discussion are used. The following is the information needed to conduct the exercise. This exercise is based on one created by Rimoldi at the Loyola University Psychometrics Laboratory. (The solution to the problem may be found in Appendix D.)

Instructions

Pretend that lutts and mipps represent a new way of measuring distance, and that dars, wors, and mirs represent a new way of measuring time. A man drives from Town A through Town B and Town C to Town D. The task of your group is to determine how many wors the entire trip took. You have twenty minutes for this task.

You will be given cards containing information related to the task of the group. You may share this information orally, but do not show your cards to anyone else.

Information for Individual Group Members

Each of the following questions and answers is typed on a three-by-five-inch index card (twenty-six cards). The cards are distributed at random among the five group members.

How far is it from A to B?
It is 4 lutts from A to B.
How far is it from B to C?
It is 8 lutts from B to C.
How far is it from C to D?
It is 10 lutts from C to D.
What is a lutt?
A lutt is 10 mipps.

What is a mipp?

A mipp is a way of measuring distance.

How many mipps are there in a mile?

There are 2 mipps in a mile.

What is a dar?

A dar is 10 wors.

What is a wor?

A wor is 5 mirs.

What is a mir?

A mir is a way of measuring time.

How many mirs are there in an hour?

There are two mirs in an hour.

How fast does the man drive from A to B?

The man drives from A to B at the rate of 24 lutts per wor.

How fast does the man drive from B to C?

The man drives from B to C at the rate of 30 lutts per wor.

How fast does the man drive from C to D?

The man drives from C to D at the rate of 30 lutts per wor.

MURDER MYSTERY EXERCISE

The following exercise is a mystery situation that can be used to study the way in which information is communicated in problem-solving groups. Each clue should be written on a separate card, and the cards should be passed out randomly to the group members. Groups of any size can be used. The same basic procedures used in the previous exercises should be used, along with the same observation forms and discussion questions. The solution is in Appendix D.

The task of the group is to solve a murder mystery by finding the murderer, the weapon, the time of the murder, the place of the murder, and the motive. Each member has some clues that will help solve the mystery. These clues may be communicated verbally, but the cards may not be shown to other group members. The clues are:

When he was discovered dead, Mr. Thompson had a bullet wound in his calf and a knife wound in his back.

Mr. Barton shot at an intruder in his apartment building at midnight.

Mr. Thompson had virtually wiped out Mr. Barton's business by stealing his customers.

The elevator operator reported to police that he saw Mr. Thompson at 12:15 a.m.

The bullet taken from Mr. Thompson's calf matched the gun owned by Mr. Barton.

Only one bullet had been fired from Mr. Barton's gun.

The elevator man said Mr. Thompson did not seem too badly hurt.

A knife found in the parking garage had been wiped clean of fingerprints.

Mrs. Scott had been waiting in the lobby for her husband to get off work.

The elevator man went off duty at 12:30 a.m.

Mr. Thompson's body was found in the park.

Mr. Thompson's body was found at 1:20 a.m.

Mr. Thompson had been dead for about an hour when his body was found, according to the medical examiner.

Mrs. Scott did not see Mr. Thompson leave through the lobby while she was waiting.

Bloodstains corresponding to Mr. Thompson's blood type were found in the basement parking garage.

Police were unable to locate Mr. Barton after the murder.

Mr. Thompson's blood type was found on the carpet outside Mr. Barton's apartment.

There were bloodstains in the elevator.

Mrs. Scott had been a good friend of Mr. Thompson and had often visited his apartment.

Mrs. Scott's husband had been jealous of the friendship.

Mrs. Scott's husband did not appear in the lobby at 12:30 a.m., the end of his normal working hours. She had to return home alone and he arrived later.

At 12:45 a.m. Mrs. Scott could not find her husband or the family car in the basement parking lot of the apartment building where he worked.

COMMUNICATING INFORMATION FOR PROBLEM SOLVING

For any problem-solving group to be effective, the members have to obtain information needed to solve the problem and put it together in such a way that an accurate or creative solution results. The previous exercises focused upon the communication of information within a group. The situation for each exercise can be seen in Figure 5.3.

FIGURE 5.3   Communication Information

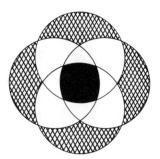

Shaded area represents information known to all group members;

crosshatched area represents information known to only one group member;

unmarked but enclosed area represents information known to two or more members of the group.

Within any communication process there are sources of "noise." How a group member is perceived, how much information a group member thinks each of the others has, how trustworthy a member has been in the past, how the messages are formulated and sent, what receiving skills are used, how cooperative the group is, and whether a member believes her information will make a contribution to the group are all sources of noise that affect the group's communication. All groups must learn that to arrive at the solution to a problem they must elicit contributions from every member and encourage effective communication between every member. Thus, each member has the responsibility to contribute his information (using effective sending skills) and the other members have the responsibility to listen carefully (using receiving skills).

The coordination of information, ideas, experiences, and opinions is an essential part of problem solving in a group. How successful a group is with such coordination depends on the skills of the group members in sending and receiving messages and on the group norms about and procedures for communicating. The patterns of communication among group members are an important aspect of group process to observe and discuss.

PATTERNS OF COMMUNICATION AMONG GROUP MEMBERS

Several patterns of communication within a group are often helpful to observe. One is the relative frequency and length of communication acts—who communicates, how often, and for how long. Observation of this pattern would show who has talked, how often, and how much of the total available time he used. A second pattern to figure out is who communicates to whom. Some people speak to those they are trying to impress, others to those from whom they want support, and still others to those from whom they expect opposition. Information on this pattern of communication among group members is often helpful in pinpointing conflicts that must be resolved or for increasing the group members' understanding of how they are relating to one another.

A third pattern of communication to observe is who "triggers" whom and in what ways. There are clear patterns of triggering, such as whenever one member speaks another always speaks next, even if the remarks are not initially directed to him. This kind of triggering may reflect either support ("Attaboy") or a desire to undo the point ("Yeabut") which has just been made. Schein (1969) quotes a businessman as saying that in group discussions in his company it takes at least three attaboys to undo the damage of one yeabut. Another type of triggering is when one member of a group interrupts other members. Knowing who interrupts whom gives the observer clues as to how members see their own status or power in the group relative to other members. Generally, high-authority members feel freer to interrupt low-authority members than vice versa. Interrupting others is one of the more common and more destructive kinds of communication behavior, and observing the patterns of interruption often reveals a great deal about relationships among members.

To check your understanding of this section, answer the following question (answer on page 137):

1. Three patterns of communication helpful to observe in a group are:
   a. Who talks, how often, and how long.
   b. Who shows the most hostility and anger.
   c. Who talks to whom.
   d. Who has the best way with words.
   e. Who triggers whom and in what ways.

EFFECTS OF COMPETITION ON COMMUNICATION

A considerable body of research shows that when a situation within a group is cooperatively structured, relevant information is communicated openly, accurately, and honestly; in a competitively structured situation, however, communication is either lacking or misleading. With a cooperative structure, each group member is interested in informing as well as being informed by others. Competition, on the other hand, gives rise to (1) espionage or other techniques to get information another group member is unwilling to communicate, and (2) diversionary tactics to mislead other group members about himself. The more intense the competition, the more likely communication will be blocked or, if group members have to communicate with one another, the more likely they will communicate only lies and threats. The very nature of competition, in which one works to gain an edge toward winning and fears the possibility of losing, promotes a great deal of defensiveness among group members.

Defensive behavior in a group is defined as behavior that occurs when a person feels threatened or anticipates a threat. Competition is inevitably accompanied by defensive behavior. And defensive people, even if they work on the group's tasks, devote a lot of energy just to defending themselves. They think about how they look to others, how they may win over or dominate their peers, how they may impress their superiors, how they may keep from losing, and how they may protect themselves from anticipated attacks. As a person becomes more and more defensive, furthermore, he becomes less and less able to see correctly the motives, values, emotions, and content involved in messages of other group members. Gibb (1961) demonstrated that defensive behavior was correlated positively with losses in efficiency and effectiveness in communication; that is, as people become less defensive, their communication behavior becomes more efficient and effective. Competitiveness in one group member breeds competition in all group members, and defensiveness will continue to spiral as long as competition thrives among group members.

Arousing defensiveness interferes with communication and makes it difficult, if not impossible, to get ideas across clearly and move purposefully toward accomplishing the group's goals. In an eight-year study of communication behavior in groups, Gibb found several factors that influence the defensiveness of group members. For example, if one group member sends messages that she is evaluating or judging other group members, they will become defensive. Descriptive messages, on the contrary, tend to arouse little uneasiness. Messages that try to control other group members increase their defensiveness, especially if the control attempts are subtle and denied. Yet if the sender is oriented toward the group problem, and communicates a desire to help in defining it and solving it, and if he also implies that he has no predetermined solution, attitude, or method to impose upon the other group members, the same problem orientation has a tendency to be created in the receivers. When the sender is seen as being engaged in a strategy involving numerous and ambiguous motives, here again the receivers tend to become defensive; no one likes to be the victim of some hidden motivation and most groups dislike deceit. Behavior that seems to be spontaneous and free of deception reduces defensiveness in the receivers.

Gibb also found that when neutrality in communication appears to the receiver to evidence lack of concern for her welfare, she becomes defensive. However, communications that are particularly persuasive in reducing defensiveness are those that show empathy with the feelings and respect for the worth of the receiver. When a person communicates that he feels superior in some way to the receiver, defensiveness is aroused; defensiveness is lessened when the sender communicates a willingness to enter into participative planning with others in mutual trust and respect. Finally, those who seem to know the answers, who need no additional information, and who see themselves as teachers rather than as coworkers, tend to arouse defensiveness in others. A person minimizes the defensiveness of receivers by communicating that she is willing to experiment with her own behavior, attitudes, and ideas. These factors are summarized below.

Behavior Characteristics of Competitive and Cooperative Orientations in Groups

Competitive Orientation	*Cooperative Orientation*
Evaluation	Description
Control	Problem Orientation
Strategy	Spontaneity
Neutrality	Empathy
Superiority	Equality
Certainty	Provisionalism

Groups with a high cooperative orientation among group members, with members who are good listeners, more accepting of ideas and less possessive of their own, generally demonstrate greater sending and receiving skills. In a cooperative group achievement will be higher than in a competitive one. More attentiveness will be paid to members' ideas and a friendlier climate will prevail than in groups where competitive orientations are present. A cooperative orientation leads to increased cohesiveness and greater group productivity. One sound means of improving the communication among group members is to increase their cooperativeness and decrease their competitiveness.

PHYSICAL BARRIERS TO COMMUNICATION

Physical factors can also block effective communication within a group. Group members should pay attention to the acoustics of the room; how members are seated; the duration of the meeting; the ventilation, temperature, and lighting in the room; what time of day it is. All these are physical factors that can easily interfere with effective communication among members. Once noted, of course, they can usually be changed or compensated for.

Again, you may check your comprehension of the preceding sections by answering the following questions (answers on page 137):

1. Several ways of improving communication among group members are (choose five):
   a. Have a training program to teach communication skills.
   b. Have a training program to train the group leaders.
   c. Analyze the communication patterns in the group.
   d. Examine the norms and traditional practices of the group.
   e. Change the goals of the group.
   f. Change the members of the group.
   g. Change the relationships in the group.
   h. Structure the group cooperatively rather than competitively.

Match the behaviors with the kind of group in which they are found:

_b_ 2. Certainty   a. Cooperative
_b_ 3. Control   b. Competitive
_a_ 4. Description
_a_ 5. Empathy
_b_ 6. Evaluation
_a_ 7. Problem orientation
_a_ 8. Spontaneity
_b_ 9. Strategy

10. Defensive behavior takes place when:
    a. A person wants to dominate a group.
    b. A person cannot meet his goals in a group.
    c. A person disagrees with the group.
    d. A person feels threatened by a group.

TRANSMISSION OF INFORMATION EXERCISE

The objectives of this exercise are to show the effect of passing information through a series of group members using one-way and two-way communication. At least ten persons and two observers are required. The time needed to complete the exercise is approximately one hour, and the procedure for the coordinator is as follows:

1. Introduce the exercise as an example of information being passed from member to member within a group.

2. Ask ten people to leave the room. They are to constitute two groups of five members each. The first group is to demonstrate one-way communication by entering the room one by one. Each is to listen to a brief story and repeat it to the next person in his own way without help from other participants or his group's observer. The receiver cannot ask questions or comment; he must simply listen to the story and then repeat it to the next person. The second group is to demonstrate two-way communication by entering the room one by one. Each is to listen to the story and ask questions about it to clarify its meaning and to make sure that he knows what the story is about. He then repeats the story to the next person in his group in his own way without help from other participants or his group's observer; the receiver can ask as many questions as he wants. You may wish to record the whole experience so that it can be played back for the participants' benefit.

3. After the ten participants have left the room, pass out two copies of the observation sheets (pp. 399 and 400) and a copy of "The Story" (pp. 327 and 328) to the observers. Discuss the use of the observation sheets and read the story. Explain the basic concepts of leveling, sharpening, and assimilation found in the section on the two-step flow of communication (page 133).

4. Begin the one-way communication demonstration by asking the first person to enter the room, read the story once, ask the second person to enter, and have the first person repeat the story to the second person, and so on until the fifth person repeats the story to the observers.

5. Begin the two-way communication demonstration by asking the first person to enter the room, read the story once, answer all questions he has about the story, ask the second person to enter and have the first person repeat the story to the second person and answer all of the second person's questions, and so on until the fifth person repeats the story to the observers.

6. Reread the original story. Using the results recorded by the observers, chart the percentages of original details retained correctly in the successive reproductions and compare one-way and two-way communications (Tables 5.1, 5.2, and Fig. 5.4). Discuss the results, including the material in the sections on the two-step flow of communication and the characteristics of communication within an authority hierarchy. Ask the group for further evidence that leveling, sharpening, and assimilation occurred. Ask the group what conclusions about one-way and two-way communication can be made based upon the results of the demonstration; ask what conclusions can be made about communication in authority hierarchies.

7. Other stories can be used in this exercise. Often the more the story differs from the listener's culture the more the story is taken in. A second story from the Eskimo culture is included in Appendix D.

TABLE 5.1 Summary Data for One-Way Communication

Person	Details Correct		Details Incorrect		Details Left Out		Total Details
	Number	Percent	Number	Percent	Number	Percent	
1							20
2							20
3							20
4							20
5							20

TABLE 5.2 Summary Data for Two-Way Communication

Person	Details Correct		Details Incorrect		Details Left Out		Total Details
	Number	Percent	Number	Percent	Number	Percent	
1							20
2							20
3							20
4							20
5							20

FIGURE 5.4 Summary Chart

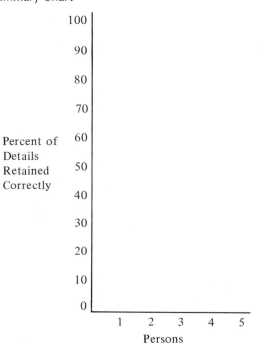

On Fig. 5.4 mark the percentages of original details retained correctly in one-way and two-way communication demonstrations. Mark the one-way results with a solid line and the two-way results with a broken line.

COMMUNICATION WITHIN AN AUTHORITY HIERARCHY

Within every organization and in many groups there is an authority hierarchy. An authority hierarchy exists when role requirements are set up in such a way that different members perform different roles and members performing particular roles supervise the other members to make sure they fulfill their role requirements. If a group, for example, is divided into several committees, each responsible for a different aspect of the group's work, its role structure would look like Fig. 5.5.

FIGURE 5.5 . A Group and Its Internal Authority Hierarchy

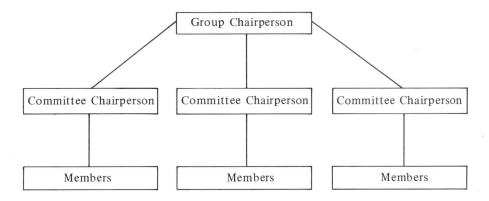

The members would be supervised by the committee chairpersons and the committee chairpersons would be supervised by the group chairperson. Within an authority hierarchy a system of rewards and punishments usually is established, to ensure that a supervisor has some power over the persons he is supervising. Although authority hierarchies are established to facilitate the effectiveness of the group, often they can interfere with its effectiveness by undermining necessary processes such as distributed participation and leadership, equalization of power, controversy procedures, and communication. In this chapter we will focus on the effect of authority hierarchies upon communication within a group and thus elaborate on the conclusions resulting from the previous exercise.

In order to organize itself to accomplish its goals, maintain itself in good working order, and adapt to a changing world, a group must structure its communication. Meetings will be scheduled; reports from group members will be requested; conferences among members will be set up; summaries of group progress may be written and sent to all members. All of these activities are structured communication opportunities. The *communication network* thus created determines the amount and type of information a group member will receive from the other members. The very nature of a group implies that communication is selective, that a communication network exists, that incentives to use it properly are present, and that members must use certain procedures for communicating with each other. Thus a college seminar will schedule meetings and teacher-student conferences as the communication network, be selective in the material communicated about, use learning and grades as incentives for using the network, and encourage certain procedures (when the teacher talks, students listen). The formal network, incentives, and procedures are established to coordinate members' efforts toward goal accomplishment. In addition to the formal communication network in many groups an informal network exists, which includes patterns of friendship and social contact among group members.

The procedures used within a formal communication network of a group can be examined in several different ways, but the one most relevant to a discussion of authority hierarchies consists of three types: one-way, one-way with feedback, and two-way. Within an authority hierarchy, a one-way communication procedure is characterized by a group chairperson giving instructions or making announcements to the other group members while they, in turn, are not allowed to communicate with him. In a one-way communication network the listener is entirely passive; communication effectiveness is determined by how the messages are created and presented. Usually there is someone higher in the authority hierarchy who communicates the message to the chairperson, who then communicates it to the group members. One-way communication takes little time compared with the other two procedures, but it is less effective. And though it is less frustrating for the sender, it is far more unsatisfactory for the receivers.

A one-way-with-feedback communication procedure is often called directive or coercive communication (McGregor, 1967). In this communication procedure within an authority hierarchy, the chairperson presents the message and the group members give feedback on how well they understand it. The exchange is completed when the group members indicate to the chairperson that they have received the message correctly. This procedure is called coercive because no provision exists for mutual influence or exchange; communication begins with the belief that the chairperson's position is correct, and the only information she needs from the group members is that they correctly understand and accept the message. The chairperson influences, while the group members merely understand. This second procedure is, in the short run, faster than two-way communication and less frustrating for the chairperson; it is also less accurate and more frustrating for the group members than two-way communication procedures.

When one-way and one-way-with-feedback communication procedures are used in groups, communication can be so poor that informal communication among group members is necessary in order to complete the group's tasks adequately. This reduces the long-term effectiveness of these procedures. The original messages can become distorted as they pass through the informal network, causing problems in coordinating member behavior. Such distortion and misunderstanding is most frequent when the most influential members of the informal network disagree with the decisions and points of view of the chairperson and his superiors (if he has them), or when distrust and competition exist among group members or between the chairperson and the group members. Unless group members have the opportunity to communicate freely with the chairperson, the informal network may become more influential, powerful, important, and effective than the group's formal network.

Two-way communication is a reciprocal process in which each member starts messages and tries to understand the other members' messages. In a two-way communication procedure the chairperson and the other group members freely exchange ideas and information in a productive discussion. Both sending and receiving skills are needed. All members are able to participate at will, and minority opinions are encouraged and more apt to be expressed. Feelings of resistance or doubt can be discussed and resolved at the time they are experienced so that they are not potential barriers to commitment. Two-way communication encourages open and candid member interaction, distributed participation and leadership, consensual decision making, and other aspects of group effectiveness. Although two-way communication is much more time consuming than the one-way procedures and more frustrating for the chairperson, it is less frustrating for the group members and much more effective in the long run. Any goal-directed, problem-solving group that hopes to be effective must use two-way communication procedures.

Even when a two-way communication procedure is encouraged, the authority hierarchy will influence communication among group members. High-authority group members usually do most of the talking and most of the messages are directed at them. Low-authority members often do not communicate very much with each other during a group meeting, preferring to address their remarks to high-authority members. Because they generally fear evaluation by those with power, members without power can be expected to take few risks, speak inconsequentially, and avoid frankness in their remarks. High-authority members often hesitate to reveal any of their own limitations or personal vulnerability, a tendency that also decreases open and effective communication among group members. Thus, several influences push the group's use of communication procedures toward practices that thwart the kind of discussion and problem solving needed for it to function effectively.

How can these tendencies be avoided so that communication within a group is effective? There are two answers to this question. The first is to establish a cooperative group climate that encourages the equal participation of all members. The second is to promote group norms that foster the feeling that a member's ideas and views, no matter what his authority level, are of real interest to other group members. If a group is to function effectively, it must adopt a two-way communication procedure and develop a cooperative group climate and group norms that facilitate interaction among members. Since communication is an interpersonal phenomenon, furthermore, anything that interferes with the relationships among group members interferes with their communication. Much attention, therefore, must be paid to the interpersonal relationships among group members.

To check your understanding of this section, please answer the following questions (answers on page 137).

1. An authority hierarchy is:
   a. the type of communication being used in the group.
   b. a specific type of problem-solving group.
   c. the way in which a group meets its deadlines and makes urgent decisions.
   d. a system of role definitions that gives supervisors power over subordinate roles.

2. A communication network consists of (choose three):
   a. several people yelling at each other.
   b. an arrangement of group members in a circle.
   c. the interaction structured among group members.
   d. the incentives to communicate in prescribed ways.
   e. the procedures for communicating when members interact.

Match the following procedures for communicating with their definitions:

b 3. one-way
a 4. one-way-with-feedback
c 5. two-way

a. Leader gives instructions; members clarify meaning.

b. Leader gives instructions; members listen.

c. Leader and members have free exchange of ideas.

6. Four characteristics of the two-way procedure is that it:
   a. takes less time than other methods.
   b. takes more time than other methods.
   c. is less frustrating for the group members.
   d. is more frustrating for the group members.
   e. is less frustrating for the chairperson.
   f. is more frustrating for the chairperson.
   g. is less effective.
   h. is more effective.

7. When some group members have more authority than other group members:
   a. high-authority members tend to talk to other high-authority members.
   b. low-authority members tend to talk to high-authority members.
   c. both high- and low-authority members talk to high-authority members.
   d. no one talks to high-authority members.

INFORMAL COMMUNICATION NETWORKS AND OPINION LEADERS

When one-way communication procedures are used in a group, comprehension of messages is often so poor that group members turn to the informal communication network to clarify what has been communicated. Often certain group members will be better able to interpret messages from higher-ups and, therefore, other members will seek them out and ask them what the higher-ups meant by the latest communication. Such members are called opinion leaders or gatekeepers because they have more influence over members' comprehension of messages than do the persons in higher-authority positions who originated the messages. There are two common types of opinion leaders: *information gatekeepers*, who receive messages from superiors, outside sources, or who read, listen, and reflect upon written reports and verbal messages to a greater extent than other group members, and *technological gatekeepers*, who read more of the theory and research literature in their field and consult more with outside sources than do the other group members.

Opinion leaders frequently serve as *translators* in taking messages from superiors and rephrasing them into more understandable form and into the specific meanings they have for different group members. When one-way communication procedures are being used the original source is often not available for questioning and clarification of messages; group members, therefore, must rely on the opinion leaders to clarify the meaning of messages and what implications they have for the specific group members. Group members, furthermore, may remember the opinion leaders' interpretations of messages they themselves have heard better than the original messages! Research on testimony in court cases indicates that people remember initial reports of events they witnessed better than the events themselves (Jones and Gerard, 1967). If the opinion leaders misconstrue the message, errors in understanding are amplified as interpretations are passed from member to member. Even within a two-way communication procedure group members will at times be unable to clarify a message and use opinion leaders to help clarify their understanding.

To check your reading of this section, answer the following question (answer on page 137).

Opinion leaders:

_____ a. are good sources of information.
_____ b. clarify the meaning and implications of messages from higher-ups.
_____ c. receive lots of messages that they read carefully.

EFFECTS ON THE MESSAGE OF A ONE-WAY PROCEDURE

Some basic research has been conducted on what happens to information when it is passed through several people with little or no clarification. Three psychological processes characterize the communication between persons who are unable to communicate directly with the original source of a message (Allport and Postman, 1945; Bartlett, 1932). These three processes are attempts to reduce the message to a simple one that has significance for the receiver in terms of his own interests, experience, frame of reference, and tasks. The more the message is passed from person to person, the more distorted and changed it will become. The three psychological processes are:

1. *Leveling:* the receiver tends to reduce the amount of information he receives by

remembering much less of the message than was presented by the sender. The message tends to grow shorter, more concise, more easily grasped and told. In successive versions, fewer words are used and fewer details are mentioned.

2. *Sharpening:* the receiver sharpens certain parts of the information so that a few high points are readily remembered while most of the message is forgotten. Sharpening is selectively retaining, perceiving, and reporting a limited number of details from a larger context. It is the reciprocal of leveling: one cannot exist without the other. This is the tendency for certain points to become dominant, and for all the others to be grouped about them.

3. *Assimilation:* the receiver takes much of the message into her own unique frame of reference and personality; thus, the receiver's interpretations and memories of what she heard are affected by her own thoughts and feelings. This process involves not only changing the unfamiliar to some known context, but leaving out material that seems irrelevant and substituting material that gives meaning in a person's own frame of reference.

Because these three processes are at work whenever one-way procedures are being used, inefficient and ineffective communication usually results. This is true even when opinion leaders supplement the one-way procedures.

In order to check your reading of this section, match the following processes with their definitions (answers on page 137).

_C_ 1. leveling
_a_ 2. sharpening
_b_ 3. assimilation

a. certain points become dominant and the others are grouped around them.

b. the material is affected by the receiver's own frame of reference.

c. the message is shortened and made more concise.

GROUP OBSERVATION

Review the material in the past three sections by taking the observation sheet used in the Bewise College Exercise and observe at least two groups of which you are a member. Find a group in which there is a chairperson (such as a teacher) who dominates the meetings, and another group in which free and open discussions are held among members. Observe the communication patterns in both groups and compare them. Write a description of the communication patterns in each group and discuss them with other members of this class.

NORMS AND COMMUNICATION EXERCISE

This exercise should develop your awareness of how group norms affect communication among group members. It needs to be used with a group that has worked together for several hours. It will take approximately one hour to complete. To conduct the exercise, an observation sheet similar to the one used in the Bewise College Exercise (page 119) is needed. Participants can construct their own observation sheets. The procedure for the coordinator is as follows:

1. Introduce the exercise as a structured experience in learning how group norms affect communication among group members.
2. For each group have two observers. The observers need to construct six copies of the observation sheet on page 119, making the number of circles on the sheets appropriate to the number of members in the group they are observing. Clarify the use of the observation sheets.
3. Hand out the discussion sheet entitled "What Is a Norm?" given on page 401, Appendix E. State that the groups have thirty minutes to discuss the topic. Give the signal to begin.
4. At the end of thirty minutes, ask the observers to report to the groups. Groups are to discuss the communication pattern within their group and how it relates to the group norms they have been listing. The groups should also discuss how the members feel about the amount of their participation and how group norms could be changed to gain more widespread participation and more effective communication among group members. Each group should then revise the list of group norms to include the discussion of their current communication patterns. They are to be allotted twenty minutes for this discussion.
5. If more than one group participates in the exercise, have the groups share their conclusions in a general discussion.

CIRCLE EXERCISE

How a group sits has a great deal of influence on how its members communicate. This exercise focuses upon the effects of sitting in a circle. The procedure consists of having the group conduct three five-minute discussions. After each one, each member writes down several adjectives to describe his feelings and reaction to the discussion. The three positions to be used for the discussions are: (1) a circle with everyone's back to the center, (2) a circle with a large table between all the members, and (3) a circle with nothing between the members.

After the fifteen minutes of discussion, compare the reactions of the members to the three positions. What were the differences in feelings and reactions? Was there any difference in how productive the discussion was? What effect did the position have upon the discussion? How was communication affected? The advantage of sitting close together in a circle with nothing between members is that an unobstructed view of one's fellow members increases the opportunities to receive and send nonverbal messages. The circular seating arrangement also encourages more equal participation because there is no podium or seat at the head of a table to suggest that a particular member should assume leadership.

TAKING A SURVEY

Group effectiveness is always improved when members have clear expectations of what kinds of behaviors are expected of them as group members. One way to clarify such expectations is the use of the survey method. In a survey any member may ask for the opinion of all others at any time; the requesting member states what he wants to know from the total group. Each member then states in two or three sentences his current position on the topic under discussion. A survey is not a vote and it does not bind the group members to a fixed position; it is a device to help communication and problem solving within a group.

IMPROVING COMMUNICATION AMONG GROUP MEMBERS

To improve communication among group members, their communication behavior must be observed in order to diagnose possible sources of difficulty. Once a diagnosis has been made and enough data have been gathered to confirm existing problems, both communication skills and the group's awareness of its present behavior need to be examined. If certain members—or all of them—lack some basic skills, the situation can be easily corrected by instituting a training program. If members have the skills but are not fully aware that they are not using them, an analysis of the communication behavior in the group can be a great help. After examining awareness and skills, the effect of group norms and traditional practices may be analyzed for the purpose of finding out if they are suppressing effective communication behavior and promoting ineffective communication behavior. Group norms can then be adjusted to increase communication effectiveness among group members.

Because communication is interpersonal, whatever interferes with the relationships among group members interferes with their communication. By changing the relationships in a group, basic improvements in communication can be made. And as we have noted before, perhaps the most powerful influence on the relationships among members and on communication in a group is the members' orientation toward participation in the group and toward its goal structure. Cooperativeness helps determine a group's effectiveness. Competitiveness, either in goal structure or member orientation, is highly destructive of communication and relationships.

YOUR COMMUNICATION BEHAVIOR

How would you now describe your communication behavior within a problem-solving group? What are your strengths in communicating and in what areas do you still wish to build skills? After completing the exercises in this chapter, take twenty minutes or so to write a description of how you see your communication behavior in problem-solving groups. Include a description of the way you formulate and send messages, the receiving skills you use, the way in which you contribute your information and ideas to the group, the way in which you receive information about group meetings and group business, and so on.

After you have written your description, meet with two persons who know you well and discuss it with them. Is it accurate? Can they add anything? Do they have other ideas that might help clarify your communication behavior?

CHECKLIST OF SKILLS

_____ I am aware of my communication tendencies within a group.

_____ I understand the difference between effective and ineffective communication.

_____ I can effectively send messages.

_____ I can effectively receive messages.

_____ I can make my messages appropriate to the frame of reference of the receiver.

_____ I can competently observe communication patterns within a group and effectively report these patterns to group members.

_____ I can recognize one-way communication procedures and predict their consequences.

_____ I can recognize one-way-with-feedback communication procedures and predict their consequences.

_____ I can recognize two-way communication procedures and predict their consequences.

_____ I can identify group norms which affect communication among group members and lead a discussion of what norms (if any) need to be changed.

_____ I can identify cooperative and competitive behaviors in the group and call attention to their effects on communication among group members.

_____ I can contribute all relevant information I have to a group's discussion.

The skills I need further work on are: _____

_____

_____

_____

_____

_____

ANSWERS

Page 112: 1: true; 2: false; 3: true; 4: true; 5: true.

Page 117: 1: a, b, d; 2: c, d; 3: c, 4: d.

Page 124: 1; a, c, e.

Page 126: 1: a, c, d, g, h; 2: b; 3: b; 4: a; 5: a; 6: b; 7: a; 8: a; 9: b; 10: d.

Page 132: 1: d; 2: c, d, e; 3: b; 4: a; 5: c; 6: b, c, f, h; 7: c.

Page 133: b.

Page 134: 1: c; 2: a; 3: b.

6

Controversy and Creativity

INTRODUCTION

Conflicts are inevitable in problem-solving groups. Involved, committed participation among heterogeneous members will produce conflicts regularly, even in the friendliest of groups. A conflict among group members is a moment of truth in group effectiveness, a test of the group's health, a crisis that can weaken or strengthen the group, a critical event that may bring creative insight and closer relationships among members—or lasting resentment, smoldering hostility, and psychological scars. Conflicts can push members away from one another or pull them into closer and more cooperative relationships. Conflicts may contain the seeds of group destruction or the seeds of a more unified and cooperative unit. Conflicts may bring aggression or mutual understanding. They have the potential for producing both highly constructive and highly destructive consequences for group functioning.

It is quite easy to find conflicts. Almost anyone can start a conflict at anytime in anyplace. Most people can easily recognize when they or others are in a conflict. Yet the concept of conflict has not been an easy one for social scientists to define. In trying to define conflict, some social psychologists have mentioned frustration, others have focused upon decisions among attractive or unattractive alternatives, and some have concentrated on the feelings of the individuals involved, such as rage and anger. The definition we shall use here is that of Deutsch's (1969); he states that a *conflict* exists whenever incompatible activities happen. An activity that is incompatible with another activity is one that prevents, blocks, interferes with, injures, or in some way makes the second activity less likely or less effective. Incompatible activities may originate in one person, between two or more people, or between two or more groups. If, for example, you want to cross the street and someone else decides to prevent, block, or interfere with your doing so, you are involved in an interpersonal conflict. If you decide that a group needs a speech on love and friendship, and another member keeps making jokes that cause your speech to be less effective, you are in conflict with that person. If you want to spend Saturday afternoon both sleeping and studying, you are in conflict with yourself. If your group decides to win a football game and another decides it also wants to win and starts tackling your ballcarriers, your group is in conflict with the other group.

In an effective group conflicts will occur regularly. Despite this fact, there seems to be a general feeling in our society that conflicts are bad and should be avoided, and that a "good" group is one in which there are no conflicts among members. Many discussions of conflict talk about it causing divorces, psychological distress, social disorder, war, violence, and the end of friendship. It is *not* the presence of conflicts that causes all these disastrous and unfortunate things, it is the harmful and ineffective management of conflicts. Conflicts are a natural and desirable part of any relationship and of any group and, when handled constructively, they are extremely valuable.

How is conflict of value? Why is conflict desirable? So many reasons exist that only a few can be listed here. First of all, without conflicts groups can become set in their ways and lose their effectiveness because they do not reexamine their procedures and their relevance to the needs and goals of both their own members and the world. Conflicts encourage not only personal but group change. Conflicts revitalize existing group practices so that the group can adjust more adequately to new conditions. Without conflicts members can become bored and uninterested in the group. Conflicts stimulate interest and spark the curiosity of group members. They provide an avenue for bringing problems out into the open, for arriving at solutions, for resolving tensions among members, and for stabilizing and integrating relationships among members. Conflicts end sources of dissatisfaction in groups by allowing the rival claims of group members to be immediately and directly resolved.

Conflicts are even fun when they become part of a process of testing and assessing oneself and experiencing the pleasure of full and active use of one's capabilities. Through conflicts groups are able to know how strong the antagonistic interests are within the group, and they can then proceed to readjust the balance of power and influence to satisfy all members. Conflicts also increase the motivation and energy of group members and encourage creativity and innovation. A group member can achieve greater self-understanding as a result of conflict with other group members, because having to talk about her position and think more carefully about how sound it is often generates greater awareness of values and identity. Internal conflicts may be worked out and managed through interpersonal conflicts within a group. Finally, when a group enters a conflict with another group, its cohesiveness increases and its sense of identity becomes clearer. These are only a few of the positive benefits that result from conflicts among group members and groups.

In this and the following chapter we are going to discuss two types of conflict: conflicts of ideas, or controversy, and conflicts of interest. They are discussed separately because they have different effects on group functioning and are resolved and managed in different ways.

You can test your understanding of this section by answering the following questions (answers on page 169).

1. A conflict exists when:
   a. People are frustrated.
   b. Incompatible activities take place.
   c. There is more than one way to solve a problem.
   d. One person hits another person over the head.
2. How can conflict help a group?
   a. It keeps everyone on his toes, dodging blows.
   b. It keeps the leaders on their toes, dodging blows.
   c. It helps everyone participate.
   d. It helps encourage change and flexibility.
3. What can participation in a conflict do for a group member?
   a. Help her self-understanding.
   b. Help promote friendly rivalry.
   c. Help in promoting satisfaction in the group.
   d. Help him find out who can hit the hardest.

NATURE OF CONTROVERSY

Participation, involvement, controversy, and creative problem solving are all closely related. To define clear, cooperative goals to which members are committed, to make effective decisions, to communicate effectively, to develop distributed leadership, all mean that every group member must actively participate in the group. Involved participation results in using fully the group's resources and in members being committed to implementing decisions. Widespread participation means that different ideas, opinions, beliefs, and information will surface—and that means that controversies among group members will occur. Controversies, are a necessary condition for creative insights and high-quality decisions.

Controversy is a form of conflict among group members. In most conflicts both substantive issues and personal emotions are involved. In a group the sources of conflict over substantive issues are differences in information, beliefs, opinions, assumptions, and ideas. Such conflicts may be labeled controversies because they involve disagreement within a problem-solving framework in which members of a group are trying to define, diagnose, and solve a problem. More precisely, a _controversy_ is a discussion, debate, or dispute in which opposing opinions clash. Decisions by their very nature suggest alternatives, argument, and controversy; basically, a decision represents ending a controversy with a particular course of action. Controversy among group members is essential because it is only through controversy that involvement, creativity, commitment to task accomplishment and to group maintenance, and high-quality decisions can evolve. Emotional responses to controversy may be positive (excitement, enjoyment, stimulation, curiosity, commitment, involvement, liking for other members) or negative (anger, distrust, resentment, fear, hurt, rejection), depending upon how the group handles the differences of opinions among members. In this chapter we will concentrate on the productive handling of controversy to increase a group's effectiveness in making creative, high-quality decisions, the kinds of decisions members commit themselves to implement and which improve the problem-solving effectiveness of the the group.

A controversy is (answer on page 169):
   a. A conflict in which people see who wins.
   b. A disagreement about the nature of the group's membership.
   c. A discussion in which opposing opinions clash.
   d. A figment of the imagination.

YOUR BEHAVIOR IN CONTROVERSIES

All of us frequently become involved in controversies. There are, however, large differences in how people react to and handle them. Some people find arguments stimulating and fun, and go around hoping to find a few every day. Other people become overly concerned about being rejected when they disagree with others and try to avoid controversies. We have all been raised to behave in certain ways in controversies. What is your behavior like in a controversy? How do you react? What are your feelings? Before you explore how to handle controversies constructively, it may be interesting for you to look at your behavior and beliefs in regard to controversies. Answer each question as honestly as possible.

1. My personal philosophy of controversy might be summarized by the statement:
   ____ "He hath conquered well that hath made his enemy fly . . . fields are won by those who believe in winning." (Translation: I like to be the only winner.)
   ✓ "Only he who is willing to give up his monopoly on truth can ever profit from the truths that others hold . . . no man has the final answer but every man has a piece to contribute." (Translation: everyone has some truth to give in an argument. No one is a winner or loser.)

2. Controversy among group members is a chance:
   ✓ to think of new, creative, and more effective alternatives for group action and problem solving.
   ____ for the strongest to dominate and a chance to see who "wins" and who "loses."

3. By disagreements being brought out into the open and faced directly, the most effective group action is discovered.
   ✓ Agree   ____ Disagree

4. A fair exchange brings no quarrel, only increased understanding of each other and of the issue being discussed.

___✓___ Agree   _____ Disagree

5. When other group members disagree with my position, I erupt into antagonism, anger, and hostile feelings.

___✓___ Agree   _____ Disagree

6. Nothing is more fun and enjoyable for me than a good argument.

_____ Agree   ___✓___ Disagree

7. Which of the following is most typical of you?

___✓___ When a controversy is taking place, I become quite curious about what others are thinking and feeling and I am concerned with getting everything out in the open.

_____ I find controversies frustrating as a rule. I usually become convinced that there is nothing I can do to resolve the issue, and I either end up smoldering with no way to break the tension or just lose interest because it's hopeless.

8. When controversies arise in the group, I speak freely and openly of my ideas, positions, and feelings.

_____ Agree   _____ Disagree

9. I am most creative in my thinking when I am working:

_____ Alone   _____ In a group

10. The way in which I help other people think creatively is to

_____ argue with them, present new and different perspectives on the issues under discussion, bring up facts they seem to have ignored.

___✓___ reinforce their ideas, give support to how well they are thinking, encourage them to apply their ideas, praise their ability to think creatively.

Check the statements that are true for you in a group:

___✓___ 11. I would rather be in a group that had a lot of controversy than one where members agree all the time.

_____ 12. A little controversy among members is all right, but I would not like to participate in it.

_____ 13. If I disagree with someone's ideas, I keep quiet.

_____ 14. If someone disagrees with my ideas, they are also rejecting me.

_____ 15. I have to know people pretty well before I will disagree with them.

_____ 16. Most people get mad at me when I disagree with their ideas.

___✓___ 17. If people argue with my ideas, I know they care enough about me to disagree.

The above questions deal with five matters related to controversy: how it is defined, how valuable or destructive it can be, how enjoyable or harmful being in one is, how open a person is with his ideas when one arises, and how it helps creative thinking. In questions 1 and 2, one alternative represents a "win-lose" orientation to controversy and the other a problem-solving orientation. Questions 3 and 4 focus upon whether controversy is positive and valuable or negative and worthless. Question 5, 6, and 7 deal with how enjoyable or distressing controversy is to you. Question 8 centers on how openly you tell of your positions, and questions 9 and 10 pertain to the way in which you help foster creativity.

Questions 11 through 17 deal with your personal reactions to controversy. Categorize yourself by your responses on each one of these issues. Then, as you reach each section in this chapter, review your responses and check to see if you still hold the same attitude and would behave in the same way.

STRANDED IN THE DESERT EXERCISE

There is nothing quite so beautiful as a desert night. And there are few places more dangerous to be stranded in than the desert during the night or day. Controversies, in helping a group make better decisions, are helpful in such dangerous situations, though the seriousness of it may intensify the emotional content of the arguments over what a stranded group should do. The purpose of this exercise is to examine the results of controversy in such a serious situation, and to determine how controversy affects the decision made by members of a group caught in a dilemma. The materials needed for the exercise include a description of the situation (page 403, Appendix E), an observation sheet with instructions on how to use it (pp. 405 and 406, Appendix E), role-playing instructions for eight group members (pp. 407 to 413, Appendix E), and a post-decision reaction form (page 404, Appendix E). Approximately an hour and a half is needed to conduct the exercise. The procedure for the coordinator is as follows:

1. Introduce the exercise and set the stage by reviewing the basic situation of being stranded in the desert and the urgent necessity to make a decision about what course of action would be best for the group's survival. State that the objective of the exercise is to focus on controversy within a group.

2. Divide into groups of ten—eight role players and two observers. Distribute a situation sheet (page 403, Appendix E) to everyone and distribute the eight role-playing sheets (pp. 407 to 413 in Appendix E) so that each group member has a different one, instructing participants not to show their sheets to each other.

3. While the group members are reading their situation sheets and their role sheets, meet with the observers. Distribute the Controversy Observer Instructions and the Observation Sheet (pp. 406 and 407, Appendix E) and discuss them until the observers clearly understand their responsibilities.

4. Give the signal for the session to begin. Groups have up to thirty minutes to make two decisions: (1) whether they will stay with the wrecked bus, or

whether they will try to walk to the ranch, and (2) whether they will or will not hunt for food. After twenty-five minutes give a five-minute warning.

5. At the end of thirty minutes stop the group discussions, hand out the Post-Decision Reaction Form (page 404, Appendix E), and instruct the participants to complete it. Collect the questionnaires and calculate the group means for each question. (Observers can help in determining the means for each question for their group.) Discuss the correct decisions and their rationale (see pp. 328 to 330, Appendix D). Then present the questionnaire data by placing it in the Summary Table (Table 6.1). Talk over the data gathered by the observers and its relationship to the questionnaire results. Discuss briefly the differences among the groups, and then ask the groups to review their experience, using the information collected by the observers, the questionnaire results, the Constructive Controversy Checklist, and the discussion questions given below. Instruct the groups to write on newsprint (if it is available) their conclusions about how they handled the controversy and how the controversy should have been handled.

6. After thirty minutes ask the groups to share their conclusions in a general session. Review the material included in this chapter on constructive controversies.

CONSTRUCTIVE CONTROVERSY CHECKLIST

1. How was the controversy defined? Was it defined as an interesting problem presenting a joint challenge that required a mutually acceptable solution or as a win-lose competition?

2. Did all members participate fully or did some members withdraw or censor their ideas and positions in order to avoid conflict?

3. Were the ideas and feelings of all the members expressed openly and honestly?

4. Were underlying assumptions and frames of reference brought out into the open and discussed?

5. Were everyone's contributions taken seriously, valued, and respected? Did members listen and pay attention to what each had to say?

6. Were quiet members encouraged to participate?

7. Was disagreement taken as personal rejection by some or all of the group members?

8. Was there adequate differentiation of positions? Did group members understand the differences among their positions? Were differences of opinion sought out and clarified?

9. Was there adequate integration of positions? Did group members understand the similarities among their positions and find ways to combine positions so that all parties were satisfied?

10. Did members in disagreement fully understand each of the others' positions and frames of reference? Did they engage in paraphrasing, negotiating for meaning, personal statements, and other forms of effective communication?

SUMMARY TABLE 6.1 Response to Controversy Questionnaire

Group	Decision 1 and 2	Understood	Influence	Commitment	Satisfaction	Learning	Feelings
1							
2							
3							
4							

Except for the first and the last columns, find the group mean to the questionnaire responses and record it in the appropriate column. To get a score for the decisions, give the group a "2" if both decisions were made correctly, a "1" if one of the decisions was made correctly, and a "0" if neither decision was made correctly. See pages 328 to 330 in Appendix D for correct answers. In the "Feelings" column put representative adjectives from the questionnaires.

11. Were emotions ignored or treated with uninvolved understanding or were they responded to with emotions?
12. Was the situational power of all members balanced?
13. Was the tension level productive or was it too high or too low for problem solving to take place?
14. Were there incentives for a creative resolution of the controversy?
15. Were conflict-reducing procedures, such as tossing a coin, voting, or bargaining, used or did the group arrive at resolutions that satisfied everyone?

DISCUSSION QUESTIONS

1. What were the results of the questionnaire responses of your group members? How do they compare with other groups? What happened to influence the responses of your group's members?
2. What are the results of the observers' information collecting? How do they compare with the questionnaire results? What happened in the group to influence members' behaviors toward the directions observed?
3. How did the group handle its controversies? Given the checklist for constructive controversies as a guide, how does the group function in controversies?
4. How did the group make its decisions? What method did it use? Why was that method used?
5. From its experience, what conclusions can the group make about the constructive handling of controversies?
6. Were opinions of members changed as a result of the discussion? Did members gain insight into other points of view? Did they learn new things about the issue?
7. What did members learn about themselves and other group members? How did you react to the controversy?

FACULTY MEETING EXERCISE

This exercise is an alternative to the Stranded in the Desert Exercise. The same basic procedures should be followed. It consists of a situation in which several teachers and a school psychologist are discussing the use of teaching machines within the school. They need to arrive at a decision about the issue. The eight specific roles for the exercise are on page 415 in Appendix E. The role descriptions are taken from an exercise developed by Dr. Lila Swell.

THINGS I VALUE EXERCISE

We all have slightly different values. Probably no one in the world has the same values as you do. How are differences in values handled in a group? How can they be constructively discussed? What can be learned by exploring another person's values? The following exercise is a chance to look at the way in which a group manages controversy about the values of its members. The exercise will take approximately an hour and a half. The observation sheets, the post-decision questionnaire, and the summary table (Table 6.1) used for the Stranded in the Desert Exercise are to be used in this and the following exercise. The What I Value sheet is on page 417, Appendix E. The coordinator's procedure is as follows:

1. Introduce the exercise as an experience in dealing with controversy.
2. Divide into groups of ten members, eight participants and two observers. Distribute the What I Value Sheet to all the participants in the exercise. Instruct the participants to read it carefully, pick out the three items they value most highly, and write a rationale for their choice. They have ten minutes to complete this part of the exercise.
3. Meet with the observers while the other participants are completing Step 2. Hand out the Controversy Observation Sheet (as used in the Stranded in the Desert Exercise) and discuss it until the observers clearly understand their responsibilities.
4. Give the signal for the session to begin. The groups have thirty minutes to discuss their value differences and arrive at a consensus about the three most important items on the What I Value Sheet, along with a rationale as to why they are the most valuable.
5. Distribute the Post-Decision Reaction Form and have group members complete it. Collect the questionnaires and compute the group means for each question. Present the questionnaire data by placing it in the Summary Table. Discuss the observations briefly. Noting the differences among groups, ask each group to discuss their experience, using the questionnaire results, the observations, the Constructive Controversy Checklist, and the discussion questions given on page 147. Ask each group to write their conclusions on the constructive management of controversy.
6. After thirty minutes ask the groups to share their conclusions in a general session. Discuss the material included in the theory sections of this chapter.

As an alternative to the What I Value list, the Fallout Shelter Situation (page 419 of Appendix E) may be used for this exercise.

VALUE OF CONTROVERSY

Effective problem solving cannot take place without conflicts over ideas and opinions. For any group to work productively toward goal accomplishment and group maintenance, its members must correct, resist, differ from, and oppose one another. Most groups waste the benefits of disputes, but every effective group thrives on what controversy has to offer.

What does controversy offer a group? In terms of effective decision making, controversy, when handled constructively, offers a group creative and high-quality decisions, the building of commitment among its members to implement the decision, and the improvement of its problem-solving ability. Controversy encourages inquiry, promotes objectivity, sharpens analysis, stimulates interest and curiosity, and increases involvement in and commitment to the group functioning. Controversy also encourages group members to search for new and better alternatives and to synthesize alternative suggestions in more imaginative and satisfying decisions. Controversy increases both the members' motivation and energy to do the group's tasks, and because of the greater diversity of the viewpoints expressed, their innovativeness. It also gives members a chance to develop a better understanding of their own contributions by forcing them to speak their views and present supporting arguments. Through controversy members may not only become more aware of their own identity as they explore what is important to them, but better managers of their own internal conflict as they release tension in arguments with other members. Controversies can also provide fun and interest, and they can give members an opportunity to air their differences in a constructive way.

Research on controversies within groups (Hoffman et al., 1962, Glidewell, 1953); has demonstrated that: (1) groups that use controversy in deciding upon their work methods produce more creative solutions than do similar, less conflicting groups; (2) members in groups that successfully resolve controversies and produce creative solutions are more satisfied with group decisions; and (3) groups that engage in controversy are different from other groups because they dig into a problem, raise issues, and settle them in ways that show the benefits of a wide range of ideas used in problem solving and a high degree of emotional involvement in and commitment to decisions.

The meaning that controversy has for group members and the method they use to handle it seem to distinguish effective from ineffective problem-solving groups. To the effective group, conflict means that the members' ideas must be elicited to a greater degree, and group thinking reexamined. To it, controversies are a necessary condition for creative insights to emerge. To the effective group, how well it manages controversy is the determining factor in whether its creative potential will be capitalized on. In effective groups, controversies keep their substantive quality without degenerating into emotional issues of "right versus wrong" or "me versus you." Effective groups seem to realize that when there is a difference of opinion, more information is needed and a closer look at the available information is required.

Unfortunately, most groups seem to operate on norms that encourage group members to suppress conflicts, to agree without commitment, and to stifle their creativity. It is characteristic of ineffective groups that they suppress and withdraw from controversy. Compromise in order to avert controversy is their rule. They often agree quickly, and believe that relationships among members are so fragile that they cannot stand the strain of prolonged differences. Norms in groups like these have to be changed if they are to develop and improve their problem-solving effectiveness.

1. List ten ways in which controversy and conflict may help a group. Refer back to the section to check your answers.

   1. _offers creative & high quality decisions_
   2. _stimulates interest & curiosity_
   3. _encourages new & better alternatives_
   4. _increases motivation & energy_
   5. _can provide fun_
   6. _produces more creative solutions_
   7. _encourages inquiry_
   8. _helps raise issues_
   9. _become aware of own identity_
   10. _satisfaction with decisions_

2. The use of conflict in problem solving results in (answers on page 169):

   (a.) More creativity.
   b. Less creativity.
   (c.) More satisfaction.
   d. Less satisfaction.
   e. More black eyes.

3. To the effective group, conflict means that (choose two):

   a. Relationships can't stand the test of argument.
   (b.) Group thinking needs to be looked at again.
   c. Group thinking has been faulty.
   d. The group should quickly agree on a compromise.
   (e.) Members' ideas need to be drawn out more.
   f. Outside resources are needed to settle the conflict.

4. To the ineffective group, conflict means that (choose two):

   (a.) Relationships can't stand the test of argument.
   b. Group thinking needs to be looked at again.
   c. Group thinking has been faulty.
   (d.) The group should quickly agree on a compromise.
   e. Members' ideas need to be drawn out more.
   f. Outside resources are needed to settle the conflict.

5. To change group norms, what must often be changed?

   a. The composition of the group.
   b. The group task.
   c. The information available to the group about the task.
   (d.) The attitudes and values of the group members.

Competing with and defeating an opponent is one of the most widely recognized aspects of interpersonal interaction in our society. The language of business, politics, and even education is filled with "win-lose" terms. One "wins" a promotion or a raise, "beats" the opposition, "outsmarts" a teacher, puts competitors "in their place." In an environment that stresses winning, it is no wonder that competitive behavior persists where it is not appropriate. It is not unusual in a group meeting for members to interrupt each other to voice their own ideas without listening to what the other member is saying, and to form power blocks in support of their position against proponents of another. The original purpose of the group becomes overshadowed by the struggle to win.

Destructive controversies are characterized by an orientation on the part of the people involved to "win" at the expense of other group members, whose ideas are defeated and they, therefore, "lose." In a win-lose situation, every action of other group members is seen in terms of one person dominating the others. The outcomes from a win-lose situation are predictable. People tend to deny the legitimacy of the other group members' interests and consider only their own needs. They try to force the other members to give in while trying to augment their own power and undermine that of the others. The loser in a win-lose situation has little motivation to carry out the actions agreed upon, resents the winner, and has no chance to contribute his resources to the problem-solving process. The winner finds it hard to enforce the implementation of her ideas. Cohesion or togetherness will decrease, and the group will have severe maintenance problems. Distrust will be rampant, communication will be limited and inaccurate, and group members will be hostile toward one another.

If any group is to function effectively, cooperation among members must be maintained at a high level. Without strong cooperation among the members, there is no coordination of behavior, no communication, no prolonged interaction. Cooperation is the most important and basic form of human interaction and, by far, the most important aspect of effective groups. The competitive, win-lose way of dealing with controversy sabotages all aspects of group effectiveness by undercutting the cooperation needed among group members. The cooperative way of dealing with them, however, helps all aspects of group effectiveness. When controversy is approached from a problem-solving point of view, members tend to recognize the legitimacy of one another's interests, and search for a solution accommodating the needs of all. They try to influence one another through persuasion, working to build up *mutual* power, not personal power.

Group members should always be concerned with finding a mutually satisfying course of action. This orientation is constructive because it (1) increases every member's motivation to implement the decisions of the group (through the principle of participation), (2) strengthens the chances of finding a high-quality solution, (3) develops critical thinking skills, (4) lessens hostility while increasing amiability among group members, (5) requires no enforcement to implement group decisions, (6) cuts out the need for power to be exercised, (7) extends trust and promotes full and accurate communication, (8) aids group cohesion, and (9) results in everyone treating everyone else with respect. Nothing is more essential to a group than making sure that differences of opinions, ideas, values, beliefs, goals, and so on are all approached from a cooperative, problem-solving orientation, not a competitive win-lose orientation.

Check your understanding of the above section by answering the following questions (answers on page 169):

(True) False 1. In a win-lose situation, every action of the other group members is seen in terms of one person dominating the others.

True (False) 2. In a win-lose situation, the loser has high motivation to carry out the group decision.

(True) False 3. Cooperation is the most important aspect of effective groups.

4. When controversy is approached in a problem-solving way (choose three):

    a. Group decisions must be enforced.

    (b.) Members try to persuade each other.

    c. Power needs to be used.

    (d.) The group tries to build up mutual power.

    (e.) Hostility is decreased and liking is increased.

    f. Trust and communication are decreased.

VALUES AND BELIEFS

The constructive management of controversy within a group requires that members generally share a common set of values and beliefs about controversy. As mentioned earlier, most people in our society have a negative conception of controversy. They regard conflicts as something undesirable and as a sign of sickness in group functioning. Groups that fight together, however, not only stay together, but function creatively and productively. Thus, group members must have a positive value system about fighting as being a productive way of handling conflicts. Verbal controversies are highly constructive and are highly desirable. When group members fight according to a proper set of rules and norms, they are able to improve their relationship to the group while enhancing group productivity and creativity. The positive values of fighting are these:

1. Controversies are a natural and desirable part of any problem-solving situation and they should *not* be avoided or repressed. Controversies are inevitable if members are involved in the group's work and committed to high-quality task accomplishment and maintenance. If differences of opinion, interests, and values are not dealt with directly, group task accomplishment and maintenance will deteriorate. Controversial discussions are a cooperative skill that requires at least two people and, when handled successfully, group members will be increasingly involved and committed to one another. Group discussion with a high rate of controversy is more productive than individual thinking. Since the goal is for the group (not the individual) to come up with creative, productive ideas, controversy is highly desirable as a means for doing so. Working through differences of opinion may lead to a more creative solution to problems than

could be achieved by any single person. All group members profit from effective controversies, both in terms of group goal accomplishment and in bettering the relationships among group members.

2. Controversies can greatly reduce the natural tension and frustration of working together. Group members can interact together with fewer inhibitions and avoidances. Fighting can provide a system for programming individual aggression. Almost everyone has aggressive feelings about other group members at one time or another, and fighting allows a person to express this aggression directly and constructively. Expressing hostile feelings is a good way to keep from withdrawing and to become emotionally involved in group work and in one's relationships with group members. Controversies allow for the expression of emotions such as anger and indignation that would interfere with group work if repressed. Feelings that are unresolved and are not dealt with make for biased, nonobjective judgments and actions. It is quite common for a person to refuse to accept a good idea because he dislikes the person who suggests it. Feelings that are unresolved affect a person's perception of events and information; threatening and unpleasant facts are often denied, ignored, or distorted, and blind spots appear that end in misinterpretation of others' ideas and actions. Finally, suppression of feelings can lead to personal barriers, irreversible conflicts, and a deterioration of relationships.

3. Controversies keep arguments up to date and help group members avoid being bothered by the past, which they cannot change. Group members who fight regularly and constructively need not carry gunnysacks full of grievances. All past conflicts have been dealt with so that they do not constrain working together and appreciating one another in the present.

4. Controversies bring information to group members about where they are, what is important to each of them, how group work can be bettered, and how their relationships can be improved. Opposition leads to greater understanding and closer relationships, not rejection and dislike.

These eight questions will help you check your understanding of the preceding section (answers on page 169).

True False | 1. Controversies are a natural and desirable part of any problem situation and should not be repressed.

True False | 2. Working through differences of opinion may lead to a more creative solution.

True False | 3. Controversies can better the relationships between group members.

True False | 4. The natural tension and frustration of working together can be greatly reduced through controversy.

True False | 5. Telling about hostile feelings is a way of withdrawing from the group.

True False | 6. Unresolved feelings affect a person's perceptions of what is going on in the group.

True False | 7. Controversy keeps the past from interfering with the present.

True False | 8. Controversy keeps group members informed on what can be improved in the group.

NORMS AND RULES

Constructive controversies require that a group agree upon norms and rules for arguing. There are no rigid cookbook rules for productive controversy behavior, but the following guidelines can help group members dispute more constructively and transform disagreement into a positive group force:

1. The right time for the controversy must be chosen. To begin a dispute five minutes before the group must end a meeting, or to bring up an issue when other members with opposing ideas are absent is bad timing. Setting a time for a controversy may involve announcing the intention to argue, stating the issues, and making sure that any emotions expressed are not misinterpreted. The full disclosure of both sides of an argument at the same time is the result of good timing.

2. There should be no winner and no loser, only a successful, creative, and productive solution to a problem.

3. Every member (within the limitations of time and other restricting factors) should take part actively in group discussions. Members should follow up their ideas, spin creative fantasies about the issues under discussion, insist on exploring the implications of their ideas, collect data to support their contentions, plan arguments to show the soundness of their ideas. A person's ideas and feelings should be expressed openly and honestly. Every person should share his position and ideas in order to get comments and reactions from other group members that will help improve the quality of group work. Every member should be free to express his ideas and feelings without defensiveness. Open, honest, accurate, complete, and effective communication should be worked upon continually. Intuition, hunches, and feelings about appropriate group action should be brought out into the open as topics for discussion.

4. The response to one another's ideas and feelings should be such that everyone's contribution is valued, respected, and taken seriously. An enthusiastic hearing should be granted to all ideas, and a warm, intense interest in all contributions should be adopted.

5. Members must be critical of ideas, not of people—and critical without intending to hurt the person who thought of the idea. Arguments should concern ideas, not personalities; there should be nothing personal in disagreement. When disagreement does occur over a member's ideas and contributions, she should treat it as an interesting point of view from which something can be learned, not as a personal attack. Members should express their disagreement without expressing rejection of the other person.

6. Appropriate pacing of the differentiation (bringing out differences of ideas) and integration (putting the different ideas together) phases of the group problem-solving process must be maintained. All different points of view must be presented and explored and then new, creative solutions sought. It is a big mistake to look for ways in which to integrate various ideas before all the

differences have been brought out. The potential for integration is never greater than the adequacy of the differentiation already achieved. Most controversies go through a series of differentiations and integrations.

7. Members who disagree with others must achieve an understanding of both the position and the frame of reference of their opponents. All participants should regularly talk about what they believe the others' position and frame of reference to be, what the others are feeling, and how they are reacting to the controversy.

8. Emotions are to be answered by emotions, not by tolerant but uninvolved understanding.

9. The situational power of all participants should be balanced. Everyone should have equal rights to participate, and contributions should be evaluated on their soundness and helpfulness in sparking thinking, not on the basis of who proposed them. Influence should be determined by ability rather than by status. People who have helpful information and interesting ideas should be listened to, regardless of formal power. Perceptions of inequality in power undermine trust, inhibit dialogue, and decrease the likelihood of a constructive outcome from a controversy. Low-power people do not trust high-power people because those with power tend to use it for their own interests. Low-power people typically inhibit and censor their own contributions; their positive intent is usually underestimated by high-power people.

10. An optimal tension level should be kept throughout the controversy. A person's maximum ability to integrate and to use information occurs at some moderate level of tension. If there is too *little* tension, a sense of urgency in resolving the controversy is lacking. If there is too *much* tension, too much distortion and defensiveness develop to block resolution of controversy. A period of substantial stress followed by an easing of tension is often the best way to achieve a productive resolution of controversies.

11. Incentives for resolving the controversies creatively must be present for all group members to be motivated toward participating and contributing.

Pick out the guidelines for constructive controversy (answers on page 169):

_____ ✓ 1. There is no winner or loser.

_____ ✓ 2. People who disagree should understand the position and frame of reference of the other.

_____ 3. Putting ideas together should start as soon as differences appear.

_____ ✓ 4. Everyone's contributions are valued.

_____ 5. Be critical of people, not of ideas.

_____ ✓ 6. Choose the right time for controversy.

_____ 7. A minimum tension level should be kept up.

_____ ✓ 8. Power should be balanced among members.

_____ 9. Emotions are answered by tolerant understanding.

_____ ✓ 10. Every member should take part in group discussions.

_____ 11. The people who disagree should be left alone to work it out.

AVOIDING CONTROVERSIES EXERCISE

People often find ingenious methods to keep from having to deal directly with controversies. How do you behave when you want to avoid a dispute? How do the other members of your group behave?

The following exercise is designed to get feedback about how other group members see your behavior when you want to avoid a controversy. Its objective is to have people examine their own behavior in relation to controversy and disagreement. Understanding avoidance behavior, or how people avoid responding, can be as helpful as increasing their awareness of constructive behaviors. The coordinator's procedure for the exercise is as follows:

1. Introduce the exercise as a chance for each group member to get feedback from other group members on his behavior.
2. Tell each group member to place a sheet of newsprint on the wall with his name clearly written at the top.
3. Have group members walk around the room writing down their impressions on the newsprint of how each of the others behaves when he wants to avoid a controversy. You may wish to use the checklist below to start ideas.
4. Each member should classify himself according to the checklist below, and then read the remarks other group members have written on his sheet.
5. Divide the participants into groups of three and have them discuss the content of the remarks written on their sheets, their own perceptions of their behavior, and the feelings generated by the exercise. Note that while all the defenses against directly facing controversy are not helpful to the group and will promote destructive outcomes, they are at times very helpful and of constructive value to the individual. Participants should ask themselves whether there are ways to protect themselves without being harmful to the group.

Defenses Against Controversy

1. Ostrich: deny the controversy exists; refuse to see the potential or actual disagreement.
2. Turtle: withdraw to avoid the issue and the people disagreeing with you.
3. Lemming: give in and accept the other person's point of view or ideas.
4. Weasel: rationalize by stating the issue is not important, you really don't hold an opposing opinion, the issue is one on which you have no expertise, and so on.
5. Gorilla: overpower the other members by forcing them to accept your ideas and point of view.
6. Owl: intellectualize about the issue and ideas so that all feelings and emotions are hidden.
7. Sheep: formulate, support, and conform to group norms forbidding oppostion and disagreement to be expressed in the group.

CONSTRUCTIVE AND DESTRUCTIVE CONTROVERSY

Controversies may be classified as constructive or destructive on the basis of (1) the processes by which they are managed and (2) their outcomes. Figures 6.1 and 6.2 summarize the differences between constructive and destructive controversies.

FIGURE 6.1 Processes

Constructive	Destructive
Defining the controversy as a mutual problem.	Defining the controversy as a "win-lose" situation.
Participation by all group members.	Participation by only a few group members; self-censorship and withdrawal.
Open and honest expression of ideas and feelings.	Closed or deceitful expression of ideas and feelings.
Everyone's contributions listened to, given attention, taken seriously, valued, and respected.	The contributions of many members ignored, devalued, not respected, and treated lightly.
Quiet members encouraged to participate.	Quiet members not encouraged to participate.
Effective sending and receiving communication skills used.	Effective sending and receiving communication skills not used.
Differences in opinions and ideas sought out and clarified.	Differences in opinions and ideas ignored or suppressed.
Underlying assumptions and frames of reference brought out into the open and discussed.	Underlying assumptions and frames of reference not brought out into the open and discussed.
Disagreement not taken as personal rejection by some or all group members.	Disagreement taken as personal rejection by some or all group members.
Adequate differentiation of positions; differences clearly understood.	Inadequate differentiation of positions; differences not clearly understood.
Adequate integration of positions; similarities clearly understood and positions combined in creative syntheses.	Inadequate integration of positions; similiarities not clearly understood and positions not combined in creative syntheses.
Emotions responded to with involvement and other emotions.	Emotions responded to by uninvolved understanding or ignored.
Equal situational power among all members.	Unequal power among group members.
Moderate level of tensions.	Tension level too low or too high for productive problem solving. *(cont.)*

Constructive	Destructive
Incentives present for creative resolution.	Incentives present for domination and "winning."
A mutually satisfying solution worked for and arrived at.	Conflict-reducing procedures—tossing a coin, voting, negotiation—used.

FIGURE 6.2 Outcomes

Constructive	Destructive
Decisions correct and of high quality.	Decisions incorrect and of low quality.
High creativity of decision.	Low creativity of decision.
Members feel understood and listened to.	Members feel misunderstood or ignored.
Members believe they exercised considerable influence on other members.	Members believe they had little or no influence on other members.
Members feel responsible and committed to group decision.	Some or all members feel no responsibility for, or commitment to, the decision.
Members highly satisfied with the decision, their participation, and the process of group work.	Members highly dissatisfied with the decision, their participation, and the process of group work.
Cohesion and member liking for one another is high.	Cohesion and member liking for one another is low.
Members feel accepted and liked by other group members.	Members feel rejected and disliked by other group members.
High level of trust among members.	Low level of trust among members.
Feelings released and dissipated; tension decreased; positive feelings dominant.	Feelings repressed, suppressed, and still present; tension increased; negative feelings dominant.
Ability to manage controversy increased.	Ability to manage controversy decreased.
High level of learning about the issue under discussion.	Low level of learning about the issue under discussion.

CREATIVITY

Creativity is a process of bringing something new into existence: Group creativity results from productive controversy during the problem-solving process. The creative process consists of a sequence of overlapping phases, such as the following:

1. Recognizing and experiencing a problem challenging enough to motivate group members to solve it.
2. Gathering the necessary knowledge and resources within the group, and planning an intense, long-term effort to solve the problem.

3. Experiencing an incubation period wherein (a) group members feel frustration, tension, and discomfort due to the failure of the group to produce an adequate solution to the problem, and (b) group members temporarily withdraw from the issue.

4. Seeing—due to productive controversy—the problem from different perspectives and reformulating it in a way that lets new orientations to a solution emerge. This phase results in a moment of insight or inspiration by one or more group members that is often accompanied by intense emotional experiences of illumination and excitement, and that leads to the formulation of a tentative solution.

5. Elaborating, detailing, and testing the solution against reality.

6. Giving the validated solution to relevant audiences.

There are three key elements in a goal-oriented, problem-solving group that bring creative approaches to goal accomplishment (Deutsch, 1969): (1) arousing an appropriate level of motivation among group members, (2) developing the conditions that allow the problem to be reformulated once an impasse has been reached, and (3) having available at the same time diverse ideas that can be flexibly put together into new and varied patterns. The best level of motivation is a level sufficient to sustain problem-solving efforts despite frustrations and dead ends, and yet not so intense that it overwhelms the group or that it keeps them too close to the problem. Group discussion must be such that members do not feel threatened and do not feel under too much pressure (Stein, 1968; Rokeach, 1960; Deutsch, 1969). Threats and excessive tension lead to closed rather than open minds. Threats bring about defensiveness and reduce both tolerance toward ambiguity and receptiveness to the new and unfamiliar. Too much tension leads to stereotyping of thought processes. Each group member needs the freedom, support, and self-confidence to express herself without being afraid of censure if she is to entertain novel ideas that may at first seem wild and implausible, and if she is to question initial assumptions or the framework within which the problem occurs. Each group member also needs to become sufficiently detached from her original viewpoint to be able to see the problem from new perspectives.

The ability to reformulate a problem and to develop creative solutions depends upon how productive the controversy is among group members and how diverse the viewpoints and knowledge are in the group. Ideas are essential for the creative solution of problems, and controversy is a useful catalyst to broaden the range of ideas and alternatives available to the people involved in solving a problem. How available the ideas are that bring about new orientations to the problem depends on such factors as the chance to communicate with and be exposed to other people with relevant and unfamiliar ideas, a social atmosphere in which innovation and originality are valued, a productive controversy in which the exchange of ideas is encouraged, and a group tradition supporting the view that, with time and effort, constructive solutions can be discovered or invented for seemingly insoluble problems.

Here again you may check your understanding of the preceding section (answers on page 169):

1. The three key elements in a group that bring creative approaches to accomplishing a goal are:
    a. A member who is an expert on creativity.
    b. Appropriately motivated group members.
    c. Conditions that allow the problem to be reformulated.
    d. Conditions that place the group under pressure until the problem is solved.
    e. Unthreatened group members.
    f. Diverse ideas available to put into new patterns.
    g. Similar ideas available to put into new patterns.
2. Closed rather than open minds are brought about by:
    a. Threat and too much tension.
    b. Confusion about the new and unfamiliar.
    c. The lack of creative alternatives.
    d. Brain surgery.

BRAINSTORMING

Within the problem-solving process there are times when divergent thinking is necessary, when it is incumbent upon members to produce many different and diverse ideas. There are other times, of course, when convergent thinking is necessary, when the group needs to agree about its course of action. Brainstorming is a procedure that encourages divergent thinking and the production of many different ideas in a short period of time. It is a method of generating ideas in quantity with the intention of getting the full participation of all group members. In essence, it represents a period of time in which all evaluation is suspended and ideas are allowed to develop freely on a particular issue. It is a time for free association of ideas and for opening new avenues of thought. Some of the reasons why brainstorming helps problem-solving groups become more creative are:

1. It increases member involvement and participation by members.
2. It provides a means of getting the most ideas in a relatively short period of time.
3. It reduces the need to look for the "right" idea in order to impress authority figures in the group.
4. It makes the session more fun, interesting, and stimulating.
5. It reduces the possibility of negative subgrouping, competition, or one-upmanship during the problem-solving process.

To assure that the brainstorming session will be a success, group members should be familiar with a number of ground rules. These ground rules are:

1. At this point all criticism or evaluation of an idea is ruled out. Ideas are suggested and placed before the group without evaluation or critical analysis.
2. Wild ideas are expected in the spontaneity that evolves when the group suspends judgment. Practical considerations are not important at this point. The session is to be freewheeling.

3. The quantity of ideas counts, not quality. All ideas should be expressed, and not screened out by any individual. A great number of ideas will increase the likelihood of discovering good ones.

4. Build on the ideas of other group members when possible. Pool your creativity. Everyone should be free to build onto ideas and to make interesting combinations from the various suggestions.

5. Focus on a *single* problem or issue. Don't skip around on problems or try to brainstorm a complex, multiple problem.

6. Promote a congenial, relaxed, cooperative atmosphere.

7. Make sure that all members, no matter how shy and reluctant to contribute, get their ideas heard.

8. Record *all* ideas.

After the period of brainstorming is over, all the ideas should be categorized and the group should critically evaluate them for possible use or application. The best critical judgment of the group members should be applied in evaluating the ideas, though members should seek for clues to something sound in even the wildest idea. Priorities should be selected and the best ideas applied.

For new groups unfamiliar with brainstorming, a warm-up session in which the rationale and rules are explained might be helpful. If groups are being formed for brainstorming, it is important that some diversity of opinion and background be present in each group.

Brainstorming is useful because many of the reasons that ideas are never born—or, once born, are quickly stifled—have nothing to do with their value. Domineering members, stereotypes of each other's expertise and intelligence, interpersonal conflicts, habitual patterns of uninvolvement and silence, fear of ridicule or evaluation can all smother the majority of members within a group. An example is a vice-president in charge of a group of managers saying: "Those opposed will signify by clearing out their desks, putting on their hats, and saying, 'I resign.' "

It is a common saying among social psychologists that there is no such thing as a creative person, only creative groups. The thinking of all of us is highly influenced by the thinking of the people with whom we talk and interact. It is almost always possible to be part of a group process that encourages, supports, and rewards our potential for creativity. The ideas of others spark our own. The theory of one group member may help build a much more creative theory by touching off all sorts of new ideas among the rest of the group members. When controversy is encouraged and diversity sought and used, a group can engage in untold amounts of creative problem solving.

BRAINSTORMING EXERCISE

The objectives of this exercise are to come up with a large number of ideas or solutions to a problem by temporarily suspending criticism and evaluation and to experience the process of brainstorming. The procedure for the exercise is:

1. The ground rules for brainstorming are reviewed by the group.
2. The group is presented with a problem: one of the authors of this book has been cast ashore nude on a desert island with nothing but a glass peace symbol on a leather thong.
3. The group is given fifteen minutes to generate ideas as to what can be done with this object.
4. The group is given another fifteen minutes to select critically their best ideas.
5. The group is asked to process how well they applied the rules of brainstorming and what the results were in their group. Was creativity enhanced? Did it help the group to discover interesting ways of using the object?

After initial exposure to brainstorming, a group should pick a specific problem it is working on and apply brainstorming to it to see if new, creative perspectives can be gained. If, however, a second practice session is desired, the following story affords another opportunity for a brainstorming experience:

A small wholesaler in the hinterland of New Mexico had called his buyer in Santa Fe and asked him to obtain a large order of pipe cleaners from Mexico. The buyer agreed. He also agreed to advance the wholesaler the money to finance the deal. A month later, just as the shipment of pipe cleaners was arriving, the buyer received a disastrous phone call from the wholesaler. His warehouse and outlet store had burned down and there simply was no more business. The buyer was suddenly faced with the prospect of trying to sell 20,000 pipe cleaners.

In one minute generate as many ideas as possible (with a recorder counting the number of different ideas) for selling pipe cleaners. (A relatively spontaneous group will create approximately twenty-five ideas in a little more than a minute; if the group creates fifteen ideas or less it should be given more training in brainstorming.)

In brainstorming a group problem, it is important that the problem be well defined and specific in nature. It must also be a problem that the group has the power to do something about. If possible the group members should be notified in advance about the issue to be explored so they will have given some thought to it.

METHODS OF GENERATING NEW IDEAS

Besides brainstorming, there are several other methods of generating new ideas (David and Houtman, 1968): part changing, checkerboard, checklist, and something similar. The *part-changing method* involves group members in identifying the parts or attributes of something that might be changed. The following is an example:

Four qualities of a chair are color, shape, size, and hardness. Invent some new kind of chair by listing fifteen different colors, ten different shapes, five sizes, and five grades of hardness. Try to think of different ideas, and do not worry about whether or not they are any good. To apply the part-changing method, group members list the main parts and then think of different ways to change each part. Recognizing that wild ideas may help others to think of good ideas, they should use their imagination. Thinking of perfect or ideal solutions can lead to good ideas.

The *checkerboard method* involves making a checkerboard figure with spaces for entering words or phrases on the vertical and horizontal axes. Different sets of properties or attributes are listed on the axes. Then the group members examine the interaction or combination of each set of two things or attributes. An example is:

Your group needs to make up a new sport or game. Place materials and equipment along the top, horizontal axis and place the things the players do (such as running, batting, kicking, hanging from their knees) down the side or vertical axis. Then examine the combination of each item on each axis with all the other items on the other axis.

The *checklist method* involves developing and using checklists to make sure that something is not left out or forgotten. David and Houtman suggest a checklist including:

1. Change color.
2. Change size.
3. Change shape.
4. Use new or different material.
5. Add or subtract something.
6. Rearrange things.
7. Identify a new design.

A group member can apply this checklist to any object or problem.

The *find-something-similar method* involves encouraging the group members to come up with new ideas by thinking of other people or animals or social units in the world that perform the same acts the group wants to perform. An example is:

Imagine your city has a parking problem. Find ideas for solving this problem by thinking of how bees, squirrels, ants, shoe stores, clothing stores, and so on store things.

Divide into a group of six to eight members. Each member should contribute a problem he would like the group to work on. Try out each of the above methods at least twice in discussing the problems generated by the group members.

CREATIVITY PROBLEM

The next problem requires creativity on the part of the group that is attempting to solve it. Divide into groups of three. The group's assignment is to connect all nine dots with only four straight and connected lines (answer in Appendix D).

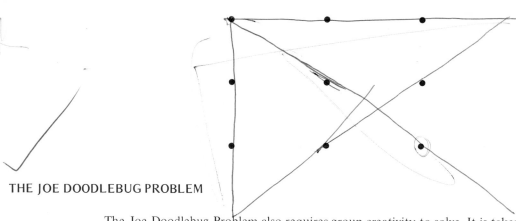

THE JOE DOODLEBUG PROBLEM

The Joe Doodlebug Problem also requires group creativity to solve. It is taken from Rokeach (1960). Divide into groups of three. The procedure is as follows:

1. Hand out the problem and state that all the information needed is on the sheet. The problem is *why* Joe *has* to take *four* jumps to reach the food, which is only three feet away. The groups are given thirty minutes to come up with an explanation. Explain that hints will be given after fifteen, twenty, and twenty-five minutes if the groups have not solved the problem.

   The Problem: Joe Doodlebug has been jumping all over the place getting some exercise when his master places a pile of food three feet directly west of him. Joe notices that the pile of food is a little larger than he. As soon as Joe sees all this food he stops dead in his tracks facing north. After all his exercise Joe is hungry and he wants to get the food as quickly as possible. Joe examines the situation and then says, "I'll have to jump four times to get the food." Why does Joe have to take four jumps to get the food?

   The conditions on Joe are as follows: Joe Doodlebug, a strange sort of imaginary bug, can and cannot do the following things: (1) he can jump only in four different directions: north, south, east, and west (he cannot jump diagonally, such as southwest); (2) once he starts in any direction he *must* jump four times in that direction before he can change direction; (3) he can only jump, not crawl, fly, or walk; (4) he cannot jump less than one inch per jump or more than ten feet per jump; (5) Joe cannot turn around.

2. After fifteen minutes give the first hint, after twenty minutes the second, and after twenty-five minutes the third.

   a. Joe does not have to always face the food in order to eat it.

   b. Joe can jump sideways and backward, as well as forward.

   c. Read the problem again. Joe was moving east when the food was presented.

3. At the end of thirty minutes, stop the groups and give them the answer (Appendix D). After clarifications of the answer are given, conduct a discussion of moving outside one's belief system to solve a problem. Then ask the group to discuss how they worked together, listened to each other, handled controversies, and so on.

For controversy to result in creativity, group members must be open minded about different beliefs, opinion, information, ideas, and assumptions. Members must seek out different perspectives, different ways of looking at the problem, different frames of reference in analyzing it. The extent to which a group member can receive, evaluate, and act on relevant information on its *own* merits (as opposed to viewing it only from one's own beliefs, assumptions, and frame of reference) defines the extent to which the person is open minded (as opposed to being closed minded). The Joe Doodlebug problem relates to open mindedness in that group members must give up a series of beliefs about the situation and replace them with a set of new beliefs. They must then synthesize the new beliefs to solve the problem.

In solving the Joe Doodlebug Problem group members must first overcome three beliefs, one by one, and replace them with three new beliefs. The first is the *facing belief*. In everyday life we have to face the food we are to eat. But Joe does not have to face the food in order to eat it—he can land on top of it. The second is the *direction belief*. In everday life we can change direction at will. But Joe is not able to do so because he is forever trapped facing north. The only way Joe can change direction is by jumping sideways and backward. The third is the *movement belief*. When we wish to change direction in everyday life there is nothing to stop us from doing so immediately. But Joe's freedom of movement is restricted by the fact that once he moves in a particular direction (north, south, east, or west) he has to continue four times in that direction before he can change it. Many group members have difficulty because they assume that Joe is at the end rather than possibly in the middle of a jumping sequence.

The replacement of old beliefs with new beliefs is called the *analytic phase* of the problem-solving process. Once new beliefs have superseded the old ones, group members must then organize the new beliefs in a way that leads them to the solution; this organizational step is called the *synthesizing phase* of the problem-solving process. The two processes are pictured in Figure 6.3. In creative problem solving, controversies and open mindedness help a group to obtain different

FIGURE 6.3   The Two-Phase Problem-Solving Process

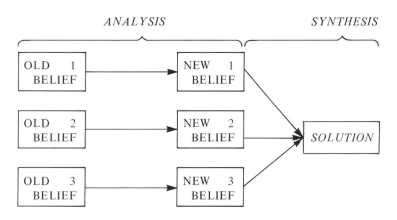

perspectives and develop appropriate beliefs that can be synthesized to help solve the problem. Controversy, replacing old beliefs with new beliefs, and synthesizing new beliefs are all essential.

How open or closed minded would each group who participated in Joe Doodlebug Exercise describe itself as being? Closed-minded groups will be characterized by (1) emphasizing the differences between what they believe and what they do not believe; (2) denying information that is contrary to what they believe; (3) having contradictory beliefs that go unquestioned; (4) discarding as irrelevant similarities between what they believe and what they reject; and (5) avoiding the exploration of differences in beliefs and distorting information that does not fit their beliefs. Open-minded groups will be characterized by (1) seeking out opposing and differing beliefs; (2) discovering new beliefs; (3) remembering information that disagrees with currently held beliefs; and (4) organizing new beliefs so that they lead to the solution of the problem. Open mindedness is an important aspect of controversy, creativity, and problem solving.

BASEBALL TEAM EXERCISE

Another test of a group's ability to utilize controversy to produce creativity is the Baseball Team Exercise developed by Al Johnson at Iowa State University. Here the problem is to determine from given information who plays what position. The procedure is to divide participants into groups of three and see how long it takes each group to solve the problem. Groups should then review the ways in which they utilized controversy to reach their solution (answer in Appendix D). The information is as follows:

a. Andy dislikes the catcher.
b. Ed's sister is engaged to the second baseman.
c. The center fielder is taller than the right fielder.
d. Harry and the third baseman live in the same building.
e. Paul and Allen each won $20 from the pitcher at pinochle.
f. Ed and the outfielders play poker during their free time.
g. The pitcher's wife is the third baseman's sister.
h. All the battery and the infield, except Allen, Harry, and Andy, are shorter than Sam.
i. Paul, Andy, and the shortstop lost $150 each at the racetrack.
j. Paul, Harry, Bill, and the catcher took a trouncing from the second baseman at pool.
k. Sam is undergoing a divorce suit.
l. The catcher and the third baseman each have two children.
m. Ed, Paul, Jerry, the right fielder, and the center fielder are bachelors; the others are married.
n. The shortstop, the third baseman, and Bill each cleaned up $100 betting on the fights.

166

o. One of the outfielders is either Mike or Andy.

p. Jerry is taller than Bill, Mike is shorter than Bill. Each of them is heavier than the third baseman.

CREATIVITY WARM-UPS

Have you ever felt in a rut? Have you ever felt embarrassed about sharing new or wild ideas? Have you ever ignored your thinking because you felt it was too far out? Do you ever enjoy letting your imagination and thoughts run wild? Have you ever been so critical of your own thoughts that you could not get started?

Here are six short, fun exercises to loosen up group thinking and warm up group creativity.

1. The group sits in a circle (limit group size to eight members or so). The person nearest the window says the first thing that comes to his mind. The statement should be short, not over a sentence or two. Without pause the person to his left says what comes to his mind; his statement must be relevant to something the first person has said. The relevance may be of any kind, an association, a contrast, an alternative, a continuation, and so on. The process continues at high speed until at least three rounds have been completed. The process is critiqued by discussing the feelings group members had during the exercise.

2. The group sits in a circle and identifies a problem or issue. The person nearest the door states his solution. Each subsequent group member (to his left) states his, using as many ideas of previous speakers' as he can. This process is continued until a plan generally acceptable to all the group members is arrived at. When a member cannot add anything new, he passes. Finally, members' reactions to and feelings about the experience are discussed.

3. The group sits in a circle and a group problem or issue is identified. The first person states his solution to the problem. The next person immediately states what his opposition to the first person's solution is. The third person immediately states his opposition to the second person's opposition. This process is continued until everyone in the group has spoken at least three times. Emphasis is upon generating creative ideas in arguments. Members' reactions to and feelings about the experience are discussed.

4. The group lies on the floor with members' heads toward the center of the room. The first person begins with a fantasy about what the group could be like. After no more than two or three minutes the fantasy is passed on to the next group member who continues it, adding his own associations and fantasies. This process continues until everyone has spoken at least three times. Members' reactions to and feelings about the exercise are examined.

5. The group has before it a number of assorted materials, such as clay, water paints, Tinker Toys, magazines, newspaper, and so on. It then creates something out of the materials—a mural, a collage, a design. If more than one group participates, they end the exercise by discussing one another's creations.

6. The group acts out a walk through the woods. Each group member takes the leadership role and directs the walk, indicating what he is experiencing and seeing. All members should direct the walk for a while. What the members learn about one another, the group, and walking through the woods should be discussed.

YOUR BEHAVIOR IN CONTROVERSIES

How do you behave in controversies? Has your behavior changed as a result of your experiences connected with this chapter? How would you now describe your behavior?

1. When I find myself disagreeing with other members of my group, I:

    ___ stand by my ideas and continue to defend my position, actively trying to get it accepted by the group and incorporated into any decisions made for as long as it takes to do so.

    ___ try to explore the points of agreement and disagreement and the feelings that other group members have about these points and why; I press a search for alternatives that take everyone's views into account.

2. Controversies are:

    ___ valuable to clear the air and enhance involvement and commitment and, when productively handled, result in increased creativity.

    ___ destructive because opposition leads to dislike, and disagreement over ideas means personal rejection of other group members.

3. When I am involved in a controversy, I:

    ___ feel rather fearful and concerned about how other members like me and whether I really like them.

    ___ feel angry at their ignorance and rather annoyed that I have to be around such stupid people.

    ___ am stimulated and feel full of excitement and fun as I think about the issues being discussed.

4. Which of the following is more typical of your behavior?

    ___ When I find myself in disagreement with other group members, I always state my position and feelings so that everything is out in the open.

    ___ When I find myself in disagreement with other group members I keep quiet and "sit the discussion out."

5. When I get involved in a good argument, I:

    ___ find my ideas becoming more and more creative as I incorporate other members' ideas and notions and begin to see the issue from different perspectives.

    ___ become more and more certain that I am correct and argue more and more strongly for my own point of view.

Compare your answers with the answers you gave to the questionnaire at the beginning of the chapter. Have you changed? How would you now describe your behavior in controversy situations? Write a description of your controversy behavior, and share it with two persons who know you well and who have participated in some of the controversy exercises with you. Ask them to add to and modify your self-description.

CHECKLIST OF SKILLS

✓ ___ I can identify when a controversy is taking place.

___ I can identify when a controversy is not taking place.

___ I can identify my defenses against dealing with controversies.

___ I can identify the norms and rules necessary for effective controversy.

___ I can identify the values and beliefs necessary for constructive controversy.

___ I can identify when persons have a "win-lose" orientation toward controversy.

___ I can identify when persons have a "problem solving" orientation toward controversy.

___ I can react to disagreement as an opportunity to explore my beliefs and opinions, not as personal rejection.

___ I can be critical of ideas without being critical of the person who has the ideas.

___ I can choose an appropriate time for a controversy.

___ I actively participate in controversies within my group(s).

___ I can manage a cycle of differentiation and integration in order to arrive at creative syntheses of opposing opinions and ideas.

___ I can help persons in a controversy understand one another.

___ I can behave in ways that facilitate the constructive processes and outcomes of controversy and reduce the likelihood of destructive processes and outcomes.

___ I can lead brainstorming sessions successfully.

The skills I need more work on are:

_____

_____

_____

_____

_____

ANSWERS

Page 141: 1: b; 2: d; 3: a.

Page 142: 1: c.

Page 150: 2: a, c; 3: b, e; 4: a, d; 5: d.

Page 152: 1: true; 2: false; 3: true; 4: b, d, e.

Page 153: 1: true; 2: true; 3: true; 4: true; 5: false; 6: true; 7: true; 8: true.

Page 155: Guidelines are: 1, 2, 4, 6, 8, 10.

Page 160: 1: b, c, f; 2: a.

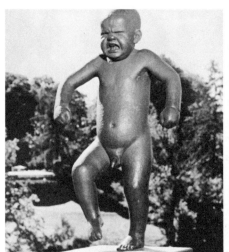

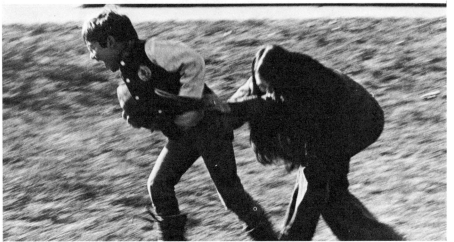

7

Conflicts of Interest

WHAT ARE CONFLICTS OF INTEREST?

Imagine you are part of a group that has just been given $1000 to spend in any way it wishes over the next two weeks. Your group has six members—Jane, Mary, Joe, John, Edythe, and yourself. Jane and Mary want to donate the money to the women's libration movement. Edythe, John, and Joe want to give a series of parties for all their friends. You want the group to use the money for a college scholarship for your younger brother. Your group is in conflict, and it is not just a controversy in which you have opposing opinions. There is a scare resource (i.e., money) that the group must decide to allocate among the competing needs of the group's members. Since different members have vested interests in spending the money in different ways, your group has a conflict of interest.

What is a conflict of interest and how do you tell one when you see it? *Conflicts of interest* are incompatible activities desired by group members based upon (1) differences in needs, values, and goals, (2) scarcities of certain resources such as power, influence, money, time, space, and position, or (3) competition or rivalry among group members. Incompatible activities are activities that prevent, block, or interfere with each other or in some way make the others less likely or less effective. If, for example, the group decides to spend its money on parties, the activity of donating the money to the women's liberation movement is prevented. Conflicts of interest are inevitable and of potential value to a group. They are also harder to manage than controversies, because they must be settled by negotiation.

All the potential values of conflict discussed in the introduction of Chapter 6 are applicable to conflicts of interest. Though not helpful in producing a creative, high-quality decision, a conflict of interest, if managed properly, can help ensure that all members are committed to implementing the group's decisions and that the group's problem-solving ability does not deteriorate during the decision-making process. In this chapter we shall focus upon the use of negotiation to resolve conflicts of interest among group members and among groups.

You may check your understanding of this section by answering the following question (answer on page 201):

What are conflicts of interest?

a. conflicts in which everyone is interested in participating.

b. conflicts that come from scarcity, rivalry, or differences in needs, values, or goals.

c. conflicts that indicate differences of opinions or ideas.

d. conflicts caused by misunderstanding and mistakes.

INTERPERSONAL CONFLICT SKILLS

Johnson, in his book *Reaching Out* (1972), has devised a program to help persons improve their skills in constructively handling interpersonal conflicts. The book gives a combination of theory and structured exercises to help in skill development, and the chapters on conflict, confrontation, and problem definition provide a foundation for the material covered in this chapter. *Reaching Out* focuses on increasing your awareness of your past and present styles of conflict management, confronting others constructively, defining a conflict constructively, getting an accurate perception of the other's position and feelings, making sure there is correct and effective communication in a conflict, developing a climate or atmosphere of trust, and structuring cooperative interdependence in resolving the conflict.

YOUR CONFLICT BEHAVIOR

How do you behave when you have a conflict of interest with other group members? What type of negotiation strategy do you use to try to resolve the conflict? How would you describe your reactions to a conflict of interest? Given below is a series of questions about behavior in conflict situations. Answer them as correctly as possible.

1. When I have a conflict of interest with other group members, I:
   ___ a. focus on the need for mutual cooperation and the areas of similarity between our needs and positions.
   ___ b. focus upon the superiority of my position and whether I win or whether they win.
2. When other group members and I have a conflict of interest, I:
   ___ a. try to increase my power and use it to push for acceptance of my position.
   ___ b. try to equalize power and push for a creative agreement that all members can live with.

172

3. When I am involved in a conflict of interest with other group members, I:

      ___ a. let members know my position is flexible in order to help in creative problem solving.

      ✓ b. let members know that I am committed to my position in order to force the other members to give in and agree.

4. When I have a conflict of interest with other group members, I:

      ___ a. use threats and express hostility to force them to accept my position.

      ___ b. avoid threats in order to reduce the other's defensiveness and express hostility to free myself from angry feelings that might interfere with cooperation in the future.

The four questions above represent a win-lose orientation and a problem-solving orientation to negotiating a settlement of conflicts of interest. Each strategy may be appropriate under certain conditions and they both are discussed at length in this chapter. To find how much your behavior reflects either or both of the strategies, mark a "1" showing the alternative you selected in the above questions.

Question	Win-Lose	Problem-Solving
1.	b. ____	a. 1
2.	a. ____	b. 1
3.	b. 1	a. ____
4.	a. ____	b. 1
Total	1	3

The highest possible score you can get in either strategy is "4." As you participate in the exercises in this chapter, keep in mind your present style of behavior to help you reflect upon how you can become more effective in conflict situations.

GROUP MEMBER EXCELLENCE EXERCISE

The objective of this exercise is to look at the dynamics of interpersonal negotiation in a group. The exercise can be conducted in less than one hour. The procedure for the coordinator is as follows:

1. Introduce the exercise as a chance to study the dynamics of negotiation among members of the same group. Divide into groups of fourteen: twelve participants and two observers. You need at least two groups. Distribute one copy of the Instruction Sheet to all members and observers, and one copy of the Observer Instructions to the observers. Without the groups knowing they are getting different instructions, give half of them copies of the Win-Lose Negotiation Instructions and the other half copies of the Problem-solving Negotiation

Instructions. (All these instruction sheets are on pages 423 to 426 in Appendix E.)

2. Meet with the observers to make sure they understand what they are expected to do.

3. Distribute a bag of marbles to each group member. Answer any questions they have about the exercise. Do *not*, however, tell them anything about the number of marbles or arrangement of colors in the bags or how to collect fifteen marbles of the same color. Collect twenty-five cents from each participant to be awarded to the members who finish the task. Announce they have fifteen minutes to do so. Give the signal to begin.

4. At the end of fifteen minutes, announce that the time is up and negotiations must end. Ask each participant to write two adjectives on her negotiation instruction sheet that describe her feelings during the negotiations. Gather the sheets and record how many participants completed the task and which type of negotiation instructions they had. Then divide the money among the members who completed the task.

5. Have each group meet separately with its observers to discuss the experience. The focus of the discussion should be upon the negotiation strategies used, how members reacted to one another's strategies, and how successful the different strategies were. Then, on a sheet of newsprint, summarize the strategies, their success, how members reacted to them, and any conclusions that can be drawn about their effectiveness.

6. Have the groups share their instructions for negotiation and the strategies members used, and ask them what conclusions they can make about the effectiveness of the different strategies. Announce how many people with win-lose instructions completed the task and how many with problem-solving instructions completed it. The adjectives win-lose participants wrote down should be compared with the adjectives problem-solving participants used. An interesting subject to explore is how often coalitions formed in which two or more members pooled their marbles and negotiated with other members as a

Distribution of Marbles for Twelve Participants

Member	.	Red	.	Blue	.	Green	.	Rainbow
1		4		3		2		1
2		1		4		3		2
3		2		1		4		3
4		3		2		1		4
5		3		3		2		2
6		3		2		3		2
7		2		3		2		3
8		2		2		3		3
9		2		2		2		4
10		2		2		4		2
11		2		4		2		2
12		4		2		2		2

block. Sometimes a member will collect two colors of marbles in order to stay flexible until the last few minutes. Summarize the major points of the discussion.

7. Have the participants read the sections on negotiation and compare their conclusions about the exercise with the material in those sections.

NEGOTIATION EXERCISE

Given below are three situations in which members of the same organization or group have to negotiate a conflict of interest. In each situation the basic procedure for the coordinator of the exercise to follow is the same. The exercise takes less than one hour to complete.

1. Introduce the exercise as one in which the dynamics of negotiation among members of a group become apparent. Divide into group of three (two participants and one observer) for Case Studies 1 and 2 and of four (three participants and one observer) for Case Study 3. You need at least two groups. Distribute the relevant background sheets and role-playing sheets to the participants and observers (see pp. 425 to 428 in Appendix E). Give each observer one copy of the Observer Instructions used in the previous exercise. Without the groups knowing they are getting different instructions, give half of them copies of the Bargaining Instructions and the other half copies of the Role Reversal Instructions. These instructions are on pp. 429 and 431, Appendix E.

2. Meet with the observers to make sure they understand what they are expected to do.

3. Give the signal to begin. Groups have up to twenty-five minutes to negotiate an agreement. If they finish before their time is up, note how long it took them to negotiate an agreement and what type of negotiation instructions they had.

4. At the end of twenty-five minutes, announce that the time is up and negotiations must end. Ask each participant to write on a sheet of paper two adjectives describing his feelings during the negotiations and hand it to you. Record how many groups negotiated an agreement and which type of instructions (Bargaining or Role Reversal) they had.

5. Ask each group to discuss their experience with their observer. The main topics of the discussion should be the negotiation strategies used, how members reacted to one another's strategies, and how successful the different strategies were. Then, on a sheet of newsprint have each group summarize their strategies, how successful they were, how members reacted to them, and any conclusions they can make about their effectiveness.

6. In a general session have each group share its instructions for negotiation, the strategies its members used, and the conclusions made about their effectiveness. You can then reveal how participants with Bargaining Instructions reacted to the negotiations compared with participants with Role Reversal Instructions, how many groups with each type of instructions completed negotiations successfully,

and how long it took them to do so. Summarize the main points of the discussion.

7. Have the participants read the sections on negotiation and compare their conclusions with the material in those sections.

DEFINITION OF NEGOTIATION

Many procedures are available in our society for managing and resolving conflicts among individuals, groups, and organizations. Legal actions, third-party roles (arbitrators, mediators, therapists, ombudsmen), violence, problem solving, bargaining, and negotiation are all examples. Negotiation is one of the most commonly used procedures. *Negotiation* is a process by which people who want to come to an agreement, but disagree about the nature of the agreement, try to work out a settlement. It is aimed at achieving an agreement that determines what each party gives and receives in a transaction between them. Bargaining and negotiation are defined in almost synonymous ways, and for all practical purposes the two terms are interchangeable. The process of the two procedures is assumed to be basically the same, whether it is between individuals, groups, or large social systems. In a negotiation process there are concrete issues, such as competitive bids for the same resources, and emotional issues that involve negative feelings between the parties, such as anger, distrust, scorn, resentment, fear, rejection. The process of negotiation focuses almost entirely on the concrete issues. The emotional issues, however, also need to be dealt with productively if agreement is to be reached. In this chapter two types of negotiations will be discussed: win-lose—based negotiations and problem-solving—based negotiations.

GOALS OF NEGOTIATIONS

The discussion of negotiations in this book focuses on the situation in which two or more members of a group (or two or more groups within the same organization) have a conflict. In this situation the goals of the negotiations are to resolve the conflict in a way that induces cooperation between the members involved, thereby helping the effectiveness of the group. More specifically, there are two basic goals for negotiating a conflict within a goal-oriented group: (1) reaching an agreement and (2) not damaging (but on the contrary, it is hoped, improving) the basic cooperative interdependence among the members.

In trying to resolve a conflict through negotiation, the group members involved must look at both the primary and secondary gains for themselves. The *primary* gain is determined by the nature of the agreement; the more favorable the agreement is to the member's short-term goals, needs, and resources, the greater the primary gain for him. The *secondary* gain is determined by the effectiveness of the group; the more effective the group, the more the member's long-term goals, needs, and resources will be met and used and, therefore, the greater the long-term gain for the member. Consequently, in negotiating a resolution to a conflict, a group member has to be concerned not only with what is more desirable for him in the short-term view, but also with what is most desirable for improving the effectiveness of the group.

There are, of course, negotiation situations in which the people in conflict have no future relationship. Buying a new car is an example where negotiation over price is usually not affected by the need for future cooperation between the buyer and the salesman. Such short-term, one-time interactions are different from conflicts in a goal-oriented goal. They are discussed later in the chapter.

To check your understanding of the preceding section, you may answer the following questions (answers on page 201):

1. Negotiation is a process by which:
   a. People who disagree work out points of disagreement.
   b. People who agree work out a settlement.
   c. People who disagree but want to agree work out a settlement.
   d. Edythe gets Buddy to ask her out to dinner.
2. What are the two basic goals in negotiating a conflict?
   a. Getting your own goals or needs met.
   b. Reaching an agreement.
   c. Keeping the conflict level down.
   d. Keeping the members cooperatively interdependent.
   e. Figuring out whether Edythe or Buddy pays for dinner.
3. In negotiation, what is a primary gain?
   a. A favorable agreement to a person's short-term goals.
   b. A favorable gain to group effectiveness.
   c. A favorable resolution to both parties.
   d. When Edythe pays the bill.
4. In negotiation, what is a secondary gain?
   a. A favorable agreement to a person's short-term goals.
   b. A favorable gain to group effectiveness.
   c. A favorable resolution to both parties.
   d. When Edythe and Buddy pay for their own meals.

THE NEGOTIATION RELATIONSHIP

Within any group conflicts of interest will arise so that members will need to negotiate agreements with each other. Yet not every group discussion involves negotiation; negotiating is just one of many types of activity that take place within a group. So how do you recognize negotiations when you see them? You can tell

whether or not you are negotiating by using the following checklist:

___ Is there another member involved?

___ Are both cooperative (we both wish to reach an agreement) and competitive elements (we both wish to have the agreement as favorable to ourselves as possible) present in the situation?

___ Does getting what you want depend upon the agreement of another member?

___ Are you in the dilemma of wanting to propose an agreement that is highly favorable to yourself but not wanting to risk making the other member so mad that she refuses to negotiate?

___ Are you dependent upon the other member to give you information about what is a reasonable agreement from her point of view?

___ Are there contractual norms on how negotiation should be conducted?

___ Do the negotiations have a beginning, a middle, and an end?

You cannot negotiate by yourself. It takes two to negotiate, whether it is two group members, two groups, two organizations, or two nations. Within any negotiations, furthermore, there are both cooperative and competitive elements. A cooperative element exists when both members believe they will gain more by negotiating than by not negotiating; a competitive element exists when both members have conflicting preferences about or contending interests in the different possible agreements. In any negotiation a range of possible agreements can be made; it is the push for one particular agreement rather than another that signifies the competitive elements in the negotiation relationship.

Because both members must commit themselves to an agreement, each is dependent upon the other for the outcome. All negotiating is aimed at achieving certain outcomes for oneself, but those outcomes are possible only if the other negotiator agrees to them. This situation is called outcome dependence. A fourth characteristic of negotiations is the dilemma that participants face: each wants an agreement as favorable to himself as possible, but for one to attempt to maximize his outcome might result in such an unsatisfactory agreement for the other member that the latter would refuse to settle and would leave the negotiation relationship. For one negotiator not to attempt to maximize his outcome, however, would provide the other with too good an agreement; one would then be settling for less than necessary. In resolving the goal dilemma, participants must decide on a "reasonable" settlement, one that will not only get the most for one participant, but have a good chance of being acceptable by the other. Both participants seek an agreement that is the best they can do in the face of the other negotiator's opposition. Inasmuch as there is rarely any obvious "correct" agreement that would be accepted immediately by both members, each must decide during the negotiations what is a reasonable outcome for himself and for the other negotiator. The problem is always that the more favorable the agreement to oneself the less favorable it is to the other person.

The fifth characteristic of a negotiation relationship is that the negotiators are not only dependent upon each other for their outcomes, they are dependent upon each other for information about a possible agreement. This information can be secured in one of two ways: each negotiator can openly and honestly share what his preferences, needs, and expectations are, or each can attempt to hide his preferences, needs, and expectations in hopes of making an agreement as favorable to himself as possible. This is a complicated issue because a negotiator often does not know what her expectations should be until she learns what the other negotiator's expectations are. To the point that negotiators know both what the other wants and what is the least the other will accept, they will be able to develop an effective negotiating position. This *information dependence* sets up two more dilemmas, the dilemma of trust and the dilemma of honesty and openness. The *dilemma of trust* involves how much a negotiator can believe of the other's communications. To trust the other negotiator is to risk potential exploitation; by telling lies one participant can reduce the outcome for the other if his lies are believed. To distrust the other negotiator means that there is no possibility of any agreement being reached. The *dilemma of honesty and openness* involves the risk of either being exploited for disclosing too much too quickly or seriously damaging the negotiating relationship by seeming to be deceitful or distrusting.

The sixth characteristic of the negotiation relationship is the development of *contractual norms* that spell out acceptable behavior. Contractual norms specify the rules to be observed and the penalties for violating them. Thus, if violations occur the penalty can be assessed without destroying the possibilities of further negotiations. Two norms quite common in negotiation situations are reciprocity and equity. The *norm of reciprocity* means that a negotiator should return the same benefit or harm given to her by the other negotiator; "an eye for an eye and a kiss for a kiss" is an example of a norm of reciprocity. The *norm of equity* means that the benefits received or the costs assessed by the negotiators should be equal. Contractual norms provide clear groundrules for conducting the negotiations and managing difficulties in reaching an agreement.

Finally, the negotiation relationship has important time dimensions. It has a beginning, a middle, and an end. Negotiation begins when the parties acknowledge that a conflict of interest exists and either formally or informally make initial moves in the direction of its resolution. Negotiation ends when one or more of the parties chooses to leave the negotiating relationship. This may occur because an agreement has been reached and the parties conclude by mutual consent, or because one or more of the parties believe no satisfactory agreement is possible. In ending a negotiating relationship, other relationships between the parties may still be active. For example, after an agreement has been negotiated, the two parties can work cooperatively toward a mutual goal. In conducting negotiations, therefore, the future relationships between the parties must always be considered; it will do no good to negotiate an agreement highly favorable to one member if future cooperation is jeopardized or if the other member becomes so resentful that the agreement cannot be implemented.

To check your understanding of the above section, answer the following questions (answers on page 201):

1. What is the cooperative element in a negotiation relationship?
    a. Both parties think they'll get more by not negotiating than by negotiating.
    b. Both parties think they'll get more by negotiating than by not negotiating.
    c. Both parties feel they have conflicting preferences or opposing interests.
    d. Both parties feel they have similar preferences or compatible interests.
    e. When Edythe and Buddy get together to study for a test.
2. What is the competitive element in a negotiation relationship?
    a. Both parties think they'll get more by not negotiating than by negotiating.
    b. Both parties think they'll get more by negotiating than by not negotiating.
    c. Both parties feel they have conflicting preferences or opposing interests.
    d. Both parties feel they have similar preferences or compatible interests.
    e. When getting to know each other interferes with studying.
3. Outcome dependence is when:
    a. The outcome depends on a third party who acts as arbitrator or decision maker.
    b. A favorable agreement for one party is the least favorable to the other.
    c. Each party depends on the other for how good an outcome he gets.
    d. Whether Edythe studies with Buddy depends on how well he does on the test.
4. A dilemma of goals is when:
    a. If one person tries for her best outcomes, the other may refuse to negotiate, and if the person doesn't try for the best outcomes, she may settle for less than is necessary.
    b. If one person tries for his best outcomes, the other may refuse to negotiate, and if the person refuses to negotiate, there will be no settlement at all.
    c. Both Edythe and Buddy want to do well on the test, but they would rather improve their relationship than study.

Match the following terms in the negotiation process with their definitions.

_C_	5.	Information dependence.
_E_	6.	Dilemma of trust.
_F_	7.	Dilemma of honesty and openness.
_A_	8.	Contractual norms.
_D_	9.	Norm of reciprocity.
_B_	10.	Norm of equity.

a. Specify the rules to be observed and what will happen if they are violated.

b. Each party should come out of the negotiations with equal settlements.

c. Each party depends on the other for the knowledge needed to structure his proposals.

d. Negotiators should return the same benefit or harm given to them by the other party.

e. What is the most and least that a person can believe of the other party's information.

f. To avoid exploitation, the least a person can tell without seeming deceitful.

STRATEGIES OF NEGOTIATION

Basically, two types of strategies may be used to negotiate a settlement in a conflict of interests: a "win-lose" strategy and a "problem-solving" strategy. In a win-lose strategy the goal of negotiations is to make an agreement more favorable to oneself than to the other negotiator. In a problem-solving strategy the goal of negotiations is to make an agreement that is the most satisfying to both negotiators.

In all negotiations a sequence of behavior occurs in which one party presents a proposal, the other evaluates it and presents a counterproposal, the first party replies with a modified proposal, and so on until a settlement is reached. This sequence of behaviors is used to obtain information that helps resolve the dilemma of goals. On the basis of his opening offer, the proposals he receives, and the counterproposals he offers, a negotiator can obtain an idea as to what sort of settlement the other will agree to. A common win-lose negotiating pattern is for both negotiators to set a relatively high but tentative goal at first; they can then change it on the basis of the other person's reactions and counterproposals. This sequence of behaviors, which allows one negotiator to assess the second negotiator's points of potential settlement, can also be used to influence the second negotiator's assessment of the first's points of potential settlement. Through his opening offer and his counterproposals a negotiator can influence the other's expectations as to what he considers a "reasonable" agreement. The more one negotiator can convince the other that he will not make an agreement unless it is highly favorable to him, the more likely it is that he will obtain a profitable agreement. Thus, an opening offer by a negotiator that is extremely favorable to him and his refusal to budge from that offer may convince the other negotiator that if an agreement is to be reached he will have to modify considerably what he originally believed was a "reasonable" agreement. Ideally, a win-lose negotiator would like to obtain the maximal information about the other's preferences while disclosing the minimal or misleading information about his own preferences.

Other win-lose strategies are changing the other's evaluation of her position, using threats and promises, and sticking doggedly to a committed position. When a win-lose negotiator makes an extreme opening offer and refuses to modify it very quickly, he must simultaneously try to convince the other negotiator of the correctness of his position. He does so by pointing out not only the validity of his own position, but the wrongness or incorrectness of the other's. He must present, in other words, convincing rebuttals to the other's statements to try to *change* her evaluation of her position. In a *threat* a negotiator states that if the other negotiator performs an undesired act (such as refusing to agree to his proposed settlement) he will make sure the other suffers harm. A negotiator may threaten that unless the other person agrees to accept a certain settlement he will not make an agreement at all. In a *promise* a negotiator states that if the other negotiator performs a desired act she will make sure the other receives benefits. A negotiator may promise that if the other person makes a certain compromise she will also compromise. Through the use of threats and promises win-lose negotiators attempt to persuade each other to make certain agreements. Finally, another way in a win-lose strategy to influence the other negotiator to accept a certain agreement is for a negotiator to *commit* himself to a proposal that makes it clear it is the other negotiator's last chance of avoiding "no agreement." Thus, he may make a proposal and plug up his ears until the other negotiator says yes.

Problem-solving strategies of negotiation are similar to the procedures used to resolve controversies (see Chapter 6) and to solve group problems (see Chapter 10). Negotiators try to clarify the basic issues, define them as a problem, diagnose the causes of the conflict, search for alternative settlements, and decide upon and implement an agreement that is the most satisfying to them both.

Figure 7.1 presents a summary of the differences between the two types of strategies.

FIGURE 7.1 Negotiation Strategies

Problem-Solving Strategy	*Win-Lose Strategy*
Define the conflict as a mutual problem.	Define the conflict as a win-lose situation.
Pursue goals held in common.	Pursue one's own goals.
Find creative agreements that are satisfying to both parties or present a mutually acceptable compromise.	Force the other party into submission.
Have an accurate personal understanding of one's own needs and show them correctly.	Have an accurate personal understanding of one's own needs, but publicly disguise or misrepresent them.

Problem-Solving Strategy	*Win-Lose Strategy*
Try to equalize power by: emphasizing mutual interdependence; avoiding harm, inconvenience, harassment, embarrassment to the other party in order to reduce his fear and defensiveness.	Try to increase one's power over the other party by: emphasizing one's independence from the other and the other's dependence upon oneself.
Make sure contacts are on the basis of equal power.	Try to arrange contact where one's own power is the greater.
Use open, honest, and accurate communication of one's needs, goals, position, and proposals.	Use deceitful, inaccurate, and misleading communication of one's needs, goals, position, and proposals.
Accurately state one's needs, goals, and position in the opening offer.	Overemphasize one's needs, goals, and position in the opening offer.
Work to have highest empathy and understanding of other's position, feelings, and frame of reference.	Avoid all empathy and understanding of other's position, feelings, and frame of reference.
Communicate a problem-solving orientation.	Communicate a win-lose orientation.
Avoid threats in order to reduce other's defensiveness.	Use threats to get submission.
Express hostility to get rid of one's feelings that may interfere with future cooperation.	Hostility is expressed to subdue the other.
Communicate flexibility of position to help in creative problem solving.	Communicate highest commitment (rigid adherence) to one's position to force the other to give in.
Behave predictably; though flexible behavior is appropriate, it is not designed to take other party by surprise.	Behave unpredictably to use the element of surprise.
Change position as soon as possible to help in problem solving.	Concede and change slowly to force concessions from the other.
Promote clarity, predictability, mutual understanding to help in problem solving.	Increase ambiguity and uncertainty in an attempt to use deception and confusion to one's advantage.
Use cooperative behaviors to establish trust and mutual cooperation.	Use cooperative behaviors to grab the chance to exploit other's cooperativeness.
Adopt a consistent posture of being trustworthy toward the other.	Adopt a posture that allows one to exploit the other whenever possible.
Seek third parties to help in problem solving.	Isolate the other to reduce the possibility of his forming a coalition with third parties.
Emphasize exploring both similarities and differences in positions.	Emphasize only differences in positions and the superiority of one's own.

The two strategies are frequently mutually exclusive. If a person uses one strategy, he automatically behaves in a manner that undermines the other strategy. A negotiator cannot be honest and deceitful at the same time, cannot use threats and simultaneously avoid threatening remarks, and so on. The difficulty in choosing between the strategies lies in the possibility of being exploited by the other person if one chooses the problem-solving strategy and the other chooses a win-lose strategy, or the danger of forcing the other into a win-lose strategy by initially adopting it. It is well to keep in mind, however, that a win-lose strategy may be necessary with certain opponents, and that cooperative relationships have to be built slowly, not just taken for granted. For one negotiator to try to use a problem-solving strategy when the other is using a win-lose strategy may only lead to his being exploited and his losing. A basic dilemma for negotiators in resolving conflicts of interest is anticipating which strategy the other will use while deciding on one's own.

For a goal-oriented group a win-lose strategy of negotiation has some fundamental shortcomings. Although it will often result in more favorable primary gains, the damage it can cause to future cooperation among group members significantly reduces its secondary gains. Because a win-lose strategy emphasizes power inequalities, it undermines trust, inhibits dialogue and communication, and diminishes the likelihood that the conflict will be resolved constructively. Attempts at creating cooperative relations between negotiators are more effective if their power is equal. Walton (1969) notes that when power is unequally distributed, the low-power person will automatically distrust the high-power person because he knows that those with power have a tendency to use it for their own interests. Usually, the greater the difference in power, the more negative the attitudes toward the high-power person. The high-power person, on the other hand, tends to underestimate the low-power person's positive intent. A negotiator's power advantage may make him more likely to interpret cooperative behavior by the other as compliant rather than volitional. The result is that the other's cooperative behavior has an effect on the high-power person less positive than it should. Unequal power can also inhibit the weaker negotiator, and, sometimes, the stronger, from giving his views in a clear and forceful way. Finally, whenever one negotiator believes the other is trying to reduce his power, he is likely to react with competition and hostility.

You may wish to check your understanding of the above section by answering the following questions (answers on page 201):

1. What is a win-lose negotiation strategy?
   a. A strategy where each person tries to influence the other.
   b. The problem is approached as a test of who is stronger.
   c. A strategy based on the fact that power is a reality and must be used.
   d. A strategy used in a conflict of opinions.
2. What is a problem-solving negotiation strategy?
   a. A strategy to solve the conflict cooperatively.
   b. A strategy to have the whole group help solve the conflict rather than just the disagreeing individuals.

c. A strategy used in a conflict of incompatible interests.

d. A strategy where each person tries to influence the other.

True (False) 3. People who use a problem-solving strategy when their opponent is using a power-based strategy will have the advantage.

True (False) 4. The power-based strategy will get more secondary gains for the user.

True False 5. A low-power person will automatically distrust a high power person.

True (False) 6. A high-power person will automatically trust a low-power person.

THE USE OF ROLE REVERSAL

Many conflicts are viewed as conflicts of interests when in fact they are not. Many people use win-lose strategies in conflicts that would be more productively resolved through the use of problem-solving strategies. One of the major problems in our society is the difficulty in establishing skillful use of effective conflict-management procedures. The use of role reversal is often helpful in changing a win-lose-oriented negotiator to a problem-solving-oriented negotiator, in helping two problem-solving-oriented negotiators understand each other, and in helping negotiators find creative integrations of their interests. Role reversal is also helpful in managing controversies.

Johnson (1971) has conducted a long series of research studies on the use of role reversal in conflict situations. He found that used skillfully role reversal increases cooperative behavior between negotiators, clarifies misunderstanding concerning the negotiators' positions, increases understanding of the other's position, and aids one's ability to perceive the issue from the other's frame of reference. He also found that role reversal skillfully used can result not only in a reevaluation of the issue and a change of attitude concerning the issue, but also in the role reverser being perceived as a person who tries to understand the other's position, as an understanding person, as willing to compromise, as cooperative, and as trustworthy. Thus, there is considerable evidence that the use of role reversal facilitates the constructive management of conflicts.

FEELINGS OF REJECTION EXERCISE

One basic aspect of any disagreement, opposition, controversy, or conflict of interest is the feelings a person has while it is taking place. A common feeling is that of being rejected, of being pushed away from the other group member. These feelings of rejection can also incur other feelings, such as hurt, anger, loneliness, and fear. It is this potential for feeling rejected that makes many people afraid of conflicts and desirous of avoiding them. The following exercise was developed by Ardyth Norem-Hebeisen. The objective of this exercise is to experience the feelings of rejection and to discuss them. It takes less than one-half hour to conduct, and the procedure for the coordinator is as follows:

1. Introduce the exercise as an experience in exploring the feelings of rejection. Then divide participants into groups of four. The groups should sit in circles.

2. Explain that we now need to cut back the membership of each group so that only three people are members. Each group needs to select one person to be rejected and excluded from the group. Then pass out the appropriate instruction sheets (page 433 in Appendix E) to each participant. Give the groups ten minutes to make their decision.

3. At the end of ten minutes, have the groups combine into groups of eight members. Present the following questions for discussion:

   a. To what extent did each person feel what it is like to be rejected by his fellow group members?

   b. What is it like to feel rejected? What other feelings result from being rejected?

   c. What are your reactions to the experience? How do you behave when someone is rejecting you? How do you handle the situation?

   d. In negotiating a conflict of interest, how can you make sure the other person does not feel rejected? How can a negotiator behave to keep the feeling of rejection minimal?

   e. What conclusions about conflict can you make from your experience?

4. Discuss with all the participants their conclusions about how rejection and conflict can be managed.

FEELINGS OF DISTRUST EXERCISE

Some conflicts of interest promote distrust among group members if a win-lose strategy of negotiation is used. Trust is always an important issue for a group. The purpose of this exercise is to focus upon feelings of mistrust and discuss their impact upon negotiating settlements in conflicts of interest. The exercise is based upon one developed by Ardyth Norem-Hebeisen. The exercise takes less than one-half hour to conduct. The procedure for the coordinator is as follows:

1. Introduce the exercise as an experience focusing upon mistrust. Divide the participants into pairs.

2. Pass out the instruction sheets, giving one person in each pair Instructions A and the other person Instructions B (pp. 435 and 436, Appendix E). Give the pairs five minutes to interact after they read their instructions.

3. Have the pairs combine into groups of eight. Ask them to discuss their experience using the following questions as guides:

   a. What were your feelings and reactions to the experience?

   b. How was distrust communicated? What behaviors specifically showed mistrust?

   c. How does distrust affect the establishment of cooperation and the resolution of conflicts?

d. What conclusions can be drawn from your experiences?

e. What are ways in which trust can be increased when a group member currently mistrusts other members?

4. Summarize the conclusions of the groups of eight with all the participants. Point out that research studies indicate that trust is very difficult to build but very easy to break. Review the chapter on trust in Johnson (1972) as additional discussion material.

BREAKING BALLOONS EXERCISE

This exercise seeks to demonstrate a nonverbal conflict—which is a complete change from the previous highly verbal activities. The coordinator's procedure is as follows: have each participant blow up a balloon and tie it to his ankle with a string; then, when you give the signal, the participants are to try to break one another's balloons by stepping on them. The person whose balloon is broken is "out" and must sit and watch from the sidelines; the last person to have an unbroken balloon is the winner. The participants can then discuss their feelings of aggression, defense, defeat, and victory. Strategies for protecting their balloon while attacking others should be noted. A variation on the exercise is to have teams with different colored balloons competing against each other.

INTERGROUP CONFLICT EXERCISE

This exercise studies the dynamics of intergroup conflict and negotiation among groups with conflicting positions. It will take two hours to conduct. The procedure for the coordinator is as follows:

1. Introduce the exercise as an experience in intergroup conflict and negotiation. Divide the participants into four groups of not less than six members, and distribute the instruction sheets (pp. 437 to 444, Appendix E) to each group. Emphasize that the exercise will determine which group is best.

2. Have each group meet separately to select a negotiator and to develop their proposals on the issue. They are given one-half hour to do this. At the end of this period give them the Reaction Form and ask them to answer only Questions 1, 2, and 5, and to write the name of their group on the top.

3. Have the negotiators meet in the center of the room with the four groups sitting behind their respective representatives. Give each group representative five minutes to present her group's proposal. After each group has completed its presentation, have all participants complete the Reaction Form, answering all questions.

4. Tell the group to reconvene separately and brief their negotiators on the best way to proceed in the further presentation of their group's position. The groups

have fifteen minutes to confer. At the end of the period they again fill out the Reaction Form.

5. Have the negotiators again meet in the center of the room with their groups seated behind them. They have up to one-half hour to reach an agreement. Group members can communicate with their negotiators through written notes. At the end of fifteen minutes stop the negotiations and have everyone again complete the questionnaire. Negotiations are to resume and at the end of the thirty-minute period everyone answers the Reaction Form for the last time.

6. Conduct a general session in which the results of the questionnaire are presented and discussed. Ask group members how they feel about the experience and focus upon the experience of the negotiators.

7. Have the groups meet separately to discuss how well they worked together and what the experience was like for them. Develop a list of conclusions about intergroup conflict and place it on newsprint.

8. Again conduct a general session in which the conclusions reached by each group are discussed.

Coordinator Instructions for Reaction Forms

1. Your major role is that of timekeeper and organizer for distributing the Reaction Form. Pick one person in each group—as many assistants as you need—to hand out and collect the Reaction Form, and to compute the average response or group mean for each question each time the forms are used.

2. Draw Tables A through D (below) on a blackboard or large sheets of newsprint. Have a different color marker or chalk for each group. After each Reaction Form question is filled out, place the group means on the large charts. The response to Question 5 should be listed for use in the discussion sessions. Do not let the participants see the results until the general session in which the results are discussed.

3. In discussing the results of each question certain trends should be looked for. For Question 1, the responses should be somewhat high in the beginning, increase after comparison with other group's proposals, and drop off if agreement is reached. If no agreement is reached it should not drop off. For Question 2, look for the "hero-traitor" dynamic: satisfaction going up if the negotiator convinces other groups that her proposals are best, and satisfaction going down if the negotiator compromises the group's position. It is often helpful to look at the notes passed to the negotiator to see how the group is reacting. For Question 3, the responses should be the reverse of satisfaction with their own group's proposals (if satisfaction with own group's proposal is high, satisfaction with other group's is low). This amounts to devaluating the other group's proposals course, a loss of objectivity in evaluation. For Question 4, overconfidence in one's own group proposal is usually demonstrated, though this sense of superiority gradually slips from an initial high as negotiations progress.

TABLE A: Satisfaction with Own Group's Proposals

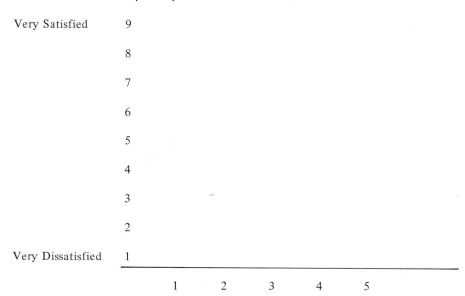

```
Very Satisfied       9

                     8

                     7

                     6

                     5

                     4

                     3

                     2

Very Dissatisfied    1  _____

                         1       2       3       4       5
```

TABLE B: Satisfaction with Negotiator

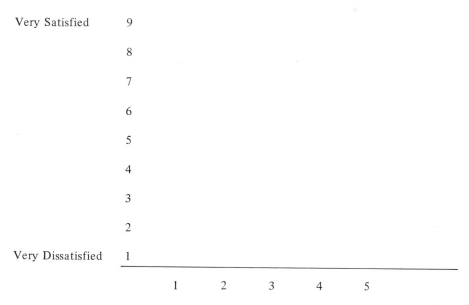

```
Very Satisfied       9

                     8

                     7

                     6

                     5

                     4

                     3

                     2

Very Dissatisfied    1  _____

                         1       2       3       4       5
```

TABLE C: Satisfaction with Other Groups' Proposals

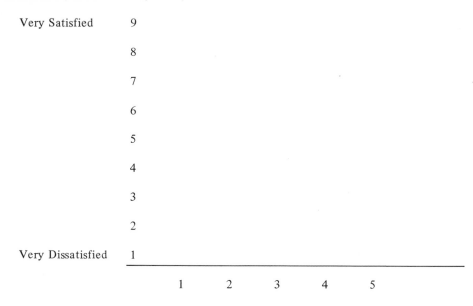

TABLE D: Satisfaction with Final Composite Proposals

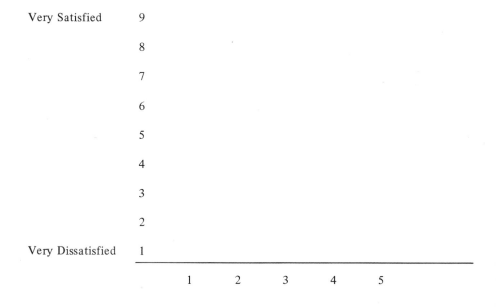

BATTLESHIP EXERCISE

This exercise is designed to increase the participants' understanding of a group's decision-making process during an intergroup conflict and to further their understanding of the dynamics of intergroup conflict. The procedure for the coordinator to follow is:

1. Divide into groups of eight (six members and two observers). Introduce the exercise as an experience in group decision making during an intergroup conflict. State that each group will have the same task, same instructions, and same time limit. Note that performance on the task will be scored objectively. Each group member is to contribute fifty cents to a pool; the group with the highest score will collect 70 percent of the pool and the group with the next highest score will collect 30 percent. After the scores of the groups have been tabulated and the pool money distributed, the two winning groups must decide how to allocate their treasure by some rule other than dividing the money equally among group members. In other words, each member of the winning groups must receive a different amount of money. Each group will have twenty minutes to plan its organization prior to performing the task; each will have thirty minutes to complete the task, including reading the instructions.

2. While the groups begin organizing, brief the observers. They are to observe the task and maintenance behaviors of the group members, note the dynamics of the decision making within the groups and record the effects of intergroup competition on intragroup functioning. These subjects are covered in this chapter and in Chapters 2 and 3. As soon as the briefing is over, the observers return to their groups.

3. At the end of twenty minutes distribute the Instruction Sheet and the Grid Sheet (pp. 445 and 446, Appendix E). Use the solution on page 331 of Appendix D as a model for drawing the correct answer anywhere on the grid. Then record the salvos fired by each group and give them their total score for each salvo. Deal only with the official spokesman of each group. Do not accept more than four salvos from each group.

4. At the end of thirty minutes stop all action. Announce the winning groups and distribute the money between them. While the winning groups are parceling out the money among their members, ask the other groups to (1) describe the process by which decisions were made, and (2) classify each person in the group in terms of the task and maintenance behaviors in which they engaged.

5. Give each group twenty minutes to analyze its effectiveness, using the information gathered by the observers as a beginning point of the discussion. Conclusions about the impact of intergroup competition on intragroup functioning should be written on newsprint and shared with the other groups during the last few minutes of the exercise.

OTHER INTERGROUP CONFLICT EXERCISES

Other intergroup conflict exercises can be made up easily or created by following the general outline given on page 187. The task can be one of stating the five most important principles of leadership, the qualities of an effective supervisor, the five most important things for a teacher to know, and so on. The dynamics of intergroup conflict are so predictable that if people are divided into groups, told to compete, develop their position, and represent that position in negotiations, the same dynamics are bound to be present.

INTERGROUP CONFLICT

How groups relate to one another within organizations has considerable bearing on the effectiveness of the organization. Groups are often in conflict and, just as cooperation is needed between different members of the same group, when two groups are part of the same organization or goal-directed effort, a high degree of cooperation between them is essential. The dynamics of intergroup conflict are about as destructive as they are predictable. And the more the intergroup conflict is defined as a win-lose situation, the more predictable are the effects of the conflict on the relationships of members within the group, on relationships between the groups, on negotiations between the groups, on the group that wins, and on the group that loses (Sherif, 1966; Blake and Mouton, 1962; Watson and Johnson, 1972).

A group in the throes of an intergroup conflict experiences a strong upward shift in cohesion as the members join together to defend their group against defeat. The group becomes more closely knit and gleans greater loyalty from its members; members close ranks and "table" or put aside some of their conflicts with one another. There is a sharpening and banding together of the ingroup power structure, as militant leaders take control, and group members become more willing to accept autocratic leadership. Maintenance needs become secondary to task needs, and the group becomes more tightly structured and organized. Satisfaction among the members runs high, along with their sense of identification or feeling of belonging with the group and with the group's position on the issues in the conflict. At the same time, the opposing group and its positions are belittled and devalued. Conformity is demanded; "a solid front" must be presented.

Between the groups an attitude of hostility develops. Each sees the other as the enemy. Inaccurate and uncomplimentary stereotypes form. Distortions in perception (see Johnson, 1972) increase; each group sees only the best parts of itself and the worst parts of the other group. Interaction and communication decrease between members of the conflicting groups. Doubt is cast upon the validity of the position of the other group; its position is seen as distinctly inferior to that of one's own group. Group members tend to listen only to that which supports their own position and stereotypes. They misperceive and fail to listen carefully to the other group's position—all of which only intensifies the conflict and deepens distrust.

In negotiations, there are distortions of judgment about the merits of the conflicting positions, with one's own position recognized as "good" and the other group's position assessed as "bad." Negotiators are relatively blind to points of agreement between their own and the others' proposals, and they tend to emphasize the differences. The orientation of the negotiators for the two sides is to win for their group, not to reach an agreement that satisfies everyone. This stance inevitably results in the hero-traitor dynamic in which the negotiator who "wins" is seen as a "hero" and the one who "loses" as a "traitor." When a neutral third party decides who is "right" and who is "wrong," the winner considers the third party to be impartial and objective; the loser views the third party as being unfair, biased, and thoughtless. Both sides see themselves as objective and rational and the other side as unjust and irrational—thereby excluding from the negotiations any signs of genuine objectivity. With the only loyalty being to one's own group position, the common result of win-lose negotiations is a deadlock. The win-lose strategy can also result, of course, in the representative being caught in a conflict between his own beliefs and perceptions and the mandate given him by his group.

The group that "wins" becomes even more cohesive. It also tends to release tension, lose its fighting spirit, become self-satisfied, casual, even playful. The leadership that was responsible for the victory is consolidated. Though there is a high concern for maintenance, there is little tendency to work. Members believe that winning has confirmed their positive stereotype of their group and the negative stereotype of the other group, and that as a result little need exists to reevaluate perceptions or reexamine group operations to learn how to improve them.

The group that "loses" frequently splinters, seeks the reasons for its defeat, and then reorganizes. Unresolved conflicts among members come to the surface in an effort to find the reasons for the defeat. Tension increases and the group begins to work even harder. Maintenance concerns abate as task concerns rise in a group effort to recover from defeat. The group often seeks someone to blame for the defeat—the leader, the judges, those who made the rules of the conflict situation, the least conforming members, and so on—and the leadership responsible for the loss is replaced. If future victories seem impossible, members may become completely demoralized, depressed, and assume a defeatist, apathetic attitude toward the group. The losing group tends to learn a great deal about itself because its positive stereotype of itself and its negative stereotype of the other group have been upset by the loss, forcing a reevaluation of perceptions. Consequently, the losing group is likely to reorganize and become more cohesive and effective once the loss has been accepted realistically.

The most important point about intergroup conflict on a win-lose basis is that it should be prevented, if at all possible. Further, it is a lot easier to prevent it on that basis by making sure there is a cooperative goal structure and problem-solving methods at work between the groups than it is to undo the conflict once the groups have gotten into a competitive, win-lose situation.

Though intergroup conflict has been discussed above from the point of view of the need to resolve it in a way that enhances cooperation among groups, it should be noted that intergroup competition can have many positive values. It often increases the involvement, fun, commitment, interest, and motivation of group members in working on tasks. For a discussion of the use of such intergroup competition in schools, see Johnson (1970) and Johnson and Johnson (1975).

To check your understanding of the preceding section, please answer the questions below (answers on page 201):

1. In a win-lose situation between groups, members become (choose two):

a. More closely knit.
b. More upset about the group.
c. Less interested in the group.
d. Less loyal to the group.
e. More loyal to the group.

2. In a win-lose situation, groups:
   a. Present their side fairly.
   b. Listen carefully to the other side.
   c. See only their best and the other group's worst.
   d. Feel that the other group has authoritarian leadership.
   e. Tell their negotiator to win or they'll beat him up.

3. In win-lose negotiations, groups:
   a. See the points of agreement between the groups.
   b. See the points of disagreement between the groups.
   c. Look for how the other group thinks about the problem.
   d. Work for a mutual agreement.
   e. Cry if they lose.

4. In a win-lose situation, when a third party decides the winner:
   a. The winner sees the decision as fair.
   b. The loser sees that the decision is fair.
   c. They both agree that the decision is fair.
   d. They both agree that the decision is unfair.
   e. They attack the third party, who then becomes the loser.

5. The group most likely to become more cohesive and effective after the decision is:
   a. The winning group.
   b. The losing group.
   c. Both groups.
   d. Neither group.
   e. All three groups.

6. The best way to solve a win-lose situation is to:
   a. Let one group win and go on to another problem.
   b. Let both groups win part of the decision.
   c. Let neither group win.
   d. Keep it from happening in the first place.

INTERGROUP CONFRONTATION: BLAKE AND MOUTON

This exercise was developed by Blake and Mouton (1962) and has since been used quite successfully in conflicts in a variety of organizations. It has probably been applied to every type of intergroup conflict one can imagine. Its purpose is to change the win-lose, competitive orientation toward intergroup conflict to the cooperative, problem-solving orientation. The exercise takes at least two or three hours to conduct (Blake and Mouton usually spend about nineteen hours conducting the exercise in actual union-management conflicts). The procedure for the coordinator of the exercise to follow is:

1. Introduce the exercise as an experience in resolving conflicts between two (or more) groups. State that the objective is to change win-lose orientations to problem-solving orientations. You might discuss the previous success Blake and Mouton have had with the exercise in difficult union-management conflicts. Use the union-management situation on page 196 to set up a role-play in trying out the procedure.
2. Have each group meet separately and develop on newsprint how it sees itself as a group and how it sees the other group. At least one hour is given for the groups to complete this task.
3. Have the two groups come together and share the results. With your help, have them compare how they see themselves with how the other group sees them. It is rather common for each group to see the other as being unreasonable, unethical, and unwilling to cooperate, while at the same time to see itself as being extraordinarily reasonable, ethical, and cooperative. The differences in the perception of how each group sees the other group are then clarified.
4. Ask the two groups to meet separately for at least one hour to diagnose their present relationship. They should answer such questions as: What problems exist? Why aren't they being constructively handled? What does the other group contribute to their mutual conflict? What does one's own group contribute to the conflict? This material is placed on newsprint.
5. Have the groups meet together to share their diagnoses. Help them try to bring together the key issues causing the conflicts between them and the main sources of friction. Keeping the material on constructive conflicts in mind, the two groups should plan the next stages for their cooperative solution of their conflicts.
6. Ask the two groups to assess their reactions to the exercise and summarize what they have learned about resolving intergroup conflict. Conclusions about preventing and resolving intergroup conflict are to be presented and discussed.

In using the procedure above, Blake and Mouton emphasize avoiding three basic traps that lead to increased, rather than decreased, conflict. The first to avoid is the *win-lose dynamic* in which every action of the other group is seen as a move to dominate. The participants must learn to recognize win-lose attitudes and behaviors and be able to set norms that stress their avoidance. The second trap to avoid is the *psychodynamic fallacy* in which the motivation for the other group's behavior is seen in terms of personality factors rather than resulting from the dynamics of intergroup conflict. It is very easy to blame the conflict upon sick, vicious, power-hungry people rather than to view the other group's behavior as a predictable result of intense intergroup conflict. Finally, they emphasize the avoidance of *self-fulfilling prophecies* in which, for example, one group assumes that the other is belligerent and then proceeds to engage in hostile behavior in an attempt to defend itself through a good offense—thereby provoking belligerence on the part of the other group, which confirms the original assumption.

UNION—MANAGEMENT EXERCISE

The teachers union of a large city has asked the local board of education for certain across-the-board increases in pay and fringe benefits. The board has refused to meet these "excessive demands," and has made an offer that the union leadership considers unacceptable. Still without a contract agreement at midnight of the day before school is to open, the union has voted to go on strike—and to remain on strike until a satisfactory agreement is reached. Divide into union and management groups and carry out the above procedures.

INTERGROUP CONFRONTATION: BECKHARD

Beckhard (1969) gives a procedure for determining the relevant, cooperative goals toward which all groups can take committed action. Because he recommends that the exercise be used when groups are in conflict and the members are experiencing stress, it becomes a conflict-management procedure. The objective of the exercise is to get the groups moving toward an action plan and a set of priorities for change and improvement that will resolve existing conflicts and establish cooperative goal accomplishment. Beckhard conducts the exercise as a one-day activity, but it can be shortened to a couple of hours when used strictly for learning. The procedure for the coordinator is as follows:

1. Introduce the exercise as an experience in setting cooperative goals among groups presently experiencing intergroup conflict. Stress that the exercise is an opportunity for the participants to influence the actions of their groups, and urge that they be open and honest with their feelings and ideas. The union-management situation as used in the previous exercise can be applied here for role-playing purposes.
2. Divide the participants into groups of five or six people. The task of these conflicting groups is to collect information. Tell them to think of ways in which life would be better in terms of their group membership and their relationship with other groups. Each group is asked to make a list of its items. This phase takes between thirty and forty-five minutes. The lists are placed on newsprint.
3. You or the participants should categorize the items listed.
4. Have the groups in conflict meet separately and ask them to complete the following tasks:
   a. Go through the entire list and select three or four items that most affect you and your group. Determine what action your group will take on them, and

the timetable for beginning work on the problems. Prepare to report your decisions in a general session.

b. Go through the list again and select those items to which you think all groups should give highest priority. These items should be things that your group cannot deal with alone.

5. In a general session have the groups share the results. Combine the lists. The groups should both outline plans for action necessary to implement their decisions and determine the necessary follow-up procedures. They should emphasize intergroup cooperation to solve the problems generated in Step 4.

6. Ask the groups to assess their reactions to the exercise and summarize what they have learned about resolving intergroup conflicts. Conclusions about preventing and resolving intergroup conflict are to be presented and discussed.

CONSTRUCTIVE MANAGEMENT OF CONFLICT OF INTERESTS

As mentioned several times in this book, if any group is to function effectively a high level of cooperation among group members must prevail. Whatever the method used to either control or resolve conflicts, it must establish as much cooperative interaction as possible among group members to be effective. The management of conflicts of interests in ways that maximize member cooperation depends upon the group having a common set of values and norms about the management of conflict and an agreed upon vocabulary to discuss conflicts among members.

As with controversies, group members in a conflict of interests must have a positive value system about fighting; they must view it as a productive way of handling differences. Members must believe that conflicts of interest are natural and desirable and should not be avoided or repressed; that the natural tension and frustration of working together can be greatly reduced through conflicts; that the conflicts keep arguments up to date and help group members avoid being bothered by the past; and that conflicts bring information to group members about how they are progressing, about what is important to each member, and about how group work and members' relationships can be improved.

The group norms needed to promote constructive management of conflicts of interests among group members include:

1. The conflict should be over issues, not between persons. Thus each group member needs to have an inner dialogue with himself to determine what the issue is, how central it is for him, how realistic the issue is, what the fight will cost the group, and how the other group members are likely to react. Current feelings should be clarified and understood.

2. Good timing should be used in scheduling the negotiations. Setting a time for negotiations may involve announcing the conflict of interest, stating the conflict, and asking for group time to negotiate the issues.

3. The circumstances that brought about the conflict should be understood by group members. Such circumstances involve both barriers to beginning negotiations and events that trigger expressions of the conflict (Walton, 1969).

Internal barriers include negative attitudes, values, fears, anxieties, and habitual patterns of avoiding conflict. External barriers may include task requirements, group norms for avoiding conflict, and faulty perceptions of own vulnerability and other's strength. Despite potential barriers, however, particular circumstances may be capable of bringing about open negotiations; these circumstances are called *triggering events*. The diagnosis of a conflict involves discovering what types of barriers usually operate and what triggers open expression of the conflict. From such knowledge groups members can help choose the time and place for negotiations. If an appropriate time is not immediately available the barriers to expressing the conflict can be increased and the triggering events can be decreased in order to temporarily avoid the conflict. Some events may trigger a destructive cycle of conflict and others may trigger problem-solving negotiations, in which case group members will want to maximize the latter. An analysis of events that surround or precede a conflict often provides clues regarding the basic issues in the conflict.

4. An open, constructive confrontation should take place at the beginning of the negotiations. *Confrontation* in this context means that the participants directly engage each other and focus on the conflict between them; they talk directly to each other about the conflict as they see it (for a detailed discussion of interpersonal confrontation, see Johnson, 1972). A confrontation is helpful in diagnosing the nature and dimensions of a conflict and in instituting a resolution process. Confrontations involve clarifying and exploring the conflict issues, the nature and strength of the underlying needs of the participants, and the current feelings of the participants.

5. The entry state of the participants should be assessed by the group. By *entry state* is meant the present ability of the participants to deal constructively with the conflict. Their level of self-awareness, their ability to control their behavior, their skills in communicating and being interpersonally effective (Johnson, 1972), their ability to withstand stress, and their ability to use their strengths for constructive conflict behavior are all important aspects of their entry state. Group support and consultation can raise the entry state of each participant.

6. A mutual definition of the conflict needs to be established. A problem-solving definition that minimizes the size of the conflict, includes current feelings of participants, avoids common misperceptions, and pinpoints the basic issues is usually the best way to define the conflict. Johnson (1972) presents a discussion of conflict definition along with several exercises to build skills in arriving at definitions.

7. Each participant should choose the negotiation strategy he will use to resolve the conflict. Either a win-lose or a problem-solving strategy may be chosen. Whenever possible the group should encourage problem-solving strategies.

8. Standards should be set on what "weapons" are to be allowed and where "beltlines" are to be established for each member. In other words, the intensity and area of attack should be kept within the member's revealed capacity to deal with the hurt.

9. Emotions should be brought out into the open and answered by emotions, not by tolerant but uninvolved understanding, and not by ridicule.

10. The situational power of all participants should be balanced. Power can involve being more verbal, having a louder voice, or having more authority. The group should help to minimize such differences so that negotiations can be conducted between equals.

11. Intermissions should take place during which participants can reflect upon the conflict and what they are learning from it.

12. There should be appropriate pacing of the differentiation and integration of the different positions. The different positions need to be clearly understood before successful compromises and integrations of the positions can be made. Remember that the potential for integration is never greater than the adequacy of the differentiation already achieved. Most conflicts go through a series of differentiations and integrations.

13. Role reversal should be used to ensure that each participant understands both the position and the frame of reference of his opponent.

14. An optimal tension level should be kept throughout the negotiations. A period of high tension to generate motivation to negotiate in good faith, followed by a reduction to a moderate level of tension, which does not interfere with a person's ability to integrate and use information, is often the best way to manage conflicts of interest.

15. The consequences of the conflict of interests should be clearly understood. Consequences can be either costs or gains. When a group is involved in negotiations among members, an appreciation of the costs and gains of the conflict is essential. Both the primary and the secondary costs and gains for the negotiators and for the group as a whole need to be correctly assessed, especially when win-lose negotiation strategies are being used. An analysis of the consequences of a conflict may give an understanding of why the conflict is tending to intensify, subside, or stay at the same pitch. An understanding of the consequences permits group members to identify the desirable and realistic outcomes of the conflict, and plan strategies accordingly. In examining the consequences of a conflict, the positive outcomes should never be ignored; it is all too easy to focus only upon the costs and not upon the benefits.

16. The negotiations should not end until an agreement is reached that specifies what each participant receives and gives, what changes the conflict has brought about, and what each has agreed to do to implement the changes.

Finally, in order for a constructive conflict of interests to be conducted within a goal-oriented group, there must be a common language about conflicts. The group language might include such terms as *win-lose, problem-solve, confront, beltline, I've-got-you-you-son-of-a-bitch,* and *gunnysack,* the last referring to the storing up of grievances for a long time and then unloading them all upon the offending group member. A common language will facilitate the identification of constructive and destructive strategies of negotiation and conflict management. Every group may develop its own vocabulary to describe conflict behaviors and procedures.

You may check your understanding of the preceding section by answering the following questions (answers on page 201):

1. What two practices are essential for managing a conflict constructively?
   a. The participants must not "hit below the belt."
   b. The other group members must stay out of the conflict.
   (c.) The participants must constructively confront each other.
   d. The participants must get the other group members to help in the conflict.
   (e.) The participants must get a mutual definition of the conflict.
   f. The participants should get a referee for the conflict.

Match the following terms with their definitions:

_C_ 2. Internal barriers.
_D_ 3. External barriers.
_E_ 4. Triggering events.
_A_ 5. Entry state.
_B_ 6. Confrontation.

a. The present ability of the participants to deal constructively with the conflict.

b. Members talk directly to one another about the problem as they see it.

c. Attitudes, values, fears, needs, anxieties, and habitual patterns of avoiding conflicts.

d. Perceptions of one's own and the other's vulnerability, task requirements, and group norms.

e. Something that brings about an open conflict, despite potential barriers.

YOUR CONFLICT BEHAVIOR

Before the topic of conflict is completed, it may be helpful to once again focus on your behavior in conflict situations. To do so, divide into groups of three with people who know you well and who have participated in some of the exercises in this book with you. Then complete the following tasks, taking at least two hours to do so.

1. Give each other feedback about the animal, song, or book the others remind you of, on the basis of how they deal with conflict. Explain why you chose the thing you did.

2. Write down your individual strengths in handling conflicts constructively. Share your lists and see what you add to the other members' lists.

3. Write down the individual skills you need to develop to handle conflict more constructively. Then share your lists and see what you can add to the other members' lists.

4. Discuss the feelings each of you have in conflict situations, and why you react the way you do. Help each other think of alternative ways of feeling or reacting to conflict situations.

5. Build a collage from magazine pictures and any other materials you have available about the way in which you behave in conflict situations. Share the collage with others in the group. Add ideas to the other members' collages.

CHECKLIST OF SKILLS

____ I can identify conflicts of interests.

____ I understand my habitual ways of dealing with conflicts.

____ I can effectively use a win-lose strategy of negotiation.

____ I can effectively use a problem-solving strategy of negotiation.

____ I can skillfully engage in role reversal.

____ I can negotiate in ways that do not make the other person feel rejected or distrusted.

____ I can effectively use several strategies for constructively managing intergroup conflicts.

____ I can apply the norms and rules for the constructive management of conflicts of interest.

The skills I need more work on are: _____

_____

_____

_____

_____

_____

_____

ANSWERS

Page   172: b.

Page   177: 1: c; 2: b, d; 3: a; 4: b.

Page   181: 1: b; 2: c; 3: c; 4: a; 5: c; 6: e; 7: f; 8: a; 9: d; 10: b.

Page   184: 1: b; 2: a; 3: false; 4: false; 5: true; 6: false.

Page 193-94: 1: a, e; 2: c; 3: b; 4: a; 5: a; 6: d.

Page   200: 1: c, e; 2: c; 3: d; 4: e; 5: a; 6: b.

8

The Use of Power

INTRODUCTION

All human interaction involves power or influence (the terms power and influence can be considered synonymous and they are used interchangeably in this chapter). It is not possible to discuss group functioning without discussing power. Group members adjust in many ways to one another. They take turns talking, they put aside individual interests to discuss mutual interests, they adjust expressions of attitudes and beliefs to take into account the reactions of other members, they speed up or slow down their activity to stay coordinated with other members. People who are interacting are constantly influencing and being influenced by one another. They constantly modify their behavior to make it fit the group in which they are participating. To be in a relationship with another person means to be influenced by and to be influencing that person. To be a member of a group means to be influencing and to be influenced by the other group members. Such influence cannot be ignored, abdicated, or denied. Every person should be aware of his power, accept it, and take responsibility for its use. The possession of power is inevitable, and it is through the exercise of mutual influence that cooperation takes place.

Within a group mutual power exists to the extent that one member can affect the goal accomplishment of other members. The more cooperative the group, the more influence members exert on one another. Through mutual influence the coordination of member behavior necessary for goal accomplishment is achieved. Leadership has been defined as the use of power to promote the goal accomplishment and maintenance of the group. Decisions cannot be made without members influencing one another. Controversies and conflicts of interest cannot be managed or resolved without the use of influence. Even communication cannot take place without mutual influence. Thus, the use of power is essential to all aspects of group functioning.

Power is the ability of one person to get others to behave in a particular way or to carry out certain actions. So, too, is influence. This ability depends not only on the forces that a person can bring to bear to get the other people to behave in the desired fashion, but on the resistances the people have to behave in that manner. When group members are taking part in cooperative activity and when their goals are compatible, they assert power in the same direction, and there is little or no resistance to accepting the influence of another member. When group members have incompatible goals, however, or are in competition with one another, then their power assertions will conflict and there will be resistance to accepting another's influence. *Resistance* is the psychological force aroused in a person that keeps her from accepting influence. It is generated by the way in which power is exerted. It can also be generated if the behavior desired by the person exerting the power fails to help the other members accomplish their goals.

In a group, members depend on one another for help in accomplishing their goals (outcome dependence) and for information about how to achieve the goals (information dependence). Outcome dependence concerns the ability of others to affect one's costs for engaging in goal-directed behavior (expenditure of energy, feelings of anxiety, fear of displeasing important people) and the benefits of one's goal directed behavior (the accomplishment of the goal). In choosing among alternative ways of attempting to accomplish one's goals, a person needs information about the potential costs of his behavior, the likelihood that a particular strategy will be successful, and his ability to carry out the necessary behaviors. When others have the information he needs to make the decision about which alternative strategy to adopt, a state of information dependence exists.

The important goals toward which all group members are working rest in the hands of other group members. Each member, consequently, tries to behave in ways that will influence other members toward accomplishing his individual goal. In such a situation two factors determine a person's power to influence other members of the group. The first is what resources the person has that the other group members need in order to accomplish their goals. The forces one member can exert on others to influence their behavior depends on how vital his resources are. The second factor is how available are alternative but similar resources. If group members can obtain the resources they need for goal accomplishment from someone else, one's power is reduced.

A final point to be made about dependence and power is that it is the *perception* of a person's resources that affect the behavior of other members, not his actual resources. A person can have large resources that are unknown or ignored by other group members; he, therefore, has little power over the others. On the other hand, a person can have few vital resources, but be seen as having many resources; he consequently has a great deal of influence over other group members.

Many people are unaware of the influence they exert on others, and many are unaware how necessary and constructive mutual influence is in building effective groups and cooperative, self-actualizing relationships. Being skillful in influencing other group members and taking responsibility for such influence are important parts of being a group member. In this chapter we shall give attention to the use of power in a group in ways that increase the group's effectiveness and clarify conflicts that can then be resolved productively. Interpersonal influence is discussed in Johnson (1972).

For many people in our society the words power and influence have negative connotations. There are individuals who say they do not wish to have power over others. This point of view is confusing the use of influence with manipulation. The authors wish to make a very clear distinction between the two concepts. All human interaction involves mutual influence; manipulation is a certain type of influence. *Manipulation* is the shrewd management or control of others, especially in an unfair or dishonest way, for one's own purpose and profit. Manipulation is the influencing of others in ways they do not fully understand and with consequences that are undesirable for them but highly desirable for oneself. It is the use of power for one's own benefit at the expense of others. People characteristically react with anger, resentment, and retaliation when they learn they have been manipulated. In proceeding through this chapter the reader should keep in mind that it focuses upon the constructive use of influence to increase cooperation and group effectiveness; the use of manipulation is destructive in that it eventually decreases cooperation and causes severe maintenance problems for a group.

To check your understanding of the preceding section, you may answer the questions below (answers on page 231):

1. Why do people join groups?
   a. To cooperate with other people in a mutual enterprise.
   b. To accomplish certain goals or to get certain rewards.
   c. To be in a position to exert power and influence.
   d. Because there's safety in numbers.

2. Power is defined as:
   a. Getting someone to do certain things.
   b. Being the president of a company.
   c. Taking over the leadership of the group.
   d. Telling other people how to behave.

3. Resistance is defined as the psychological forces that:
   a. Keep a person from being influenced.
   b. Keep a person from joining the group.
   c. Keep a person influenced.
   d. Keep a person from trying to influence another person.

4. What two things determine a person's power?
   a. Her past accomplishments.
   b. How dependent she is on the group.
   c. Availability of alternative resources.
   d. How susceptible she is to influence.
   e. The resources she has that others need.
   f. How much bigger and stronger she is than everyone else.
5. In accomplishing goals, members are dependent upon others for (pick two):
   a. Behavior.
   b. Outcome.
   c. Income.
   d. Information.
   e. Energy.

True False 6. Manipulation is the same thing as influence.
True False 7. Manipulation is good for a group.
True False 8. Manipulation is shrewdly managing or controlling others for one's own purposes and profit.
True False 9. Being manipulated makes people angry.

YOUR POWER—ORIENTED BEHAVIOR

How aware are you of the power you have over other group members? How do you usually express your power in a group? How do you react to being influenced by other members? The way in which a person handles power and influence has a strong bearing on his functioning in a group. The questions below are aimed at helping you clarify your power-oriented behavior in a group.

1. When other group members try to influence my behavior, I am likely to do the things they want me to do because (Rank the following six items from most important to you "1" to least important to you "6"):

   ___ I admire them for their personal qualities, and I want to act in a way that merits their respect and admiration.

   ___ I respect their ability and good judgment about things with which they are more experienced than I am.

   ___ They can give special help and benefits to those who cooperate with them.

   ___ They can apply pressure or penalize those who do not cooperate.

   ___ They have a legitimate right, considering their position, to expect that their suggestions will be carried out.

   ___ They have information I need in order to accomplish my goals and, therefore, I listen carefully and use what they have to say.

206

2. When I participate in a group, I am completely conscious of how much power I have and how I can use it to make sure my needs and wants are met.

    Never 1 : 2 : 3 : 4 : 5 : 6 : 7 : 8 : 9 Always

3. When it comes time to set group priorities, I seek out other group members who have compatible goals and try to form coalitions to increase my power and, therefore, the likelihood of my influencing the priorities in the way I want.

    Never 1 : 2 : 3 : 4 : 5 : 6 : 7 : 8 : 9 Always

4. I am quite comfortable dealing with power; I like influencing other group members and I enjoy being able to build enough power to get what I want from the group.

    Never 1 : 2 : 3 : 4 : 5 : 6 : 7 : 8 : 9 Always

5. The way in which I would describe my power-oriented behavior in a group is

_____

_____

_____

The questions above deal with the feelings you have when influencing other group members, your power-oriented behavior, your inclination to form coalitions to increase your power, your consciousness of power issues in the group, and the bases of power that are most important to you. At this point your answers will not be analyzed or discussed. Keep them in mind, however, as you go through the exercises and material in this chapter.

PERSONAL POWER AND PERSONAL GOAL ACCOMPLISHMENT*

A basic need of every group member is to have some influence over what takes place in the group. A person joins a group to accomplish goals he cannot achieve, or cannot achieve as easily, without group membership. The power a person needs within a group is the power to ensure that his personal goals are accomplished.

There is a definite process by which a person's power is mobilized to help in accomplishing his goals. The steps in the process consist of (1) determining his goals, (2) assessing his resources and information level, (3) determining what coalition is necessary to obtain the needed information and resources to accomplish the goals, (4) contracting a coalition committed to them, and (5) carrying out the necessary activities for the goal accomplishment. The next sections will examine this process step by step in order to help you acquire experience with it.

DETERMINING YOUR PERSONAL GOALS

The first step in using your power within a group is to clarify your personal goals. Goals are based upon a person's needs, wants, and self-interests. The term "goal" is

*The following sections were inspired by the work of George Peabody in this area.

used here in the broadest possible sense to refer to the rewards consciously sought as well as the rewards obtained unconsciously through relationships with other group members. In order to consciously plan for attaining your goals, you must be *aware* of them and accept them as valuable and worthwhile. Because many people work for power they do not need and for goals they do not really want, it is essential that you first be clear about what you want. Group members have to deal realistically with what each of them wants, and an effective group is one in which most members have their goals met. So, it is essential that a group member is clear about his goals, accepts them as worthwhile, and is willing to enlist the aid of other group members to accomplish them. As an important part of building and keeping trust, it is also essential that a group member be honest and accurate in his statements about his personal goals and that he be willing to work openly for their accomplishment.

At this point divide into groups of four. Each person should first state all possible desires, needs, wants, goals, and so on that he might work toward in this group. After everyone has had their say, each should then state which three goals they would like the group to accomplish first. Write these on newsprint, indicating the person and the goals. Then go on to the next section.

DETERMINING YOUR PERSONAL RESOURCES

The second step in the process of mobilizing your power is to affirm the resources you bring to the group. You must be aware of and accept your resources in order to tell others about them. Moreover, an awareness and acceptance of your resources are basic to an understanding by others of what you can contribute toward the accomplishment of your goals and the goals of other group members. Using the resources of members is a key issue for effective groups. Not only should the group as a whole take an inventory of its resources before beginning work, but the individual member should also take a personal inventory to determine her ability to accomplish her own goals.

Everybody has *many* different strengths upon which they base their interactions with others. All group members have solid strengths that are often unidentified and unused, both by the group and by themselves. The word *strength* refers to any skill, talent, ability, or personal trait that helps one function more productively. The objective of the exercise below is to increase your awareness of your strengths. The procedure is as follows:

1. Individually, each of you in your group of four should think of all the things you do well, all the things you are proud of having done, all the things for which you feel a sense of accomplishment. List all your positive accomplishments and successes.
2. Share your lists with one another. Then, with the help of the other three members, examine your past successes to identify the personal strengths you used to achieve them. Make a list of these strengths.

3. After you have all made your lists of strengths, give one another feedback about additional strengths. Add to each person's list the qualities, skills, and characteristics he has overlooked or undervalued.

4. Each member should then discuss the question "What might be keeping me from using all my strengths?" The group helps each person explore the ways in which he can free himself from factors that limit the use of his strengths.

5. If possible, review the material on self-acceptance and the acceptance of others in Johnson (1972).

DETERMINING YOUR NEEDED COALITIONS

The third step in the process of mobilizing your power in a group is to assess what coalitions with other members are necessary to secure the information and resources needed to accomplish your goals. The question to ask yourself is "Who has the information and resources I need and how can I ally myself with them to help my goal accomplishment?" After identifying the people, ask yourself "What are their goals, and how might I contribute resources and information they need for their goal accomplishment?" Then ask yourself "What coalitions can I make with members who have compatible, similar, or complementary goals?"

To begin this step, take out the personal goal sheets you composed in Step 1. Review your goals and change them in any way you believe appropriate. Then, as a group of four, look for similarities among your goals. As a group, decide upon the three goals that are in most accord with the personal goals of each member. List them on newsprint. Then review the strengths listed in Step 2. Try to determine what resources are needed to accomplish each of the three goals and who has them. In determining these resources, it may be helpful to read the Bases of Power section (below) and apply it to the strengths of your group members. What are your bases of power? What are your resources? In what ways can you influence the goal-achievement of your other group members? In what ways can they influence your goal achievement? How can you use your power to guarantee that your goals are met? In deciding on which coalitions are necessary to help your goal accomplishment, all these questions should be considered.

In participating in this exercise, you may experience either the frustration of finding little or no compatibility between your own goals and those of the other group members or the rejection of having your resources overlooked, undervalued, or underused. You may also experience the disappointment of finding that other members are more skillful in making coalitions. It is possible that two members will find themselves in basic disagreement with the other two group members. It is from such situations that conflicts are born. In the previous chapter we discussed at length the nature of such conflicts and how they can be managed productively. At this point the group should make such conflicts explicit, bring them out in the open, and be very clear about how they are dealt with.

Do not at this point make any formal coalitions among group members. Limit yourself to determining what coalitions are needed. Then go on to the next section.

CONTRACTING HELP WITH YOUR GOALS

The interdependence among group members should now be obvious. In contributing resources to achieve the group's three top goal priorities, different members have different levels of motivation and different levels of energy in working toward goal accomplishment. The degree to which your personal goals are reflected in the group's goals, and the degree to which your resources are recognized and used will usually determine the amount of energy you will contribute to accomplishing the goal. In planning how resources will be utilized to help achieve a goal, group members often develop formal or informal contracts with one another. The forming of a contract is Step 4 in the mobilization of one's power in a group, and it usually includes at least three items: (1) what I want from the group members, (2) what the other group members want from me, (3) what we exchange so that everyone can accomplish his goals.

In the previous three steps you set group goals, surveyed resources, and made judgments about what coalitions needed to be formed to help your goal accomplishment. Now, in Step 4, consciously work out formal contracts with other group members and form open coalitions. In doing so, specifically focus on the three items involved in a contract. Write your contracts on newsprint so that all members can see and read them. In essence, these contracts are a plan for cooperative action among group members to apply their resources in certain ways toward the achievement of the group's goals. Step five, implementing the contracts, will not be discussed.

DISCUSSION OF PERSONAL POWER
AND PERSONAL GOAL ACCOMPLISHMENT

After completing the five steps, the group should discuss their experiences. The following questions may be used to stimulate discussion:

1. How was power developed in the group?
2. How was power used in forming the group's goals and in identifying needed resources?
3. What was the outcome of the above steps? To what extent were everyone's goals integrated in the group's goals and to what extent were everyone's resources committed to the accomplishment of the group's goals?
4. What are the present reactions and feelings of each group member to the five steps?
5. With the help of the other group members, each member should answer the following questions:
   a. What are my goals?
   b. What are my sources of power in the group?
   c. How did I apply my power to make sure my goals were accomplished?

d. How successful was I?

e. How can I do better for myself next time?

6. What conclusions can be made about the use of power within a group on the basis of the group's experiences? Write these on newsprint. When all groups have finished their discussion, the conclusions should be shared.

BASES OF POWER

In discussing how power is developed and used, many behavioral scientists have given particular attention to its sources or bases (French and Raven, 1959; Raven and Kruglanski, 1970). According to their formulations, there are six possible bases of a person's power: his ability to *reward* and to *coerce*, his *legal* position, his capacity as a *referent*, his *expertise*, and his *information*.

1. A person has *reward* power over other group members if she has the ability to deliver positive consequences or remove negative consequences in response to their behavior. Her power will be greater the more the group members value the reward, the more they believe that she can dispense the reward, and the less their chances appear of getting the reward from someone else. The successful use of reward power will generally produce a "moving toward" the person. Group members will comply with the person's requests, seek her out, increase their liking for her, and communicate effectively with her. Under certain conditions, however, the reward power can backfire. Too many rewards or the development of suspicions on the part of the group members that they are being bribed or conned into going along can lead to a "moving away" or "moving against" the person.

2. A person has *coercive* power over other group members if she can mete out negative consequences or remove positive consequences in response to the behavior of group members. Punishment for a member who fails to get the group to go along with her wishes often increases the pressure on group members to engage in the desired behavior. Coercive power, however, frequently causes the group to avoid the person and to like her less. Group members may do what she wants, but they may tend to avoid interacting with her in the future. Only when the use of coercive power brings a conflict out into the open to be resolved can it have many positive effects.

3. When a person has *legitimate* power, group members believe he ought to have influence over them because of his position in the group or organization (such as an employer), or because of his special role responsibilities (such as those of a policeman). Group members invariably believe it their duty to follow the commands of a person with legitimate power, or perform a limited set of behaviors. Often legitimate power is used to reduce conflict—when the person with it plays the role of an arbitrator or mediator or when those with less power simply conform to his wishes.

4. When a person has *referent* power, group members identify with or want to be like him and therefore do what he wants out of respect, liking, and wanting to be liked. Generally, the more the person is liked, the more the group members will identify with him.

5. When a person has *expert* power, group members see her as having some special knowledge or skill and as being trustworthy. The group members believe she is not trying to deceive them for selfish purposes. The successful use of expert power results in the "movement toward" the person, for the group members are convinced of the correctness of her request. Only if her expertise fosters feelings of inadequacy in the group members will it have negative effects.

6. When a person has *informational* power, group members believe that he has resources of information that will be useful in accomplishing the goal and which are not available anywhere else. This power is based upon the logic of a person's arguments or the superiority of his demonstrated knowledge; it has effects similar to those that result from the use of expert power.

Review the sources of power used in the previous exercise on personal power and personal goal accomplishment. Classify them according to the bases of power discussed in this section. What power bases do you usually rely upon?

Match the following bases of power with their definitions (answers on page 231):

_C_ 1. Reward.

_f_ 2. Coercive.

_b_ 3. Legitimate.

_e_ 4. Reference.

_d_ 5. Expert.

_a_ 6. Informational.

a. Group members believe the person has useful knowledge not available elsewhere.

b. Group members believe the person ought to have power because of his position or responsibilities.

c. A person can deliver positive consequences or remove negative consequences.

d. Group members believe the person has a special knowledge or skill and is trustworthy.

e. Group members do what the person wants out of respect, liking, and wanting to be liked.

f. A person can deliver negative consequences or remove positive consequences.

UNEQUAL RESOURCES EXERCISE

This exercise provides a chance to observe how groups (1) use resources that have been unequally distributed and (2) negotiate to obtain the resources they need. The exercise may be conducted with groups of from two to four members. If necessary, others may participate without being group members. Should more than one cluster of four groups participate in the exercise, the coordinator may wish to add the element of competition between the groups as well as within the clusters. The exercise should take less than one hour. The coordinator's procedure for the exercise is as follows:

1. Introduce the exercise as an experience with the use of resources needed to accomplish a task that have been unequally distributed among groups. Form the groups. For each cluster have at least two observers. Groups should be placed far enough away from each other so that their negotiation positions are not compromised by casual observation.

2. Meet briefly with the observers and discuss what they might focus upon. Any aspect of negotiation and problem solving can be observed.

3. Distribute an envelope of materials and a Tasks Sheet (page 447, Appendix E) to each group. Explain that each group has different materials, but that each must complete the same tasks. Explain that they may negotiate for the use of materials and tools in any way that is agreeable to everyone. Emphasize that the first group to finish all tasks is the winner (if clusters are competing, there will be both a group winner and a cluster winner). Give the signal to begin.

4. Stop the process when winners have been declared and the groups have been allowed to complete their tasks. Then conduct a discussion on using resources, sharing, negotiation, competition, and the use of power. Ask the observers to participate in the discussion. Then ask the clusters to summarize their conclusions about the use of power that manifested itself during their experience in this exercise.

Group Materials

Group 1: Scissors, ruler, paper clips, pencils, and two 4″ squares of red paper and two of white.

Group 2: Scissors, glue, and two sheets of gold paper, white paper, and blue paper, each 8½″ by 11″.

Group 3: Felt-tipped markers and two sheets of green paper, white paper, and gold paper, each 8½″ by 11″.

Group 4: Sheets of paper, 8½″ by 11″—one green, one gold, one blue, one red, and one purple.

POWER POLITICS EXERCISE

The objective of this exercise is to examine the dynamics of negotiating for power. Group members with different amounts of power are to negotiate for power coalitions with other group members. The exercise takes one and one-half hours to conduct. The procedure for the coordinator to follow is:

1. Introduce the exercise as a situation in which different group members have different amounts of power and are negotiating power coalitions to complete a task. Divide the participants into groups of twelve. Each participant needs a pencil and a pad of paper for sending notes.

2. Hand out the Power Politics Instruction Sheet (page 449, Appendix E), to each participant and have them read it. Randomly hand out slips of paper with numbers on them to each participant. The number per slip is to range from 100

to 1,200. Then announce that there will be two rounds of negotiations before the first vote is taken. The first round will be a fifteen-minute period in which members write notes to each other. No verbal communication is permitted. Members may write as many notes to as many other members as they wish. Notes should indicate the name of the sender and of the receiver. Notes are not to be read until the end of the fifteen-minute period. Give the signal to begin Round 1.

3. At the end of fifteen minutes stop all note passing and allow members to read their notes. After all notes are read announce the beginning of Round 2. The same rules apply. Round 2 lasts fifteen minutes.

4. At the end of Round 2 ask the groups if they are ready to vote on their chairperson. If seven members want to vote, a vote is taken. All voting takes place by secret ballot. Members note the number of votes they control and how they commit them. If the group is not ready to vote or if no one has enough votes to become chairperson, go to Round 3.

5. In Round 3 members may negotiate verbally with one another. There are no restrictions on negotiations during this round. The round lasts for fifteen minutes.

6. At the end of Round 3 call for a vote. The vote is again a secret ballot. If no one has enough votes to become chairperson allow another ten-minute free negotiation period. Then take a final vote.

7. Have the groups discuss their experience using the following questions as guides:

   a. What deals were made for the 100 units of patronage? How was power used in making those deals?

   b. What negotiation strategies were used?

   c. How did people make decisions about whom to commit their votes to? What criteria were used to make the decision?

   d. What were the feelings and reactions of the members to the experience?

   e. What feelings arose from the unequal distribution of votes? How did it feel to control a small number of votes? How did it feel to control a large number of votes?

   f. How did members proceed to create allies and develop power blocks? What strategies were used?

   g. Who felt powerful? Who felt powerless?

   h. What conclusions can you make about the use of power? (Write these on newsprint to share with other groups.)

POWER AND PROBLEM SOLVING

In the previous exercises the resources of the group were distributed unequally among its members. For most problems a group faces, this will be the case. Yet because resources are unequally distributed does not mean that there are members who are powerless. Every group member has some power, every group member is able to influence other group members in some way. Different group members will have different bases of power; some, for example, may have a high degree of informational power, others may have legitimate power. How a group manages the influence aspects of member relationships is an important part of group effectiveness.

The effectiveness of any group is improved when (1) power is relatively balanced among its members, and (2) power is based upon competence, expertise, and information. Influence needs to be generally balanced or equal among all group members. A member's commitment to implementing a group decision depends upon her believing that she has influenced the decision. The ability of the group to solve problems increases as all group members come to feel that they share equally in influencing the direction of the group effort, and as the group climate becomes relatively free of domination by a few of the most powerful members. When members have equal power they are more cooperative in their interactions and more responsive to the cooperative initiatives of other members. Even within organizations, studies have found that the satisfaction of subordinates increases when they believe they can influence particular aspects of the organization's decision making. Unequal power interferes with the trust and communication necessary to manage group conflicts constructively. Thus, the problem-solving ability of a group is improved when the group has flexible and changing power patterns that, in the long run, equalize influence among group members.

A group's decisions are invariably of higher quality when power is based upon competence, expertise, and relevant information—not upon authority or popularity. The problem-solving capacity of many groups is seriously damaged when the member with the most authority is most influential at a time that calls for expertise and accurate information as the bases of power. The participation and involvement of all group members is dependent upon their being able to share the bases of power to influence the decisions made by the group.

When power is not shared and equally distributed among group members, or when the use of authority dominates and expertise and informational bases of power are ignored, group effectiveness is undermined. The following exercise deals with the unequal distribution of power and the consequences it can have for both high- and low-power group members.

To check your understanding of the preceding section, you may answer the questions below (answers on page 231):

1. When people or groups have equal power compared with groups with unequal power, they are:

   a. More frustrated.
   b. More constrained.
   c. More competitive.
   d. More feminine.
   e. More cooperative.

2. The ability of a group to solve problems increases as (choose two):

a. The low-power members form strong coalitions against the high-power members.

b. There are members in authority responsible for making the decisions.

c. Group members believe they have an equal chance to influence the decision.

d. Influence is based upon expertise and possessing relevant information.

e. The number of women members increases.

POWER TO THE ANIMALS EXERCISE

The objective of this exercise is to examine the interaction among groups of different power in negotiating with one another. The exercise takes two hours to conduct. The coordinator should read the Distribution of Marbles Instructions (below) and then follow this procedure:

1. Introduce the exercise as one that highlights interaction among unequal power groups. Divide into groups of twelve members. Explain that within each group are three animals, four birds, and five fish; who will remain in each group is determined by how well they negotiate—for marbles. Hand out a copy of the General Instructions Sheet (page 451, Appendix E) to every participant.

2. Distribute twelve bags of marbles randomly within each group. Make sure that they understand the instructions. Give them time to examine what marbles they have, warning them not to let other group members see the marbles. Then begin Negotiation Session 1, which is to last five minutes.

3. During the negotiation session place on newsprint three headings: animals, birds, and fish. After five minutes stop the negotiating and have the participants compute their scores. Take the three highest scores and place them, along with the persons' initials, under the heading of "Animals." Take the next four scores and place them, together with the persons' initials, under the heading of "Birds." Take the next five scores and place them, with the persons' initials, under the heading of "Fish." Have each person make a name tag indicating what he is and put it on.

4. Begin Negotiation Session 2. After five minutes end it and ask for scores. Read just the individual scores so that the three highest are in the animals column, the next four in the birds column, and the next five in the fish column. People who change columns need to exchange their name tags.

5. Conduct Negotiation Session 3 in the same way.

6. Conduct Negotiation Session 4 in the same way.

7. Announce that the animals now have the authority to make the rules for the exercise and that though anyone else can suggest rules the animals will decide which will be implemented. Inform the animals that they may make any rules they wish, such as that all marbles must be redistributed so that everyone has equal points, all fish and birds must give animals the marbles they ask for whether they want to or not, and so on. Have the animals record their rules on newsprint.

216

8. After the new rules are established, conduct Negotiation Session 5. Then allow five minutes for the animals to discuss and make any rule changes.

9. Repeat this cycle twice. Then distribute the sheet entitled Strategies for Influencing High-power Group (page 453, Appendix E). Give the birds and the fish ten minutes to discuss the strategies and decide upon which ones to adopt. Then continue with the exercise.

10. After a variety of strategies have been tried by the birds and the fish, or after they refuse to continue, conduct a discussion of the experience. The following questions may be used as guides:

   a. What were the feelings and reactions of the members to the experience?

   b. Are there any parallels between the system set up by the game and the system in which we live?

   c. Would it have made much difference if the members who were fish had been the animals?

   d. Were the animals acting with legitimate authority?

   e. Are there any parallels between the exercise and the relations among racial groups, rich and poor, and adults and students?

   f. What negotiation strategies were used?

   g. What feelings arose from the unequal distribution of power? How did it feel to have high power? How did it feel to have low power?

   h. How did the strategies for changing the high-power group work? What contributed to their effectiveness or ineffectiveness?

   i. What conclusions about the use of power can be made from your experiences in the exercise?

Marbles Required for the Exercise

1. The total number of marbles needed is seventy-two (six times the number of group members).

2. The number of green marbles needed is five (number of animals plus two).

3. The number of yellow marbles needed is ten (number of birds plus the number of fish plus one).

4. The number of red, white, and blue marbles needed is fifty-seven; nineteen of each.

Distribution of Marbles Instructions

Each participant is given six marbles. The coordinator should distribute at random five bags each containing one green marble, one yellow marble, and four randomly selected from the colors of red, white, and blue. The coordinator should distribute at random three bags, each containing one yellow marble and five randomly selected from the colors red, white, and blue. The coordinator should distribute four bags containing a random assortment of red, white, and blue marbles.

UNEQUAL POWER

When the distribution of power is obviously unequal within a group, both the high- and low-power members have troubles. As discussed previously, overall group effectiveness suffers, the gains members receive from being members decrease, and severe maintenance problems result. In discussions of theory and research pertaining to high and low power, the usual reference is to our society rather than to a small, problem-solving group. Yet the same dynamics between high-power and low-power people can be found in any size group, even one as large as our society. In the previous exercise, you yourself experienced, depending on your marbles, what it means to have a great deal of power or what it means to have very little power. Compare your experience with the following discussion:

Life generally seems good for high-power people. Everything goes right, every problem is easily solved, everyone seems to like and appreciate high-power people and everything they do. High-power people are typically happy with their situation and tend not to see how much the use of power is involved in their relationships. They are convinced that low-power people really do like them, that everyone communicates honestly with them, that no one hides information from them, and that they are really seen as "nice" people. When this enjoyable world is threatened by expressed dissatisfaction on the part of low-power people, however, the high-power people have a tendency not to react benevolently. They are hard to move toward cooperation, conciliation, and compromise, and they will largely ignore the efforts of low-power members to increase cooperative problem solving. To them, somehow, low-power persons never learn to "know their place" and they insist on "rocking the boat" out of ignorance and spite.

1. There are at least two strategies that high-power group members will use to make it less possible for low-power members to reduce the differences in power between them (Jones and Gerard, 1967). The first is to institute norms or rules in the group that legitimize or make right their power and make illegitimate or wrong any attempt by others to change the status quo. As may have been noticed in the previous exercise, the first action taken by most groups who attain power is to make their holding of it legitimate and to establish regulations and norms that make illegitimate any change in the power relationships. For example, in most communities the white power structure has established strong norms about where minority group members may live, what occupations they may be employed in, and where they must go to school—as well as procedures for making both whites and nonwhites believe that the status quo is "legitimate" and "right." This strategy may be described as the "power defines justice" strategy, or the "might is right" strategy.

2. The second strategy high-power members employ to solidify their position is to make the risk of attempting to change status quo so great that the low-power members are deterred from trying to do so. They can invoke this strategy by establishing severe penalties against those who might attempt to change the status quo, and by offering the low-power members a variety of benefits or rewards on condition that they refrain from rebelliousness. Of the two, the second seems to be more effective. The threat of punishment has never worked effectively to deter behavior, but the paternalistic leadership that tries to keep everyone happy has been applied successfully in combatting labor and racial unrest in many parts of the country. This strategy may be defined as the "this hurts me more than it will hurt you" strategy, or the "if only you would behave, neither one of us would go through this suffering" strategy.

In America, high power is believed to result in arrogance and corruption. "Power corrupts" is a common household saying, and most people have seen the arrogance of those who have more power than they do (usually a secretary in the office of their boss). There are many exceptions to these correlations, of course, but perhaps not nearly so many as high-power people like to believe. Halle (1967) also provides the interesting idea that the greater a person's power becomes, the more insufficient it is likely to seem, simply because the claims upon it increase faster than the power to fulfill them. The Ford Foundation, for example, while by far the richest of American foundations, is undoubtedly the most inadequately endowed in terms of the expectations it is called on to meet. High power may also bring difficulties in handling small problems; it may become easier to drop an atom bomb on a mosquito than to use a can of bug spray.

Generally, a person or group continually subjected to the power of another finds such a relationship threatening and debilitating. To defend himself against the threat of the high-power person, a low-power person will often emphasize and exaggerate (1) the degree to which the high-power person likes him and (2) the goodwill of the high-power person (Cartwright and Zander, 1968). Low-power people have been found to direct much of their communication and attention to high-power people and to keep on good terms with them. On the other hand, people subjected to authoritarian leadership have been observed to be apathetic and submissive or, alternatively, hostile and rebellious. The lack of freedom that the low-power person has in setting his own goals and deciding how they should be accomplished will have damaging effects on his behavior.

Given the resistance and defensiveness that people in high power have, what can low-power members of a group do to change the distribution of power? One strategy is to endear themselves or to try to "get in good" with those who have more power. This strategy is accomplished by giving the high-power person compliments, signs of agreement, indications of admiration, respect, and so on. It is a strategy that does not do much for a low-power person's self-perception, though it may increase the high-power person's dependence on him. Deutsch (1969) assumes that the goal of low-power members is to establish authentic, cooperative relationships with the high-power members in which the two have equal power. He states that the ability to offer and engage in authentic cooperation means that the low-power people are aware that they are neither helpless nor powerless, even though they are at a relative disadvantage. Cooperative action requires a recognition that a person has the capacity to "go it alone" if necessary; unless a person has the freedom to choose not to cooperate, there can be no free choice to cooperate. Thus, the low-power people need to build enough cohesiveness and strength to function independently of the high-power people if it is necessary. In addition, the high-power members must be motivated to cooperate with the low-power members so the latter must find goals important to the high-power members and ones the high-power members cannot accomplish without the cooperation of the low-power members.

Deutsch (1969) notes that a variety of strategies are available to low-power members for influencing high-power members. By building their own organizations and developing their own resources, low-power members not only can make themselves less vulnerable to exploitation, but can add to their power by providing themselves with alternatives that preclude their being solely dependent upon the high-power members. Low-power members can also add to their power by allying themselves with third parties. Another strategy they can employ is to try to use existing legal procedures to bring pressures for change. Further, low-power members can search for other kinds of attachments with the high-power members which, if made more obvious, could increase their positive feelings toward or outcome dependence upon the low-power members. Low-power members can try to change the attitudes of those in high power through education or moral persuasion. Finally, the low-power members can use harassment techniques to increase the high-power members' costs of staying with the status quo. For low-power members of a group to plan how to increase their power in relation to the high-power members, they should first clarify their goals, then completely inventory their resources, and finally study how to make the high-power members more aware of their dependence on them and of their compatibility (if any) of goals.

You may check your understanding of the preceding section by answering the following questions (answers on page 231):

True ~~False~~   1. High-power people are usually eager to cooperate and compromise.
True ~~False~~   2. The greater a person's power becomes the more sufficient it is likely to seem.

Match the groups with the strategies they use:

_a & b_ 3. They find that goals important to the other group cannot be done without them.

_b_ 4. They try to change attitudes through education or moral persuasion.

_a_ 5. They make rules to legitimize power.

_a_ 6. They punish attempts to change things.

_b_ 7. They try to get in good with the other group.

a. High-power group.
b. Low-power group.

220

a & b 8. They build up their organizations and resources.

9. People subjected to authoritarian leadership have been observed to be:
   a. Apathetic.
   b. Submissive.
   c. Hostile.
   d. Rebellious.
   e. All of the above.
   f. None of the above.

10. To plan how they can increase their power, members of a low-power group need to (choose two):
   a. Show the high-power group how incompatible the goals of the two groups are.
   b. Plan how to make the high-power group more aware of its dependence on them.
   c. Clarify the goals of the high-power group.
   d. Clarify their goals and inventory their resources.
   e. Get a third party to intervene.

THE SEVENTEEN GIRLS EXERCISE

The following exercise is based upon an actual study of seventeen girls living in a college dormitory. The exercise provides a chance for a group discussion of the formation of groups, the development of leadership, and the use of power within peer groups. The exercise takes two hours to conduct. The coordinator's procedure for the exercise is as follows:

1. Introduce the exercise as a vehicle to discuss group formation, leadership, and power. Divide into groups of six members.
2. Within each group study the information given on the following pages about each girl. Then take thirty minutes to draw a picture of the social system formed by the seventeen girls, giving attention to: (a) the location of the subgroups formed within the social system (there are four); (b) the identity of the leader(s) of subgroups; and (3) the interaction patterns occurring between girls as well as between subgroups, noting in particular the frequency and quality of the interaction(s).
3. When they have finished Step Two, instruct the groups to write a one-page description of leadership. What are the qualities they believe are pertinent to leadership, and how do the girls identified as leaders exemplify these qualities? The groups have thirty minutes to complete this step.
4. Next, instruct the groups to write a one-page description of power as it relates to social systems. Utilizing the seventeen girls as examples, discuss the ways in which power structures are built in social organizations such as schools, colleges, churches, businesses, and so on. Discuss how the girls exert influence and what their bases of power are. The groups have thirty minutes to complete this step.
5. Share the conclusions of each group in a general session.

TABLE 8.1 Objective Characteristics of the Seventeen Girls

Characteristic	Girl Number					
	1	2	3	4	5	6
Religion	Presbyterian	Baptist	Baptist	Jewish	Episcopalian	Jewish
Attendance	Rare	Frequent	Frequent	Occasional	Never	Occasional
Sorority	No	No	No	No	Yes	No
Allowance	High	Low	Medium	High	Medium	Medium
Major	Radio	Phys. Ed.	Home Econ.	Journalism	Home Econ.	Sociology
Grade Average	B	D	C	A	C	C
Hometown Population	100,000	2,500	Rural	100,000	2,500	1,000
	7	8	9	10	11	12
Religion	Methodist	Nonsectarian	Jewish	Jewish	Methodist	Christian
Attendance	Frequent	Never	Occasional	Frequent	Never	Often
Sorority	No	No	No	No	Yes	No
Allowance	Medium	Medium	Medium	High	High	Medium
Major	Home Econ.	Arts & Sc.	Commerce	English	Languages	Home Econ.
Grade Average	B	B	B	C	D	B
Hometown Population	100,000	25,000	2,000	100,000	25,000	8,000
	13	14	15	16	17	
Religion	Nonsectarian	Baptist	Baptist	Baptist	Jewish	
Attendance	Never	Often	Never	Often	Occasional	
Sorority	No	No	Yes	No	No	
Allowance	Medium	Medium	High	Medium	High	
Major	Music	Education	Arts & Sc.	Home Econ.	English	
Grade Average	A	C	C	C	A	
Hometown Population	10,000	3,000	2,500	2,000	100,000	

General Description of Characteristics and Activities

Girl No. 1 dates frequently—sometimes double-dating with No. 5 or No. 11. She attends movies, dances, smokes, and drinks—sharing liquor with Nos. 5, 11, 15, and sometimes No. 17. She also shares food with these same girls; that is, Nos. 5, 11, and 15. Sometimes Nos. 2 and 17 participate in these food-sharing activities. She stays out of the dormitory after hours, but always seems to get back into the dormitory unaided and uncaught. When she goes home for the weekend, she sometimes takes No. 5 with her. After 11 p.m. (when the gabfests begin) she may be found in either her own room, or in No. 11's room. When she has problems, however, she will be found in No. 8's. The girl is quite attractive and is a good dresser. In this respect, she sometimes borrow clothes from No. 8. She has a very high "origination rate"—that is, she generally originates conversation with the other girls, and she generally does most of the talking.

Girl No. 2 does not attend the movies. She does not smoke, drink, or dance. She is afflicted with a thyroid condition that keeps her body plump and her face pimpled and blemished. She is the gushy type that tries to be friendly with everyone. She is very accommodating, taking telephone calls and notifying the other girls of all calls and messages. Although she borrows clothes from No. 8, she does not know how to dress well. It appears that No. 8 is the only one who will loan clothes to No. 2. After 11 p.m. she can generally be found in her own room, but she will sometimes be in No. 11's or No. 12's. When she has a personal problem, she often goes to see No. 16. She does, in fact, spend a great deal of her time with No. 16.

Girl No. 3 dates seldom. She attends the movies. She does not smoke, drink, or dance. She shares food with Nos. 7, 12, and 14—sometimes with Nos. 2 and 16. Her problems are shared with No. 12, in whose room she can generally be found after 11 p.m.

Girl No. 4 has strong traditional values. She is a good talker and has the facility for outdebating most of the other girls. She is well versed in such subjects as dates, men, home, clothes, and even some academic subjects. She dates frequently. She also smokes, drinks, and dances. Food and liquor are shared with Nos. 6, 9, 10, and sometimes 17. Clothes are borrowed from Nos. 6, 9, and 10, and in turn loaned to those girls. Her problems are shared with either Nos. 8 or 17, but mostly with No. 8. After 11 p.m. she can be found in her own room, or sometimes in No. 10's.

Girl No. 5 occasionally dates—sometimes double-dating with Nos. 1 or 11. She dances, smokes, and drinks—sharing liquor with Nos. 1, 11, 15, and sometimes No. 17. Food is shared with Nos. 1, 11, 15, and sometimes 2 and 17. Her troubles are shared with No. 1. Sometimes she stays out of the dormitory after hours and is helped back in by No. 1. After 11 p.m. she may be found in the room of Nos. 1 or 11.

Girl No. 6 dates occasionally also—some of these dates being double dates with No. 9. She dances, smokes, and drinks. Food and liquor are shared with Nos. 4, 9, 10, and sometimes 17. Clothes are borrowed from Nos. 4, 9, and 10. She, in turn, loans her clothes to these same three girls. When she has a problem, she generally goes to No. 4 in whose room she can be found after 11 p.m.

Girl No. 7 attends the movies. She does not smoke, drink, or dance. Food is shared with Nos. 3, 12, 14, and sometimes 2 and 16. Her troubles are shared with No. 12 in whose room she can generally be found after 11 p.m. This girl does not date.

Girl No. 8 seldom dates and never double-dates. She smokes, but neither drinks nor dances. She borrows clothes from no one, but loans them to Nos. 1, 2, 17, and 16.

Her troubles, unlike her clothes, are her own; she shares them with no one. No. 8 has a very adaptable personality. She listens readily but never puts herself forward. She has a very perceptive mind and sees most situations very clearly. She feels that those in authority are usually correct, that rules should be obeyed. After 11 p.m. she can be found in her own room. Usually, however, she is not alone. Some girls drop in to borrow clothes, others to talk about various subjects, or to discuss personal problems. This girl goes home on weekends quite a bit, but never takes any of the other girls with her.

Girl No. 9 dates occasionally—sometimes double-dating with No. 6. She smokes, dances, and drinks. Food and liquor are shared with Nos. 4, 6, 10, and sometimes 17. Her troubles are shared with No. 4. She borrows clothes from Nos. 4, 6, 10 and loans clothes to these same girls. After 11 p.m. she can be found in either Nos. 4 or 10's room.

Girl No. 10 dates occasionally. She smokes and dances. She sometimes brings into the dormitory liquor, which is shared with Nos. 4, 6, 9, and sometimes 17. Clothes are borrowed from Nos. 4, 6, and 9. She also lends clothes to these same girls. Her problems are shared with No. 4. Although she sometimes shares food with No. 2 she apparently dislikes No. 2 and also No. 12. She is pleasant, but not overly attractive. Apparently, she has more money than is good for her, because she tries to buy friendship and seems to believe that she can buy her way through life. Though capable of carrying on a serious and intelligent discussion, she sometimes tries to attract attention by telling dirty stories. After 11 p.m. she can be found in her own room or in No. 4's.

Girl No. 11 often dates—sometimes double-dating with Nos. 1 and 5. She dances, smokes, and drinks; she is, in fact, the procurer of liquor that is shared with Nos. 1, 5, 15, and sometimes 17. Her troubles are shared with No. 1. Sometimes this girl stays out after hours and is aided in entering the dormitory by No. 1. She seldom studies—when she does, it is a cram session with No. 15. She is a very flashy person who talks at a terrific rate about men, clothes, and parties and enjoys telling dirty stories. Apparently she dislikes No. 16 and sometimes talks about her in a derogatory manner. After 11 p.m. she can be found in her own room or in No. 1's.

Girl No. 12 seldom dates. She does not smoke, drink, or dance. She is very active in her student religious council. She studies hard—sometimes reminding the other girls about study or quiet hours. When she does say something about quiet hours, Nos. 1 and 10, who seem to resent her presence, generally make some sarcastic remark to one of their friends. This girl shares food with Nos. 3, 7, 14, and sometimes 2 and 16. She lends clothes to No. 14. She is a "nice, clean-cut" young lady—neat, ladylike, modest, and possessed of strong moral convictions. When she has a personal problem, she goes to see either No. 8 or her religious leader. After 11 p.m. she can be found in her own room.

Girl No. 13 is quite attractive, but never dates. She smokes, but does not drink or dance. She borrows clothes from no one; neither does she lend clothes. In her room are a number of books (both fiction and nonfiction), but no one ever asks to borrow any of them. Just as her books are her own, so are her problems—she shares with no one. After 11 p.m. she may be found in her own room. Although she has an "A" average, she never reminds the other girls about quiet hours. It has been said that if she did there would be some sort of an explosion.

Girl No. 14 seldom dates. She does not smoke, drink, or dance. Clothes are sometimes borrowed from No. 12. Food is shared with Nos. 3, 7, and 12, and sometimes Nos. 2 and 16. Her problems are shared with No. 12. After 11 p.m. she can generally be found in room No. 12.

Girl No. 15 dates occasionally but never double-dates. She dances, smokes, and drinks—sharing liquor with Nos. 1, 5, 11, and sometimes 17. Food is shared with these same three girls and also with No. 2 and sometimes 17. Occasionally this girl stays out of the dormitory after hours and is helped in by No. 1. She borrows clothes from No. 11 and sometimes shares her problems with this girl. She also shares her problems with No. 1. After 11 p.m. she can generally be found in the room of either Nos. 1 or 11.

Girl No. 16 is the oldest one on the floor. She is rather mannish and aggressive and is not interested in men. Consequently, she never dates. Neither does she smoke, drink, or dance. She apparently likes to wrestle with the other girls, especially with No. 2. She does, in fact, spend a great deal of time with No. 2. She sometimes shares food with Nos. 3, 12, 7, 14, and 2. After 11 p.m. she can be found in the room of either Nos. 2 or 11. When she has a problem, she goes to Nos. 2 or 11. No. 11, however, would not readily invite No. 16 to one of her parties.

Girl No. 17 has occasional dates, but never double-dates. She smokes, drinks, and dances. She is wealthy, well-traveled, and sophisticated, and has been characterized as a skeptic. Sometimes she borrows clothes from No. 8, with whom she shares her problems. The girl has an inquiring mind and is quite mature. She never seems to condemn anyone for their actions. In her room are a number of "nontext" books that no one seems to borrow. After 11 p.m. she can be found in the room of either Nos. 4, 8, or 11.

CAMPUS DEVELOPMENT EXERCISE

The following exercise is a modification of an exercise developed by Allen Zolb. The exercise involves five organizations that own a total of sixteen plots of land. They must trade, buy, and sell land from one another in order to achieve their objectives. During this activity a wide range of phenomena occur within each group and among groups; besides a focus on power and intergroup conflict internal decision making and controversy may be examined. The situation is such that five organizations are attempting to reach specified objectives and can do so only by interacting with one another. The objectives of the exercise are to examine the management of power among groups and to examine all aspects of group problem solving. The procedure for coordinator of the exercise is as follows:

1. Have the participants form into five groups of eight members (six members and two observers). Then give the observers the Observation Note Form, page 455 in Appendix E. Read the following statement to the participants: "Our activity for this session is called 'Campus Development.' The exercise is concerned with five organizations that own a total of sixteen plots of land just north of the central campus of a college. The organizations represent a fraternity, the college faculty club, the college housing office, a private investment company, and the local city government. Each group holds a certain combination of the plots and desires to own land in a different combination. Each group begins with a statement of its present position and goal, its deeds to each piece of land owned, its option forms, and, in some cases, its financial assets. From this point on, the groups must depend on their own resources." Activity in each group is to be closely followed by the observers. The observers are not to take part in the activity—they simply watch it and report back later.

2. Explain option forms and their use as follows:

   a. According to Webster, an option is "a stipulated privilege of buying or selling a stated property, security, or commodity at a given price within a specified time."

   b. For this privilege (or option) the buyer pays an agreed upon sum of money. This money, depending upon the agreement, may or may not be applied against the total purchase price.

   c. During the time the option is in effect, the property owner may not dispose of the property to any party other than the option holder unless the option holder has specifically released the owner from the option obligations.

   d. If, after taking an option, the prospective buyer does not complete the purchase within the specified time (five minutes or less), the property and the money paid for the option are the sole possession of the property owner.

   e. In short, the option may be considered a binder or perhaps a nonrefundable down payment.

   f. In using the option, an Option-to-Buy agreement should be written and given to the prospective buyer.

3. State and clarify the following ground rules:

   a. Land held by each group at the beginning should be marked by shaded areas on a large map posted above each group's meeting place.

   b. All plots are equal in land area and desirability. (Mountains and swamps have a way of appearing when this is not pre-established.)

   c. There is no problem in gaining access to any plot. (Easements are assumed.)

   d. Whole plots must be sold.

   e. Some of the organizations involved will be trying to get "adjacent" plots. For this exercise, two plots are adjacent if they have a common side (not just a common point). If more than one adjacent plot is required, the combinations are limitless because each additional plot becomes adjacent to the preceding one, which is already adjacent.

    f. If any agreements are reached, the actual deeds, money, option forms, etc., should change hands.

    g. Advise the participants that you can answer questions and rule on disagreements during the exercise.

    h. Set a definite time for the groups to reassemble. It is important that the groups feel pressed for time.

4. Ask for and answer any questions on the ground rules.

5. Distribute the prepared envelopes containing information and assets to the five participating groups (pp. 457 to 465, Appendix E) and start exercise.

6. Allow thirty minutes for negotiations.

7. End exercise and begin feedback and critique, relying heavily upon observers. Give each group a chance to comment on its operations. Focus on the use of power among groups.

GROUP POWER EXERCISE

The group stands in a circle. Each person helps with one hand to hold a sheet of paper. No talking or verbal communication is allowed in this exercise. At a prearranged signal, the paper represents "power." See what happens and discuss.

DOMINANCE AND SUBMISSIVENESS EXERCISE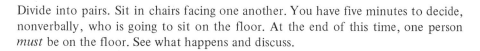

Divide into pairs. Sit in chairs facing one another. You have five minutes to decide, nonverbally, who is going to sit on the floor. At the end of this time, one person *must* be on the floor. See what happens and discuss.

POWER FANTASY

Sit in a circle. Each of you close your eyes and picture the group in which you are a member. Now, in your fantasy, begin a game of follow-the-leader. At first see yourself as leader and note what happens among the followers. Now shift leaders and see someone else at the head of the line. Keep going until all members of your group have had a chance to be the leader. Then open your eyes and discuss the following questions: What kinds of things did different people ask the group to do? What feelings did you imagine among the followers? How did you picture the group behaving when you were the leader? Who seemed to most "natural" in the role? Who seemed the least "natural" in the role?

LOW–POWER FANTASY

Sit in a circle. Each of you close your eyes and imagine yourself as someone who lives in a small rural village. You have been handed an important message to deliver to someone in a neighboring, much more powerful village. You begin to walk to the other village. You pass a girl on a bridge. You pass a man on a bicycle. You pass a family having a picnic. You hear the sound of birds singing, trees moving in the breeze, you smell the grass and the earth. Rounding a bend, you suddenly come upon a wall. It continues in both directions as far as you can see. The village you need to get to is beyond the wall. Think of what happens for a few minutes. Then open your eyes and share stories of what happened at the wall. Discuss, from the standpoint of power.

PICTURE EXERCISE

Divide into groups of four members. Make a picture or collage of power, using resources available—such as magazines, pencils, paints, crayons, newspapers, and so forth. At the end of thirty minutes discuss the pictures of each group. If Polaroid cameras are available, instead of making a picture of power go out and take a picture of power. Then come back and discuss.

INFLUENCE LINEUP

This exercise is for a group that has been working together on a task. Stand in a line according to how you see yourselves as most powerful to least powerful. Before beginning mark one end of line as the spot for the most powerful so that everybody will know how to arrange themselves. After the line has stabilized, ask if anyone wants to move himself to a different location from where he is now. Discuss the self-perceptions and perceptions of others. How does your power as perceived by other members compare with how you see it? Were there disagreements among members about who is the most powerful? Does the group have certain biases about power, such as the richest person being seen as the most powerful?

POWER AND CONFLICT

An intimate relationship exists between power and conflict. The use of power is always present in personal and group interaction. Group conflict does not exist, however, unless a group member wants something to happen that she does not have the power to make happen. If a person wants group members to do something and has the power to make them do it, there is no conflict. Also, if the person wants group members to do something and they want to do it, though she does not have the power to make sure they do it, there is no conflict. But if a person wants other group members to do something and they do not want to do it, and she does not have enough power to overcome their unwillingness, then a state of conflict exists. The successful attempt to use power can often end a conflict. The successful attempt to influence the group is one that helps resolve conflicts, whereas the unsuccessful attempt can increase the conflict. Conflicts are also increased when the desire to influence is not matched by the capacity to influence.

The destructive management of conflict is characterized by less and less mutual influence among group members. In a conflict situation that is being badly managed, information and expertise power are apt to be rejcted because each participant sees the other as being untrustworthy and as trying to use his knowledge or expertise for personal goals. Hostility and distrust undermine legitimate power. The emphasis on differences among group members decreases mutual referent power. Reward power can arouse suspicions of bribery or of being attempts to increase one's dependence upon another. When the bases for these kinds of influence deteriorate, those with power begin to rely more and more on the use of coercive power.

The use of a coercive power base is destructive in managing conflicts for many reasons. It exacerbates the conflict, thereby increasing hostility, resentment, lies, threats, retaliation, revenge, and distrust. Threats often lead to aggression and counterthreats. Coercion and threat can sometimes cut short or control a conflict simply by getting behavioral compliance or by forcing a group member to leave the situation, but it will never lead to a productive resolution and cooperation. Communication decreases and becomes less reliable. Mutual influence also decreases, and the likelihood of a mutually satisfying settlement is diminished. Thus, whenever possible, attempts to exercise influence through the use of a coercive power base should be avoided in conflicts. One central strategy to resolve or control a conflict is to reestablish mutual influence among all those in the group.

Below is a test of your understanding of the preceding section (answers on page 231):

1. In which instance does conflict exist?
   a. If a person wants the other group members to do something and has the power to make them do it.
   b. If a person wants other group members to do something, does not have the power to make them do it, but they want to do it.
   c. If a person wants other group members to do something they don't want to do, and the person doesn't have enough power to make them do it.

True False   2. The successful use of power can end a conflict.

True False   3. In a conflict situation that is badly managed, information and expertise are apt to be the only powers accepted.

True False   4. The use of coercive power lessens the conflict.

True False   5. The more punishment is used, the less chance there is of an agreement being reached.

True False   6. A central strategy to resolve a conflict is to reestablish mutual influence in the group.

YOUR POWER BEHAVIOR

You have now participated in a series of exercises on power as well as having read a summary of much of the current theory and research on the use of power. Power has been discussed in several previous chapters. At this point divide into groups of three. Within the group, discuss what you have learned about yourself and your behavior in relation to power situations. What are your feelings when you are being opposed and have to rely upon power to further your goals? How do you feel when others quickly conform to what you wish them to do? How do you react when other people force you to comply to their wishes? What basis of power do you usually rely upon? Have you ever been manipulated or conned? What did it feel like? Any question about power and its use should be discussed if it increases your self-understanding and your understanding of the other members of your group. Write down your conclusions about yourself and your use of power.

CHECKLIST OF SKILLS

____ I can apply my knowledge of power to my group behavior.

____ I can tell the difference between influence and manipulation.

____ I can use both outcome and information dependence in influencing other individuals.

____ I know how to determine my goals for being a member of a group.

____ I can identify my resources for accomplishing my goals.

____ I can negotiate coalitions with other group members to help achieve my goals.

____ I can influence others through reward, coercive, legitimate, referent, expert, or informational power, depending upon the situation.

____ I can improve the problem solving of a group by promoting equalization of power.

____ I can improve the problem solving of a group by promoting the use of expert and informational power rather than legitimate or referent power.

____ I can identify the problems both high- and low-power members have when power is unequally distributed within a group.

____ I can control myself and avoid the use of coercive power when I am in a conflict.

____ I can help establish mutual influence between two group members who are in conflict.

The skills I need more work on are: _____

_____

_____

_____

ANSWERS

Page 205:   1: b; 2: a; 3: a; 4: c, e; 5: b, d; 6: false; 7: false; 8: true; 9: true.
Page 212:   1: c; 2: f; 3: b; 4: e; 5: d; 6: a.
Page 215:   1: e; 2: c, d.
Page 220:   1: false; 2: false; 3: b; 4: b; 5: a; 6: a; 7: b; 8: b; 9: e; 10: b, d.
Page 229:   1: c; 2: true; 3: false; 4: false; 5: true; 6: true.

9

Cohesion and Norms

Two important aspects of group effectiveness are the cohesion of the group and the group norms. In this chapter we will review the process by which cohesion and group norms are developed and maintained within a group. Because cohesion is the primary factor in keeping a group in existence, it is of particular interest and significance when discussing group effectiveness. And because group norms influence the behavior of all members, they, also, are of particular significance in examining group effectiveness. The cohesion and norms of the group largely make up the working climate within which members function. We shall take up group cohesion first and then group norms.

What is group cohesion? How do you tell when your group has a sufficient amount of cohesion? How do you tell when your group does not have sufficient cohesion? The attractiveness of group membership for each member refers to the cohesion of the group. *Group cohesion* can be defined as the sum of all the factors influencing members to stay in the group; it is the result of the positive forces of attraction toward the group outweighing the negative forces of repulsion away from the group.

A person's attraction to a group is determined by his assessment of the desirable and undesirable consequences of group membership. The more favorable the outcomes he can expect from membership, the more he will be attracted to the group. The outcomes expected from membership in a given group depend upon such factors as the nature of the group and its goals, how clearly the goals are stated, how clearly the paths for goal attainment are marked, how likely it is that the goal will be successfully achieved, how the characteristics of the group relate to the person's needs and values, how well the group members cooperate, and whether membership in other groups would provide greater benefits. Cohesion is constantly changing because different members will be attracted to the group in different degrees and the same person's attraction toward the group will vary at different times. Each event that occurs in the group alters the cohesion of the group to some extent.

The level of group cohesion is indicated in several ways. Attendance by group members, whether members arrive on time, the trust and support present among group members, the amount of individuality accepted in the group, the amount of fun members have, all may reflect the cohesion of the group. Cohesion can also be measured just by asking members whether they like one another, whether they want to continue their membership, whether they are sure they can work effectively with the other group members in the future.

How is group cohesion increased? There are several methods for doing so. Probably the most effective is to structure cooperative relationships among group members. Because this method was analyzed in the chapter on group goals, it will not be discussed here. Other ways in which group cohesion can be strengthened are to deepen the trust among group members, to further the affection expressed among members, to increase the expressions of mutual inclusion and acceptance among group members, to expand the mutual influence of group members, and to promote group norms that encourage the expression of individuality among group members. Each of these will be discussed in this chapter.

Quickly check your reading of this section by answering the following questions (answers on page 255):

1. What is group cohesion?
   a. The result of all forces acting on members to stay with the group.
   b. The result of all forces acting on groups to stay with the task.
   c. The result of all forces acting as a deterrent on negative behavior.

True   False   2. Cohesion rarely changes in a group.

3. How can you tell if a group has cohesion?
   a. By how often a group meets.
   b. By how well the group accomplishes its tasks.
   c. By whether members like either other and want to stay in the group.

4. How can cohesion be built in a group?
   a. By having divergent members express their feelings openly.
   b. By cooperativeness, trust, and acceptance.
   c. By everyone working hard on the task.

YOUR COHESION BEHAVIOR

How does your behavior affect group cohesion? When you want to increase group cohesion what do you do? How would you describe your behavior in influencing group cohesion? The following questions should help you reflect upon how your behavior influences the cohesion of the groups to which you belong. Answer each question as honestly as possible.

1. I try to make sure that everyone enjoys being a member of the group.
   Never 1 : 2 : 3 : 4 : 5 : 6 :(7): 8 : 9 Always
2. I disclose my ideas, feelings, and reactions to what is currently taking place within the group.
   Never 1 :(2): 3 : 4 : 5 : 6 : 7 : 8 : 9 Always
3. I express acceptance and support when other members disclose their ideas, feelings, and reactions to what is currently taking place in the group.
   Never 1 : 2 : 3 : 4 : 5 : 6 :(7): 8 : 9 Always
4. I try to make all members feel valued and appreciated.
   Never 1 : 2 : 3 : 4 : 5 : 6 :(7): 8 : 9 Always
5. I try to include other members in group activities.
   Never 1 : 2 : 3 : 4 : 5 : 6 :(7): 8 : 9 Always
6. I am influenced by other group members.
   Never 1 : 2 : 3 : 4 :(5): 6 : 7 : 8 : 9 Always
7. I take risks in expressing new ideas and current feelings.
   Never 1 : 2 : 3 : 4 : 5 : 6 : 7 :(8): 9 Always
8. I express liking, affection, and concern for other members.
   Never 1 : 2 : 3 : 4 :(5): 6 : 7 : 8 : 9 Always
9. I encourage group norms that support individuality and personal expression.
   Never 1 : 2 : 3 : 4 : 5 : 6 : 7 : 8 : 9 Always

The questions above focus upon several aspects of increasing group cohesion. The first question deals with a general attempt to keep cohesion high. Questions 2 and 3 pertain to the expression of ideas and feelings and the support for others expressing ideas and feelings; such personal participation is essential for cohesiveness and for the development of trust. Questions 4 and 8 also focus upon support for, and liking of, other group members. Question 5 refers to including other members, and Question 6 takes up one's willingness to be influenced by other members. Questions 7 and 9 center on the acceptance of individuality within the group. All these factors are important for group cohesion. Discuss your answers with another group member. Then add all your answers together to get a total cohesion score. Keep your responses to these questions in mind as you proceed through this chapter.

MEMBER NEEDS AND GROUP DEVELOPMENT EXERCISE

People need other people. A person is a social being who depends on other individuals for his humanness (Johnson, 1973). All human beings, because they live in a society, must establish a social balance between themselves and their associates. This social nature of man gives rise to certain interpersonal needs. Three are basic: inclusion, control, and affection (Schutz, 1958). Every group, no matter what its purpose or who its members are, has to deal with these three needs. The *inclusion* need centers around membership, who is "in" and who is "out," who is included and who is excluded, who belongs and who does not, who is part of togetherness and who is not. Some people want the group to be very inclusive, other members want it to be loosely knit. The *control* need pertains to power relations in the group, who has influence over the other group members, who has authority. Some members will want a great deal of influence, others may not want to influence anyone. The *affection* need has to do with how close and personal the relations in the group will be. Some members may want a close, warm group, other members may want a rather cool and distant group atmosphere.

You may check your reading of this section by answering the following question (answers on page 255):

Match the three basic interpersonal needs with their examples.

c 1. Inclusion.
b 2. Control.
a 3. Affection.

a. Linda wants a warm group and Ralph and Jack do not.
b. Roger influences the group and Jeanne does not.
c. Sam belongs to the group and John does not.

The following exercise developed by Duane Meyer highlights these three areas of personal needs and group issues. Its purpose is to provide direct experiences with inclusion, control, and affection. It can be conducted within two hours. For the coordinator, the procedure is as follows:

1. Introduce the exercise as a microlab on the three needs of inclusion, control, and affection. A brief review of the material above may be helpful. Explain that the exercise has three rounds.

2. *Round 1:*
   a. Have the participants mill around the room for awhile, and then form into groups of three. They are to decide in their minds who was the most influential in bringing the triad together, point at that person, and talk about how they decided to be together.
   b. The participants should again mill around the room. Ask them to close their eyes, continue milling, and with eyes closed find the other two members of their triad. When all the groups are reformed, have them talk about the experience.
   c. Each triad should decide on which one of its members is to leave. They have two minutes to eliminate a member. The person eliminated from the group should move to the end of the room and sit quietly, reflect on his feelings, and not interact with the others. Publicly interview the "orphans" to find

out what kind of decision-making process resulted in their being selected as the ones to leave the threesome.

    d. Ask the pairs to decide on which new person they will invite to join them. They may not claim back the person they have just eliminated. At your signal, pairs should move to the end of the room and claim the person they want to join them.

    e. Have the threesomes verbally express some sort of affection to one another.

    f. Combine the triads into groups of six and have them share their feelings about their experiences so far.

3. *Round 2:*

    a. Have the triads decide on who in their group is to be A, who is to be B, and who C—and reflect on how their decisions were made. Who influenced the decisions the most?

    b. The C's, without talking, are to take a pose representing a statue. The A's are to continue building the statue by assuming a posture in harmony with C's. Prohibit talking while this is going on. The B's are to complete the statue by assuming a pose in harmony with C's and A's. Now break up the statue. Have them talk with one another about their nonverbal interaction while creating a statue, and how they influenced one another by the poses they assumed.

    c. Allow the triads two minutes to again decide on which one of them will leave the group. The "singles" are to gather at the far end of the room for instructions. Tell the pairs to sit knee to knee with each other, talk to each other about their feelings and reactions to the exercise thus far, or to hold a conversation about whatever interests them both. Instruct the singles (out of hearing of the pairs) to pick a pair, approach it, and watch in what ways they are or are not included by the pair. When all or most of the singles have become a part of the ongoing conversation, stop the participants and have a general discussion on the experiences of the "newcomers."

    d. Have the triads express nonverbally some sort of affection to one another.

    e. In groups of six, ask them to talk about their feelings and reactions to Round 2.

4. *Round 3:*

    a. Ask each triad to find quickly something that makes it unique and distinctive from all others in the room and announce what they have picked.

    b. Have each member recall an impressive moment of quiet beauty and share that memory with the others in their triad.

    c. Give each triad two minutes to decide which one of its members shall leave. Have those cast adrift gather in the center of the room and sit quietly on the floor; the pairs are to form a circle around them. Inform the participants that the pairs are to whisper together to decide (1) whether to pick anyone from the center and (2) if they do, who it should be (it cannot be their former triad member). Ask the singles to decide (1) whether to pick a new group to join and (2) which group it should be (it cannot be their former group). All are asked to make clear decisions and stick to them. At your signal, everybody is asked to demonstrate the choice they have made. If anyone is left (individuals or pairs who did not choose and were not chosen), they are to be interviewed about the result of their choices and the feelings they are having about their immediate situation. Then ensure that everyone is in triads.

d. Have triad members find some way to express verbally and nonverbally their affection toward one another.

e. In groups of six, have them discuss their feelings and reactions to Round 3.

5. Ask the participants to reflect on the experiences of all three rounds and tell what they have learned personally to the other members of their final triad. They should use the following questions as a guide:

a. What were all the feelings they remember having throughout the exercise?

b. Around each feeling, what was happening? Were there any patterns of reactions in the situations?

c. When approaching a new group what were they usually feeling?

d. When approaching a new group what was their usual behavior?

e. When eliminating a member of their group what were they usually feeling?

f. When they were being eliminated from a group what were they usually feeling?

g. When they were expressing affection what did they usually feel in addition to the affection?

h. When they were receiving affection what did they usually feel?

i. When they were influencing a decision, how did they usually feel and behave?

j. When they were being influenced, how did they usually feel and behave?

INCLUSION, CONTROL, AND AFFECTION

The need for inclusion is the need people have to keep a satisfactory relationship between themselves and others with respect to interaction or belongingness. This is the membership issue of groups. Some people like to be with other people all the time; others seek much less contact, preferring to be alone and keep their privacy. Membership behavior has two aspects: trying to include other members in what is taking place within the group, and wanting other members to try to include you. Because inclusion involves the process of forming relationships, it usually comes first in the life of a group. A person with little need for inclusion may be called undersocial; he tends to be introverted and withdrawn. The oversocial person is the opposite extreme; she tends toward extraversion. During the membership phase of the group's formation and development, it is important for the question "Who am I with these other people?" to be answered by each member. When all have a sense of identification with the group, the membership issue is resolved. A group observer will notice this when statements shift from "I—others" to "we."

Control problems usually follow those of inclusion in the development of a group. Once a group has formed, it begins to differentiate among members.

Different people take or seek different roles, and often power struggles and influence become central issues. The need for control is the need people have to keep a satisfactory relation among themselves with regard to power or influence. Every person has a need to control his environment to some degree, so that it will be predictable for him. Ordinarily, this amounts to controlling others, because people are the main agents that threaten an individual's environment and create an unpredictable and uncontrollable situation. This need for control varies from those who want to control their entire environment, including all the people around them, to those who want to control no one in any situation, no matter how appropriate control would be. The person who is extremely low on control—an "abdicrat"—is one who tends to be submissive and does not accept power and responsibility in her interpersonal behavior. This person drifts toward the subordinate position where she will not have to take responsibility for making decisions, and where someone else takes charge. The person who is extremely high on control is called an "autocrat" and is a person who is very dominating. This person wants to be at the top of a power hierarchy. She is the power seeker, and is afraid people will not be influenced or controlled by her and will therefore come to dominate her. The person in the middle feels comfortable both in giving or receiving influence, as it fits the situation. There are two aspects of control in a group: the degree to which one controls others, and the degree to which one wants to be controlled. Often, issues of control are centered around decision making, with members asking the question "Does it make any difference if I am here or not?" Every member has a preference about the degree to which he needs to control or influence other members and the degree to which he wishes to be controlled or influenced by other members. If leadership is distributed throughout the group, all members will control and be controlled.

Affection is based on the building of emotional ties. As a consequence, it is usually the last phase to emerge in the development of a group. In the inclusion phase, members must encounter one another and decide to continue their relationship. Control needs then require them to confront one another and work out how they will be related. To continue the group relationship, ties of affection must form, and people must embrace one another in order to form a lasting bond. The need for affection is the need a person has to keep a satisfactory relationship between himself and other people regarding love and affection. At one extreme are people who like close, personal relationships with every person they meet. At the other extreme are those who prefer their personal relationships to be quite impersonal and distant, perhaps friendly, but not close and intimate. Affection also has two aspects: the degree to which a person expresses affection toward others, and the degree to which a person wants others to express affection toward him. In a group the issue is one of feeling valued and respected; being accepted is a vital part of membership in the group. The question for members is "How much do I care for these others and how much do they care for me?" Many times this question is answered in the moments after a task is completed successfully by the group—when each member feels he has been working with good people, when there is an awareness of warm feelings and pride in "our" accomplishments. At other times it is answered with just a nice feeling of affection and satisfaction in being together.

You can check your understanding of this section by answering the following questions (answers on page 255).

Match the needs with their definitions:

 1. Inclusion.
 2. Control.
 3. Affection.

a. The need to keep a satisfactory relationship regarding power and influence.

b. The need to keep a satisfactory relationship regarding belonging and interacting.

c. The need to keep a satisfactory relationship regarding liking and loving.

(True) False   4. The two aspects of membership behavior are wanting other members to include you and wanting to be included by other members.

True (False)   5. The two aspects of control are the degree to which you control others and the degree to which others control you.

(True) False   6. The two aspects of affection are the degree to which you express affection toward others and the degree to which you want others to express affection toward you.

(True) False   7. Inclusion involves the process of forming relationships.

(True) False   8. Everyone needs to control his environment.

True (False)   9. If leadership is distributed throughout the group, some members will control and others will be controlled.

True (False)   10. Inclusion needs require people to confront one another and work out how they will be related.

The next nine exercises deal with the three interpersonal needs of group members. Each outlines the procedure for a coordinator to follow.

INCLUSION EXERCISE 1

After the group has had some time together, indicate that the center of the room is for those who definitely feel a part of this group. Have group members place themselves in the room in relation to how they feel. To obtain further information, ask them to stand nearest the people to whom they feel closest. They should then share feelings and perceptions about the placements.

INCLUSION EXERCISE 2

When someone indicates he feels excluded from the group, ask the group to stand in a circle with arms around one another's waist. The excluded person is outside the circle and is instructed to try to get inside. After he succeeds in doing so—or after he tries very hard to do so—discuss his feelings of trying to get inside the circle and the feelings of those who were part of the circle. Have the participants exchange views on what they learned about the group and how it deals with inclusion and exclusion.

AFFECTION EXERCISES

1. Ask each group member to think of an imaginary, meaningful gift for each of the other members. Each member describes the gifts she has selected.

2. Ask group members to focus on one another with three statements: (1) When I look at you I see . . . , (2) I wish you would . . . , and (3) What I really like about you is . . . .

3. Ask the group to stand in a circle and give itself a big hug.

CONTROL EXERCISE 1

Ask the participants to pick an imaginary spot in the center of the room that is theirs. At the signal, each is to try to sit on his spot. Once settled, the group members are to turn to a neighbor and discuss the experience.

CONTROL EXERCISE 2

Ask group members to stand in a circle and touch fingertips with the person on either side of them. Then ask each member to pick a spot in the room to which she would like the group to go. Make it clear to the group members that they must keep fingertip contact and that they may not talk. At the signal, everyone tries to get the group to her chosen spot. Discuss what was learned about the group and how it deals with the control issue.

COHESION EXERCISE 1

Divide the participants into several groups. Give each group fifteen minutes to develop and construct a group symbol, such as a flag or a drawing of the group, and to develop several group traditions that will be carried out in the future. Ask the groups to share these symbols and traditions with one another, each presenting its symbols and traditions in turn. Then ask the groups to analyze the effect these activities have had upon cohesion.

COHESION EXERCISE 2

Review the exercises in the previous chapters. Find exercises in which participants were asked to indicate their satisfaction with the group, their liking for group members, their desire to continue as a member of the group, and other indexes of group cohesion. The exercise on group maintenance in Chapter 2 and the main controversy exercises are examples. Based upon the results of those exercises, have the participants build a theory as to how cohesion may be developed in groups.

COHESION EXERCISE 3

Divide participants into small groups of four to six members. Have them sit with their backs to the center of the group and talk about their impressions of the group. They should then sit facing one another with their eyes closed and discuss who the members of the group are. Ask them to open their eyes and look at one another's hands and discuss what are the most significant things that have recently happened to group members. They are to lie down with their heads toward the center of the group and with your shoulders touching, and describe what they were doing when they were ten and what they were doing when they were fifteen. Raise one arm up and have a group hand dance. Have them discuss what effect each procedure and topic had upon group cohesion. And then say good-bye in a nonverbal way.

COHESION EXERCISE 4

The better relationships are among group members, the more cohesive the group will be. Relationships improve as they become more "open." This exercise focuses upon explaining the difference between open and closed relationships. Have the participants study the diagram on open and closed relationships (Figure 9.1), and then consider in their groups whether the relationships among members are open or closed. They should also discuss how relationships can become more open. Ask for volunteers to practice behaviors that will make relationships among group members more open.

YOUR TRUST–BUILDING BEHAVIOR

Are you building trust in your group? How does your behavior contribute to a high level of group trust? The following is an exercise aimed at providing a comparison between the way in which you see your trust-building behavior and how it is perceived by other group members. The exercise can be conducted in one hour. The procedure for the coordinator is as follows:

1. Introduce the exercise as an opportunity to diagnose the level of group trust and the ways in which the behavior of each member contributes to building and maintaining trust in the group.
2. Instruct the participants to complete the questionnaire "My Group Behavior" given below. After completing the questionnaire the participants are to turn to page 331, Appendix D for scoring instructions. Their scores on the questionnaire are to be entered in Figure 9.2.

3. Instruct the participants to take slips of paper (one for each member of the group) and write on them: (1) Openness and sharing and (2) Acceptance and support. Each group member should fill out a slip on every other group member by giving them ratings between 1 and 7 on the two dimensions (Low 1 : 2 : 3 : 4 : 5 : 6 : 7 High). An example of a completed slip is:

Member receiving feedback: Edythe Johnson
1. Openness and sharing: 1
2. Acceptance and support: 7

---

4. Collect the slips of paper and sort them by name of member to receive the feedback. Compute a group mean for each member by adding the numbers together for each of the dimensions and dividing the totals by the numbers of slips of paper. Then give the group members their means and have them draw the means (using dotted lines) in Figure 9.2.

5. Each member has the results of the questionnaire and the results of the feedback received from his fellow group members. Both have been recorded in Figure 9.2 (self-perception in solid lines, feedback in dotted lines). Ask each group member to answer the following questions. How similar are they? Is there a close match? If not, what factors do you think contribute to the other group members' seeing your behavior differently from the way that you do? How could you modify

FIGURE 9.1 Open and Closed Relationships

Closed ← ——————————————————————————— → *Open*

Content being discussed	The content is of concern to no one within the group, e.g., weather talk.		The content is of concern to some group members.	The content is of concern to all group members.
Time reference	No time reference, e.g., jokes and generalizations	Distant past or future being discussed.	Recent past or future being discussed.	The immediate "here and now" is being discussed.
Disclosure of feelings	Feelings are excluded as irrelevant and inappropriate to group functioning.		Feelings are included as helpful information for group functioning.	
Disclosure of personal information	Personal information is never mentioned; discussion focuses upon generalizations, abstract ideas, and intellectualizations.		Personal information such as attitudes, values, preferences, experiences, are discussed and focused upon.	
Disclosure of relationship information	Relationships among group members are never mentioned; discussion focuses upon generalizations, abstract ideas, and intellectualizations.		Relationships among group members are openly discussed and focused upon.	

your behavior to create a better match between your view of your behavior and theirs? Ask the other group members to discuss their ratings of you and help you brainstorm suggestions for improving the effectiveness of your behavior.

FIGURE 9.2   Johnson Trust Diagram, Part One

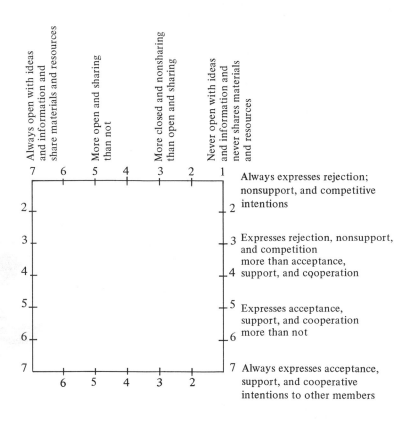

FIGURE 9.3   Johnson Trust Diagram, Part Two

	High Acceptance, Support, and Cooperative Intentions	Low Acceptance, Support, and Cooperative Intentions
High Openness and Sharing	Trusting and trustworthy	Trusting but untrustworthy
Low Openness and Sharing	Distrustful but trustworthy	Distrustful and untrustworthy

MY GROUP BEHAVIOR

The following are a series of questions about your behavior in your group. Answer each question as honestly as you can. There are no right or wrong answers. It is important for you to describe your behavior as accurately as possible.

1. I offer facts, give my opinions and ideas, provide suggestions and relevant information to help the group discussion.

    Never 1 : 2 : 3 : 4 : 5 :(6): 7 Always

2. I express my willingness to cooperate with other group members and my expectations that they will also be cooperative.

    Never 1 :(2): 3 : 4 : 5 : 6 : 7 Always

3. I am open and candid in my dealings with the entire group.

    Never 1 : 2 : 3 :(4): 5 : 6 : 7 Always

4. I give support to group members who are on the spot and struggling to express themselves intellectually or emotionally.

    Never 1 : 2 : 3 : 4 : 5 :(6): 7 Always

5. I keep my thoughts, ideas, feelings, and reactions to myself during group discussions.

    Never 1 :(2): 3 : 4 : 5 : 6 : 7 Always

6. I evaluate the contributions of other group members in terms of whether their contributions are useful to me and whether they are right or wrong.

    Never 1 : 2 : 3 :(4): 5 : 6 : 7 Always

7. I take risks in expressing new ideas and current feelings during a group discussion.

    Never 1 : 2 : 3 : 4 : 5 :(6): 7 Always

8. I communicate to other group members that I am aware of, and appreciate, their abilities, talents, capabilities, skills, and resources.

    Never 1 : 2 : 3 :(4): 5 : 6 : 7 Always

9. I offer help and assistance to anyone in the group in order to bring up the performance of everyone.

    Never 1 : 2 :(3): 4 : 5 : 6 : 7 Always

10. I accept and support the openness of other group members, supporting them for taking risks, and encouraging individuality in group members.

    Never 1 : 2 : 3 : 4 : 5 :(6): 7 Always

11. I share any materials, books, sources of information, or other resources I have with the other group members in order to promote the success of all members and the group as a whole.

    Never (1): 2 : 3 : 4 : 5 : 6 : 7 Always

12. I often paraphrase or summarize what other members have said before I respond or comment.

    Never 1 : 2 : 3 : 4 : 5 :(6): 7 Always

13. I level with other group members.

        Never 1 : 2 : 3 : 4 : (5) : 6 : 7 Always

14. I warmly encourage all members to participate, giving them recognition for their contributions, demonstrating acceptance and openness to their ideas, and generally being friendly and responsive to them.

        Never 1 : 2 : 3 : (4) : 5 : 6 : 7 Always

EXPRESSING SUPPORT EXERCISE

Every group member has considerable positive qualities and resources that can be used to facilitate the accomplishment of the group's goals. Group cohesion and trust are increased when these positive qualities are recognized and utilized. The following exercise is aimed at increasing group members' awareness of own and other's positive resources. The procedure for the coordinator is as follows:

1. Introduce the exercise as an opportunity to increase awareness of the positive resources available in the group. Positive resources refer to any skill, talent, ability, or personal trait of a member that helps the group accomplish its goals.
2. Ask each member to think of all the things she does well, all the things she is proud of having done, all the things for which she feels a sense of accomplishment. Each member is to list all her positive accomplishments and successes of the past.
3. Ask each member to share her list with the group. Group members are to help each other identify the positive resources utilized to accomplish past successes. Group members are then to add any other positive resources they perceive the person to have. A final list of positive resources is made for each group member.
4. Each member next asks the group what might be keeping her from utilizing all her positive resources. The group then explores the ways in which each member can free herself from factors that limit the utilization of positive resources.
5. The group then reviews its current goals and tasks. A discussion is held, which focuses upon how the group can more effectively utilize the positive resources of members to facilitate the accomplishment of the group's goals.

DEVELOPING AND MAINTAINING TRUST

An essential aspect of increasing a group's cohesion is developing and maintaining a high level of trust among group members. The development and maintenance of trust is discussed at length in Johnson (1972) and, therefore, will be only briefly reviewed at this point. If possible, readers should review the treatment of trust in the earlier text before going ahead with this chapter.

Why is trust important? Trust is a necessary condition for stable cooperation and effective communication. The higher the trust the more stable the cooperation and the more effective the communication. A group member will more openly express his thoughts, feelings, reactions, opinions, information, and ideas when the trust level is high. When the trust level is low, group members will be evasive, dishonest, and inconsiderate in their communications. Group members will more honestly and frequently announce their cooperative intentions and contribute to a cooperative effort when they believe they are dealing with highly trustworthy persons. Cooperation and group effectiveness rest upon every member's sharing resources, giving and receiving help, dividing the work, and contributing to the accomplishment of mutual goals. Such behaviors will occur when there is trust that everyone else is contributing to the group's progress and not using members' openness and sharing of resources for personal rather than group gain.

What is trust? Making a choice to trust another member involves the perception that the choice can lead to gains or losses, that whether you will gain or lose depends upon the behavior of the other member, that the loss will be greater than the gain, and that the other member will probably behave in such a way that you will gain rather than lose. Sounds complicated doesn't it? There is nothing simple about trust; it is a complex concept and difficult to explain. An example may help. Imagine you are part of a small group supposed to decide which teachers to rehire for next year. You begin to contribute to the discussion knowing you will gain if you contribute good ideas that other members accept but will lose if your ideas are laughed at and belittled. Whether you gain or lose depends upon the behavior of the other group members. You will feel more hurt if you are laughed at than you will feel satisfaction if your ideas are appreciated. Yet you expect the other group members to consider your ideas and accept them. The issue of trust is expressed in the question every member asks, "If I openly express myself, will what I say be used against me?"

In a goal-oriented group the crucial elements of trust are openness and sharing on the one hand and acceptance, support, and cooperative intentions on the other. Cooperative group work requires openness and sharing, which, in turn, are determined by the expressions of acceptance, support, and cooperative intentions in the group. *Openness* is the sharing of information, ideas, thoughts, feelings, and reactions to the issue the group is pursuing. *Sharing* is the offering of your materials and resources to others in order to help them move the group toward goal accomplishment. *Acceptance* is the communication of high regard for another person and his contributions to the group's work. *Support* is communicating to another person that you recognize her strengths and believe she has the capabilities needed to manage productively the situation she is in. *Cooperative intentions* are the expectations that you are going to behave cooperatively and that every group member will also cooperate in achieving the group's goals. From these definitions, *trusting behavior* may be defined as openness and sharing and *trustworthy behavior* may be defined as expressing acceptance, support, and cooperative intentions. In considering members' trustworthy behavior, it is important to remember that accepting and supporting the contributions of other group members does not mean that you will agree with everything they have to say. You can express acceptance and support for the openness and sharing of other members while at the same time expressing different ideas and opposing points of view. This is an important point in building and maintaining trust.

You may check your understanding of this section by answering the following questions (answers on page 255):

1. Which of the following has some of the elements of trust?
   a. a close friendship developed in the group over a period of time.
   b. a group has decided to tell everything about one another.
   c. there is a risk involved with another person with possible gains or losses.
   d. a mountain climber hanging on a rope over a cliff with his wife holding the other end.
2. In developing and maintaining trust, group members must:
   a. be open about why they joined the group and what their personal problems are.
   b. be open about their reactions to other members and their past relationships with them.
   c. be open about their ideas, thoughts, feelings, and reactions to the issue the group is pursuing.
   d. dangle over a cliff with other group members holding the rope.
3. Trustworthy behavior is defined as:
   a. revealing how you are reacting to the group interaction.
   b. the openness and sharing among group members.
   c. the expression of acceptance, support, and cooperative intentions among group members.
   d. keeping all your appointments with other group members.
4. Trusting behavior is defined as:
   a. loaning your favorite records to other group members.
   b. expressing support, acceptance, and cooperative intentions to other group members.
   c. being open in the group and sharing with other group members.
   d. making sure everyone in the group participates.
5. Support is defined as:
   a. showing another person that you recognize her strengths.
   b. showing another person that you feel he is likable.
   c. showing another person that he is accepted as a group member.
   d. finding the right wall to lean on.

GROUP NORMS

To build and maintain cohesion, groups must institute norms. The way in which positive behaviors become implemented and stabilized in a group is for them to become supported by norms that show what behavior is expected of good group members. Such norms will focus on encouraging trusting and trustworthy behavior;

the expression of individuality and ideas, feelings, and reactions to the group's situation; and the expression of concern and affection among group members.

Norms refer to the common beliefs of the group regarding appropriate behavior for members; they tell, in other words, how members are expected to behave. They are the prescribed modes of conduct and belief that not only guide the behavior of group members, but help group interaction by specifying the kinds of responses that are expected and acceptable in particular situations. All groups have norms, set either formally or informally. A group of students that often parties together, for example, will have common ideas about what is acceptable and unacceptable behavior at a party, about what is expected of everyone. More formally organized groups, such as classrooms, will have norms about absence, arriving late, accomplishing assigned work, about when it is permissible to speak. In any group some norms specify the behavior expected of all group members, and others apply only to people in specific roles. In the classroom, for instance, some norms govern both the teacher's and the students' behavior, but other norms may apply only to the teacher or only to the students. Because norms refer to the expected behavior sanctioned (rewarded or punished) by a group, they have a specific "ought to" or "must" quality: group members must not disrupt the group's work, group members ought to participate in discussions, and so on. The norms of any group vary in importance. Those that are less important for the objectives and values of the group usually allow for a greater range of behavior, and bring less severe pressures for people to conform than do norms that are highly relevant for group functioning.

For a group norm to influence a person's behavior, he must recognize that it exists, be aware that other group members accept and follow the regulation, and accept and follow it himself. At first a person may conform to a group norm because the group typically rewards conforming behavior and punishes nonconforming behavior. Later the person may internalize the norm and conform to it automatically, even when no other group members are present. A regulation that all members should be on time for group meetings, for example, becomes a norm only to the extent that the individual group member accepts it, sees other group members accepting it, and sees them enforce the regulation among themselves. For a more detailed discussion of norms see Johnson (1970) and Watson and Johnson (1972).

Below is a brief check of your understanding of the preceding section (answers on page 255):

1. Norms refer to:
   a. The common beliefs that encourage the expression of individuality in the group.
   b. The common beliefs that encourage conforming behavior in the group.
   c. The common beliefs that tell members how they are expected to behave in the group.

True False   2. Group norms build and keep group cohesion.
True False   3. All groups have norms.
True False   4. Group norms are the same for all the members.

249

In every group certain group norms are vitally necessary for its cohesion and its effectiveness functioning. The following short exercises focus upon diagnosing the norms of your group.

NORM EXERCISE 1

Divide into triads and list five "dos" and five "don'ts" for group members. Then meet as a group and have each triad present its list. In the group as a whole decide on which three norms about "dos" and which three norms about "don'ts" affect group cohesion the most.

NORM EXERCISE 2

Given below is a list of behaviors. For each behavior please indicate how appropriate or inappropriate you think it would be as a norm for your group. Write in the number that shows your best estimate of how the group would feel. Write a "5" if the behavior is definitely appropriate as a norm, write a "4" if the behavior is somewhat appropriate, a "3" if it is questionable, a "2" if it is somewhat inappropriate, and a "1" if it is definitely inappropriate.

_____ 1. Said little or nothing in most meetings.

_____ 2. Talked about the details of her sex life.

_____ 3. Brought up problems he had with others who weren't in the group.

_____ 4. Kissed another group member.

_____ 5. Asked for reactions or feedback (how do you see me in this group?).

_____ 6. Talked mostly about what was going on in the group.

_____ 7. Frequently joked.

_____ 8. Pleaded for help.

_____ 9. Challenged other members' remarks.

_____10. Said she was not getting anything from being in the group.

_____11. Described his reactions to what was taking place in the group.

_____12. Highlighted opposition among ideas.

_____13. Formed a contract with another member about the use of each other's resources in meeting both their needs and goals.

_____14. Refused to be bound by a group decision.

_____15. Asked for the goal to be clarified.

_____16. Noted competition in the group and asked how it could be reduced.

_____17. Gave advice to other group members about what to do.

_____18. Interrupted a dialogue going on between two members.

_____19. Told another member that she was unlikable.

_____20. Was often absent.

_____ 21. Shouted with anger at another member.

_____ 22. With strong feelings, told another member how likable he was.

_____ 23. Tried to manipulate the group to get her own way.

_____ 24. Hit another group member.

_____ 25. Acted indifferently to other members.

_____ 26. Dominated the group's discussion for more than one session.

_____ 27. Encouraged other group members to react to the topic being discussed.

_____ 28. Tried to convince members of the rightness of a certain point of view.

_____ 29. Talked a lot without showing his real feelings.

_____ 30. Told the group off, saying that it was worthless.

_____ 31. Showed she had no intention of changing her behavior.

_____ 32. Resisted the suggestions of other members on procedures.

_____ 33. Commented that the decision-making procedure was not appropriate to the nature of the decision.

_____ 34. Asked that the causes of a group problem be analyzed.

_____ 35. Expressed affection for several group members.

After reacting to these items the group members may think of other behavioral norms to include. Once each member has rated the group norms, the group should discuss them and decide how each affects the cohesion of the group.

NORMS AND POWER

Group norms often serve as substitutes for influence among group members (Thibaut and Kelley, 1959). Both the weaker and the stronger members tend to gain from having mutually acceptable norms that introduce regularity and control into their relationship without making direct interpersonal application of power necessary. The high-power members do not encounter the resistance and lack of wholehearted cooperation that often comes from applying power in forceful ways. And the low-power members have more of a chance to influence the high-power members through the norms that specify their expected behavior and the limits to the use of power. Norms are a protection against the capricious or inconsistent use of influence by high-power members, and they free the high-power members from constantly checking the behavior of low-power members to make sure they are conforming. Norms carry weight because they embody some of the personal power given up by group members. People let themselves be influenced by norms in ways that they would never permit themselves to be influenced by others, as norms often take on the characteristics of moral obligations. At the very least, conformity to group norms is a requirement for continued membership in the group.

At this point stop and think about your group. What group norms serve as a substitute for the use of power? Ask other group members what their answers are to this question. Try to build a set of conclusions about how norms influence group members and serve as a substitute for the direct application of power.

IMPLEMENTATION OF GROUP NORMS

There are several ways in which norms can be started in a group (Johnson, 1970). Frequently, a norm is initiated into a group by a member directly stating it and telling other members to accept it. A member, for example, might say "I think we should express our feelings openly about this topic" and tell other members to do so. Norms can also be initiated through modeling, wherein members learn to conform to a group norm by watching others conform. Modeling is discussed in Johnson (1970 and 1972). Norms can also be imported from other groups. People usually learn cultural norms of social responsibility (you should help someone who is in need of help), fair play (don't kick someone when he's down), reciprocity (if someone does you a favor, you should do her a favor in return) from others, and these cultural norms can be incorporated into one's own group. All in all, however, perhaps the most effective way of starting group norms is through group discussion.

Johnson (1970) presents a set of general guidelines for the establishment and support of group norms. They are:

1. For members to accept group norms, they must recognize that they exist, see that the other members accept and follow them, and feel some internal commitment to them.
2. Members will accept and internalize norms to the extent that they see them as helping accomplish the goals and tasks to which they are committed. It is helpful, therefore, for a group to clarify how conformity to a norm will help goal accomplishment.
3. Members will accept and internalize norms for which they feel a sense of ownership. Generally, members will support and accept norms that they have helped set up.
4. Group members should enforce the norms on each other immediately after a violation. Enforcement should also be as consistent as possible.
5. Appropriate models and examples for conforming to the group norms should be present. Members should have the chance to practice the desired behaviors.
6. Cultural norms that help in goal accomplishment and group maintenance and growth should be imported into the group.
7. Because norms exist only to help group effectiveness, they should be flexible so that at any time more appropriate norms can be substituted.

In your group review the material above. Divide into groups of three and plan how to implement at least two norms in the group. Then reconvene as a large group and discuss any topic of interest while each triad attempts to implement its norms into the group.

CONSEQUENCES OF GROUP COHESIVENESS

A variety of research studies indicate that group cohesiveness has several definite consequences upon a group (Cartwright, 1968; Watson and Johnson, 1972). As cohesiveness increases, so, too, does the capacity of a group to keep its members—and the longer the group keeps its members, the greater the likelihood is that the group will achieve its goals. Highly cohesive groups are characterized by low turnover in membership and low absenteeism. They are less likely to be disrupted as a group when one member does decide to leave. Members of highly cohesive groups attend meetings more faithfully and remain members longer. As cohesiveness increases, there is a corresponding rise in the participation of all group members—and the greater the participation of members, the more resources are available to the group to help goal accomplishment. Members of cohesive groups participate more readily in group meetings.

As cohesiveness increases, members also become more committed to the group's goals, accept assigned tasks and roles more readily, and conform to group norms more frequently. Members of cohesive groups put a greater value on the group's goals and stick more closely to the group's norms than do members of groups lacking cohesion. They are also more eager to protect the group's norms by putting pressure on or rejecting people who violate them. They are more loyal to the group and more willing to work toward a common goal. Unlike members of loosely assembled groups, members of cohesive groups more often take on group responsibilities, persist longer in working toward difficult goals, are more motivated to accomplish the group's tasks (if for no other reason than to live up to the expectations of their fellow group members), and are more satisfied with the work of the group. When the norms of a group favor productivity, those that are highly cohesive are more productive in accomplishing goals and in completing assigned tasks. Moreover, group members communicate more frequently and effectively in highly cohesive groups. They are more likely to influence one another in making decisions, to be more willing to listen to other members, to be more willing to accept the opinions of the other members, and to be more willing to be influenced by other members. They are also more willing to endure pain or frustration in behalf of the group and more willing to defend the group against external criticism or attack.

Highly cohesive groups are a source of security for members; they serve to reduce anxiety and to heighten self-esteem. Members of highly cohesive groups experience greater security and relief from tension in the group than do members of noncohesive groups. The awareness that one is liked, accepted, and valued, and that other people hold similar goals and values, are important aspects of psychological health. A person's acceptance by other group members is related to his participation in the group in an important way—the greater the group's acceptance, the more likely he is to participate, and the acceptance of the group becomes much more important psychologically *after* a person has disclosed himself to the group through participation. Acceptance and approval are of utmost importance for any group member.

Although cohesive groups may show greater acceptance, intimacy, and understanding, there is also evidence that they allow greater development and expression of hostility and conflict than do noncohesive groups. Unless antagonism is openly expressed and conflicts are openly resolved, persistent and impenetrable hostile attitudes may develop that will increasingly hamper effective member cooperation and interaction. The result of a hostile attitude is often an avoidance of and an irrational dislike for the ideas of other members—and a refusal to communicate with them. At the most fundamental level, a person simply does not enjoy being with someone she dislikes, and the resulting lack of communication bars chances for the conflict to be resolved. These circumstances have been found to apply between groups as well as between members of a group. Cohesiveness affects such behavior, because when the degree of cohesiveness is considerable, the members must mean enough to one another that they are willing to bear the discomfort of working through the conflict. Regardless of how angry they become, members of cohesive groups are more apt to continue communication, which enables a group to resolve conflicts and capitalize upon controversies, both of which increase its productivity. Not only are members of cohesive groups better able to express hostility, but there is also evidence that they are better able to express hostility toward the leader (Pepitone and Reichling, 1955; Wright, 1943). All in all, cohesiveness in a group results in a better group, where members work more cooperatively on the task and work out group difficulties.

Here is a brief true-and-false test to check your understanding of the above section (answers on page 255):

True (False) 1. Highly cohesive groups will have low membership turnover and high absenteeism.

(True) False 2. Highly cohesive group members stick closely to the group norms.

(True) False 3. Members of highly cohesive groups work harder.

True (False) 4. Members influence each other less in highly cohesive groups.

True (False) 5. Members have more anxiety and less self-esteem in highly cohesive groups.

(True) False 6. Highly cohesive groups have greater expressed hostility and conflict.

YOUR COHESION BEHAVIOR

Review your experiences in the exercises in this chapter. At this point how would you describe your behavior relating to building and maintaining a high level of cohesion in the group? How would other members describe it? What skills do you still need to develop to be able to build and maintain a high level of cohesion in groups to which you belong? Think about these questions. Write down your responses. Then meet in a group of three and review one another's answers. Add anything that will be of help to the other members of your triad.

CHECKLIST OF SKILLS

___ I can increase a group's cohesion.

___ I can decrease a group's cohesion.

___ I can build and maintain trust within a group.

___ I can increase others' feelings of inclusion within the group.

___ I can increase others' feelings of affection within the group.

___ I can increase others' feelings of having influence within a group.

___ I can establish norms in a gorup.

___ I can use group cohesiveness to increase the group's effectiveness.

I need more work on the skills of: _____

_____

_____

_____

_____

_____

_____

ANSWERS

Page 234: 1: a; 2: false; 3: c; 4: b.

Page 236: 1: c; 2: b; 3: a.

Page 240: 1: b; 2: a; 3: c; 4: true; 5: false; 6: true; 7: true; 8: true; 9: false; 10: false.

Page 248: 1: c; 2: c; 3: c; 4: c; 5: a.

Page 249: 1: c; 2: true; 3: true; 4: false.

Page 254: 1: false; 2: true; 3: true; 4: false; 5: false; 6: true.

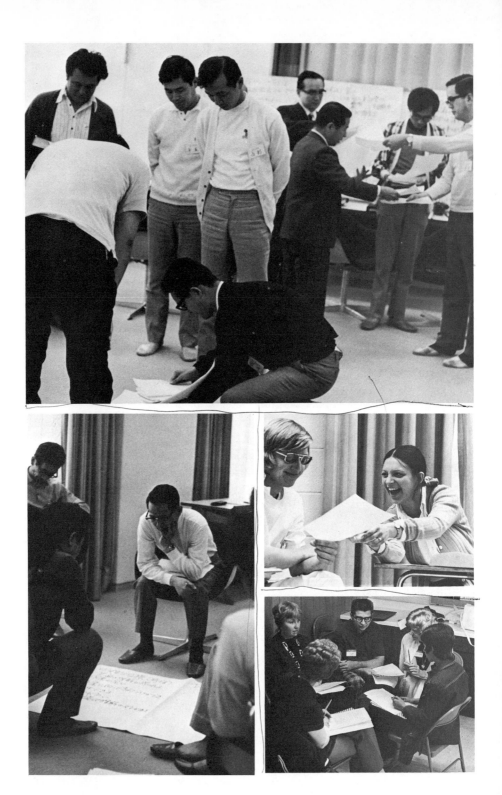

10

Problem Solving

INTRODUCTION

Every chapter of this book deals with some aspect of solving group problems effectively. The adequacy of group problem solving is the primary focus of group skills. Before we proceed further in examining the problem-solving process, it may be helpful to define several key concepts. For our purposes, a *problem* may be defined as a discrepancy or difference between an actual state of affairs and a desired or ideal state of affairs. *Problem solving* is the process of resolving the unsettled matters, of finding an answer to a difficulty; it is a process that results in a solution to a problem, and it involves changing the actual state of affairs until it is identical with the desired state of affairs. Thus, there are four concerns in solving a problem: (1) determining the actual or current state of affairs, (2) specifying the desired state of affairs, (3) determining the best means of moving the group from the actual to the desired state of affairs, and (4) doing so. Problem solving requires both an idea about where the group should be and correct information about where it is now. Every group, furthermore, can be evaluated on the basis of its problem-solving adequacy. *Problem solving adequacy* has four elements: (1) general agreement about the desired state of affairs; (2) structures and procedures to produce, understand, and use relevant information about the actual state of affairs, (3) structures and procedures for inventing possible solutions, for deciding upon and implementing the best solution, and for evaluating its effectiveness in having permanently eliminated the problem; and (4) accomplishing these three activities without deteriorating—preferably while augmenting—the effectiveness of the group's problem-solving capabilities.

You can test your understanding of this section by answering the following questions (answers on page 275):

1. A problem is defined as a:

   a. Difference of opinion between group members.
   b. Difference between the actual and ideal state of affairs.
   c. Process that results in a solution to the problem.

2. Problem solving is defined as:

   a. Resolving differences of opinion between group members.
   b. A difference between the actual and ideal state of affairs.
   c. A process that results in a solution to the problem.

3. What are the four parts of solving a problem?

   a. Solving the problem.
   b. Giving up and going home.
   c. Figuring out the current state of affairs.
   d. Figuring out the desired state of affairs.
   e. Figuring out how to change the current state to the desired state.
   f. Figuring out how to gather the resources necessary for solving the problem.
   g. Having the members solve the problem by themselves.

YOUR PROBLEM—SOLVING BEHAVIOR

When your group is struggling with a problem, how do you behave? Before beginning a discussion of problem solving, consider for a moment how you behave while your group is trying to arrive at a proper solution to a problem. The analytical statements below should be helpful.

1. When a problem comes up in a meeting, I try to make sure it is thoroughly explored until everyone understands what the problem is.
   Never 1 : 2 : 3 : 4 : 5 : 6 : 7   Always

2. I ask why the problem exists and what the causes are.
   Never 1 : 2 : 3 : 4 : 5 : 6 : 7   Always

3. I tend to accept the first solution that is proposed by a group member.
   Never 1 : 2 : 3 : 4 : 5 : 6 : 7   Always

4. When a group decides upon which solution to adopt and implement, I make certain it is clear what the decision is, who should carry it out, and when.
   Never 1 : 2 : 3 : 4 : 5 : 6 : 7   Always

5. I do not take the time to really study or define the problem the group is working on.
   Never 1 : 2 : 3 : 4 : 5 : 6 : 7   Always

6. I have a tendency to propose answers without really having thought the problem and its causes through carefully.
   Never 1 : 2 : 3 : 4 : 5 : 6 : 7   Always

7. I make sure that the group discusses the pros and cons of several different alternative solutions to a problem.

Never 1 : 2 : 3 : 4 : 5 : 6 : 7 Always

8. I tend to let decisions remain vague—as to what they are and who will carry them out.

Never 1 : 2 : 3 : 4 : 5 : 6 : 7 Always

9. I push for definite follow-ups on how decisions reached at earlier meetings work out in practice.

Never 1 : 2 : 3 : 4 : 5 : 6 : 7 Always

10. I know if the results of the group's work are worth the effort.

Never 1 : 2 : 3 : 4 : 5 : 6 : 7 Always

FIVE STEPS IN PROBLEM SOLVING

There are five basic steps in the problem-solving process: (1) defining the problem, (2) diagnosing how big it is and what causes it, (3) formulating alternative strategies or plans for solving it, (4) deciding upon and implementing the most desirable strategies, and (5) evaluating the success of the strategies used. Every step in this process is vitally important for different reasons, and they are all interrelated. How the problem is defined at the start, for example, may affect how committed the group members are to implementing the strategies decided upon. In the statements above on your problem-solving behavior, there are two dealing with each step. Numbers 1 and 6 pertain to problem definition, 2 and 7 on diagnosing the problem, 3 and 8 on formulating alternative strategies, 4 and 9 on deciding upon and implementing a strategy, and 5 and 10 on evaluation. Some statements are worded so that they should be scored positively; others should be scored negatively. Think about your self-analysis in terms of these statements, and how it relates to the problem-solving adequacy of a group. Then continue reading this chapter.

DEFINING THE PROBLEM

The clearer and more accurate the definition of the problem, the easier it is to do the four other steps in the problem-solving processes. The discussion in Chapter 4 on group goals is relevant to defining the problem in order to begin the problem-solving sequence. A problem exists, as we have just noted, where there is a difference between the actual and the desired state of affairs; accordingly, the definition of a problem begins with getting everyone in the group to agree on what the desired state of affairs is. The next step is to obtain valid, reliable, and correct information about the existing state of affairs. The difference between the desired and actual state of affairs should be thoroughly discussed, because it is from the awareness of this discrepancy that the commitment and motivation to solve the problem is built. Because problem-solving groups often progress too quickly toward a solution to the problem without first getting a clear, consensual definition of the problem itself, members of the group should see to it that everyone understands what the problem is before going on to the next step. The direction a group first takes in defining the problem may keep it from finding a successful solution (Maier, 1930); therefore, the group should be careful not to agree prematurely on the definition of its problem.

Defining a workable problem is perhaps the hardest stage of the problem-solving process. Suggestions for procedures are as follows:

1. List a series of statements about the problem. Describe it as concretely as possible by mentioning people, places, and resources. There should be as many different statements of the problem as the members are willing to give. Write them on a blackboard where everyone can see them. Avoid arguing about whether the problem is perfectly stated.
2. Restate each problem statement so that it includes a description of both the desired and actual state of affairs. Take out alternative definitions that are beyond the resources of the group to solve, and choose the definition that the group members agree is most correct. The problem should be important, solvable, and urgent.

For a discussion of how to define an interpersonal problem, see Johnson (1972). In processing how a group has defined a problem, the following questions may be helpful:

1. Is the problem clearly defined?
2. How specific is the problem definition? Is it overly abstract? How is the actual situation different from the desired situation?
3. Does the definition allow for alternatives or does it imply a solution? Does it mistake a solution or goal for the problem?
4. Is the problem stated in a way that does not arouse defensiveness?
5. Who initiates the problem statement? Who clarifies it?
6. Are all members agreed upon the problem statement? Does the group check to ascertain agreement?

Here is a quick test of your understanding of the above section (answers on page 275):

True False 1. The first problem-solving step in a group is to get valid, reliable, and correct information about the present state of affairs.

True False 2. Problem-solving groups often progress too quickly toward a solution to the problem.

True False 3. The direction a group first takes in defining a problem may keep it from finding a successful solution.

True False 4. Defining a workable problem is one of the easiest stages of the problem-solving process.

5. You are in a group that needs to define the problem in a workable way. Being the expert in the group, you are asked to lead the group in doing this. Write down the two suggested procedures you will undoubtedly follow:

a. _____

b. _____

DIAGNOSING THE PROBLEM

The second step in the problem-solving process is diagnosing the dimension and causes of the problem. The objective here is to identify the nature and magnitude of the forces helping the group to move toward the desired state of affairs as well as the forces hindering this movement. Determining what forces are acting upon the problem situation is called *force field analysis* (Lewin, 1945; Myrdal, 1944). In force field analysis the problem is seen as a balance between forces working in opposite directions—some helping the movement toward the desired state of affairs and others restraining such movement. The balance that results between the helping and restraining forces is the actual state of affairs, a "quasi-stationary equilibrium" that can be altered through changes in the forces. Figure 10.1 illustrates the basic notions of force field analysis.

FIGURE 10.1   Force Field Analysis

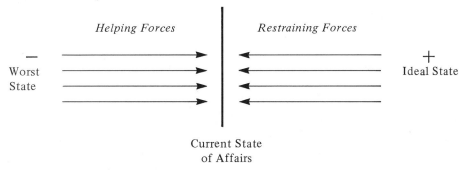

Current State
of Affairs

The ideal state of affairs toward which the group is working is on the right side of Figure 10.1 and is represented by the plus sign. The worst state of affairs, on the left side of the figure, is represented by the minus sign. The vertical line in the middle signifies the current state of affairs. On any problem numerous forces are at work, some restraining change and others helping change. There are two basic steps for a group to follow in doing a force field analysis:

1. Make up lists of forces by first brainstorming all the helping forces and then all the restraining forces. The list should include all possible forces, whether psychological, interpersonal, organizational, or societal. If a force seems to be a complex of variables, each variable should be listed separately. Critical judgment

should be avoided; it is essential that every member's ideas are publicly requested and aired.

2. Rank the forces according to their importance in affecting the present situation. Agree on the most important helping and restraining forces, which may total from three to six each. Rate the important forces according to how easily they can be resolved, and avoid spending time discussing those that the group cannot influence with their current resources.

Without defining the problem correctly and specifically, it cannot be adequately diagnosed. And without an accurate and precise diagnosis of the forces involved, the alternative strategies for the solution of the problem cannot be formulated.

Below is a quick check of your comprehension of the section above (answers on page 275):

1. In force field analysis, the problem is seen as:

   a. A movement toward the desired state of affairs.

   b. Something out of a science fiction story.

   c. A balance between helping and hindering forces working in opposite directions.

   d. A balance between helping and hindering forces working in similar directions.

2. You did a brilliant job in helping the group define the problem in a workable way. The members are so impressed with your expertise that they have asked you to again lead the group, this time in a force field analysis of the problem. You confidently lead the group in the two major steps of a force field analysis, which are:

   a. _____

   b. _____

A PROBLEM–DIAGNOSIS PROGRAM

This program is designed to help you in diagnosing a problem that involves people working together in a group. In this program twelve separate steps are presented. each of which contains a complete and separate idea, question, or instruction. Be sure that you understand and complete each step before going on to the next one.

1. Identify the problem you wish to work on. Describe the problem as you now see it. _____

   _____

   _____

   _____

2. Most problem statements can be rephrased so that they describe two things:

   a. The situation as it is now.

b. The situation as you would like it to be (the ideal).

Restate your problem situation in these terms. _____

_____

_____

_____

3. Most problem situations can be understood in terms of the forces that push toward improvement—in other words, helping forces and restraining forces (see Figure 10.1). It is useful to analyze a problem by making lists of the helping and restraining forces affecting a situation. Think about these now, and list them. Be sure to list as many as you can, not worrying at this point about how important each one is. Use additional paper if you need to.

Helping Forces	*Restraining Forces*
_____	_____
_____	_____
_____	_____
_____	_____
_____	_____

4. Review the two lists. Underline those forces that seem to be the most important right now, and that you think you might be able to influence constructively. Depending on the problem, there may be one specific force that stands out, or there may be two or three helping forces and two or three restraining forces that are particularly important.

5. Now, for each restraining force you have underlined, list some possible courses of action that you might be able to plan and carry out to reduce the effect of the force or to eliminate it completely. Brainstorm. List as many action steps as possible, without worrying about how effective or practical they would be. You will later have a chance to decide which are the most appropriate.

Restraining Force A:

Possible action steps to reduce this force: _____

_____

_____

Restraining Force B:

Possible action steps to reduce this force: _____

_____

_____

Restraining Force C:

Possible action steps to reduce this force: _____

_____

_____

7. Now do the same with each helping force you underlined. List all the action steps that come to mind that would increase the effect of each helping force.

Helping Force A:

Possible action steps to increase this force: _____

_____

_____

_____

Helping Force B:

Possible action steps to increase this force: _____

_____

_____

_____

Helping Force C:

Possible action steps to increase this force: _____

_____

_____

_____

8. You have now listed possible action steps to change the key forces affecting your problem situation. Review these possible action steps and underline those that seem promising.

9. List the steps you have underlined. Then for each action step list the materials, people, and other resources available to you for carrying out the action.

Action Steps	*Resources Available*
_____	_____
_____	_____
_____	_____
_____	_____

10. Review the list of action steps and resources and think about how each might fit into a comprehensive action plan. Take out those items that do not seem to fit into the overall plan, add any new steps and resources that will round out the plan, and think about a possible sequence of action. _____

_____

_____

_____

11. Plan a way of evaluating the effectiveness of your action program as it is implemented. Think about this now, and list the evaluation procedures you will use. _____

_____

_____

_____

12. You now have a plan of action to deal with the problem situation. The next step is for you to implement it.

FORMULATING ALTERNATIVE STRATEGIES

The third step in problem solving is identifying and drawing up alternative ways to solve the problem. Creativeness, divergent thinking, opposition among ideas and inventiveness are essential for this phase; these are discussed in Chapter 6. Each alternative solution needs to be concretely specified. The theory of force field analysis is a particularly useful way to specify alternative strategies for solving a problem. According to the theory, changes in the present situation will occur only as the helpful and restraining forces are changed so that the level where they are balancing is altered. There are two basic methods for changing the equilibrium point between the two sets of forces: increasing the strength or number of the helping forces and decreasing the strength or number of the restraining forces. Of the two, the preferable strategy is to get rid of the restraining forces or reduce their strength.

Experience has shown that as pressure builds up for a change in the present situation by increasing the helping forces, natural resistances also increase, reducing the effectiveness of that strategy. Reducing the restraining forces, therefore, is usually the more effective of the two strategies. The fewer the forces acting upon the present situation, furthermore, the lower the tension level of the people in the situation. Often people who use force field analysis try to reduce restraining forces and increase helping forces at the same time. When this can be done, it is very effective. One way of intervening simultaneously with both types of forces is to change a restraining force so that it becomes a helping force.

One of the most successful strategies for changing the direction of a restraining force is to involve the group members who are resisting the desired changes in diagnosing the problem situation and in planning the solutions (Watson and Johnson, 1972). People enjoy and affirm the changes they make themselves, and they resist changes imposed upon them by others. Involvement of resisters in the diagnosing and planning of change often means a more difficult planning process, but it virtually guarantees that they are committed to the proposed changes. It also helps clear up any misunderstandings and differences of opinion before the strategies are implemented, and it uses the resources of the "opposition."

Force field analysis is useful for two reasons. First, it avoids the error of a single-factor analysis of a problem; using it will keep attention on the problem situation until a number of relevant factors are identified. Second, by helping to identify a number of problem-related factors, it gives group members several points at which they may intervene in their attempt to produce a change. Because any change is the result of a number of factors, an effective change strategy involves plural actions that are directed toward several of those factors. When an approach is made through modifying several factors at the same time, the possibility is increased that the improvement will be permanent.

In specifying alternative strategies for change, group members should think of as many ways as possible in which the forces holding the group from moving toward the desired state might be reduced. They should obtain ideas from everyone in the group. If group members do not have many ideas, outside consultants can always be invited to lend assistance. Bringing in an expert who knows a lot about the substance of the problem is often extremely helpful at this point. Group members should try to take each restraining force in turn and think up ways to reduce its strength or to eliminate it altogether. Brainstorming is useful and divergent thinking should be encouraged.

To determine how well your group has formulated alternative strategies, the following questions may be helpful:

1. Does a persistent "set" inhibit idea production? Do members feel free to produce deviant ideas?
2. Do dominant members or coalitions stifle the ideas of other members?
3. Is the group comfortable with silence?
4. Does the group direct its attention toward soluble aspects of the problem or does it endlessly attempt a solution to an insoluble aspect?
5. Are ideas combined or improved to produce still other ideas?
6. Do all members participate? Are minority opinions given a full hearing?
7. Do the group atmosphere and norms encourage expression of disagreement?
8. Are some members overly protective of their own ideas?
9. Does the group have appropriate methods for testing ideas?
10. Does the group search for both the positive and the negative consequences that might be attached to various alternatives?

Here are four questions to check your understanding of the preceding section (answers on page 275):

1. According to the force field analysis theory, changes in the present situation will happen only when:
    a. The forces are changed so the level where they are balancing is changed.
    b. The forces are changed so the helping ones balance the hindering ones.
    c. The forces are seen as agents that help in the problem-solving process.
    d. Force is used.
2. The more effective way to change the force field is to:
    a. Increase the strength of the helping forces.
    b. Decrease the strength of the hindering forces.
    c. Decrease the strength of both forces.
3. When people are a restraining force, a successful strategy is to:
    a. Ignore them until they give in.
    b. Explain to them why they are wrong.
    c. Involve them in planning the solution.
4. Force field analysis is useful for two reasons:
    a. It avoids single-factor analysis of a problem.
    b. It avoids use of standard solutions to a problem.
    c. It produces permanent change.
    d. It gives the group more than one point where it can work at changing the problem.
    e. It gives the group the best solution to the problem.

DECIDING UPON AND IMPLEMENTING A STRATEGY

Once all the possible strategies have been identified and formulated in specific terms, the group needs to select the strategies it will implement. This procedure involves two central aspects of problem solving: decision making and decision implementation. *Decision making* is a process that results in a choice among alternative courses of action; it is discussed at length in Chapter 3. *Decision implementation* is a process of taking the necessary actions that result in the execution of the decision; it is also discussed in Chapter 3. Decision making requires alternatives from which a group can choose, and decision implementation requires internal commitment by group members to the decisions made. During this fourth step in the problem-solving process, the group should use critical judgment and convergent thinking to build concrete plans for implementation. The following points may be helpful:

1. Select the alternatives that seem best. List three positive values in adopting each alternative.
2. List the materials and other resources needed to implement the strategy. The cost of implementation, in terms of time, people, and material resources, should be specified.

3. Evaluate how realistic the strategy is; the necessary variables should be within the power of the group members to influence.
4. Weigh the probabilities for success against the cost of implementation.
5. Try to anticipate all the barriers to implementation and how the group members will handle them.
6. Put the ideas and actions of the strategy into a time sequence and estimate specific dates for the actions to occur.
7. Assign responsibilities to group members for implementing the strategy.
8. Begin taking the first steps.

The following questions may be useful in processing how well your group has decided upon and implemented a strategy:

1. Does premature voting occur?
2. Are all the members ready for a decision? Has there been adequate testing of ideas?
3. Does the group make any effort to summarize its progress?
4. How is the decision made? What method is used?
5. Are feelings of the members adequately explored?
6. How does the group handle conflict? Is conflict smoothed over or brought out into the open?
7. Does the group explore the implications of the decision from points of view outside the group?
8. Is there a detailed plan of action?
9. Does the group assign responsibilities for various action steps?
10. Does the group pause for reality testing, refinement, and replanning? Does it anticipate potential problems in implemention?
11. Are all of the members committed to the decision? Which members appear to have reservations or to be displeased?
12. Does the group allow time for a critical examination of its process of arriving at a decision?

EVALUATING THE SUCCESS OF STRATEGIES

The fifth and final step in problem solving is evaluating the success of the strategies the group has decided to implement. To do that, the group members must figure out (1) whether the strategies were successfully implemented and (2) what the effects were. The first activity is sometimes called process evaluation because it deals with the process of implementing a strategy; the second is called outcome evaluation because it involves assessing or judging the consequences of implementing the strategy. Planners should establish criteria for or ways in which to judge the effectiveness of their actions in implementing the strategy, and review their progress as each action step occurs. The major criterion for assessing the outcome of an implemented strategy is whether the actual state of affairs is closer to the desired state of affairs than it was before the strategy was carried out.

If the group finds that its strategies have been successfully implemented, but have failed to change substantially the current situation into the ideal state of affairs, they may develop new strategies until they find one that is effective. The solution of one set of problems, however, often brings other problems into the open, and in trying out various strategies the group may find that it has not been working for the solution of the most critical problem in the situation. The final result of the evaluation stage, therefore, should be to show the group what problems have been solved and to what extent, what problems still need to be solved, and what new problems have come up. Evaluation should result in a new definition of a problem, a rediagnosis of the situation, and the beginning of a new problem-solving sequence.

BLOCKS TO PROBLEM—SOLVING EFFECTIVENESS

There are eight blocks to problem-solving effectiveness to which group members should be alerted. They are as follows:

1. *Lack of clarity in stating the problem.* Much of the initial effort of groups in solving a problem is directed toward orienting members to what the problem is. This phase is extremely important, and it deserves sufficient time and effort to identify the problem, to define it, and, through this process, to get the members involved in and committed to solving it. Often, groups are doomed to failure when they inadequately define the nature of their problem.

2. *Not getting the needed information.* When information is minimal, the definition of the problem will be inadequate, fewer alternative strategies for the solution will be generated, and the potential consequences of those alternatives will not be properly explored. The result is relatively low-grade solutions. Great emphasis must be placed on fact finding in order to solve a problem effectively.

3. *Poor communication within the group.* Poor communication among group members has the same effect as the lack of information—with the added problem that it makes it difficult to implement any action that requires coordination among group members. Effective communication among all group members is necessary for effective problem solving.

4. *Premature testing of alternative strategies, or premature choice.* For most people, ideas are fragile creations, easily blighted by a chill, or even indifferent, reception. As groups proceed in their problem-solving activities, they must avoid all tendencies to evaluate each idea as it comes along; instead, they should create an atmosphere that supports the presentation and the pooling of a wide assortment of ideas. Only then can the group critically evaluate the alternatives.

5. *A critical, evaluative, competitive climate.* A supportive, trusting, coopera-

tive atmosphere is necessary for solving problems successfully. If group members are afraid of the way in which other members are evaluating their ideas, effective problem solving is destroyed.

6. *Pressures for conformity.* Pressures for conformity and compliance slow down the development of different and diverse ideas. Divergent thinking as well as convergent thinking are necessary for sound problem solving.

7. *Lack of inquiry and problem-solving skills.* Some groups may need special training in how to use inquiry and problem-solving methods to advantage. Training may be accomplished through an expert member of the group, or the group may wish to call in an outside consultant.

8. *Inadequate motivation.* Any problem-solving group must have the motivation to solve its problems. If the group members are not motivated, they must be persuaded into seeing the importance of the problem and the necessity for seeking a solution. Members who leave work to others clearly lack motivation.

Here are two quick questions to check your comprehension (answers on page 275):

1. Because of your brilliant and knowledgeable leadership, the group is now ready to evaluate the success of its strategies. To do so, what two things must the group figure out?

   a. _____

   b. _____

2. After the evaluation, the group realized that the problem was not successfully solved. In an attempt to keep them from blaming your leadership, you search desperately in your mind for possible blocks to problem-solving effectiveness. These blocks are:

   a. _____

   b. _____

   c. _____

   d. _____

   e. _____

   f. _____

   g. _____

   h. _____

GROUPTHINK AND PROBLEM SOLVING

As we have seen in Chapter 3, group performance in problem-solving activities is much better than individual performance. This superiority is not to imply, of course, that group performance is always successful. For example, Janis (1971) has published the results of his studies which indicate that, under certain conditions, groups can prevent effective problem solving from taking place through a state of "groupthink." He studied the groups advising presidents of the United States and found powerful social pressures brought to bear whenever a dissident began to voice his objections to what otherwise appeared to be a group consensus. Group norms were present that bolstered morale at the expense of critical thinking. One of the most common norms was that members should remain loyal to the group by sticking with the policies to which the group had already committed itself even when those policies were obviously working out badly and had unintended consequences that disturbed the conscience of each member. Groupthink is a problem-solving process in which proposals are accepted without a careful, critical scrutiny of the pros and cons of the alternatives, and in which considerable suppression of opposing thoughts takes place. The suppression of opposition, however, takes on a rather unique form: a dissenting member is not shouted down; rather, each group member decides himself that his misgivings are not relevant and should be set aside. Janis lists eight main symptoms of groupthink:

1. Most or all of the members of the group share an illusion of being invulnerable that gives them some degree of reassurance about obvious dangers and leads them to become overoptimistic and willing to take extraordinary risks. It also causes them to fail to respond to clear warnings of danger.

2. The group collectively constructs rationalizations in order to discount warnings and other forms of negative feedback that would, if it were taken seriously, lead members to think again about their assumptions each time they recommit themselves to past decisions.

3. Members have an unquestioning belief in the moralness of their group. This belief results in their tendency to ignore the ethical or moral consequences of their decisions.

4. Group members hold stereotyped views of the leaders of enemy groups. Enemy leaders are assumed to be either so evil that genuine attempts at negotiating differences with them are unwarranted, or so weak or so stupid that they cannot deal effectively with whatever attempts, however risky, the group makes to defeat their purposes.

5. The group applies direct pressure to any member who momentarily expresses doubts about any of the group's shared illusions, or who questions the validity of the arguments supporting a policy alternative favored by the majority.

6. Members avoid deviating from what appears to be group consensus. They keep silent about their misgivings and even minimize to themselves the importance of their doubts. A great deal of self-censorship takes place within the group.
7. Members share an illusion of unanimity within the group about almost all judgments expressed by members who speak in favor of the majority view.
8. Members sometimes appoint themselves as "mindguards" to protect the leader and themselves from adverse information that might break the complacency they share about the effectiveness and morality of past decisions.

Janis also lists six poor decision-making practices of groups that are caught in the trap of groupthink. They are:

1. The group limits its discussions to a few alternative courses of action (often only two) without an initial survey of all the alternatives that might be worthy of consideration.
2. The group fails to reexamine the course of action initially preferred by the majority after they learn of risks and drawbacks they had not considered originally.
3. The members spend little or no time discussing whether there are covert gains they may have overlooked, or ways in which to reduce the seemingly prohibitive costs of rejected alternatives.
4. The group makes little or no attempt to get information from experts within their own organization, members who might be able to supply more precise estimates of potential losses and gains.
5. Members show positive interest in facts and opinions that support their preferred policy and tend to ignore facts and opinions that do not.
6. Members spend little time considering how their chosen policy might be hindered by bureaucratic inertia, sabotaged by political opponents, or temporarily derailed by common accidents. They fail to work out contingency or alternative plans to cope with foreseeable setbacks that could endanger the overall success of their decision.

To check your understanding of groupthink, you may wish to answer the questions below (answers on page 275):

1. Groupthink is a process whereby:
   a. Everyone in the group thinks of ways to solve the problem.
   b. Proposals are accepted without careful consideration of alternatives.
   c. Proposals aren't accepted until every alternative is considered.
   d. A considerable amount of evaluation takes place.
2. The suppression of opposition in groupthink takes the form of:
   a. A member's ideas being shouted down.

b. A member deciding that his ideas aren't relevant.

c. A member deciding that other's ideas aren't relevant.

d. An authority making the decisions.

3. Some symptoms of groupthink are (choose four):

a. Members think they are invulnerable.

b. Members agree with the authority who makes the decision.

c. Members have stereotyped views of enemy leaders.

d. Members avoid deviating from what seems to be group consensus.

e. Members have stereotyped views of other members.

f. Members are surprised when things go wrong.

g. Members don't question the group's basic assumption.

4. Some poor decision-making practices of groupthink are (choose three):

a. The group limits itself to only a few alternatives.

b. The group does not reexamine the initial course of action.

c. The group cannot decide on an alternative.

d. The group does not consult experts.

e. The group ignores facts that support their preferred policy.

CLIMATE

Another critical aspect of effective group problem solving is the climate or atmosphere in the group. Group climate is primarily a consequence of its goal structure and the orientation of its members. Climates can be either cooperative or competitive. Review Table 4.2, which lists the effects of the differences between cooperative and competitive group climates on group problem solving.

GROUP MEMBERSHIP

Groups can be composed either of people who are much alike (homogeneous) or people who are different from one another (heterogeneous). There is a good deal of evidence to show that heterogeneous groups are superior to homogeneous groups in solving problems effectively and in arriving at creative solutions. The usual explanation for the superiority of heterogeneous groups is that they generate a wider variety of ideas on, and different possible approaches to, the problem. Effective groups must not only have a diversity of viewpoints and backgrounds to consider, they must also provide conditions under which these varied viewpoints can be heard. One of the most effective barriers to hearing all points of view in a group is the tendency of members to evaluate suggested solutions as they appear, one by one, instead of waiting until all suggestions are in and then making their choice. A period of idea production, free from evaluation, can lead to a solution of high quality if the members can refrain from instant criticism and avoid focusing on particular strategies before exploring many possible solutions. Hall and Williams (1966), furthermore, found that as individual opinions before discussion became more diverse, group members had a greater tendency to produce and incorporate into their decisions judgments they had not held before. Thus, the appearance of creative solutions to problems is helped by the diversity of opinion represented in the group—as long as the conflict among opinions is managed constructively.

Opposition and a diversity of viewpoints are essential for effective problem solving. These differences bring about involvement, creativity, and high-quality solutions. Controversy among ideas is a prerequisite for effective problem solving, and the best way to structure it into the group is by having a heterogeneous membership.

YOUR PROBLEM—SOLVING BEHAVIOR

To end our discussion of problem-solving procedures, it may be helpful to once again review your own behavior in problem-solving groups and determine how you now behave and how you would like to behave. You may also wish to make some plans for eliminating differences between the two. Divide into groups of three. Take each problem-solving step and write down, as a group, the task and maintenance behaviors most needed in each step. Note the behaviors that are typically yours and the behaviors in which you rarely, if ever, engage. Within the group, decide on how each person can behave in the future to help the problem-solving process of groups to which he belongs.

CHECKLIST OF SKILLS

——— I can effectively use problem-solving procedures.

——— I am aware of and understand my behavior in problem-solving situations.

——— I can define a problem.

——— I can diagnose the helping and restraining forces involved in a problem.

——— I can formulate alternative strategies to solve a problem.

——— I can decide on and implement a strategy to solve a problem.

——— I can evaluate the success of a strategy implemented to solve a problem.

——— I can avoid the symptoms and dangers of groupthink.

I need further work on the following skills: _____

_____

_____

_____

_____

ANSWERS

Page 258: 1: b; 2: c; 3: c, d, e, f.

Page 260: 1: false; 2: true; 3: true; 4: false; 5: (a) list a series of problem statements, (b) rephrase the statements to include a description of both the desired and the actual states of affairs.

Page 262: 1: c; 2: (a) make up lists of helping and hindering forces by brainstorming, (b) rank the forces in order of importance in affecting the present situation.

Page 267: 1: a; 2: b; 3: c; 4: a, d.

Page 270: 1: (a) whether the strategies were successfully implemented, (b) what the effects of the strategies were on the problem; 2: See pages 269 and 270.

Page 272: 1: b; 2: b; 3: a, c, d, g; 4: a, b, d.

11

Leading Discussion Groups

NATURE OF A DISCUSSION GROUP

Many groups have as their purpose the learning of specific materials or procedures by their members. Group learning occurs in all sorts of educational ways—from preschool programs to postgraduate seminars, from athletic teams to special conferences and workshops. A discussion group is a group whose purpose is mastering a particular subject. Yet learning in a discussion group should be viewed differently because it depends to such a great extent upon the orientation of the people involved and their specific goals. Some discussions can be aimed at drawing forth facts and knowledge known to the members. Others can be aimed at promoting new conclusions from known material. Such "inquiry" discussions involve leading the group members, through questions, to the "right" answer to a problem—the right answer usually being a new concept. Some discussions can be open-ended, their purpose being to encourage members to think and value their own ideas as well as the ideas of others. There are no right or wrong answers in an open-ended discussion, only conclusions made through applying critical thinking procedures. Finally, a discussion can be aimed at solving a problem the group faces in a way that promotes the learning of procedures, skills, and knowledge by members.

NECESSITY OF GROUP SKILLS

Despite all the instances of learning in groups in our society, very little specific training is given to educators on how to conduct discussion groups in ways that maximize members' learning. The all too common practice of simply asking persons to sit around a table and carry on a "meaningful" discussion is all too often unproductive. One major difficulty here is that though people spend much of their lives talking with one another, most of them have failed to develop the aptitudes and attitudes necessary for carrying on a worthwhile discussion for the purpose of learning new material, skills, or knowledge. People tend to be self-conscious, to be overly concerned with what others may think of their ideas, to listen carelessly to others, and to look for others to provide the direction and leadership.

Productive discussion groups require the conscious development of an effective group. A review of the model of group effectiveness presented in Chapter 1 might be helpful at this point, as well as a review of previous chapters that focus upon the skills necessary to develop an effective group. Group members must be taught the fundamental skills and attitudes necessary for group effectiveness if they are to learn anything in a discussion group. They must know how to build an effective group. Thus, an emphasis in any discussion group has to be upon developing the necessary skills among its members for a productive discussion to be held.

BASIC PROCEDURE FOR DISCUSSION GROUPS

In conducting productive group discussions, certain basic procedures must be followed. These procedures organize and coordinate members' behavior so that cooperative interaction can transpire. They also orient members as to what is expected of them at different points in the discussion. Goal-directed behavior cannot take place in the absence of perceived goals or in the absence of clear procedures for accomplishing the goals. If the goals and procedures are obscure, even the most highly motivated member will have difficulty being influential simply because he has no conceptual model or firm understanding of the kind of behavior that contributes to productive discussions and effective groups. A prerequisite for a group discussion, therefore, is the development of a clear understanding of the group's goals, the criteria against which the performance of the group is to be evaluated, the behaviors needed to ensure an effective learning group, the expectations of the coordinator, and what is expected of the group members.

Before a learning session begins, members must be prepared. They can best prepare themselves by having a copy of the seven-step discussion outline listed below and by writing down ideas wherever they think they will best fit into the discourse. Members should not hesitate to look up and learn the meaning of new words and concepts. After carefully examining the material to be discussed, they should again go through the discussion outline and jot down what else they might say during each step. It is important that members not only know the material to be discussed, but also map out their participation in the discussion.

Hill (1962), in an excellent book on discussion groups, has outlined a series of steps for conducting a group discussion. A slight modification of his steps is as follows:

1. *Definitions of terms and concepts.* To take up a subject, a group must have a shared understanding of the language that will be used. New terms need to be studied and their meanings agreed upon before the discussion can proceed. In this step the members may wish to make up a list of the words and concepts with which they have some difficulty, develop a shared definition of the words on the list, give examples to clarify the meaning of each word, and double-check all members on their understanding of the words.

2. *Establish discussion goals; identify major themes to be discussed.* At the start, the goals or objectives of the learning session need to be clear and the criteria used to determine goal accomplishment need to be specified. With learning the objective of the group, what the group hopes to be taught should be specified and how the group determines the extent to which members have learned it should be understood. As part of this process, everyone should know the major themes to be reviewed. The purpose of this step is to get a grasp of both the overall discussion and the desired outcomes. In reaching agreement on the themes to be talked over, group members should state in their own words what they think the group should accomplish during the session, question each other about the points to be taken up, and arrive at a general consensus about the nature of the discussion to take place. Each major theme can be broken down into subtopics. An overall outline of the themes to be covered should be clear before the session begins.

3. *Allocation of time.* Time should be allocated or set aside for each of the remaining steps, and a timekeeper should be appointed to see to it that the allocations are observed. The themes should be ranked according to their priority, with the most important themes given more time than the less important themes. Often a discussion group will spend so much time on minor topics that the major themes never get reviewed.

4. *Discussion of the major themes and subtopics.* The discussion of each theme and subtopic now begins within the time limit specified in the previous step. Members contribute their information, analyses, opinions, ideas, feelings, and reactions. Controversy is encouraged to increase the involvement, excitement, and fun of the members, and to arrive at creative syntheses of the material to be learned. Every group member should be able to say what the major themes are and what the group has concluded. Quoted sources supporting or questioning the validity of the conclusions made should be presented. Questions should be framed to help group members test the usefulness of specific conclusions.

5. *Integration of the material.* The purpose of this step is to guard against learning that is fragmentary and isolated from other knowledge. It may be that there is little with which to integrate the new information, but usually this step increases in importance as the group has more and more sessions. Relating the material to previous topics; showing its relationship to future topics for discussion; adding one's ideas about the meaning or usefulness of new material in understanding other ideas or concepts; stating how the new material contradicts, substantiates, or amplifies some previously-developed point; summarizing into compact statements the points others have made; reviewing puzzling aspects of the material being discussed—all these are useful procedures in this step.

6. *Application of the material.* Group members should try to identify the implications of the material for their own lives, the work they do, and their relationships with other people. The personal relevance of the material being learned should be clear. Group members may wish to share an experience that emphasizes the point being discussed; they should look carefully to see if the learning can be applied in the here-and-now situation—that is, what is taking place in the discussion group that can be related to the topic of discussion. They should

also state how the learning might be applied in a future situation in which many or all of the group members might find themselves. As much as possible, discussion topics should be applied to the life situations of the group members.

7. *Evaluation of the quality of discussion.* Here group members should take a critical look at their performance as a group and as individual members. They should try to solve problems that hamper the learning within the discussion group. The criteria for evaluating the discussion are given in the next section. This evaluation should include a review of the behaviors necessary for a productive discussion and the aspects of an effective group given in Chapter 1.

CHARACTERISTICS OF PRODUCTIVE DISCUSSION GROUPS

To evaluate how it is functioning, a discussion group must have some notion of how it should operate, some standard of performance, and some ground rules for productive discourse. Besides the group effectiveness model presented in Chapter 1, the following criteria may be helpful (Hill, 1962).

1. The group climate should be warm, accepting, and nonthreatening. This kind of climate is of particular importance because it is invariably necessary for members to expose their ignorance, take risks with their ideas, and engage in controversy with other group members. Good discussions are possible only if members are protected by a warm, understanding group climate.

2. Learning should be approached as a cooperative enterprise. The only way in which a discussion group can function is for a high level of cooperation to prevail among group members. Members should help each other develop an understanding of the material being presented. They must feel free to ask for help from one another without social stigma, and be willing to offer it whenever it is needed. Rewards for group participation must be given on the basis of cooperative behaviors, which promote the learning of all members. Competitive behaviors—one-upmanship, status seeking, ridicule—are all unhelpful in a discussion group. All controversy should be approached as a fun activity that results in solutions to mutual problems and a more creative synthesis of the material to be learned.

3. Learning should be accepted as the primary purpose of the group. The material must be adequately and efficiently covered, and members must learn it. The whole point of having a discussion is to promote the learning of the members, and if such learning is not taking place, the group cannot be considered productive.

4. Every member should participate in the discussion. A group in which only a few members take part is obviously not a productive discussion group. Members will not all participate to the same degree; even so, all should take part some of the time. If a member does not participate, he may not be getting anything from the group; more important, he is not contributing anything to the group. When silent members are asked about their lack of participation they typically respond that although they are not talking they are getting a lot out of the group discussion. The question they are avoiding, however, is what are they contributing? A group discussion is successful only if all members contribute—especially those who do not fully understand the material or what is being discussed. If only those who fully

understand it do the talking, it would be more efficient to get the material from an expert in the first place.

5. Leadership functions should be distributed. Responsibility for making the group operate productively should not be delegated or usurped by one or a few members. If all members are going to learn, they must all participate, interact, and perform leadership functions.

6. Group sessions and the learning tasks should be enjoyable. Group sessions are meant to be lively and pleasant experiences. If no one is having fun, something is wrong. One of the major functions of controversy is often to spark more involvement and enjoyment in a discussion.

7. Evaluation should be accepted as an integral part of the group operation. A productive group is one that accepts the fact that there will be process problems, and is willing to evaluate its progress from time to time. Through evaluation, group members learn what is required to improve the group's functioning, and they gain a better understanding of how and when to contribute to its needs. Group skills, in other words, are improved through evaluation.

8. Members should attend regularly and come prepared. A productive group discussion is one in which members are present and prepared to discuss the material; only then can the resources they have to offer be used fully. Absenteeism, moreover, often demoralizes other members.

REQUIRED MEMBER BEHAVIORS

Any member should feel free to behave in any way that will increase the productivity of a discussion group. Some suggested behaviors are:

1. Initiating and contributing ideas, and information.
2. Giving and asking for information, ideas, opinions, feelings.
3. Clarifying, synthesizing, and giving examples.
4. Periodically summarizing what has taken place and the major points discussed.
5. Encouraging and supporting participation by all members.
6. Evaluating the effectiveness of the group and diagnosing difficulties in group functioning.
7. Process observing.
8. Giving direction to the discussion.
9. Energizing the discussion.
10. Helping the sending skills of the members.
11. Helping the receiving skills of the members.
12. Being an active listener.
13. Testing whether decisions have been made and what the procedure has been.
14. Moderating controversies by disagreeing with others in ways that promote intellectual disagreement without personal rejection and helping other members disagree in the same manner.
15. Beginning, ending, and keeping on time during the meeting.

DISCUSSION LEADER OR COORDINATOR

For every discussion group there is usually a designated leader or coordinator. Often this person is the teacher or the educator in charge of the instructional program. The responsibilities of such a person are hard to define specifically because the coordinator needs to promote discussion without controlling or dominating it; he needs to help in a process where a group of people learn from their discussion and interaction with one another. Some of the coordinator's responsibilities are to introduce the discussion session; to be a task-oriented timekeeper who keeps the group moving so that it does not get sidetracked or bogged down; to restate and call attention to the main ideas of the discussion so that learning is focused; to promote a climate of acceptance, openness, warmth, and support to facilitate learning; and to know when to provide a sense of closure.

Though all group members are responsible for behaving in ways that help one another learn, the coordinator may be more qualified than most other members to use three particular types of helpful behaviors. The first is the instructional behavior of resource expert. In most cases the coordinator will best know the materials, information, and readings that are most relevant and helpful for the group. His second type of helpful behavior is that of teacher—teaching the members the group skills they need to function effectively in a discussion group. The coordinator may hold skill sessions in which members are given practice in fulfilling different functions in the group, or in which he makes periodic evaluations of the functions present and those needed to improve the quality of the group's performance. The third behavior is that of process observer. As such, the coordinator must not only diagnose present functioning of the group, but intervene in the group in ways that improve its effectiveness. The observation skills needed to diagnose group effectiveness, and the questionnaires helpful in gathering the members' perceptions of current group functioning are included in the previous chapters of this book. The intervention skills needed to improve group functioning are also covered in the previous chapters.

Finally, the coordinator may be the keeper of the group's physical structure. It is the discussion leader who will check to see that the group is sitting in a circle without tables or desks between members, fairly close together, in a comfortable, pleasant room—perhaps with refreshments. This task is a vital part of promoting a productive session, for the physical setting can do much to help or obstruct learning in a discussion group.

In addition to the above responsibilities, there are other ways in which a coordinator can assist the group. He can be helpful, for example, in beginning a discussion session, in keeping it going, and in ending it. As stated previously, in the early part of a session members are usually concerned about what is expected of them and what the goals of the session are. A discussion of these points provides a basis for orienting and directing group members. Furthermore, as the meeting progresses, the coordinator may occasionally test to ascertain whether the group clearly knows what the goals are. Group members also need to be clear about the coordinator's responsibilities and why she is there. A coordinator never wants to be in the position of having all group maintenance and goal accomplishment left up to her. One of the easiest ways to make sure that all members will fulfill the responsibilities expected of them is to have the coordinator's role well defined.

Another aspect of beginning a discussion is setting a helpful climate. As we have noted previously, group members will not "open up" until they feel secure in expressing their attitudes and ideas, until they know they won't be ignored, ridiculed, criticized, or otherwise embarrassed by the other group members. Some of the ways in which coordinators can promote a free and friendly climate are by helping members become better acquainted; dispensing with unnecessary formalities, such as raising hands for permission to speak; listening attentively to what each group member is saying; not evaluating the contributions of members or commenting on every contribution made; ruling out preaching, teaching, or moralizing; and avoiding forcing members into participation before they are ready.

A good discussion leader is also one who is prepared with several questions and stimulating comments to begin a discussion, though he should not be in a hurry to use them. One of the critical points in a discussion group's development is freeing the members from dependence upon the coordinator's ideas and direction. Silence, therefore, should not disturb the coordinator. Many a discussion has never gotten started because the coordinator didn't stop talking long enough for the group to "pick up the ball."

During the discussion the coordinator should help establish norms of participation by all members, model good communication skills, promote member-to-member interaction, and maintain the group's direction and agenda. He can encourage productive participation by watching for signs of a member's efforts to be heard and giving her an opportunity to contribute; by being wary of those too eager to talk as they can monopolize all the group's time, by encouraging and supporting all members who participate; by summarizing and clarifying the contributions, and by not dominating the discussion or commenting too frequently. Above all else, a coordinator should show enthusiasm for the discussion and a sincere interest in the group members.

Often in a discussion group there are times when one member obstructs the functioning of the group. And almost as often the other group members are not able to solve the problem constructively; they either support the obstructer or reject him—both of which are undesirable. The coordinator, then, may have to intervene if the situation is to be handled productively. The skills in handling interpersonal conflicts are discussed in chapters 6 and 7 in this book and in Johnson (1972). The important point for the group to remember in such a conflict situation is that it must be processed, negotiated, and resolved to everyone's satisfaction.

Finally, a coordinator needs to be concerned with how the meeting is ended. A few minutes before the group discussion is scheduled to close, or when it appears that the group has exhausted the subject, the session can be concluded with a summarization of the significant points by a member or by the coordinator. This summary should be brief, but it should not be a last-minute statement given to the tune of moving chairs and scuffling feet. The summary is helpful and vital because it leaves the group with a sense of achievement, it clarifies group thinking, and it tests the conclusions of the summarizer against those of other group members. After the summary, the group should evaluate how it has functioned as a group. Finally, the coordinator may express her appreciation to the group. If the group is to meet again, she may wish to explain where and when. And if a final report is required, it should be done before the fine points of the discussion are forgotten.

If you would like to review this chapter to make sure you know the more important points, try answering the following questions. Check back in the chapter for the answers.

1. The purpose of a discussion group is: _____

2. The purpose of following basic procedures in a group are:

   a. _____

   b. _____

3. Below are the steps for conducting a productive discussion. Because the order is important for many of these steps, see if you can put them in the order suggested in the chapter.
   ___ Allocation of time.
   ___ Application of the material.
   ___ Discussion of major themes and subtopics.
   ___ Evaluation of the quality of the discussion.
   ___ Definition of terms and concepts.
   ___ Integration of material.
   ___ Establish discussion goals; identify major themes to be discussed.

4. The chapter suggests eight criteria for how a group should function. See if you know them well enough to fill in the blanks.

   The group climate should be _____ and

   _____.

   Learning should be approached as a _____ enterprise.

   _____ should be accepted as the primary purpose of the group.

   Every member should _____.

   Leadership functions should be _____.

   Group sessions and the learning tasks should be _____.

   _____ should be accepted as an integral part of the group operation.

Members should _____ regularly   and   come

_____ .

5. What are three types of behaviors the coordinator may be more qualified to use than the group members?

a. _____

b. _____

c. _____

6. List as many ways as you can in which the coordinator may help the group. You should come up with at least ten.

_____

_____

_____

_____

_____

_____

_____

_____

_____

_____

12

Leading Growth Groups

INTRODUCTION

Literally tens of thousands of people each year now participate in small groups for the purpose of increasing their interpersonal effectiveness, self-actualization, group skills, personal awareness, and ability to function within organizations. In the last twelve years there has been an explosion of such groups, and more than a hundred "growth centers" in the United States now offer a wide variety of opportunities to join a small group for a weekend, week, or longer. Special group experiences have been designed to help improve couples' relationships, to bridge the gap between parents and children, to strengthen the communion and unity that have characterized religious organizations in the past, to help people handle conflict more constructively, and to increase their ability to meditate, "center," and communicate through touch. Training in human relations is becoming mandatory for potential teachers, and intercultural experiences between blacks and whites, Indians and whites, middle class and poor, are frequently offered to improve teaching and ethnic relations. There are sensitivity training groups, encounter groups, confrontation groups, personal growth groups, strength groups, and such a variety of other groups that no one can keep up with current labels. All such groups are generally referred to as *growth groups* in this book. With such a demand for small-group experiences, and such an expasnion in the type of group experiences available, it is difficult to conceive of a book on groups that does not cover growth groups.

To be an effective growth-group leader, a person needs three models: (1) of interpersonal and group effectiveness, self-actualization, humanness, and so on (of where he is going), (2) of how these goals are to be achieved (of how he will get there), and (3) of leadership conduct (of how he will behave along the way). Models of interpersonal and group effectiveness have been presented in this book and in Johnson (1972), and models of self-actualization and humanness have been described in Johnson (1973); these goals, however, will be briefly reviewed in the next section. The method of reaching these goals is almost universally the inquiry-experiential method of learning discussed in Chapter 1. Inasmuch as this book is based on such a model, the subject is not reviewed here. The reason why such a variety of group experiences can all be lumped together under the label of "growth group" is because they all use the inquiry-experiential approach to learning. Finally, this chapter will focus upon presenting briefly a model for how a growth-group leader—hereafter termed a *facilitator*—behaves in order to promote learning by group members.

GOALS

Growth groups have many different stated goals. All these goals cannot be discussed here, but they can all be put into three main categories: the personal exploration of self, interpersonal interaction, and group dynamics. The major difficulty in discussing the goals of growth groups in general is that most such group experiences focus upon creating a highly flexible setting for learning, one in which a wide variety of personal learning goals can be pursued simultaneously by different members. Each member of such a group may be working toward achieving different goals; if there are ten members, there may be ten different goals. We shall limit the discussion in this section, therefore, to three types of generally desired outcomes: increasing the "humanness" of the participants, promoting self-actualization, and increasing interpersonal and group effectiveness.

One major goal of growth groups is to humanize interpersonal relationships and to increase the participant's abilities and capacities for creating humanizing relationships. Based upon definitions in Webster's dictionary and in Johnson (1972, 1973) for humanization and dehumanization, what makes us "human" is the way in which we interact with other people. A *humanizing* relationship is one that reflects the qualities of kindness, mercy, consideration, tenderness, love, concern, compassion, responsiveness, friendship, and so on. A *humane* relationship is one in which we are sympathetic and responsive to human needs, invest each other with the character of humanity, and treat and regard each other as human. It is the positive involvement with other people that is labeled humane. A *dehumanizing* relationship is one in which the qualities noted above are lacking in people, in which people become machinelike. In a dehumanizing relationship people are treated in impersonal ways, in ways that reflect indifference to human values. To be *inhumane* is to be unmoved by the suffering of others, to be cruel, brutal, and unkind. It is the impersonality of the relationship and the cruelty to and destruction of the other person that is labeled inhumane. One is dehumanized when he loses the human attributes of kindness, love, compassion, tenderness, concern, mercy, consideration, caring, helping, and responsiveness. There are a variety of forces in our society that work to dehumanize us (Johnson 1973). The bureaucratic nature of our organizations, the increasing reliance upon machines, the mobility that creates short-term relationships, the complexity and largeness of our social organizations, are among the factors that contribute to feelings of depersonalization and dehumanization. Not surprisingly, growth-group experiences have become one of the principal methods in our society of feeling and enlarging one's humanness; of experiencing growth-oriented, fulfilling, meaningful, self-actualization; of expanding one's human relationships with others.

Advocates of growth groups make the assumption that people, through their self-awareness and intentionality, have self-actualization or self-realization as their end goal in life. *Self-actualization* may be defined as the psychological need for growth, development, and utilization of potential (Maslow, 1954); a self-actualizing person will be moving toward the full use of his talents, capacities, and potentialities. Self-actualization involves both self-development and self-utilization—that is, potentialities are developed and then used in order to actualize oneself. Much of the focus on self-actualization in growth groups is aimed at greater personal understanding and awareness, and an increased sensitivity to both the surrounding environment and other people. There is an emphasis on being more alive and aware in the immediate present, while keeping a continuity with one's past, present, and future. There is an emphasis upon being more autonomous, upon *not* having one's behavior rigidly determined by a few inner principles or by pressure from other people, but upon having a flexible approach to any situation based upon our knowledge of ourselves and our awareness of the requirements of the situation. Self-actualizing relationships are promoted. They are characterized by mutual help in the development and use of personal resources and potential, in the experiencing of positive emotions, and in the feelings of personal fulfillment. For a much more complete discussion of self-actualization, the reader is referred to Johnson (1973).

Interpersonal and group skills are based upon a person's interpersonal effectiveness. *Interpersonal effectiveness* may be defined as the extent to which the consequences of a person's behavior match his intentions (Johnson, 1972). When we interact with another person we have no choice but to make some impact, stimulate some ideas, arouse some impressions and observations, or trigger some feelings and reactions. Sometimes we make the impression we want to, but at other times we find that people react to our behavior much differently than we would like. An expression of warmth, for example, may be misunderstood as being condescension, and an expression of anger may be misunderstood as being a joke. A person's interpersonal effectiveness depends upon such factors as his self-awareness of his intentions, his self-acceptance of those intentions, his self-disclosure of those intentions to others, his ability to put to use constructive feedback in order to maximize his awareness of the consequences of his behavior, and his willingness to experiment with new behaviors if the consequences of his present behaviors fail to match his intentions. Growth groups are ideal settings in which to work on increasing one's interpersonal effectiveness. From an awareness of one's behavior and its consequences, and from an awareness of the alternative behaviors available that might also produce the desired consequences, a person becomes free to choose how he wishes to behave in any given situation.

To be interpersonally effective, a person must have certain basic skills—generally four. A specific skill-training pogram to develop them is presented in Johnson (1972). Most growth-group experiences involve these skills. The four interpersonal skills are: (1) initiating, building, and maintaining relationships with other people that are fulfilling and trusting (this skill includes self-disclosure, giving and receiving feedback, trust, and self-acceptance); (2) communicating ideas and feelings correctly and unambiguously both verbally and nonverbally; (3) influencing and supporting other people; and (4) constructively resolving problems and conflicts in ways that bring people closer together and help the growth and development of the relationship.

The group skills focused upon in growth groups are summarized in the previous chapters of this book.

LEADING A GROWTH GROUP

A facilitator needs several sets of complex skills in order to lead a growth group. The first set involves his being able to develop a growth-oriented climate in the group—that is, a climate of psychological safety that promotes openness, trust, and experimentation with alternative behaviors. A climate of psychological safety is built by communicating an authentic warmth and support for, an empathy with, and an accurate understanding and acceptance of the group members as individuals. A member is psychologically safe when he feels supported, accepted, understood, and liked. Being *supportive* is, basically, communicating to other individuals a recognition of their strengths and capabilities and the belief that they have the capacity to handle productively the situation they face. Being *accepting* is, basically, communicating a high regard for other people and a disposition to react to their behavior in a nonevaluative way. The specific skills involved in being warm, supportive, empathetic, and accepting are presented in Johnson (1972). Much research on psychotherapy, experimental social psychology, and growth groups substantiates the necessity for such behavior. Leiberman, Yalom, and Miles (1973), for example, found that the most effective growth-group leaders cared a great deal (demonstrated such behaviors as protection, friendship, love, affection, support, praise, encouragement) for group members.

A second set of skills required of an effective group leader involves his being a resource expert, an educator using inquiry-experiential methods, and a diagnoser of personal-interpersonal-group dynamics. Any growth-group facilitator should be skilled in the use of inquiry and experiential methods for learning, a subject discussed in Chapter 1 and in Appendix A. Almost all types of growth groups emphasize inquiring into the experiences of the group members. This inquiry is usually based upon diagnosing the personal, interpersonal, and group dynamics being experienced, by applying a conceptual framework based upon theory and research to the behavior of the group members. To make such diagnoses, the facilitator must provide expertise in one of the behavioral sciences such as psychology or sociology. The presentation of conceptual frameworks enables members not only to gain insight into their behavior and their internal reactions to what occurs within the group, but to understand more fully the interpersonal and group dynamics they are involved in. Thus, a facilitator must have a solid knowledge of one of the behavioral sciences, an expertise in inquiry-experiential learning methods, and the ability to use his knowledge and expertise to help the members understand what they are experiencing. Leiberman, Yalom, and Miles found that the most effective leaders had a great ability to present conceptualizations that gave meaning to the experiences the members were undergoing. This one ability was the most important variable for promoting member learning found in their study. Such conceptualizations are especially useful to members after the group experience has ended, and they are able to use them to understand more fully their day-to-day interpersonal and group situations. The conceptualizations presented in this book and in Johnson (1972) are examples of the type of conceptual frameworks a facilitator must be able to communicate to members.

A third set of facilitator skills pertains to his making sure that members are provided with constructive feedback and confrontations. Helpful feedback means the sharing, upon request, of a description of how a person sees another person's behavior and its consequences, and a description of how the person is reacting to the other person's behavior. A confrontation is a deliberate attempt to help another person examine the consequences of some aspect of his behavior; it is an invitation to engage in self-examination. A confrontation originates from a desire to involve oneself more deeply with the person one is confronting, and it is intended to help the person behave in more fruitful or less destructive ways. The specific skills of feedback and confrontation are presented in Johnson (1972). The important point to keep in mind when feedback and confrontations are being facilitated is the difference among the behavior being observed, the conceptual framework the observer is using, and the inferences and interpretations made about the person engaging in the behavior. A facilitator should never let group members confuse these three elements involved in giving feedback and in confronting other members. The actual behavior being observed will be the same to all group members (given that the observations are valid), but the conceptual frameworks used to understand the behavior and to make interpretations and inferences about it can be widely disparate. Selling other group members on one interpretation of what is taking place is a much different activity from arriving at a consensus of what behavior is taking place.

A fourth set of skills required of a facilitator concerns his being able to model the behaviors he hopes members will learn from their group experience. Social-learning theory (Bandura, 1969) emphasizes the importance of modeling desired behaviors and then reinforcing group members (e.g., giving recognition and approval for imitating the facilitator); this procedure is probably the most effective way to teach new skills. The behaviors a facilitator may model are discussed in this book and in Johnson (1972). This would include such behaviors, for example, as sending and receiving communications, self-disclosure, giving and receiving feedback, experimenting with alternative behaviors, expressing acceptance and support for others. A willingness to model desired skills means that the facilitator will take an active part in interacting with other group members. Some research indicates that activeness on the part of the facilitator is to be preferred to passiveness (which, when it pertains to members, is associated with anxiety, dissatisfaction, silence, poor attendance, discontinuance, and lack of learning), except when the activeness turns into domination (Bierman, 1969). Peters (1966), in addition, found that members who imitate the facilitator learn more from growth groups than those who do not. Thus the facilitator may want to be the "ideal member" in the group in order to promote members' skill development. Finally, it should be noted that simply being an "authentic person" does not systematically present effective skills to be imitated by group members; a facilitator must be able to be interpersonally effective so she can model desired skills.

A fifth set of skills involves a facilitator's being able to engineer a problem-solving process with respect to the concern of members. This subject has been discussed in Chapter 10 of this book as well as in other chapters. In such a problem-solving process it may be important to bring in information about the person's past behavior and feelings as well as his behavior and feelings in the group (Leiberman, Yalom, and Miles, 1973).

A sixth set of skills a facilitator needs is to be able to promote corrective or reparative emotional experiences in the group. Highly personalized and relevant learning often arouses emotions, of anxiety while the learning is taking place and of happiness and satisfaction when it is achieved. To give and receive feedback, to confront and be confronted, to experiment with new behaviors, to bring out personal concerns to be problem solved, all promote considerable emotional reaction. High levels of warmth, anger, frustration, and anxiety are all found in most growth-group experiences. A facilitator may stimulate emotional reaction by confronting group members, by supporting attempts at experimenting with alternative behaviors, by promoting feedback and problem solving, by disclosing highly personal material about herself, and by expressing warmth and support for the members of the group. The most effective leaders in the Leiberman, Yalom, and Miles study engaged in a moderate amount of emotionally stimulating behavior. Though emotional experiences do not mean that learning will take place, genuine learning is often accompanied by emotionality. The facilitator needs to be certain that the members not only experience deep emotion, but also are helped to look at the experience objectively, in such a way as to give it meaning for the future. She should place emphasis upon reflection as well as experience, and guide members in applying their present experiences. In managing the emotionality of the group, the facilitator must also moderately stimulate learning that arouses emotions and provide conceptualizations that will promote learning from emotional experiences.

The seventh set of skills facilitators should be able to demonstrate concerns the social engineering of an effective group. All the skills discussed in this book are relevant to this point. Only in an effective growth group can the learning of members take place. The cohesion of the group; group norms that favor moderate emotional intensity, confrontation, and supportive peer control; the distribution of participation and leadership; the quality of communication; the management of conflict; and all the other aspects of group effectiveness are extremely important for productive growth groups. A facilitator must be able to promote effective group behavior among the members.

It is sometimes useful for a facilitator to have a clear contract with members concerning their responsibilities as group members. The contract might provide, for example, that members agree (1) to be completely open about themselves to the group with respect to both past and current behavior, (2) to take responsibility for themselves once they enter the group and not to blame others or circumstances for their predicaments, and (3) to get involved with the other group members and cooperate in increasing their learning. When an explicit contract is made, the facilitator becomes the "keeper of the contract" and should see to it that it is enforced.

Finally, a facilitator may have a variety of executive functions to carry out. Organizing the group, arranging for facilities in which it is to meet, providing it with needed materials, conducting an evaluation of its success, and so on may be the responsibility of the facilitator, all of which require a range of administrative and evaluation skills.

BECOMING A FACILITATOR

In the past decade more and more people have wanted to become qualified to conduct growth groups. One does not have to be a qualified growth-group facilitator to conduct inquiry-experiential learning activities. This book has organized material on group skills so that many different types of educational ventures can use it without a highly qualified staff. Yet being skilled in conducting inquiry-experiential learning activities does not mean that a person is qualified to conduct growth groups.

A person interested in being a facilitator should ask himself four basic questions. The first question is "Do I have an adequate training in a behavioral science?" A facilitator should have a background in an applied behavioral science (such as social psychology) that places a heavy emphasis upon interpersonal relations and group dynamics. Ideally, he should have a basic knowledge of personality theory, psychopathology, group processes, and interpersonal dynamics. Ideally, he should be connected with some organization, institution of higher education, or other agency that confirms his professional status. He should have a serious commitment to growth groups as part, but not all, of his professional activity. He should be clear about his intentions and goals as a facilitator, and he should understand all the ramifications of the client-facilitator relationship. A familiarity with the research on growth groups is also necessary.

The second question is "How much experience have I had as a participant and a facilitator in growth groups?" Larkin (1972) recommends that before a person can legitimately function as a facilitator, she should have had a three-year training sequence something like the following: she should (1) participate as a member in at least two growth groups, (2) observe group meetings of at least five growth groups and meet after the sessions with their facilitators to discuss the interactions of members and other relevant processes, (3) co-lead five groups with experienced facilitators, (4) lead five groups as sole facilitator, but be observed and discuss her functioning in the facilitator role with the observer, (5) have had either psychotherapy or some equivalent sustained experiential self-study, (6) be evaluated by local, experienced, well-qualified facilitators who not only focus upon her general fitness of character and her background of preparation, but review with care evaluations others have made of her and their recommendations, and (7) be required to keep up to date by periodically becoming involved in local seminars, supervision, and discussions of the ethics of the facilitator role and function.

The third question is "What is my personal level of sensitivity, self-awareness, self-understanding, and self-actualization?" No matter how much training a person has as a facilitator, if he is not self-aware and self-understanding, he will not be able to resist indulging his own personal needs for such things as power and positive responses from participants. The personal qualities of sensitivity to and respect and liking for others are crucial for facilitators. Finally, Maslow (1962) states that a need-deficient person tends to see others in terms of the ways in which they can be of use; the self-actualized person, who is freer and more disinterested, is able to stand off and see others as they are—unique people with their own problems who can be helped in various ways by various means.

The final question is "Am I certified by a professional organization?" There are many professional organizations that to some extent certify members as being competent as growth-group facilitators. Also many states license or certify practicing psychologists. A serious facilitator will take the time and trouble needed to become certified by a professional organization or licensed by his state.

FEELINGS, INTUITION, AND CONCEPTUAL FRAMEWORKS

One major requisite of an effective facilitator is the ability to assess accurately his feelings, intuition, and conceptual frameworks. To a capable, well-trained, and experienced facilitator, the three become quite intergrated. Among poorly trained and inexperienced facilitators, feelings and intuition may be given a "mystical" sense of rightness and followed blindly as a form of emotional anarchy. Though this issue is closely related to the discussion of creativity in Chapter 6, it is important enough to be briefly reviewed at this point.

A person's feelings are great sources of information about what is happening within the group and what sorts of problems are now occurring in the relationships among members. But feelings are not infallible. They are susceptible to bias, distortion, and misunderstandings, especially in situations where the person is threatened, defensive, anxious, or tense. Moreover, all people have their blind spots and in certain situations, or under certain conditions, their feelings can be a reflection of their own fears and anxieties rather than a reflection of what is actually taking place in the group. It is important, therefore, for a facilitator to "calibrate" himself on the validity and reliability of his feelings in different situations, in relation to different types of events, and under different conditions. When a person becomes highly emotional, he should be cautious about relying on the accuracy of his feelings, because it is then that they are most susceptible to distortion and bias. Understanding oneself and the potential causes of various feelings is important in learning when to take action on the basis of one's intuitions, hunches, and feelings.

Awareness of one's feelings and knowledge of the areas in which one can trust one's feelings lead to the issue of intuition as a base for judging what is taking place in the group and how and when to intervene in certain situations. Intuitive hunches often prompt a facilitator to intervene without his being able to explain the basis of its appropriateness. Intuition is a preconscious process in which the person does not know quite how the conclusions or impulses were determined. Intuitive thinking characteristically does not advance in careful, well-defined steps; the person has an emotional and cognitive reaction to the total situation and arrives at an answer. He rarely can provide an adequate account of how the answer evolved, and he may be unaware of just what aspects of the problem situation he is responding to. Intuition results from an immersion in the group process and the members, and a strong identification with and empathy for what is occurring in the group. The greater the familiarity a person has with the issues that concern the group, the greater the likelihood of his intuitions being correct. A wide understanding of and acquaintance and empathy with both human nature and the nature of the group members will help more in intuition about the participants than will factual knowledge. As in calibrating one's emotions, experience in calibrating one's intuitive abilities is also needed because one will find that on certain types of issues one's intuition is sound, whereas on others it is misleading.

The overuse of intuition in leading growth groups has several shortcomings. Facilitators who, through lack of training or self-discipline, do not have conceptual frameworks from the behavioral sciences and who do not have the skills to use conceptual frameworks in gathering information about what is taking place in the group and its members, are ignoring the shortcomings of intuition. First, intuitive hunches often confuse observation with inference; a facilitator begins defending his intuitive inferences as if they were observations and facts. One cannot, for example, *prove* that a member is projecting his feelings into others. Second, facilitators may overrate the validity of their personal observations, believing them more accurate than they usually are. Research on rumors and testimony, for example, indicates that quite often eyewitnesses' perceptions, memory, and inferences are completely false and inaccurate even though they are convinced that they know exactly what happened. Third, the history of medicine and clinical psychology gives overwhelming evidence of the folly of treatments based upon intuition. For several centuries, for example, it was intuitively obvious that not only were insane people possessed by demons, but all diseases were in the blood and a sick person, therefore, could be cured by bleeding. What was intuitively obvious yesterday is often laughed at today. Fourth, the research on self-fulfilling prophecies indicates that one quite often engages in behavior that makes an originally false conclusion or perception become valid. Thus, a facilitator whose intuition is wrong may misunderstand a situation but set in action certain dynamics that create the very situation she is trying to correct but which confirm her original false intuition. A fifth shortcoming is that a person's intuitions give her no adequate basis for knowing whether they are accurate. The major fallacy in intuitive thought is not that it may be inaccurate, though we know that many hunches turn out to be mistaken; a person's intuitions may be quite accurate. But no basis exists for knowing if it is right or wrong. A facilitator who takes action on the basis of her intuition takes action before she can verify whether or not the actions are appropriate. Finally, it must be recognized that intuition represents an internal logic based upon one's culture and frame of reference. Making intuitive judgments about another culture or another frame of reference is a very poor practice.

The need to use feelings and intuitions as a basis for action within the group, even though the dangers of doing so are recognized, points up the necessity for conceptual frameworks and data-gathering skills in order to verify hunches. Facilitators must have the ability to clarify their intuitions to the degree that they are able to formulate hypotheses that can be verified or disproved. It is through conceptualizing what is happening within the group and among its members that effective interventions are usually derived. It is through communicating one's conceptualizations, furthermore, that much of the learning of members takes place. While facilitators vary according to how much reliance they place upon behavioral science conceptualizations and their feelings and intuitions, all have some conceptualization of what is taking place. One always has a set of assumptions from which to operate; the only question is how well formulated and explicit the conceptual framework is, and how systematically it is used to verify one's hunches.

A conceptual framework is nothing more than a way of looking at pieces of behavior in order to make some kind of sense out of them. Individual behaviors, when examined one by one, often have little or no value. When the pieces are conceptually connected, however, they become understandable and useful. A conceptual framework is used to see the connections among and meaning of the individual behaviors of group members. All conceptualizations involve understanding relationships, grasping inherent meaning, or comprehending a structure. The value of conceptualization is that it provides an instrument for decision making; a facilitator is able to use her theoretical system to bring her interventions under rational control. She plans her actions in accordance with a system of related hypotheses rather than on the basis of an intuited procedure. The knowledge now available in the behavioral sciences provides facilitators with the means of organizing their perceptions, of making observations systematically to promote member learning, of checking out their hunches, and of communicating their expertise to the members. There is no way to overemphasize the importance to facilitators of explicit conceptual schemes that they can use systematically in helping members learn from their experiences.

As with intuition, however, if facilitators use only conceptualizations without using their feelings and intuitions, their effectiveness may suffer. Their behavior in a group may become uncreative and overly structured. They may be pretending that the group is at a level of sophistication and knowledge that it is not, and they will be repressing their capacity for the kind of creativity that provides insights and alternative solutions to the problems the group faces. Though conceptual frameworks do help organize observation and help in understanding and communication, they do not always help people harness their creativity in arriving at insights into members' behavior and in putting fire and zest into their own personal growth and actualization.

An effective facilitator should be aware of and accept his feelings. He should use them to spark his intuition about what is taking place in the group and among its members. He should also have expertise in using conceptual frameworks to verify hunches, to observe systematically member behavior, and to communicate with members in ways that facilitate their learning. Intuition and theory are both necessary and useful in generating effective interventions within a growth group. Neither should be slighted; neither should be overvalued when employed separately.

13

Team Building

In large organizations—schools, churches, businesses, government—many decisions are made and implemented by small groups or teams. Most of their decision making, problem solving, policy making, and planning transpires in small groups. The effectiveness of an organization cannot be discussed, therefore, without also examining the effectiveness of its subgroups, for the quality of their work has a direct bearing on the effectiveness of the organization as a whole. Schools, for example, may foster team planning and team teaching. Administrative decisions may be made by teams such as school boards, city councils, and executive groups. Any organization, whether it is an industrial corporation, a university, or a national charity, can be viewed as being made up of overlapping teams. One team might be composed, for example, of a president and her vice-presidents, another of a vice-president with his managers, a third of a manager with her supervisors, another of a supervisor with his foremen, another of a foreman with her workers, and so on. Teams are also made up of interdepartmental personnel to coordinate the functioning of different departments and of temporary task forces, committees, and project teams.

All organizations accomplish their work through a number of teams of different kinds. And to function effectively, they must make sure that their work teams are productive. A work team of competent and cooperating people who have the same general goals and who have resources on which to draw is the principal resource an organization has. Thus, it is vital that organizations strive to improve the effectiveness of their teams.

There are many real payoffs for team development in organizations, especially in large corporations. Today's large company often faces such problems as the lack of real commitment from its employees, avoidance of responsibility and risk taking by members, lack of clear and operational objectives, destructive competition among executives, poor communication, loss of young managerial talent, and resistant employees. The solution to many of these problems lies in team development. The meaning and significance of one's work and the interpersonal rewards of being an organization member are usually found in the work group. Through participation on a team where there is effective communication, shared leadership and decision making, cooperative goals to which everyone is committed, and chances for quality production and personal responsibility, meaning and significance are put back into a person's work life.

One major tool used to improve organization functioning is, therefore, team building (also called team development and team training). Team building refers to a method under which groups experientially learn to increase their skills for effective teamwork by examining their structures, purpose, setting, procedures, and interpersonal dynamics. This learning takes place with the members of an existing group within the organization, usually made up of a superior and his subordinates.

To begin a process of team building, a model of what constitutes the ideal, effective team must be available. The one of group effectiveness presented in Chapter 1 is such a model. Thus, an effective team would have clear, cooperative goals to which every member is committed; accurate and effective communication of ideas and feelings; distributed participation and leadership; appropriate and effective decision-making procedures; productive controversy; high levels of trust, acceptance, and support among its members and a high level of cohesion; constructive management of power and conflict; and adequate problem-solving procedures. Once this model of group effectiveness has been established, the team needs to structure self-renewing procedures. These procedures consist of:

1. Gathering data about the present functioning of the team
2. Analyzing the data in such a way that the team can compare its current functioning with the desired group functioning as specified by the model.
3. Initiating a problem-solving process about the best means of improving its functioning to make it more in line with desired group functioning.
4. Increasing members' skills, attitudes, and interpersonal effectiveness and establishing normative and structural supports to encourage and reinforce the desired changes.
5. Gathering new data about current group functioning to see how successful the group has been in implementing the changes.

As part of the problem-solving process in Steps 3 and 4, two essential questions need to be dealt with: (1) Do the group members have the necessary skills and attitudes to work together cooperatively and effectively? and (2) Do the group norms, role definitions, values, and structures encourage and support the use of the needed skills? If the group members do not have the necessary skills for maximizing group effectiveness, a specific skill-training program—this book, for example, could serve—should be started. Because groups function as their members make them function, effective groups first of all need to be made up of effective people. Interpersonal effectiveness can be defined as the degree to which the consequences of a person's behavior match his intentions; the skills involved in interpersonal effectiveness are dealt with at length in Johnson (1972). Learning effective skills is more than just learning the specific behaviors involved and then practicing them. There is also a set of values, beliefs, and attitudes that must be considered in conjunction with the development of a skill. For instance, a person may learn the procedures for consensual decision making, but unless she believes that involvement of effective group members will improve the quality of the decision and help its implementation, she will not tend to use her skills in promoting decisions by consensus. A skill-development program must focus on both the actual skills to be learned and the beliefs, values, and attitudes of the people learning the skills.

Once it is established that team members have the necessary skills and attitudes, careful attention must be directed toward how these skills are encouraged, reinforced, and supported. The normative structure of the team, the expectations for appropriate behavior, the reinforcements given for engaging in skillful and effective behavior, and the way in which a group structures specific role responsibilities and time for both assessing its effectiveness and implementing desired changes all influence the extent to which individual members will engage in needed behavior in skillful ways.

Every consultant will probably approach the implementation of team building in different ways. A few studies, however, indicate the effects of various team-building programs on the team's effectiveness and the effectiveness of the organizations within which the teams function. Harrison (1962) found that the members of a managerial team, after training, described one another in more "human" emotional terms, but did not use these terms to describe other associates who had not attended the training program. Friedlander (1967) found that managers who had attended team training reported a greater increase in their participation, personal involvement, mutual influence, and problem-solving effectiveness than did managers who had no training. A more detailed follow-up (Friedlander, 1968) demonstrated that the team that had the most extended pre- and post-training contact with an outside consultant showed the greatest change. Morton and Wight (1964) found that managers trained with their teams reported more factors involving improved team functioning than did managers trained in groups other than their own teams. Zenger (1969) studied the effects of two years of team training on a sales organization consisting of a six-man top team plus related subordinate teams; he found improvements in sales, income of sales agents, and company standing. Zenger concluded that these changes were accompanied by improved perceptions of one's self, one's superior, one's work group, and one's organization. Finally, Beckhard and Lake (1971) analyzed the effects of an intensive two year organization-development program aimed at establishing a team approach to management in a large banking organization. The division within the firm they worked with most intensively (in comparison with the control divisions) improved productivity, reduced turnover and absenteeism, developed better internal communication and greater structural inventiveness, and improved problem-solving capacities. Data from superiors of the managers most closely affected by the intervention indicated that innergroup conflicts were reduced and that more problem-oriented and productive work was being accomplished. The subordinates of the same managers reported that they had more frequent access to their superiors, whom they perceived as more egalitarian, less closely supervising, more open to suggestion, and more influential with their own superiors. The improvements in team effectiveness were, in general, being maintained when studied four years later.

FEEDBACK EXERCISE

One of the most necessary activities of a work team is for the members to give and receive feedback about their behavior. Unless members get feedback from other members, the chief resource for improving their functioning is lost; unless members give feedback to other members, the chance for them to improve their effectiveness is denied. The purpose of this exercise is to start a feedback session in which members exchange information and gain increased clarity and understanding of their impact on the other team members. The exercise is adapted from one developed by Richard Byrd. The procedure is as follows:

1. In your team or group, you and your colleagues should discuss the following ground rules:
   a. You may use the questions attached or any others you want to ask.
   b. You do not have to ask any questions at all if you do not wish to.
   c. You may ask certain people to respond to your questions.
   d. You should not expect everyone to have an answer to your questions, but do ask for more than one reaction.
   e. If you are not sure of or are concerned about someone's unstated feelings toward you, or toward others, ask him directly, by name, to respond.

2. Manner of responding:
   a. Be specific in answering your team colleague's questions (i.e., "When you do such and such I see you thus and so.")
   b. Don't give a superficial answer. If you have no answer, don't create one.
   c. Answer directly and candidly any questions asked of you, even if the answer is that you have no answer.
   d. Make sure everyone gets her chance to participate, at least once.
   e. Don't answer in terms of right or wrong. Share your own feelings about what

your colleague does. You are giving her information about her impact on you.

3. Once the ground rules are clear, begin the process of asking questions of one another. It usually helps the group climate if the team leader herself begins asking a question about her behavior. If she sincerely wants to get feedback, an open climate will tend to be established. Use the questions imaginatively.

FEEDBACK QUESTIONS

Make sure people give you illustrations or examples of your behavior when answering your questions. Illustrations of behavior make a point quickly and graphically.

1. Do I help others to express their ideas?
2. Do I listen alertly and with understanding to what others are saying?
3. Do I communicate my ideas well?
4. Do I avoid conflict when I shouldn't?
5. Am I overly stubborn about my opinions?
6. Do I often provide leadership for our team?
7. Do I seek and use other people's ideas well?
8. Am I overly aggressive?
9. Do I give in too quickly when I'm opposed?
10. Am I sensitive to others' feelings?
11. Do I take responsibility readily?
12. Am I more often disruptive than constructive?
13. Am I too quiet?
14. Do I participate enough?
15. Do I appear to believe people?
16. Am I tolerant of opposition viewpoints?
17. Do I dominate the conversation?
18. Do I appear willing to support other people's ideas?
19. Do I "own" my ideas and feelings?

BEGINNING A NEW TEAM EXERCISE

People do not just walk into a room, introduce themselves as members of the same team, listen to their group goals, and begin productive work. An effective team develops just as any other group develops—by establishing relationships among members as well as norms and procedures for the group, and by clarification of and commitment to goals. The purpose of this exercise is to provide a model for beginning a new team.

1. *Forming the team* or *Who are we?* Team members should share their expectations about what the team is to do, their individual needs and desires that the group may help meet, and how they are feeling "right now." Several incomplete sentences can be used to start the discussion, such as: (1) "When I first enter a new group I feel. . . . "; (2) "I usually try to make people think I am. . . . "; (3) "What I am afraid is going to happen is. . . . "

2. *Deciding upon procedures* or *How will we work together?* One of the first things a group has to do is to formulate its procedures, such as how decisions are going to be made and how it is going to approach its goals and tasks. Members should discuss which procedures seem appropriate. They should also predict some problems that might block the team from working effectively, and decide on methods for working through the blocks. Members should then share impressions of one another. Many problems are avoided if procedures are established before work begins.

3. *Clarifying goals and tasks* or *What are we going to do together?* Many team problems can be avoided by clearly establishing at the outset just what goals the group is going to accomplish. To achieve a goal, a high level of coordination must exist among tasks needed to accomplish it and the resources of the group and its members. A team should fantasize about the ultimate, maximum results it hopes to accomplish—in other words, dream about the potential ideal results. It should then explore the strengths and resources of each group member, and, finally, the different ways of stating its goal. It might also review its "commission" or stated purpose, probe differences in member understanding, discuss the relationship of goal and tasks to personal needs and "dream" lists, and bring out any hidden agendas present in the group. The criteria presented in Chapter 4 for an effective goal should be used.

4. *Analyzing the helping and obstructing factors that affect goal achievement.* As a group, members should do a force field analysis on the forces they expect to affect the achievement of the goal.

5. *Planning the tasks necessary for goal accomplishment* or *How will we get there?* The team may first want to brainstorm action steps necessary for goal accomplishment and then rank different plans in terms of desirability (see brainstorming section in Chapter 6). After choosing one plan and working out the procedure for its implementation, it is often desirable to go back and work out another alternative, as "Plan B."

6. *Planning evaluation* or *How will we know when we get there?* Team members must plan the evaluation of its efforts and the criteria to be used to signify the degree of goal accomplishment.

7. *Team Processing.* Members must process how effectively they have worked as a team throughout this exercise.

8. *Summarizing.* Team members should summarize their conclusions concerning team building that can be made on the basis of their experiences in doing this exercise.

14

Epilogue

Group skills and knowledge are vital for creating effective groups, which in turn are vital for developing a high quality of life and psychological health. As noted in Chapter 1, groups are of incalculable importance in the life of every person and skills in group membership are absolutely essential for effective functioning within any society, family, organization, or relationship. We are not born with these skills, they must be developed. You have now completed a variety of experiences aimed at increasing your group skills and knowledge. It is hoped that you are now more skillful in leading decision-making activities to accomplish group goals. During such activities, it is hoped that you will be able to promote effective communication, controversy, conflict management, mutual influence and other aspects of group effectiveness. It is also hoped that you will be able to apply your increased skills and knowledge in a variety of groups and under a variety of conditions. You may wish to repeat many of the exercises in this book to reinforce your knowledge and to reread much of the material to gain a more complete understanding of how to utilize group skills. There are, however, two concluding exercises that may be helpful in applying the material covered in this book to the memberships you hold in groups.

TERMINATING A GROUP

The goals of this exercise are to (1) complete any unfinished business in a group, (2) relive and remember the positive group experiences the group has had, (3) synthesize what group members have received from being part of the group, and (4) describe and express constructively group members' feelings about the termination of the group. The theme of the exercise is that though every group ends, the things you as a member have given and received, the ways in which you have grown, the skills you have learned, all continue with you. Terminating relationships may be sad, but the ways in which you have grown within your relationships with other group members can be applied to group situations in the future. Here is the procedure for the group to follow in the exercise:

1. Discuss the topic, "Is there anything that needs to be resolved, discussed, dealt with, or expressed before the group ends?"
2. Discuss these questions: "What have been the most significant experiences of the group? What have I gotten out of being a member of the group? How has being a part of this group facilitated my growth as a person? What skills have I learned from being in this group?" As alternatives to a discussion, group members might make a painting, a collage, or a poem describing their experiences.
3. Discuss how you feel about the group winding up its activities and what feelings you want to express about the termination. Personal styles of handling the dissolution of a group may be discussed. If you cannot discuss this issue, the following alternatives may generate a productive discussion:
   a. Each of you in turn says good-bye to the group and leaves. Each of you then spends five minutes thinking about your feelings and returns to express anything you wanted to but did not express before.
   b. Each of you nonverbally shows how you felt when you first joined the group and then shows nonverbally how you feel now.
4. As a closing exercise, stand up in a close circle. You are all to imagine that you have the magical power to give anything you wish to another group member. You are then to give the person on your right a parting gift, each taking your turn so that everyone in the group can hear what the gifts are. Examples of what individuals might give are moonbeams, a flower, a better self-concept, an ability to commit oneself to a relationship, comfort with conflict, more empathy with others, the perfect love affair, and so on. When giving the gift, extend your hands as if actually passing something to the other person. When receiving the gift, extend your hands as if actually receiving something from the other person.
5. Have a group hug.

SELF—CONTRACT

Write a description of yourself as a group member. Mention all the strengths and skills you can think of and mention the areas in which you need to increase your skills. Then make a contract with yourself to make some changes in your life; the contract can involve starting something new, stopping something old, or changing some present aspect of your life. It should involve applying your group skills to the actual group situations you are now facing, or working to develop certain skills further. It may involve joining new groups and terminating old group memberships. In making the contract, pick several group memberships you now have and set a series of goals concerning how you will behave to increase your effectiveness and satisfaction as a group member. Write the contract down, place it in an envelope, address the envelope to yourself, and open it three months later.

A

Conducting Skill-Training Exercises

TYPICAL SKILL—TRAINING SESSION

To discuss how to conduct a skill-training session, it may be helpful to first review the overall structure of a group exercise. A typical session would involve the following procedures:

1. Participants are presented with an introduction by a coordinator, who then conducts a warm-up discussion. The introduction should include the objectives of the session, an outline of what will happen, and a description of the specific skills with which the participants will be concerned during the exercise. The warm-up is to set the stage for the exercise, engender participant involvement, and promote some sort of emotional connection among participants. The warm-up discussion could take the form of a brief exchange of current feelings among participants or of the coordinator telling an interesting anecdote or story about group skills. The expectations of the participants should be set at this point.

2. The exercise is then conducted.

3. After the exercise is completed, the participants are asked to conceptualize, analyze, and summarize their experience. This step may be structured through discussion questions or data feedback about how each person and the group behaved. The personal learnings of each participant, their application to his life, and the theoretical principles into which the participants gain insight as a result of their experience can be focused upon.

4. In a general session participants should talk over the experience and summarize the nature of their ideas of their experience. The coordinator should integrate appropriate theory and cognitive frameworks into the participants' statements.

The emphasis at this point is upon integrating the important learnings, theory, and research with their experiences.

5. The coordinator should then discuss the issues of applying the learnings and skills to the participants' specific life situations.

6. An evaluation of the success of the session in accomplishing its objectives should be made.

7. At the end of the session, a sense of closure needs to be provided by the coordinator. It may be achieved by concluding with a short, fun, involving experience or by the coordinator simply saying the training exercise is over.

DESIGNING A SKILL—TRAINING SESSION

A skill-training program could involve any number and combination of the exercises presented in this book. It could consist of a single exercise or of several exercises drawn from different chapters. It could last a few minutes or several days. Whatever the length of the session and the number of exercises used, the basic design of the training process is the same. The following elements need to be considered by the coordinator in designing a skill-training session:

1. The coordinator-participant relationship must be examined. Useful questions to be cleared up include: What is the purpose of the session? Why is the coordinator conducting it? What is the contract between the coordinator and the participants? What is the relationship between the coordinator and the participants? Your motivation as coordinator, hidden agendas (if any), explicit and implicit assumptions about the session and the participants, and your limitations and competencies should be reviewed. It is also helpful to know the following information about the participants:

   a. Expectations: What do the participants hope, believe, or fear will happen or not happen?

   b. Experience: What kind of previous training have the participants had?

   c. Relevance: How might the learnings be used after the session?

   d. Relationships: What are the participants past and future relationships with each other?

   e. Needs: What specific learnings, and what general kinds of learnings, do the participants want or need?

   f. Vital data: sex, age, marital status, general attitudes, physical or emotional problems and pressures, back-home support possibilities, and so on.

   g. Motivation: What is the level of the participants' motivation?

   h. Recruitment: How were the participants recruited? Did they all voluntarily agree to attend the session?

2. The desired outcomes of the session should be specified; they are usually discussed as objectives or goals. They should specify who is to be trained and what is the direction and magnitude of the desired learning. Clearly specified

goals are useful in deciding upon the components of the session and its evaluation. All the criteria for clear goals given on page 104 in Chapter 4 are of importance in stating the session's objectives. Participants should be able to spell out the learnings they will try to achieve.

3. Detail the constraints on the session. These include the time periods available, the location, the facilities, the range of competencies in the coordinator(s), and so on.

4. Generate a list of alternative exercises and activities that can be used in the skill-training session. These alternatives may include a variety of exercises and theory sessions. This list can be put together from two sources: the desired outcomes of the session and the resources and preferences of the coordinator(s). All the exercises in this book and in *Reaching Out* are possibilities.

5. Make a tentative design for the session. Evaluate it in terms of these questions:
   a. Is it appropriate to accomplish the desired outcomes?
   b. Are the activities within your range of competencies?
   c. Is there an opportunity for participants to express their needs or expectations or both?
   d. Does it enable the participants to make the transition from the "outside" world to the session and back to the "outside" world?
   e. Does it encourage the transfer of learnings?
   f. Does it have high personal relevance for the participants, and will it enable them to function better in their day-to-day life?
   g. If there is more than one coordinator, does it allow time for you to check signals with each other?
   h. Are high- and low-tension activities appropriately placed within the design?
   i. Are the assumptions about the skill and background of the participants appropriate?
   j. Does the overall design provide a sense of continuity, appropriate transitions among activities, a good "flow"?
   k. Are participants able to see the relationship between the exercises and the desired outcomes of the session?
   l. Does it allow for a logical flow of experiences?
   m. Does it offer flexibility/maneuverability to meet unexpected and emerging needs?
   n. Is it consistent with the principles of experiential learning?
   o. Is there opportunity for ongoing participant feedback and evaluation?
   p. Are you as coordinator prepared to recognize and deal with unanticipated learning outcomes?
   q. Are all the necessary materials and facilities available?

6. Make sure you are highly committed to the final design. If there is more than one coordinator assign responsibilities. Arrange for the materials and facilities.

7. If there is more than one coordinator process how you function as a staff. Check to see if any team development needs to take place among the staff before the skill-training session begins.

EVALUATION

Evaluation is the process of determining how successful—or unsuccessful—a group was in achieving its goal or objective. In the case of a skill-training session, it is the process by which evidence is gathered about whether the desired outcomes of the session were accomplished, what unanticipated learnings were accomplished, how the activities involved in the session contributed to its success or failure, and what the coordinator(s) could do to improve their competencies. In an evaluation there must be a clear, operational statement of the desired outcomes, ways to measure how nearly the desired outcomes were achieved and what activities and coordinator behaviors contributed to the session's success or failure, time within the design for the participants to give feedback on the effectiveness of the session, and time following the session for the data to be analyzed and conclusions drawn.

In evaluation it is helpful to know such things as the emotional reactions of the participants (how do they feel now), the specific or significant learnings the participants have obviously achieved, the amount of increased participant competence in performing the skills, what sort of future experiences the participants now see the need for, the degree to which the desired outcomes were accomplished, the participants' reactions to various parts of the session, and what the coordinator(s) did that was helpful or unhelpful to the participants.

A variety of data-collection procedures can be used by the coordinator(s) to evaluate a session: interviews, general statements made by the participants, questionnaire responses, observation of how skills were applied, and so on. All sessions do not have to be evaluated at a high level of proficiency, but more than the general impressions of the coordinator(s) should be used. At the very least the coordinator(s) should be able to direct the same session in the future in a more effective and efficient way.

HELPFUL GUIDELINES

In conducting the exercise in this book the coordinator will have a set of general responsibilities. They include:

1. Organizing the materials, procedures, and facilities needed to manage the exercise.
2. Introducing, ending, and tying together the experiences involved in the exercise.
3. Keeping time in a task-oriented way to prevent the participants from getting sidetracked.
4. Restating and calling attention to the main learnings of the exercise, which include relating the experiences to the theory.

5. Setting a climate of experimentation, acceptance, openness, and warmth so that participants will be encouraged to try out new skills and improve their competencies.

6. Serving as an anchor point by being reliable, knowledgeable, trustworthy, and responsible.

7. Modeling the skills he wishes to teach.

8. Following the general outlines of experiential learning.

9. Being enthusiastic about the value of the exercise.

10. Knowing and understanding the material well.

11. Checking to make sure everyone understands their instructions and responsibilities.

12. Being sensitive to the differences in participation, needs, and styles of the participants.

13. Remaining flexible so that the preplanned procedures do not interfere with participant learning.

14. Enjoying himself and making sure that he also learns and benefits from the exercises.

B

Ethics of

Experiental Learning

All learning activities require a code of ethics, either implicit or explicit. A great deal of attention has been paid to the ethics of growth-group leaders, but little consideration has been given to the ethics of conducting experiential-learning activities. Some of the ethical issues relevant to the type of skill-training exercises included in this book are as follows.

A. THE CONTRACT

1. The coordinator's intentions and objectives should be clearly communicated to the participants. The participants should understand that they are going to participate in an experiential exercise in which they will be expected to examine their own behavior and the behavior of others, and analyze the behaviors for purposes of learning.
2. The nature of the contract should be easily understood by the coordinator and the participants. The number of experiences, the length of each session, the appropriateness and the objectives of each exercise all should be agreed upon.
3. The coordinator should have the competencies, preparation, and training necessary to conduct the program for which he is contracting.
4. The point at which the contract is terminated should be clear to both coordinator and participants.

B. THE ACTIVITIES

5. The participants' freedom of choice should be respected. Participation should be on a voluntary basis. An individual's freedom to choose whether or not to

become involved in an exercise or part of an exercise should be respected. This freedom includes advising the participants on how they can say "no" to the instructions of the coordinator.

6. The coordinator should have an explicit reason for conducting the exercise and be prepared to state it publicly.

7. Only exercises the coordinator is competent to direct should be conducted. If the coordinator lacks certification and competence in psychotherapy, for example, exercises aimed at exposing deep psychodynamics of participants should not be held (and there are no such exercises in this book).

8. The coordinator should present relevant theory and research when it is appropriate to the participants' learning and increased effectiveness.

9. The coordinator should be constantly aware of his behavior styles and personal needs, and deal with them productively in the performance of his role. He should also be aware of the impact of his needs and style on the participants.

10. All experiences should be processed by discussing the participants' feelings and reactions to them and by asking the participants what can be learned from the experiences. Adequate time must be programmed into the design of the session for this purpose.

11. The coordinator should not initiate confrontations between participants, which may damage their future relationship. This admonition does not mean that coordinators should discourage risk taking in giving feedback, and making honest process comments, or instituting attempts at facing conflicts and improving the relationship. It simply means that confrontations should originate with the participants, not the coordinator.

12. If any personal information is revealed, the coordinator should make sure that the possibility of it being used in any way to damage the participants is minimized.

13. Ideally, the coordinator should be able to recognize symptoms of serious psychological stress and be able to make responsible decisions when such problems arise. At the very least the coordinator should know where emergency psychological services are available.

14. Sessions should be evaluated to provide the coordinator with feedback to improve his performance. The sessions should be open to scrutiny by competent professionals interested in the effectiveness of experiential learning.

15. Follow-up interviews with the participants should be possible so that the impact of the sessions on them can be assessed and their feelings and reactions to the sessions can be discussed.

The statements above are meant to be guidelines, not rigid rules. The only effective way to enforce ethical standards in educational activities is for the persons conducting the educational programs to enforce their code of ethics on themselves and use good judgment in what they do. As long as a coordinator's behavior is based upon caring, respect, and regard for the participants, ethical violations will probably be avoided. It is hoped that the above guidelines will be provocative in helping the users of this book build a personal code of ethical conduct.

How to Compute a Group Average

To find a group average, simply total the individual scores of the group members and divide by the number of members in the group. The following is an example:

Members	*Score*
Tom	5
Jane	6
Dennis	4
Pat	7
Roger	3
David	6
Edythe	6
Dale	5
8 members	42

$$\text{Average} = 5.25$$
$$8\overline{\smash{\big)}42.00}$$

Answers

HOLLOW SQUARE EXERCISE

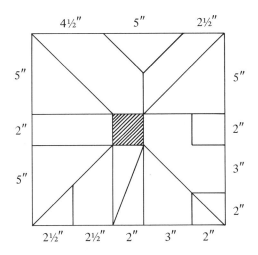

REDUCING RESISTANCE TO CHANGE

The case study on which you have just reached a decision was an actual situation studied by Coch and French (1948) in the late 1940s. From the results of their studies and the studies conducted by Lewin (1947), the correct ranking is considered to be: 4, 3, 2, 5, 1. The two principles involved are (1) group discussion is more effective than lectures and memorandums in influencing change, and (2) if employees believe they are really participating in decision making, they become more committed to putting the decision into practice. The results of this exercise will most likely confirm and extend the findings of the groups on the effects of participation in decision making.

WINTER SURVIVAL EXERCISE

Background Information

None of the information here should be given to participants until after they have completed the decision-making parts of the exercise. Mid-January is the coldest time of the year in Minnesota and Manitoba. The first problem the survivors face, therefore, is to preserve their body heat and protect themselves against its loss. This problem can be met by building a fire, minimizing movement and exertion, and using as much insulation as possible.

The participants have just crash-landed. Many individuals tend to overlook the enormous shock reaction this has upon the human body, and the death of the pilot and copilot increases the shock. Decision making under such conditions is extremely difficult. Such a situation requires a strong emphasis upon the use of reasoning not only to make decisions, but also to reduce the fear and panic every person would naturally feel. Along with fear, shock reaction is manifested in the feelings of helplessness, loneliness, and hopelessness. These feelings have brought about more fatalities than perhaps any other cause in survival situations. Through the use of reasoning, hope for survival and the will to live can be generated. Certainly the state of shock means that movement of individuals should be at a minimum and that an attempt to calm them should be made.

Before taking off a pilot always has to file a flight plan. The flight plan contains the vital information regarding the flight, such as the course, speed, estimated time of arrival, type of aircraft, number of people on board, and so on. Search-and-rescue operations would begin shortly after the plane failed to arrive at its destination at its estimated time of arrival.

The eighty miles to the nearest known town is a very long walk even under ideal conditions, particularly if one is not used to walking such distances. Under the circumstances of being in shock, dressed in city clothes, having deep snow in the woods and a variety of water barriers to cross, to attempt to walk out would mean almost certain death from freezing and exhaustion. At the temperatures given, the loss of body heat through exertion is a very serious matter.

Once the survivors have found ways in which to keep warm, their most immediate problem is to provide signaling methods to attract the attention of search planes and search parties. Thus, all the items the group has must be assessed according to their value in signaling the group's whereabouts.

Winter Survival Exercise Scoring Key

The correct ranking of the survivors' items was made on the basis of information provided by Mark Wanig and supplemented from Rutstrum (1973). Wanig was an instructor for three years in survival training in the reconnaissance school in the 101st Division of the U. S. Army and later an instructor on wilderness survival for four years at the Twin City Institute for Talented Youth. He is now conducting wilderness-survival programs for Minneapolis teachers.

1. *Cigarette lighter (without fluid).* The gravest danger facing the group is exposure to the cold. The greatest need is for a source of warmth and the second greatest need is for signaling devices. This makes building a fire the first order of business. Without matches something is needed to produce sparks to start a fire. Even without fluid the cigarette lighter can be used to produce sparks. The fire will not only provide warmth, it will also provide smoke for daytime signaling and firelight for nighttime signaling.

2. *Ball of steel wool.* To make a fire, a means of catching the sparks made by the cigarette lighter is needed. Steel wool is the best substance with which to catch a spark and support a flame, even if it is a little bit wet.

3. *Extra shirt and pants for each survivor.* Clothes are probably the most versatile items one can have in a situation like this. Besides adding warmth to the body they can be used for shelter, signaling, bedding, bandages, string when unraveled, and tinder to make fires. Even maps can be drawn on them. The versatility of clothes and the need for fires, signaling devices, and warmth make this item number three in importance.

4. *Family-size Hershey bar (one per person).* To gather wood for the fire and to set up signals, energy is needed. The Hershey bars would supply the energy to sustain the survivors for quite some time. Because they contain basically carbohydrates, they would supply energy without making digestive demands upon the body.

5. *Can of shortening.* This item has many uses—the most important being that a mirrorlike signaling device can be made from the lid. After shining the lid with the steel wool, the survivors can use it to produce an effective reflector of sunlight. A mirror is the most powerful tool they have for communicating their presence. In sunlight, a simple mirror can generate 5 to 7 million candlepower. The reflected sunbeam can be seen beyond the horizon. Its effectiveness is somewhat limited by the trees but one member of the group could climb a tree and use the mirror to signal search planes. If the survivors have no other means of signaling, they would still have better than 80 percent chance of being rescued within the first twenty-four hours.

Other uses for the item are as follows: The shortening can be rubbed on the body to protect exposed areas, such as the face, lips, and hands, from the cold. In desperation it could be eaten in small amounts. When melted into an oil the shortening is helpful in starting fires. Melted shortening, when soaked into a piece of cloth, will produce an effective candlewick. The can is useful in melting snow to produce drinking water. Even in the wintertime water is important as the body loses water in many ways, such as through perspiration, respiration, shock reactions, and so on. This water must be replenished because dehydration affects the ability to make clear decisions. The can is also useful as a cup.

6. *Flashlight.* Inasmuch as the group has little hope of survival if it decides to walk out, its major hope is to catch the attention of search planes. During the day the lid-mirror, smoke, and flags made from clothing represent the best devices. During the night the flashlight is the best signaling device. It is the only effective night-signaling device besides the fire. In the cold, however, a flashlight loses the power in its battery very quickly. It must therefore, be kept warm if it is to work, which means that it must be kept close to someone's body. The value of the flashlight lies in the fact that if the fire burns low or inadvertently goes out, the flashlight could be immediately turned on the moment a plane is heard.

7. *Piece of rope.* The rope is another versatile piece of equipment. It could be used to pull dead limbs off trees for firewood. When cut into pieces, the rope will help in constructing shelters. It can be burned. When frayed it can be used as tinder to start fires. When unraveled it will make good insulation from the cold if it is stuffed inside clothing.

8. *Newspaper (one per person).* The newspaper could be used for starting a fire much the same as the rope. It will also serve as an insulator; when rolled up and placed under the clothes around a person's legs or arms, it provides dead-air space for extra protection from the cold. The paper can be used for recreation by reading it, memorizing it, folding it, or tearing it. It could be rolled into a cone and yelled through as a signal device. It could also be spread around an area to help signal a rescue party.

9. *.45-caliber pistol.* This pistol provides a sound signaling device. (The international distress signal is three shots fired in rapid succession.) There have been numerous cases of survivors going undetected because by the time the rescue party arrived in the area the survivors were too weak to make a loud enough noise to attract attention. The butt of the pistol could be used as a hammer. The powder from the shells will assist in fire building. By placing a small bit of cloth in a cartridge, emptied of its bullet, a fire can be started by firing the gun at dry wood on the ground. At night the muzzle blast of the gun is visible, which also makes it useful as a signaling device.

The pistol's advantages are counterbalanced by its dangerous disadvantages. Anger, frustration, impatience, irritability, and lapses of rationality may increase as the group waits to be rescued. The availability of a lethal weapon is a real danger to the group under these conditions. Although it could be used for hunting, it would take a highly skilled marksman to kill an animal and then the animal would have to be transported through the snow to the crash area, probably taking more energy than would be advisable.

10. *Knife.* A knife is a versatile tool, but it is not too important in the winter setting. It could be used for cutting the rope into desired lengths, making shavings from pieces of wood for tinder, and many other uses could be thought up.

11. *Compress kit (with gauze).* The best use of this item is to wrap the gauze around exposed areas of the body for insulation. Feet and hands are probably the most vulnerable to frostbite, and the gauze can be used to keep them warm. The gauze can be used as a candlewick when dipped into melted shortening. It would

also make effective tinder. The small supply of the gauze is the reason this item is ranked so low.

12. *Ski poles.* Although they are not very important, the poles are useful as a flag pole or staff for signaling. They can be used to stabilize a person walking through the snow to collect wood, and to test the thickness of the ice on a lakeshore or stream. Probably their most useful function would be as supports for a shelter or by the fire as a heat reflector.

13. *Quart of 85-proof whiskey.* The only useful function of the whiskey is to aid in fire building or as a fuel. A torch could be made from a piece of clothing soaked in the whiskey and attached to an upright ski pole. The danger of the whiskey is that someone might try to drink it when it is cold. Whiskey takes on the temperature it is exposed to, and a drink of it at minus thirty degrees would freeze a person's esophagus and stomach and do considerable damage to the mouth. Drinking it warm will cause dehydration. The bottle, kept warm, would be useful for storing drinking water.

14. *Sectional air map made of plastic.* This item is dangerous because it will encourage individuals to attempt to walk to the nearest town—thereby condemning them to almost certain death.

15. *Compass.* Because the compass may also encourage some survivors to try to walk to the nearest town, it too is a dangerous item. The only redeeming feature of the compass is the possible use of its glass top as a reflector of sunlight to signal search planes, but it is the least effective of the potential signaling devices available. That it might tempt survivors to walk away from the crash site makes it the least desirable of the fifteen items.

Winter Survival Exercise: Key

The correct ranking of the survivors' fifteen items is as follows:

11	Compress kit (with 28-ft., 2-in. gauze)
2	Ball of steel wool
1	Cigarette lighter (without fluid)
9	Loaded .45-caliber pistol
8	Newspaper (one per person)
15	Compass
12	2 Ski poles
10	Knife
14	Sectional air map made of plastic
7	30 feet of rope
4	Family-size Hershey bar (one per person)
6	Flashlight with batteries
13	Quart of 85-proof whiskey
3	Extra shirt and pants for each survivor
5	Can of shortening

WRECKED ON THE MOON EXERCISE: KEY

15	Box of matches	Little or no use on moon
4	Food concentrate	Supplies daily food required
6	Fifty feet of nylon rope	Useful in tying injured together, help in climbing
8	Parachute silk	Shelter against sun's rays
13	Portable heating unit	Useful only if party landed on dark side
11	Two .45-caliber pistols	Self-propulsion devices could be made from them
12	One case dehydrated Pet milk	Food, mixed with water for drinking
1	Two 100-pound tanks of oxygen	Fills respiration requirement
3	Stellar map (of moon's constellations)	One of principal means of finding directions
9	Life raft	CO_2 bottles for self-propulsion across chasms, etc.
14	Magnetic compass	Probably no magnetized poles; thus, useless
2	Five gallons of water	Replenishes loss by sweating, etc.
10	Signal flares	Distress call when line of sight possible
7	First-aid kit containing injection needles	Oral pills or injection medicine valuable
5	Solar-powered FM receiver-transmitter	Distress signal transmitter possible communication with mother ship

GRIEVANCES OF BLACK CITIZENS: KEY

The ordering of the grievances given by the National Advisory Commission on Civil Disorders is as follows:

- 4 Inadequate education
- 7 Disrespectful white attitudes
- 10 Inadequate municipal services
- 1 Discriminatory police practices
- 3 Inadequate housing
- 12 Inadequate welfare programs
- 5 Poor recreational facilities
- 2 Unemployment and underemployment

8   Administration of justice
   9   Inadequate federal programs
  11   Discriminatory consumer and credit practices
   6   Unresponsive political structure

HAZARD POTENTIAL OF SOME COMMON DRUGS EXERCISE: KEY

The correct ranking as established by Samuel Irwin is as follows:

   3   Alcohol
   5   Barbiturates
   4   Cigarette smoking (tobacco)
   6   Codeine
   2   Dexedrine
   1   Glue sniffing
   6   Heroin
   5   Hypnotics
   7   LSD-25
   8   Marijuana
   7   Mescaline
   2   Methamphetamine

Glue sniffing was rated highest because of the ensuing rapid loss of control and consciousness leading to possible overdosage and death from respiratory arrest, and to its ability to produce irreversible damage to the brain and bodily tissues.

Methamphetamine and Dexedrine (or "Speed," especially when taken intravenously) was rated second because of its high psychological dependence liability (it is too pleasurable). It also predictably produces a paranoid schizophrenic state with greatly impaired judgment, excitement and a tendency for violence after repeated use of doses three or more times what a physician might prescribe. Especially with the stimulants, users are tempted to seek more intense effects by taking the drug by injection. This leads to further impairment of functioning, a possibility of hepatitis (serious inflammation of the liver), of septicemia (infection of the veins by bacteria) from the use of unsterile materials, and a probable need for protective hospitalization. All of this is summarized by the common catch phrase, "speed kills."

Alcohol was ranked third because it has high potentials for psychological

*This rating is based on a paper by Samuel Irwin, Ph.D., "Drugs of Abuse: An Introduction to Their Actions and Potential Hazards," in *Starting Point*, a booklet published by the Florida State Department of Health and Rehabilitative Services. Dr. Irwin is a professor of psychopharmacology at the University of Oregon Medical School.

dependence, greatly impairs judgment and coordination (a leading cause of driving accidents), increases aggressiveness and violent behavior, often produces marked social deterioration, and causes irreversible damage to the brain, liver and other body tissues. The withdrawal symptoms (delirium tremens) from alcohol abuse are also often life-threatening and difficult to treat.

Cigarette smoking (tobacco) is listed next (fourth) because of the high incidence of irreversible damage (to lungs, heart and blood vessels) and cancer formation accompanying its prolonged use. These hazards greatly reduce the life span and often debilitate the individual long before death.

Barbiturates and hypnotics were ranked fifth because, although similar to alcohol in their overall effects and dependence liabilities, they do not cause as much extensive tissue damage. A greater danger with the hypnotics, however, is the increased possibility of death from overdose.

Heroin and related narcotics (Codeine) were rated sixth because, unlike alcohol and the barbiturates, they do not impair coordination and judgment in normal doses, do not produce extensive tissue damage, and are more likely to inhibit aggressive behavior. When taken intravenously, these drugs are potentially very addictive, both psychologically and physically, and their continued use can lead to social deterioration. But, the physical dependence would be of relatively little consequence if the drug were available, and sufficient tolerance develops to the depressant effects so that it is possible to function more productively under the influence of heroin than with alcohol or barbiturates. The main danger from heroin (or morphine) is acute respiratory failure and death from overdoses among unexperienced users, as a very narrow margin exists between the effective dose and the lethal dose. With illicit supplies varying greatly in potency, this represents a serious danger. Because unsterile materials are often used for injection, there is also the possibility of developing hepatitis and septicemia.

LSD-25 and other hallucinogens (Mescaline) are seventh on the list because, although they can cause psychotic reactions, such occurrences are relatively rated (less than 1% of volunteers in clinical settings have prolonged adverse reactions; and the rate of psychotic reactions for the general population of illicit users is probably less than 5%). LSD is not an addictive drug in the usual sense; it is taken intermittently and its use is usually gradually discontinued. The hallucinagens produce no physical dependence, but pose hazards in individuals, and opening up the possibility of flashbacks of LSD-like effects even months after the last dose (attributed by some physicians to hysterical reactions associated with unresolved conflicts). For some, the LSD experience can profoundly alter personal attitudes and life-styles, not necessarily detrimentally. The lethal dose is so high that no human deaths have been reported from overdosage.

Marijuana is ranked last in intrinsic hazard because there have been fewer untoward reactions from its use requiring treatment of hospitalization than from any other type of psychoactive drug. Also, marijuana is more prone to reduce aggressiveness than to increase it. Psychologic dependence to the drug is not as great a hazard as it is with alcohol; there is little tolerance development, no danger of physiological dependence and no significant tissue damage associated with its use. In small and moderate doses there seems only minor impairment of judgment or coordination and hallucinogenic effects are relatively difficult to achieve by smoking (they can occur when the drug is taken orally, a route which leads to much less predictable drug effects). Like LSD, the lethal dose of marijuana is so high that it is extremely difficult to kill oneself from overdose.

BROKEN SQUARES EXERCISE: DIRECTIONS FOR MAKING A SET OF SQUARES

You need a set of five envelopes containing pieces of cardboard that have been cut in different patterns and that, when properly arranged with pieces from some of the other four envelopes, will form five squares of equal size. One set should be provided for each five-member group.

To prepare a set, cut out five cardboard squares of equal size, approximately six-by-six inches. Place the squares in a row and mark them as below, penciling the letters a, b, c, etc., lightly so they can later be erased.

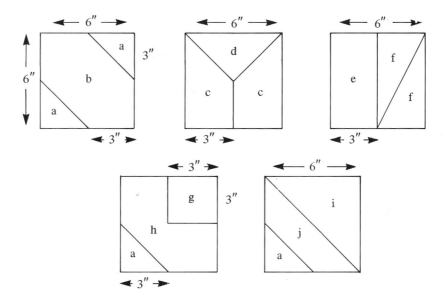

The lines should be so drawn that when cut out, all pieces marked "a" will be of exactly the same size, the pieces marked "c" will be of the same size, and the pieces marked "f" will be of the same size. By using multiples of three inches, several combinations will be possible that will enable participants to form one or two squares, but only one combination is possible that will form five squares six-by six inches.

After drawing the lines of the six-by-six-inch squares and labeling them with the lowercase letters, cut each square as marked into smaller pieces to make the parts of the puzzle.

Mark each of five envelopes A, B, C, D, and E. Distribute the cardboard pieces in the five envelopes as follows:

Envelope A has pieces i, h, e.

Envelope B has pieces a, a, a, c.

Envelope C has pieces a, j.

Envelope D has pieces d, f.

Envelope E has pieces g, b, f, c.

Erase the penciled lowercase letter from each piece and write on it, instead, its appropriate envelope letter. This relabeling will make it easy to return the pieces to the proper envelope for later use when a group has completed the task.

BEWISE COLLEGE PROBLEM SOLUTION

Name	Background	Education degree	Teaching experience	Public relations experience	Administrative experience
David Williams	Black-American	Masters	13 years	*none*	8 years
Roger Thornton	*Upper-class*	B.A., Masters	7 years	9 years; politician	16 years
Edythe James	Community center director	*none*	8 years	2 years	7 years
Frank Pierce	Neighborhood center worker, community relations	Masters	*none*	14 years	14 years
Helen Lucy	Childhood in slums	B.A., Masters	4 years	5 years	15 years
Keith Collins	Volunteer work; Book	B.A.	5 years	13 years	*none*

Andrews College is the smallest college in the state and therefore it had a 100% black-American student body in 1952.

Every candidate but Helen Lucy is disqualified because they lack the qualifications outlined in the position statements.

ENERGY INTERNATIONAL EXERCISE: SOLUTION

Name	Age	Education	Nationality	Language Spoken	Experience
Illin	38	New York School of Mines	American	Portuguese	*2 years*
Hule	45	*New Mexico Institute of Earth Science*	American	Portuguese	7 years
Gadolin	44	New York School of Mines	American	Portuguese	6 years
Samar	36	Massachusetts Institute of Sciences	American	Portuguese	5 years

Name	Age	Education	Nationality	Language Spoken	Experience
Lute	39	New York School of Mines	American	*No* Portuguese	9 years
Noddy	46	*Saint Francis University*	American	Portuguese	14 years
Lanta	39	Massachusetts Institute of Science	*Canadian*	Portuguese	4 years

The New Mexico Institute of Earth Sciences and Saint Francis University require three special subjects for graduation and are therefore smaller than the Massachusetts Institute of Sciences or the New York School of Mines. Saint Francis is not the smallest; therefore the New Mexico Institute of Earth Sciences must be. This makes NMIES a women's university. Brazilians hold a feudal attitude toward women.

Seismology and paleontology are essential for general membership. Saint Francis does not offer seismology; therefore no graduate of Saint Francis can qualify for general membership.

None of the Brazilian staff understands English, nor do the government inspectors; therefore, before the general manager can countersign the inspector's report, he must be able to read Portuguese.

The person must have at least three years' experience.

Minimum age is 38.

Each candidate except Gadolin is disqualified because he lacks the qualifications outlined.

DISTRIBUTED INFORMATION EXERCISE SOLUTION

The answer to the problem is 23/30 wors.

MURDER MYSTERY EXERCISE SOLUTION

After receiving a superficial gunshot wound from Mr. Barton, Mr. Thompson stepped on the elevator and was killed by Mr. Scott (the elevator man) with a knife at 12:30 a.m. because Mr. Scott was jealous.

TRANSMISSION OF INFORMATION EXERCISE

The Story*

A *farmer* in *western Kansas* put a *tin roof on his barn*. Then a *small tornado blew* the roof off, and when the farmer found it *two counties away*, it was *twisted and mangled* beyond repair.

*This story by Samuel J. Sackett, entitled "Tin Lizzie," is included in Botkin (1957). The title of the story should not be mentioned until after the demonstration.

A *friend and a lawyer* advised him that the *Ford Motor Company* would pay him a *good price* for the scrap tin, and the farmer decided he would *ship the roof* up to the company to see *how much he could get for it*. He crated it up in a *very big wooden box* and sent it off to *Dearborn, Michigan*, marking it plainly with his *return address* so that the Ford Company would know where to *send the check*.

Twelve weeks passed, and the farmer didn't hear from the Ford Company. Finally he was just on the *verge of writing them* to find out what was the matter, when he *received an envelope* from them. It said, "We don't know *what hit your car*, mister, but we'll have it fixed for you by the *fifteenth of next month.*"

The War of the Ghosts

One night two young men from Egulac went down to the river to hunt seals, and while they were there it became foggy and calm. Then they heard war cries, and they thought: "Maybe this is a war party." They escaped to the shore, and hid behind a log. Now canoes came up, and they heard the noise of paddles, and they saw one canoe coming up to them. There were five men in the canoe and they said:

"What do you think? We wish to take you along. We are going up the river to make war on the people."

One of the young men said: "I have no arrows."

"Arrows are in the canoe," they said.

"I will not go along. I might be killed. My relatives do not know where I have gone. But you," he said, turning to the other, "may go with them."

So one of the young men went, but the other returned home.

And the warriors went on up the river to a town on the other side of Kalama. The people came down to the water and they began to fight, and many were killed. And presently the young man heard one of the warriors say: "Quick, let us go home. That Indian has been hit." Now he thought, "Oh, they are ghosts." He did not feel sick, but they said he had been shot.

So the canoes went back to Egulac, and the young man went ashore to his house and made a fire. And he told everybody: "Behold I accompanied ghosts, and we went to fight. Many of our fellows were killed, and many of those who attacked us were killed. They said I was hit, but I did not feel sick."

He told it all, and then he became quiet. When the sun rose he fell down. Something black came out of his mouth. His face became contorted. The people jumped up and cried.

He was dead.

STRANDED IN THE DESERT EXERCISE

Important Facts about Surviving in the Desert*

The group has just been through a traumatic situation that has had a shocking

*This information was taken from Paul Nesbitt, Alonzo Pond, and William Allen, *The Survival Book* (New York: Funk & Wagnalls, 1959).

impact on all members. The fact that their adviser was killed would increase the shock reaction. Most, if not all, members of your group need to receive treatment for shock. The group also needs to make some very clear and correct decisions about what it should do next.

The most vital problem for the group is dehydration—from exposure to the sun, from bodily activity causing perspiration and respiration, and from the hot, dry air circulating next to the skin. Thus, a sunshade needs to be rigged from the canvas, and everyone needs to wear his jacket (without wearing the jackets, trousers, socks, and so on, survival time will be shortened by at least a day). Once the sunshade is up, everyone should be as calm and inactive as possible. The canvas will also be a signaling device once it is spread out as a sunshade. Any activity increases heartbeat, respiration, and perspiration, all of which speeds up dehydration. Taking care to remain calm and under cover, the group could probably survive three days without water.

The most important items for survival, however, are the mirror and the flashlight. Their use is to signal search parties who may enter the area. The mirror is especially useful as it can generate from 5 to 7 million candlepower—which can be spotted even beyond the horizon. By using the mirror, the group has an 80 percent chance of being rescued within twenty-four hours.

The water is not enough to significantly extend survival time, but it will help in postponing the more severe effects of dehydration. Because the group must make important decisions soon after the accident, the water should be drunk as members become thirsty. There is not enough water to reverse the effects of dehydration once they begin, so saving or rationing the water serves no purpose. In late July, furthermore, the cacti contain very little water; a member would probably use up more water through respiration in breaking up the cacti than he would get from sucking its inner fibers. The belief that salt tablets help retain water is a myth; blood salinity increases with dehydration, and in taking the tablets members would need large amounts of water (far more than a quart) for the body to rid itself of increased salinity. If a member took the salt tablets he would get the same effect as drinking sea water.

Starvation is not the issue; the issue is dehydration. Increased activity in hunting would result in increased dehydration. It would also be very hard to kill an animal with enough meat to feed the group; the animals of the desert survive by "lying low." They are seldom seen. If the group got lucky and killed an animal, the protein in the meat would require increased amounts of water to process it. Thus, eating would hasten dehydration and do far more harm than good. The book is worthless. The pistol is good only as a signaling device. The group should not hunt.

If the group decides to walk out, even walking only at night, all members will probably be dead on the second day. They will have walked less than thirty-three miles during the two nights. If group members decide to walk during the day, they would probably be dead by the next morning—after walking less than twelve miles. For the group to walk out—having just gone through a traumatic experience that has had a considerable impact on the body, having few if any members who have walked forty-five miles before, and having to carry the canvas and wear the jackets to prevent dehydration—would be disastrous. One further fact of great importance:

once members started walking, the group would be much harder to spot by search parties.

CREATIVITY PROBLEM: SOLUTION

The ability to solve this problem is based upon the ability to go outside the obvious boundaries in reaching the solution. The correct answer is:

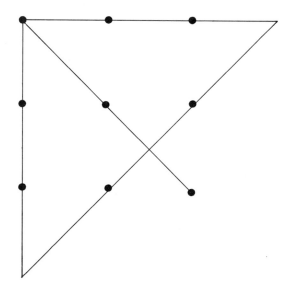

JOE DOODLEBUG PROBLEM: SOLUTION

At the moment Joe's master set down the food, Joe had already jumped once to the east. He therefore has to jump sideways three times more to the east, and once sideways back to the west, landing on top of the food. He can now eat.

BASEBALL TEAM EXERCISE: SOLUTION

Catcher: Allen.
Pitcher: Harry.
First baseman: Paul.
Second baseman: Jerry.
Third baseman: Andy.
Shortstop: Ed.
Left field: Sam.
Center field: Bill.
Right field: Mike.

BATTLESHIP EXERCISE: SOLUTION

	A	B	C	D	E	F	G	H	I	J
1										
2										
3										
4				1						
5			1	3	1					
6			1	5	1					
7			1	5	1					
8			1	3	1					
9				1						
10										

SCORING OF MY GROUP BEHAVIOR QUESTIONNAIRE

To score this questionnaire add the scores in the following way, reversing the scoring on the questions that are starred. Find the average response by dividing the total scores by seven.

Openness and Sharing	*Acceptance and Support*
1. ____	2. ____
3. ____	4. ____
*5. ____	*6. ____
7. ____	8. ____
9. ____	10. ____
11. ____	12. ____
13. ____	14. ____
Total ____	Total ____
Average ____	Average ____

*Reverse the scoring on these questions.

APPENDIX

E

Exercise Materials

OBSERVATION SHEET FOR TASK BEHAVIORS

Behaviors	*Group Members*									
Information and Opinion Giver										
Information and Opinion Seeker										
Starter										
Direction Giver										
Summarizer										
Coordinator										
Diagnoser										
Energizer										
Reality Tester										
Evaluator										
Other:										
Other:										
Other:										
Other:										

OBSERVATION SHEET FOR MAINTENANCE BEHAVIORS

Behaviors	*Group Members*									
Encourager of Participation										
Harmonizer and Compromiser										
Tension Reliever										
Communication Helper										
Evaluator of Emotional Climate										
Process Observer										
Standard Setter										
Active Listener										
Trust Builder										
Interpersonal Problem Solver										
Other:										
Other:										

OBSERVATION SHEET FOR TASK BEHAVIORS

Behaviors	Five-Minute Time Blocks									
Information and Opinion Giver										
Information and Opinion Seeker										
Starter										
Direction Giver										
Summarizer										
Coordinator										
Diagnoser										
Energizer										
Reality Tester										
Evaluator										
Other:										
Other:										
Other:										
Other:										

OBSERVATION SHEET FOR MAINTENANCE BEHAVIORS

Behaviors	*Group Members*									
Encourager of Participation										
Harmonizer and Compromiser										
Tension Reliever										
Communication Helper										
Evaluator of Emotional Climate										
Process Observer										
Standard Setter										
Active Listener										
Trust Builder										
Interpersonal Problem Solver										
Other:										
Other:										

OBSERVATION SHEET FOR MAINTENANCE BEHAVIORS

Behaviors	Five-Minute Time Blocks									
Encourager of Participation										
Harmonizer and Compromiser										
Tension Reliever										
Communication Helper										
Evaluator of Emotional Climate										
Process Observer										
Standard Setter										
Active Listener										
Trust Builder										
Interpersonal Problem Solver										
Other:										
Other:										
Other:										
Other:										

OBSERVATION SHEET FOR TASK BEHAVIORS

Behaviors	*Five-Minute Time Blocks*										
Information and Opinion Giver											
Information and Opinion Seeker											
Starter											
Direction Giver											
Summarizer											
Coordinator											
Diagnoser											
Energizer											
Reality Tester											
Evaluator											
Other:											
Other:											
Other:											
Other:											

OBSERVATION SHEET FOR MAINTENANCE BEHAVIORS

Behaviors	*Five-Minute Time Blocks*									
Encourager of Participation										
Harmonizer and Compromiser										
Tension Reliever										
Communication Helper										
Evaluator of Emotional Climate										
Process Observer										
Standard Setter										
Active Listener										
Trust Builder										
Interpersonal Problem Solver										
Other:										
Other:										
Other:										
Other:										

OBSERVATION SHEET FOR TASK BEHAVIORS

Behaviors	*Group Members*									
Information and Opinion Giver										
Information and Opinion Seeker										
Starter										
Direction Giver										
Summarizer										
Coordinator										
Diagnoser										
Energizer										
Reality Tester										
Evaluator										
Other:										
Other:										
Other:										
Other:										

OBSERVATION SHEET FOR MAINTENANCE BEHAVIORS

Behaviors	Five-Minute Time Blocks									
Encourager of Participation										
Harmonizer and Compromiser										
Tension Reliever										
Communication Helper										
Evaluator of Emotional Climate										
Process Observer										
Standard Setter										
Active Listener										
Trust Builder										
Interpersonal Problem Solver										
Other:										
Other:										
Other:										
Other:										

OBSERVATION SHEET FOR TASK BEHAVIORS

Behaviors	Five-Minute Time Blocks									
Information and Opinion Giver										
Information and Opinion Seeker										
Starter										
Direction Giver										
Summarizer										
Coordinator										
Diagnoser										
Energizer										
Reality Tester										
Evaluator										
Other:										
Other:										
Other:										
Other:										

INSTRUCTION SHEET FOR OBSERVERS

You will be observing a situation in which a planning team decides how to solve a problem and gives instructions to an implementing team. The problem consists of assembling sixteen flat pieces into a square containing an empty square in its middle. The planning team is supplied with a general diagram of the assembled pieces. The planners are *not* allowed to put the puzzle together themselves; they are to instruct the implementing team on how to assemble the pieces in minimum time. You will be silent observers throughout the process. Half of you should observe the planners throughout the entire exercise and half of you should observe the implementers. Observation sheets focusing upon task and maintenance leadership behaviors are provided to help you observe. Make sure you understand the behavioral roles before you begin.

Some suggestions for observers are:

1. Each observer should watch the general patterns of leadership behavior.
2. During Phase I, consider the following questions:
   a. What kinds of behavior block or help the process?
   b. Are the team members participating equally?
   c. How does the planning team divide its time between planning and instructing?
   d. What group functions are not provided by the group members?
3. During the instructing process, note these behavioral questions:
   a. At the beginning of the instruction, how do the planners orient the implementers to their task?
   b. What assumptions made by the planning team are not communicated to the implementing team?
   c. How effective are the instructions?
   d. Does the implementing team appear to feel free to ask questions of the planners?
   e. What leadership functions are present and absent?
4. During the assembling period, seek answers to the following questions:
   a. How does the implementing team show that instructions were clearly understood or misunderstood?
   b. What nonverbal reactions do planning team members show as they watch their plans being implemented or distorted?
   c. What leadership functions are present and absent?
5. You should each have two copies of the observation sheets, one for Phase I and one for Phase II.

342

INSTRUCTION SHEET FOR PLANNERS

Each of you will be given a packet containing four pieces of a puzzle. When all the pieces from all four packets are properly assembled, they will form a large square containing an empty place in the middle. A sheet bearing a diagram of the completed puzzle is provided for your team. Your task is to:

1. Plan how the sixteen pieces distributed among you can be assembled to solve the puzzle.
2. Decide on a plan for instructing your implementing team on how to carry out your plan for putting the puzzle together.
3. Call the implementing team and begin instructing them at any time during the next forty minutes.
4. Give them at least five minutes of instructions; the implementing team must begin assembling the puzzle forty-five minutes from now.

Before you begin, read these rules:

1. During planning:
   a. Keep the pieces from your packet in front of you at all times.
   b. Do not touch the pieces nor trade any with other persons, either now or during the instruction period.
   c. Do not assemble the square; that is the implementers' job.
   d. Do not mark any of the pieces.
2. During instruction:
   a. Give all instructions in words. Do not show the diagram to the implementers; hide it. Do not draw any diagrams yourselves, either on paper or in the air with gestures. You may give your instructions orally or on paper.
   b. The implementing team must not move the pieces until the signal is given to start Phase II.
   c. Do not show any diagram to the implementers.
   d. After the signal is given for the assembly to begin, you may *not* give any further instructions; stand back and observe. You may not touch the pieces or in any way join in the implementers' work.

HOLLOW SQUARE PATTERN

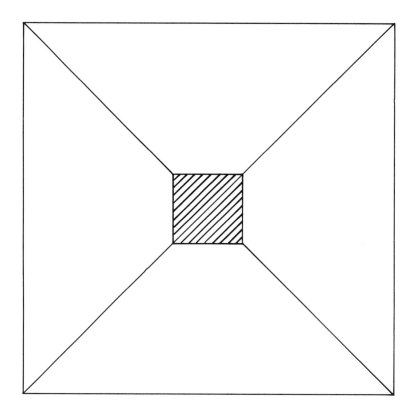

INSTRUCTION SHEET FOR IMPLEMENTERS

1. Your team will have the responsibility of carrying out a task in accordance with instructions given you by your planning team.

2. Your task will begin forty minutes from now.

3. Your planning team may call you in for instruction at any time during the next forty minutes.

4. If they do not call you during the next forty minutes, you must report to them on your own at the end of that time.

5. You may send notes to the planners and they may send notes in reply.

6. Once you have begun the task of assembling the puzzle, your planning team will not be allowed to give you any further instructions. Finish the assigned task as quickly as possible.

7. While you wait for a call from your planning team, do the following:

   a. Individually, write on a piece of paper the concerns you feel while waiting for instructions.

   b. As a group, think of anything you can that might help you follow instructions or keep you from doing so. Write actions that will help you on one sheet of paper and those that will hinder you on another.

   c. Make notes on how the four of you can organize as a team to receive and follow the instructions.

   d. Keep handy the sheets on which you have written these notes. You may find them useful during the discussion that takes place after you have completed the task.

INSTRUCTIONS TO ROLE PLAYERS

North Vietnamese Representative

You are a member of a negotiation team that has been sent to arrange a truce in the Vietnam conflict. You represent the North Vietnamese government, and you firmly believe that the United States government has been an aggressor against your nation. Your purpose is to get the United States out of South Vietnam and to force the United States to stop its military raids that have been destroying your country's resources and facilities. You are ready to negotiate with the United States under any conditions, but you will work for the removal of its forces.

UN Mediator

You are a member of a team that has been sent to negotiate a truce in the Vietnam war. You are a United Nations mediator in the truce talks, and your only purpose is to keep the talks going. You are willing to abide by any agreement the conflicting parties can reach, as long as peace is established.

United States Representative

You are a member of a negotiation team that has been sent to discuss truce terms in the Vietnam conflict. You represent the Unites States. You are concerned with stopping North Vietnamese infiltration into South Vietnam, and you are committed to getting a positive, decisive statement from the North Vietnamese assuring you that they will halt the movement of men and supplies into the South. You will not accept any offer short of a total commitment by them to stop this practice. You are willing to negotiate with anyone, and you firmly believe that if the negotiations can only continue, an agreement is likely. You also believe, therefore, that the talks must not be cut off because of disagreement between the negotiators. Your goals and your commitment, nonetheless, are clear: the removal at all costs of the North Vietnamese from South Vietnam.

Viet Cong Representative

You are a member of a negotiation team that has been sent to reach a truce in the Vietnam conflict. You represent the Viet Cong guerrilla fighters who are committed to the removal of U. S. forces and influence from South Vietnam, and you are angry about devastating raids the United States has been staging against North Vietnam. Your firm belief is that the South Vietnam government has been involved in the manipulation of resources and aid, that it is an illegal government engaging in illegal activities, and that it is not an instrument of the people. You also firmly believe that the South Vietnam government will eventually give way to a true "people's government," and that the best way to realize this goal is to continue your guerrilla activities in the South until you have an army capable of overcoming the Saigon government and replacing it with one that will again unify North and South Vietnam, this time under one Communist regime. You are opposed to U. S. efforts to help the government in Saigon; you firmly believe that there will be no peace until both the United States and the Saigon government are removed; and you are not willing to negotiate.

Saigon Government Representative

You are a member of a team that has been sent to negotiate a truce in the Vietnam conflict. You represent the South Vietnam government. When the Communists took over the North, you moved your family to the South, where you now enjoy certain economic comforts. Your family owned a rice farm in the North before you emigrated, and though you were not at all wealthy, you managed to harvest a large enough crop to feed your family comfortably. You believe that the Communists in the North should be removed and also that the government in the South represents the best government for the people there. You are committed to seeing that your government continues to hold power so that help from the United States will continue, thereby gaining continued economic growth for your nation. You feel that United States military assistance to your country is necessary if the Communists in Hanoi are to be contained. You are not at all opposed to negotiating with North Vietnam, because your major goal is to have the fighting over as soon as possible. Your major desire, however, is to have the United States guarantee that the South Vietnamese government will remain in power.

Chinese Representative

You are a member of a negotiation team that has been sent to arrange a truce in the Vietnam conflict. You represent the Red Chinese government in Peking. You are committed to supplying whatever arms and military help are needed to the North Vietnamese and the Viet Cong in their fight against the government of South Vietnam.

You believe that the United States is an aggressor in Vietnam, that it has no legal reason to be there. Its action against North Vietnam and the presence of its military in South Vietnam are expressions of American imperialistic policy. You will not negotiate unless the United States agrees to end its aggression in Vietnam. You are interested in using the conflict to reveal to the world the imperialistic policies of the United States. You want to capitalize on the conflict for your own purposes.

Russian Representative

You are a member of a negotiation team that has been sent to reach agreement on a truce in the Vietnam war. You represent the Soviet Union. You are in a difficult position in Vietnam. You are afraid that the extremist policies of China are too incendiary, and may lead to a major world conflict. You have been disturbed by how aggressively the Chinese interpret the need for world communism. At the same time, you do have some commitment to support Red China if she does take on the capitalists. Your relations with the United States have been improving, however, and you are now enjoying positive trade, cultural, and scientific relations with the United States. You believe that this new relationship is of great help in the long run to the development of the Soviet Union. You also believe that communism is a better form of government than capitalism—and that eventually communism will triumph. For the present, however, you believe that an agreement must be reached and the Vietnam war ended. Thus, you advocate a middle-of-the-road compromise between the extreme position of Red China and the aggressive policy of the United States in Vietnam.

OVERCOMING RESISTANCE TO CHANGE

In American industry competition makes change necessary—like changing products and the way in which jobs are done. One of the most serious production problems at the Sleep-Eze Pajama factory has been that production workers have resisted necessary changes. The upshot has been grievances about the piece rates that went with the new methods, high job turnover, low efficiency, restriction of output, and marked aggression against management. Despite these undesirable effects, methods and jobs must continue to change at the Sleep-Eze company if it is to remain a competitor in its field.

The main plant of the Sleep-Eze Manufacturing Corporation is in a small town in a southern state. The plant produces pajamas and, like most sewing plants, hires mostly women; there are about 500 women and 100 men employees. The workers are recruited from the rural areas around the town, and they usually have no industrial experience. Their average age is twenty-three, and their average education is ten years of formal schooling. Company policies in regard to labor relations are liberal and progressive. A high value has been placed on fair and open dealing with the employees, and they are encouraged to take up any problems or grievances with the management at any time. Sleep-Eze has invested both time and money in employee services, such as industrial music, health services, lunchroom facilities, and recreation programs.

The employees of Sleep-Eze work on an individual-incentive system. Piece rates are set by time study, and are expressed in terms of units. One unit is equal to one minute of standard work: 60 units per hour equal the standard efficiency rating. The amount of pay received is directly proportional to the weekly average efficiency rating achieved. Thus, an operator with an average efficiency rating of seventy-five units an hour (25 percent more than standard) would receive 25 percent more than the base pay. The rating of every piece worker is computed every day, and the results are published in a daily record of production that is shown to every operator.

The average relearning time for workers who are transferred to a new job is eight weeks. The relearning period for experienced operators is longer than the learning for a new operator.

The company now recognizes that the time has come to make changes again. Although they are to be minor ones, changes heretofore have been met with extreme resistance by the employees involved. Such an expression as "When you make your units (standard production), they change your job" is heard all too frequently. As in the past, many operators will refuse to change, preferring to quit.

Some examples of the changes to be made are:

1. Eighteen hand pressers have formerly stacked their work in half-dozen lots on a flat piece of cardboard the size of the finished product. The new job calls for them to stack their work in half-dozen lots in a box the size of the finished product. An additional two minutes per dozen will be allowed (by the time study) for this new part of the job.

2. Thirteen pajama folders have heretofore folded coats with prefolded pants. The change calls for the pants to be folded too. An additional two minutes per dozen will be allowed.

3. Fifteen pajama examiners have been clipping threads and examining every seam. The new job calls for pulling only certain threads off and examining every seam. An average of 1.2 minutes per dozen will be subtracted from the total time.

What is the best procedure for management to take to make sure the least amount of resistance results from these needed changes? Listed below are several different ways of handling this problem. Rank these alternatives in terms of their effectiveness for bringing about the least resistance to change. Place a "1" by the most effective alternative, "2" by the second most effective, and so on through "5," the least effective.

___ By written memo, explain the need for a change to the employees involved and allow extra pay for transfers, to make up for the usual drop in piece rate after a change.

___ Before any changes are made, hold meetings with large groups of the employees involved and give a lecture explaining that the change is necessary because of competitive conditions. Have the time-study man thoroughly explain the basis of the new piece rate. Then put in the change as planned.

___ Before any changes take place, hold meetings with large groups of the employees involved. Using demonstrations, dramatically show the need for change. Present a tentative plan for setting the new job and piece rates, and have the groups elect representatives to work with management in making the plan final.

___ By written memo, explain the need for the change, put the change into operation, and make layoffs as necessary on the basis of efficiency.

___ Before any changes occur, hold meetings with small groups of the employees involved. Employing demonstrations, dramatically present a tentative plan for setting the new job and piece rates, and ask everybody present to help in designing the new jobs.

INDIVIDUAL REACTION FORM

1. How much did you participate in making the decisions reached by your group?

   I participated:

   9 — Completely.

   8 — Quite a lot.

   7 — A little more than moderately.

   6 — Moderately.

   5 — Neither very much nor very little.

   4 — Less than expected.

   3 — Moderately less than expected.

   2 — Quite a lot less than expected.

   1 — Not at all.

2. How satisfied did you feel with the amount and quality of your participation in reaching a joint decision?

   I felt:

   9 — Completely satisfied.

   8 — Quite satisfied.

   7 — Moderately satisfied.

   6 — A little more satisfied than dissatisfied.

   5 — Neither very satisfied nor very dissatisfied.

   4 — A little more dissatisfied than satisfied.

   3 — Moderately dissatisfied.

   2 — Quite dissatisfied.

   1 — Completely dissatisfied.

3. How much responsibility would you feel for making the decision work?

   I would feel:

   9 — Completely responsible.

   8 — Quite responsible.

   7 — Moderately responsible.

   6 — A little more responsibile than not responsible.

   5 — Neither very responsible nor very irresponsible.

   4 — A little more irresponsible than responsible.

   3 — Moderately irresponsible.

   2 — Quite irresponsible.

   1 — Completely irresponsible.

4. How committed do you feel to the decision your group made?

   I feel:

   9 — Completely committed.

   8 — Quite committed.

   7 — Moderately committed.

   6 — A little more committed than uncommitted.

   5 — Neither very committed nor very uncommitted.

   4 — A little more uncommitted than committed.

   3 — Moderately uncommitted.

   2 — Quite uncommitted.

   1 — Completely uncommitted.

5. How much frustration or fulfillment did you feel during the work on the decision?

I felt:

9 — Completely frustrated.
8 — Quite frustrated.
7 — Moderately frustrated.
6 — A little more frustrated than fulfilled.
5 — Neither very frustrated nor very fulfilled.

4 — A little more fulfilled than frustrated.
3 — Moderately fulfilled.
2 — Quite fulfilled.
1 — Completely fulfilled.

6. How good was the decision your group made?

It was:

9 — The best possible.
8 — Quite good.
7 — Moderately good.
6 — A little more good than bad.
5 — Niether very good nor very bad.

4 — A little more bad than good.
3 — Moderately bad.
2 — Quite bad.
1 — The worst possible.

7. How much influence did you have on the group's decision?

9 — A great deal.
8 — Quite a lot.
7 — A little more than moderately.
6 — Moderately.
5 — Neither very much nor very little.

4 — Less than expected.
3 — Moderately less than expected.
2 — Quite a lot less than expected.
1 — None at all.

8. When members had differences of opinion, to what extent were all sides carefully listened to and the conflict directly faced and resolved?

9 — Always.
8 — Almost always.
7 — Usually.
6 — A little more than half the time.
5 — Half the time.

4 — A little less than half the time.
3 — Not very often.
2 — Rarely.
1 — Never.

9. To what extent do you believe you could work effectively with this group in the future?

9 — A great deal.
8 — Quite a lot.
7 — A little more than moderately.
6 — Moderately.
5 — Neither very much nor very little.

4 — Less than expected.
3 — Moderately less than expected.
2 — Quite a lot less than expected.
1 — None at all.

WINTER SURVIVAL EXERCISE

The Situation

You have just crash-landed in the woods of Northern Minnesota and Southern Manitoba. It is 11:32 a.m. in mid-January. The small plane in which you were traveling has completely destroyed except for the frame. The pilot and copilot have been killed, but no one else is seriously injured.

The crash came suddenly before the pilot had time to radio for help or inform anyone of your position. Since your pilot was trying to avoid a storm you know the plane was considerably off course. The pilot announced shortly before the crash that you were eighty miles northwest of a small town that is the nearest known habitation.

You are in a wilderness area made up of thick woods broken by many lakes and rivers. The last weather report indicated that the temperature would reach minus twenty-five degrees in the daytime and minus forty at night. You are dressed in winter clothing appropriate for city wear—suits, pantsuits, street shoes, and overcoats.

While escaping from the plane your group salvaged the fifteen items listed on page 353. Your task is to rank these items according to their importance to your survival.

You may assume that the number is the same as the number in your group and that the group has agreed to stick together.

Winter Survival Decision Form

Rank the following items according to their importance to your survival, starting with "1" for the most important and proceeding to "15" for the least important:

_11_ Compress kit
(with 28-ft., 2-in. gauze)

_2_ Ball of steel wool

_1_ Cigarette lighter (without fluid)

_9_ Loaded .45-caliber pistol

_7_ Newspaper (one per person)

_15_ Compass

_12_ Two ski poles

_10_ Knife

_14_ Sectional air map made of plastic

_7_ 30 feet of rope

_4_ Family-size chocolate bar
(one per person)

_6_ Flashlight with batteries

_13_ Quart of 85-proof whiskey

_3_ Extra shirt and pants for each survivor

_5_ Can of shortening

p. 318-321

WINTER SURVIVAL: GROUP SUMMARY SHEET

Items	Members												Summary
	1	2	3	4	5	6	7	8	9	10	11	12	
Compress kit													
Ball of steel wool													
Cigarette lighter													
.45-caliber pistol													
Newspaper													
Compass													
Ski poles													
Knife													
Sectional air map													
Piece of rope													
Chocolate bars													
Flashlight													
Whiskey													
Shirt and pants													
Shortening													

INSTRUCTIONS TO OBSERVERS

The Survival in Winter Exercise looks at the process by which groups make decisions. Crucial issues are how well the group uses the resources of its members, how much commitment is mustered toward implementing the decision, how the future decision-making ability of the group is affected, and how members react to and feel about what is taking place. As an observer, you may wish to focus on these issues:

1. Who does and does not participate in the discussion? Who participates the most?
2. Who influences the decision and who does not? How is influence determined (expertise, sex, loudness of voice)?
3. Who is involved and who is uninvolved?
4. What are the dominant feelings of the group members? How would you describe the group atmosphere during the meeting?
5. What leadership behaviors are present and absent in the group? You may wish to use the Task- and Maintenance-behavior Sheets presented in the preceding chapter.
6. What are the basic causes for the members' resources being used or not used?

INSTRUCTIONS: DECISION BY CONSENSUS

This is an exercise in group decision making. Your group is to employ the method of group consensus in reaching its decision. This means that the ranking for each of the fifteen survival items *must* be agreed upon by each group member before it becomes a part of the group decision. Consensus is difficult to reach. Therefore, not every ranking will meet with everyone's complete approval. Try, as a group, to make each ranking one with which all group members can at least partially agree. Here are some guidelines to use in reaching consensus:

1. Avoid *blindly* arguing for your own individual judgments. Present your position as clearly and logically as possible, but listen to other members' reactions and consider them carefully before you press your point.

2. Avoid changing your mind just to reach agreement and avoid conflict. Support only solutions with which you are able to agree to at least some degree. Yield only to positions that have objective and logically sound foundations.

3. Avoid "conflict reducing" procedures such as majority vote, tossing a coin, averaging, or bargaining in reaching decisions.

4. Seek out differences of opinion. They are natural and expected. Try to involve everyone in the decision process. Disagreements can help the group's decision because a wide range of information and opinions improves the chances for the group to hit upon more adequate solutions.

5. Do not assume that someone must win and someone must lose when discussion reaches a stalemate. Instead, look for the next most acceptable alternative for all members.

6. Discuss underlying assumptions, listen carefully to one another, and encourage the participation of *all* members—three important factors in reaching decisions by consensus.

INSTRUCTIONS: DECISION BY LEADER

This is an exercise in how a leader makes decisions after participating in a group discussion. Your group is to have a discussion as to what the ranking of the survival items should be, but the final decision rests with the designated leader of your group. At the end of the forty-five-minute period, your group's leader will hand in what he considers to be the best ranking of the items. The role of the group member is to provide as much help as the leader wants in trying to determine how the items should be ranked.

HIDDEN—AGENDAS PROBLEM SHEET

Fact-Finding Committee of the CAP Governing Board

The participants:
- a. Marvin Turner, shoe-store owner-operator.
- b. Roberta Stevens, ADC mother of five.
- c. Louis Haber, dentist.
- d. Jack Simon, Middleburg Chamber of Commerce vice-president.
- e. Carol Stone, social worker, Middleburg Department of Welfare.

The problem:
   You are at a meeting of a special fact-finding committee of the Community Action Program (CAP) Governing Board. Your committee was established to study the suggestion that CAP revise its procedure for electing representatives of the poverty group to its governing board. At present, representatives are selected for three years, through a general-area election. Your committee group has been authorized to come up with specific recommendations for the board to act upon at its next meeting. The board has advised your committee to consider two issues:

1. What would be the best electoral basis for selecting poverty representatives?
    - a. Keep the present system (general area-wide election).
    - b. Institute smaller district elections.
    - c. Institute even smaller neighborhood elections.
2. How long should representatives serve on the governing board?
    - a. Keep the present system (three-year term).
    - b. Institute a one-year term.

   The chairman of the committee is Marvin Turner, who will report your recommendations to the city council.

INSTRUCTIONS FOR ROLE PLAYERS

You are Carol Stone, a social worker with the Middleburg Department of Welfare, who would like some of your welfare clients to become active in the Community Action Program (CAP). You feel that if you help some of your personal clients get elected as representatives to the CAP Governing Board, your department head will be impressed with your efforts and you will have more power generally in the CAP program. Since your territory as a social worker covers a district, you want the district basis of election to be recommended and the terms of board representatives to remain at three years.

***

You are Marvin Turner, a shoe-store owner and operator, who is an ambitious community leader. You want the poverty representatives on the CAP Governing Board to show a lack of unity and goals, so that the professional and governmental members can run things more their way. You feel the poor are just "lazy." Therefore, you support general-area elections for board representatives—so that there will be more representatives without any specific support from a small-area interest group, and without many specific goals in mind. You also support one-year terms to minimize continuity among members from poverty areas.

***

You are Roberta Stevens, a mother of five getting welfare aid to dependent children (ADC) who wants a greater role for poverty representatives on the CAP Governing Board. You would also like different people from poverty areas to have a chance to get on the board. You support the concept of neighborhood or small-unit elections for one-year terms. You also want more poverty representatives on the board than there are currently to counteract some of the professional and governmental members.

***

You are Louis Haber, a dentist, who is also on the City Council of Middleburg. You feel that local government, as well as professional people "who know what they are doing," should have a larger say on the CAP Governing Board. Therefore, a weaker voice from the poverty representatives is what you seek. You support general-area elections and a one-year tenure for representatives. Your objective is a weaker group of poverty representatives on the board.

***

You are Jack Simon, vice-president of the Middleburg Chamber of Commerce, who is not really concerned with the work of your fact-finding group. You joined the committee for one reason only: to meet Carol Stone and eventually ask her for a date. During the meeting you plan to agree with, and support, every point that Carol makes. Your behavior is guided by your desire to impress Carol Stone.

INSTRUCTIONS TO EACH MEMBER OF THE COOPERATIVE GROUP

Each member of your group has an envelope containing pieces of cardboard for forming squares. When the signal is given to begin, the task of the group is to form one square in front of each member. Only parts of the pieces for forming the five squares are in each envelope. The exercise has two goals: your individual goal of forming a square in front of yourself as fast as possible and the group's goal of having squares formed in front of every member as fast as possible. The individual goal is accomplished when you have a completed square in front of you. The group goal is accomplished when all group members have completed squares in front of them.

You are to role play a member of a group in which members are all highly cooperative. To you the group goal is far more important than the individual goal. Your job is to cooperate with the other group members as much as possible in order to accomplish the group goal in the shortest period of time possible. To you the other group members are your partners, and you are concerned with helping them put together a completed square. All members of your group have received the same instructions.

The specific rules for the exercise are:

1. No talking, pointing, or any other kind of communication among the five members of your group.
2. No person may *ask* another member for a piece of the puzzle or in any way signal that another person is to give him a puzzle piece.
3. Members may *give* puzzle pieces to other members.
4. Members may not throw their pieces into the center for others to take; they have to give the pieces directly to one person.
5. Anyone may give away all the pieces of his puzzle, even if he has already formed a square.
6. Part of the role of the observers is to enforce these rules.

INSTRUCTIONS TO EACH MEMBER OF THE COMPETITIVE GROUP

Every person in this group has an envelope that contains pieces of cardboard for forming squares. When the signal is given to begin, your task is to form a square in front of you. Only parts of the pieces for forming the five squares are in each envelope. The exercise has two goals: your individual goal of forming a square in front of yourself as fast as possible and the group's goal of forming squares in front of every member as fast as possible. The individual goal is accomplished when you have a completed square in front of you. The group goal is accomplished when all group members have completed squares in front of them.

You are to role play a member of a group in which the members are all highly competitive. To you the individual goal is far more important than the group goal. Your job is to compete with the other group members to see who can get a completed square in front of himself first. At the end of the exercise group members will be ranked on the basis of their speed in completing their square. The member finishing first will be labelled as the "best" person in the group, the person finishing second will be labelled as "second best" person in the group, and so on with the last person finishing being labelled as the "worst" person in the group. The other group members are your competitors, and you are concerned with completing your square before they do. If you complete your square and then decide to give a piece of it away, you lose your previous rank in terms of the order of members completing their squares and must start over. All members of your group have received the same instructions.

The specific rules for the exercise are:

1. No talking, pointing, or any other kind of communicating among the five members of your group.
2. No person may *ask* another member for a piece of the puzzle or in any way signal that another person is to give him a puzzle piece.
3. Members may *give* puzzle pieces to other members.
4. Members may not throw their pieces into the center for others to take; they have to give the pieces directly to one person.
5. Part of the role of the observers is to enforce these rules.

INSTRUCTIONS FOR OBSERVERS

Your job is part observer, part recorder, and part rule enforcer. Do your best to enforce strictly the rules on the instruction sheet for participants. Then as accurately as possible, record and observe the items listed below. The information you record will be used to help discuss the results of the exercise.

1. Did the group complete the task?   _____Yes;   _____ No
2. How long did it take the group to complete the task:
   _____ Minutes,   _____ Seconds

3. Number of times a group member took a puzzle piece from another member:	Number of times a group member gave a puzzle piece to another member:

4. Number of members who finished their square and then divorced themselves from the struggles of the rest of the group? _____

5. Were there any critical turning points at which cooperation or competition increased?_____

   _____

   _____

   _____

6. What behaviors in the group show cooperativeness or competitiveness?_____

   _____

   _____

   _____

CLEAR AND UNCLEAR GOALS EXERCISE: OBSERVATION GUIDE

During this exercise the groups will work on two tasks. The first task will be unclear, the second will be clear. Your job as an observer is to make careful notations of group behavior on the two tasks. After you understand the form below, return to your groups, but sit outside the circle.

	First Task	Second Task
1. Number of times the goal was clarified or asked to be clarified.		
2. Assessment of "working" climate of the group. Was it cooperative, hostile, pleasant, critical, accepting, and so forth?		
At the beginning?		
At the middle?		
At the end?		
3. Frequency of verbal behavior not directly related to getting the job done (side conversations, jokes, comments).		
4. Frequency of nonverbal behavior not related to getting the task done (looking around the room, horseplay, bored withdrawal, hostility).		
5. How much progress did the group make in getting the task done? (Make an estimate.)		

Bewise College Data Sheet

Your group is a committee consisting of college board members, administrators, faculty, and students of Bewise College. Your group has been authorized by the Board of Regents to select a new president of the college from among the list of candidates.

Each of the represented groups (Board of Regents, administrators, faculty, students) has its own list of requirements for the new president. Insofar as possible, your group is pledged to select a candidate who meets these requirements.

Bewise College was established in 1969. It is located in the heart of an industrial city with a population of about 100,000. In addition to a standard liberal arts curriculum, Bewise College offers a curriculum in which students can receive college credit for work and learning experiences outside of the college. Bewise College was established to provide higher education for persons such as minority group members, working-class and lower-class students, the elderly, and dropouts from other colleges and universities.

The new president faces a series of challenges. The Board of Regents is most concerned about the ability of the president to be a public relations person for the college and raise money. The college has been losing money for the past two years of teaching at Bewise College and want a president who is qualified to judge the teaching ability of faculty members. The latter are having a very difficult time in the classroom and want to make sure the new president has a background that includes experience in working with the type of students attending Bewise College.

BEWISE COLLEGE EXERCISE

Briefing Sheet

1. This is the first meeting of your group.
2. Basically, the data you bring with you are in your head.
3. Assume there is one solution.
4. Assume that all information is correct.
5. There must be substantial agreement within the group when the problem has been solved.
6. You must work on the problem as a group.

Bewise College Data Sheet

Your group is a committee consisting of college board members, administrators, faculty, and students of Bewise College. Your group has been authorized by the Board of Regents to select a new president of the College from the list of candidates. .

Each of the represented groups (Board of Regents, administrators, faculty, students) has its own list of requirements for the new president. Insofar as possible, your group is pledged to select a candidate who meets these requirements.

Bewise College was established in 1969. It is located in the heart of an industrial city with a population of about 100,000. In addition to a standard liberal arts curriculum, Bewise College offers a curriculum in which students can receive college credit for work and learning experiences outside the college. The faculty at Bewise College is made up primarily of young and dedicated but not highly experienced teachers.

The new president faces a series of challenges. The Board of Regents is most concerned about the ability of the president to be a public relations person for the college and raise money. The college has been in the "red" for the past two years and may have to close it it cannot balance its budget. The new president will be expected to make many public speeches to raise money from the community. The students are angry about the quality of teaching and want a president who can judge the teaching ability of faculty. Members of the college administration have nightmares about getting a president who is an incompetent administrator.

BEWISE COLLEGE EXERCISE

Briefing Sheet

1. This is the first meeting of your group.
2. Basically, the data you bring with you are in your head.
3. Assume there is one solution.
4. Assume that all information is correct.
5. There must be substantial agreement within the group when the problem has been solved.
6. You must work on the problem as a group.

Bewise College Data Sheet

Your group is a committee consisting of college board members, administrators, faculty, and students of Bewise College. Your group has been authorized by the Board of Regents to select a new president of the college from among the list of candidates. . .

Each of the represented groups (Board of Regents, administrators, faculty, students) has its own list of requirements for the new president. Insofar as possible, your group is pledged to select a candidate who meets these requirements.

Bewise College was established in 1969. It is located in the heart of an industrial city with a population of about 100,000. In addition to offering a standard liberal arts curriculum, Bewise College also provides a curriculum in which students can receive college credit for work and learning experiences outside of the college. Since universities are always larger than colleges, Bewise is smaller than the State University, but it is growing rapidly.

The new president faces a series of challenges. The students are dissatisfied with the faculty's teaching and have stated that the only qualification they will recognize as valid for judging faculty teaching ability is for the president to have an education degree. The faculty, on the other hand, demands that the new president have experience in working with the type of student attending Bewise. The Board of Regents sees the need for a president who can raise money to support the college.

BEWISE COLLEGE EXERCISE

Briefing Sheet

1. This is the first meeting of your group.
2. Basically, the data you bring with you are in your head.
3. Assume there is one solution.
4. Assume that all information is correct.
5. There must be substantial agreement within the group when the problem has been solved.
6. You must work on the problem as a group.

Bewise College Data Sheet

Your group is a committee consisting of college board members, administrators, faculty, and students of Bewise College. Your group has been authorized by the Board of Regents to select a new president of the college from among the list of candidates. . . .

Each of the represented groups (Board of Regents, administrators, faculty, students) has its own list of requirements for the new president. Insofar as possible, your group is pledged to select a candidate who meets these requirements.

Bewise College was established in 1969. It is located in the heart of an industrial city with a population of about 100,000. In addition to offering a standard liberal arts curriculum, Bewise College also provides a curriculum in which students can receive college credit for work and learning experiences outside of the college. Within the state, only Brown College, Samuels College, and Holubec College are larger, which makes Bewise one of the largest colleges in the state; Andrews is the smallest.

The new president faces a series of challenges. The Board of Regents wants a president who can raise money for the college. The college administration will not accept a new president who does not have administrative experience. The faculty is upset about the difficulty in teaching the students and, therefore, wants a president with experience in teaching the type of student who attends Bewise. Teaching experience is also considered crucial because it would make the president sympathetic to the problems of the faculty.

BEWISE COLLEGE EXERCISE

Briefing Sheet

1. This is the first meeting of your group.
2. Basically, the data you bring with you are in your head.
3. Assume there is one solution.
4. Assume that all information is correct.
5. There must be substantial agreement within the group when the problem has been solved.
6. You must work on the problem as a group.

Bewise College Data Sheet

Your group is a committee consisting of college board members, administrators, faculty, and students of Bewise College. Your group has been authorized by the Board of Regents to select a new president of the college from among the list of candidates. . . . .

Each of the represented groups (Board of Regents, administrators, faculty, students) has its own list of requirements for the new president. Insofar as possible, your group is pledged to select a candidate who meets these requirements.

Bewise College was established in 1969. It is located in the heart of an industrial city with a population of about 100,000. In addition to offering a standard liberal arts curriculum, Bewise College also provides a curriculum in which students can receive college credit for work and learning experiences outside of the college. There is only one other college in the same city; it is the smallest college in the state and until 1954 all students attending it were black Americans.

The new president faces a series of challenges. The Board of Regents wants a president who can raise money for the college, as the college is now in a desperate financial position. The college administration is very much afraid of a president who will not be a competent administrator. Students are dissatisfied with faculty teaching, and faculty members are dissatisfied with student unresponsiveness to their teaching. Both students and faculty see the necessity of having a president who comes from a background that would provide insights into the type of student attending Bewise.

BEWISE COLLEGE EXERCISE

Briefing Sheet

1. This is the first meeting of your group.
2. Basically, the data you bring with you are in your head.
3. Assume there is one solution.
4. Assume that all information is correct.
5. There must be substantial agreement within the group when the problem has been solved.
6. You must work on the problem as a group.

Bewise College Candidate Summary Sheet

Name:	David Williams
Education:	Graduated from Andrews College in Liberal Arts in 1952; Masters of Education from Wolcott University in English in 1954; Doctorate in Political Science from Wolcott University in 1958.
Employment:	Instructor in English at Wolcott University, 1954–1958; taught Political Science at James University, 1958–1967; representative in state legislative, 1960–62; chairperson of Political Science Department at James University, 1967–1972; Dean of Students at James University, 1972 to present.
Other:	Is well known for his scholarship and intelligence.

Name:	Roger Thornton
Education:	Graduated from Samuels College in industrial arts in 1950; Master of Education in Chemistry from Smith University in 1952; Doctorate in administration from Smith University in 1966.
Employment:	High school chemistry teacher, 1952–1959; high school principal, 1959 to 1966; school superintendent, 1966 to present.
Other:	Very innovative and efficient administrator; very successful political speaker (superintendent of schools is an elected office in his district); his father is vice-president of a large bank.

Name:	Edythe James
Education:	Graduated from Holubec College in Liberal Arts in 1955; Master's in accounting from Smith University in 1960; doctorate in administration in 1968 from Smith University.
Employment:	Insurance Agent, 1955–1960; certified public accountant, 1960–1968; vice-president of finance, Williams College, 1968 to present.
Other:	Taught accounting in night school for 8 years; volunteer director of a community center in a lower-class neighborhood for 4 years; has a competing job offer from a public relations firm; has worked part time for this firm for 2 years.

Name:	Frank Pierce
Education:	Graduated from Smith University in Liberal Arts in 1958; Master of Education in math in 1961 from Smith University; doctorate in administration from Johnson Institute in 1972.
Employment:	Neighborhood worker, 1958–1961; coordinator of parent volunteer program for school system, 1961–1965; assistant superintendent for community relations, 1965–present.
Other:	Has written a training program for industrial education.

Name:	Helen Lucy
Education:	Graduated from Brown College in social studies education in 1956; Master of Education in social studies in 1960 from Brown College.
Employment:	Teacher of basic skills in a neighborhood center run by school system, 1956–1960; chairperson of student teaching program, Smith University, 1960–1964; dean of students, Smith University, 1964–1970; vice-president for community relations, Smith University, 1970–present.
Other:	Grew up in one of the worst slums in the state; has written one book and several scholarly articles.
Name:	Keith Collins
Education:	Graduated in biology education from Dale University in 1957; Master's in administration from Dale University in 1959.
Employment:	Biology teacher in a high school, 1957–1962; consultant in fund-raising, public relations firm, 1962–present.
Other:	Is well recognized in the state as one of the best fund-raisers available; has written a book on teaching working-class students; extensive volunteer work in adult education.

Energy International Data Sheet

Your group is a committee made up of the general managers of Energy International, a young, medium-sized, growing organization. The prime mission of EI is to locate and develop mineral deposits (copper, uranium, cobalt, and so forth).

The company's business has grown very rapidly, especially in South America, where your organization has been made welcome by the governments. In a recent meeting the board of directors decided to develop a new property near Fortaleza, in northeastern Brazil. This operation will include both mining and milling.

The date is April 1, 1975. You have come from your respective plants in different locations. This is the initial session of your annual meeting, and your first order of business today is to select a new general manager for the Brazilian plant from among the candidates on the attached list.

Fortaleza has a hot climate, one railroad, a scheduled airline, a favorable balance of trade, a feudal attitude toward women, considerable unemployment, a low educational level, a low literary rate, and a strongly nationalistic city government. The government has insisted that the company must employ Brazilians in all posts except that of general manager. It has also installed an official inspector from whom it will receive monthly reports. This report must be signed by the company's representative, who must be a Fellow of the Institute of Mineralogy.

There are a number of schools offering degrees in mineralogy; the most recently founded is the New Mexico Institute of Earth Sciences, an institute established under a special grant and opened in 1945. To earn a bachelor's degree in mineralogy, this school requires geology, seismology, and paleontology, in addition to the usual courses.

ENERGY INTERNATIONAL EXERCISE

Briefing Sheet

1. Instructions to the group:
   a. You are a committee made up of the general managers of Energy International.
   b. You have just flown into town.
   c. This is the first meeting of the group.
   d. You have just learned that EI will open a new plant in Brazil, and your first job is to select a general manager from among the seven applicant candidates.
   e. Basically, the data you bring with you are in your head.
2. Assumptions which need to be made:
   a. Assume that there is one solution.
   b. Assume that all data are correct.
   c. You have one hour to work the exercise.
   d. Assume that today's date is April 1, 1975.
   e. There must be substantial agreement when the problem has been solved.
   f. You must work the problem as a group.

Energy International Data Sheet

Your group is a committee made up of the general managers of Energy International, a young, medium-sized, growing organization. The prime mission of EI is to locate and develop mineral deposits (copper, uranium, cobalt, and so forth)..

The company's business has grown very rapidly, especially in South America, where your organization has been made welcome by the governments. In a recent meeting the board of directors decided to develop a new property near Fortaleza, in northeastern Brazil. This operation will include both milling and mining.

The date is April 1, 1975. You have come from your respective plants in different locations. This is the initial session of your annual meeting, and your first order of business today is to select a new general manager for the Brazilian plant from among the candidates on the attached list.

Fortaleza has a hot climate, one railroad, a scheduled airline, a favorable balance of trade, a feudal attitude toward women, considerable unemployment, a low education level, a low literacy rate, and a strongly nationalistic city government. The government has ruled that the company must employ Brazilians in all posts except that of general manager. It has also installed an official inspector, from whom it will receive a monthly report countersigned by the general manager. By law, the general manager must have had at least three years' experience as a manager in charge of a mining operation.

There are a number of schools offering a degree in mineralogy, a degree essential to qualify for general membership in the Institute of Mineralogy. The smaller universities require three, the larger four, of the following special subjects as a part of their graduation requirements: geology, geophysics, oceanography, paleontology, seismology. The smallest is a women's university.

ENERGY INTERNATIONAL EXERCISE

Briefing Sheet

1. Instructions to the group:
    a. You are a committee made up of the general managers of Energy International.
    b. You have just flown into town.
    c. This is the first meeting of the group.
    d. You have just learned that EI will open a new plant in Brazil, and your first job is to select a general manager from among the seven applicant candidates.
    e. Basically, the data you bring with you are in your head.
2. Assumptions which need to be made:
    a. Assume that there is one solution.
    b. Assume that all data are correct.
    c. You have one hour to work the exercise.
    d. Assume that today's date is April 1, 1975.
    e. There must be substantial agreement when the problem has been solved.
    f. You must work the problem as a group.

Energy International Data Sheet

Your group is a committee made up of the general managers of Energy International, a young, medium-sized, growing organization. The prime mission of EI is to locate and develop mineral deposits (copper, uranium, cobalt, and so forth)...

The company's business has grown very rapidly, especially in South America, where your organization has been made welcome by the governments. In a recent meeting the board of directors decided to develop a new property near Fortaleza, in northeastern Brazil. This operation will include both mining and milling.

The date is April 1, 1975. You have come from your respective plants in different locations. This is the initial session of your annual meeting, and your first order of business today is to select a new general manager for the Brazilian plant from among the candidates on the attached list.

Fortaleza has a hot climate, one railroad, a scheduled airline, a favorable balance of trade, a feudal attitude toward women, considerable unemployment, a low educational level, a low literacy rate, and a strongly nationalistic city government. The government has ruled that the company must employ Brazilians in all posts except that of general manager. It has also installed an official inspector, from whom it will receive a monthly report countersigned by the company's representative. None of the government inspectors can read or write any language but his own.

There are a number of schools offering degrees in mineralogy, but a passing grade in paleontology is essential to qualify for general membership in the Institute of Mineralogy. The largest university is the New York School of Mines, which requires the following special subjects for graduation: geology, paleontology, geophysics, and seismology.

ENERGY INTERNATIONAL EXERCISE

Briefing Sheet

1. Instructions to the group:
   a. You are a committee made up of the general managers of Energy International.
   b. You have just flown into town.
   c. This is the first meeting of the group.
   d. You have just learned that EI will open a new plant in Brazil, and your first job is to select a general manager from among the seven applicant candidates.
   e. Basically, the data you bring with you are in your head.
2. Assumptions which need to be made:
   a. Assume that there is one solution.
   b. Assume that all data are correct.
   c. You have one hour to work the exercise.
   d. Assume that today's date is April 1, 1975.
   e. There must be substantial agreement when the problem has been solved.
   f. You must work the problem as a group.

Energy International Data Sheet

Your group is a committee made up of the general managers of Energy International, a young, medium-sized, growing organization. The prime mission of EI is to locate and develop mineral deposits (copper, uranium, cobalt, and so forth)....

The company's business has grown very rapidly, especially in South America, where your organization has been made welcome by the governments. In a recent meeting the board of directors decided to develop a new property near Fortaleza, in northeastern Brazil. This operation will include both mining and milling.

The date is April 1, 1975. You have come from your respective plants in different locations. This is the initial session of your annual meeting, and your first order of business today is to select a new general manager for the Brazilian plant from among the candidates on the attached list.

Fortaleza has a hot climate, one railroad, a scheduled airline, a favorable balance of trade, a feudal attitude toward women, considerable unemployment, a low educational level, a low literacy rate, and a strongly nationalistic city government. The government has ruled that the company must employ Brazilians in all posts except that of general manager. It has also installed an official inspector, from whom it will receive a monthly report countersigned by the company's representative. None of the company's employees or staff can read or write any language but Portuguese.

There are a number of schools offering degrees in mineralogy, and a passing grade in seismology is essential to qualify for general membership in the Institute of Mineralogy. The Massachusetts Institute of Sciences requires the following special subjects for graduation: geology, seismology, oceanography, and paleontology.

ENERGY INTERNATIONAL EXERCISE

Briefing Sheet

1. Instructions to the group:
   a. You are a committee made up of the general managers of Energy International.
   b. You have just flown into town.
   c. This is the first meeting of the group.
   d. You have just learned that EI will open a new plant in Brazil, and your first job is to select a general manager from among the seven applicant candidates.
   e. Basically, the data you bring with you are in your head.
2. Assumptions which need to be made:
   a. Assume that there is one solution.
   b. Assume that all data are correct.
   c. You have one hour to work the exercise.
   d. Assume that today's date is April 1, 1975.
   e. There must be substantial agreement when the problem has been solved.
   f. You must work the problem as a group.

Energy International Data Sheet

Your group is a committee made up of the general managers of Energy International, a young, medium-sized, growing organization. The prime mission of El is to locate and develop mineral deposits (copper, uranium, cobalt, and so forth).....

The company's business has grown very rapidly, especially in South America, where your organization has been made welcome by the governments. In a recent meeting the board of directors decided to develop a new property near Fortaleza, in northeastern Brazil. This operation will include both mining and milling.

The date is April 1, 1975. You have come from your respective plants in different locations. This is the initial session of your annual meeting, and your first order of business today is to select a new general manager for the Brazilian plant from among the candidates on the attached list.

Fortaleza has a hot climate, one railroad, a scheduled airline, a favorable balance of trade, a feudal attitude toward women, considerable unemployment, a low educational level, a low literacy rate, and a strongly nationalistic city government. The government has ruled that the company must employ Brazilians in all posts except that of general manager. It has also installed an official inspector, from whom it will receive a monthly report countersigned by the company's representative, who must be an American citizen.

Fellowship in the Institute of Mineralogy can be obtained by men over thirty-eight years of age who have otherwise qualified for general membership in the institute. Saint Francis University, which is not the smallest school, requires the following special courses for graduation: paleontology, geophysics, and oceanography.

ENERGY INTERNATIONAL EXERCISE

Briefing Sheet

1. Instructions to the group:
   a. You are a committee made up of the general managers of Energy International.
   b. You have just flown into town.
   c. This is the first meeting of the group.
   d. You have just learned that EI will open a new plant in Brazil, and your first job is to select a general manager from among the seven applicant candidates.
   e. Basically, the data you bring with you are in your head.
2. Assumptions which need to be made:
   a. Assume that there is one solution.
   b. Assume that all data are correct.
   c. You have one hour to work the exercise.
   d. Assume that today's date is April 1, 1975.
   e. There must be substantial agreement when the problem has been solved.
   f. You must work the problem as a group.

Energy International Candidate Summary Sheet

Name:	R. Illin
Date of birth:	March 2, 1937
Passport:	L3452 U.S.A.
Education:	New York School of Mines, degree in mineralogy, 1957.
Employment:	Research assistant, New York School of Mines; 1958–1960
	Lecturer, Mineralogy, University of Bonn, 1966–1970
	Manager, Utah Copper Mining Co. Plant, 1970 to date
Language command:	English, French, German, Portuguese

Name:	S. Hule
Date of birth:	May 4, 1929
Passport:	H4567 U.S.A.
Education:	New Mexico Institute of Earth Sciences, degree in mineralogy, 1955
Employment:	Uranium Unlimited, management trainee, 1955–1957
	Anaconda Copper Co., Montana area, geology officer, 1958–1965
	Manager, Irish Mining Co. Ltd., 1965 to date
Language command:	English, French, Portuguese

Name:	T. Gadolin
Date of birth:	June 5, 1930
Passport:	L7239 U.S.A.
Education:	New York School of Mines, degree in mineralogy, 1955
Employment:	United Kingdom Mining Board, management trainee, 1955–1957
	Assistant Manager, NDB Cheshire plant, 1958–1966
	Manager, Idaho Cobalt Minerals, 1966 to date
Language command:	English, Portuguese

Name:	U. Samar
Date of birth:	April 6, 1938
Passport:	H6259 U.S.A.
Education:	Massachusetts Institute of Sciences, degree in mineralogy, 1959
Employment:	Junior Engineer, West Virginia Mining Research Station, 1959–1968
	General manager, Liberian State Mining Plant, 1968 to date
Language command:	English, German, Swahili, Portuguese

Name:	V. Lute
Date of birth:	August 6, 1935
Passport:	K62371 U.S.A.
Education:	New York School of Mines, degree in mineralogy, 1956
Employment:	Junior Development Mineralogist, Ontario Mining Construction, Ltd., 1956–1959
	Assistant chief mineralogy officer, Canadian Development Board, 1960–1963
	Plant manager, Welsh Mining Co., Ltd., 1964 to date
Language command:	English, French, Welsh, Pekingese

Name:	W. Noddy
Date of birth:	August 7, 1928
Passport:	H63241 U.S.A.
Education:	Saint Francis University, degree in mineralogy 1953
Employment:	Assistant manager, Socïeté Debunquant d'Algérie, 1953–1957
	Manager, Kamchatka Mining Co., 1958 to present
Language command:	English, Portuguese, Russian, Arabic

Name:	X. Lanta
Date of birth:	September 8, 1935
Passport:	Q123YB Canada
Education:	University of Quebec, diploma in English, 1955
	Massachusetts Institute of Sciences, degree in mineralogy, 1958
Employment:	Technical Officer, Sardinia Mining Corporation, 1960–1968
	Manager, Moab Valley Mining Plant, 1968 to date
Language command:	Spanish, English, Portuguese

OBSERVATION SHEET: ONE-WAY COMMUNICATION

List in the first column the twenty specific details of the story. Verify the list when the coordinator reads the story to the first person. As Person One repeats the story to Person Two, note the mistakes in Person One's version by writing the wrong words or phrases in the proper row and column. To help scoring, use a check mark for details correctly reported and a zero for the details left out. Repeat this procedure for the rest of the participants.

Item	Original Story	Version 1	Version 2	Version 3	Version 4	Version 5
1						
2						
3						
4						
5						
6						
7						
8						
9						
10						
11						
12						
13						
14						
15						
16						
17						
18						
19						
20						

OBSERVATION SHEET: TWO-WAY COMMUNICATION

List in the first column the twenty specific details of the story. Verify the list when the coordinator reads the story to the first person. As Person One repeats the story to Person Two, note the mistakes in Person One's version by writing the wrong words or phrases in the proper row and column. To help scoring, use a check mark for details correctly reported and a zero for details left out. Repeat this procedure for the rest of the participants.

Item	Original Story	Version 1	Version 2	Version 3	Version 4	Version 5
1						
2						
3						
4						
5						
6						
7						
8						
9						
10						
11						
12						
13						
14						
15						
16						
17						
18						
19						
20						

WHAT IS A NORM?

Norms develop in groups so that members will know how they are expected to behave and what is appropriate member behavior. They are common rules or customs followed by group members, which specify acceptable behavior. In some groups, for example, members address each other by their last names and in other groups first names are used. All groups have norms, and usually they become so automatic that they are followed without conscious thought. Norms can develop so that every member does the same thing (we will all dress formally for a group meeting) or so that every member does something different (we will all dress differently for a group meeting).

Norms are not built from scratch. They develop from the values, expectations, and learned habits that the members bring with them when the group is first formed. "Don't interrupt the chairperson" is a norm that expresses respect for authority, which most persons bring with them into new groups. Norms can also be implied by the setting in which the group meets. Most persons do not sit on the floor when they find themselves in a room that appears to be arranged formally. Most people do not remain standing when the group is meeting at a beach.

Norms have a powerful influence upon communication within a group. Such influences are seldom examined. It is even rarer that a group attempts to change their norms to facilitate their goals and needs. Usually, group members simply follow norms without question. This does not mean that norms do not change. Norms do change, as expectations of appropriate member behavior change, but this is commonly an unobstructive process.

What norms have developed in your group? Do you all sense where you are supposed to sit? Do you all sense who should be listened to and who should be ignored? Do you interrupt each other, or is politeness a group norm? Are jokes allowed, or is the tone of the group serious? How do discussions usually start out? How are boredom or frustration generally expressed, if at all? Are certain things permissible to talk about and others avoided? Is the emotional involvement of members supposed to be high or low? In answering these questions you will become more conscious of the norms that are present in your group.

Spend the next thirty minutes discussing your group norms and make a list of what they are.

STRANDED IN THE DESERT EXERCISE

Situation

You are one of eight members of a geology club that is on a field trip to study unusual formations in the New Mexico desert. It is the last week in July. You have been driving over old trails, far from any road, in order to see out-of-the-way formations. At 10:47 a.m. the specially equipped minibus in which your club is riding overturns, rolls into a fifteen- to twenty-foot ravine, and burns. The driver and the professional adviser to the club are killed. The rest of you are relatively uninjured.

You know that the nearest ranch is approximately forty-five miles east of where you are. There is no other place of habitation closer. When your club does not report to its motel that evening you will be missed. Several people know generally where you are, but because of the nature of your outing they will not be able to pinpoint your exact whereabouts.

The area around you is rather rugged and very dry. You heard from a weather report before you left that the temperature would reach 110 degrees, making the surface temperature 130 degrees. You are all dressed in lightweight, summer clothing, although you do have hats and sunglasses. Before your minibus burned, you were able to salvage the following items:

Magnetic compass	One jacket per person
Large, light-blue canvas	Accurate map of the area
Book, *Animals of the Desert*	A .38-caliber pistol, loaded
Rearview mirror	Bottle of 1,000 salt tablets
One flashlight	Four canteens, each containing two quarts of water

The group needs to make two decisions: (1) to stay where it is or to try to walk out, and (2) to hunt for food or not to hunt. To make these decisions, it will be necessary to rank the salvaged items in the order of their importance. And in making the group decisions, your group must stay together.

Post-Decision Reaction Form

1 What did your group decide?

_____ Stay where you are   _____ Walk out   _____ Could not decide

_____ Hunt   _____ Not to hunt   _____ Could not decide

2. How understood and listened to did you feel in the group?

Not at all 1 : 2 : 3 : 4 : 5 : 6 : 7 : 8 : 9 Completely

3. How much influence do you feel you had on the group's decision?

None at all 1 : 2 : 3 : 4 : 5 : 6 : 7 : 8 : 9 Complete

4. How responsible and committed do you feel to the decisions that were made?

Not at all   1 : 2 : 3 : 4 : 5 : 6 : 7 : 8 : 9 Completely

5. How satisfied are you with your group's performance?

Very dissatisfied 1 : 2 : 3 : 4 : 5 : 6 : 7 : 8 : 9 Very satisfied

6. I would assess my learning about the issue under discussion to be:

None at all 1 : 2 : 3 : 4 : 5 : 6 : 7 : 8 : 9 A great deal

7. Write two adjectives describing the way you now feel. _____

_____

Stranded in the Desert Exercise: Observer Instructions

This exercise is concerned with the process by which group members manage controversy. Critical issues to observe are as follows:

1. Do the participants have a problem-solving or a win-lose orientation toward the controversy? A problem-solving orientation is characterized by an approach to the controversy as a mutual problem presenting a challenge for all to arrive at a mutually acceptable solution. A win-lose orientation is characterized by the attempt by certain group members to dominate others and have them submit to a particular position.

2. Is everyone participating by presenting ideas, information, positions, and opinions?

3. Is the basic situation the group faces being clarified? To make a high quality and creative decision, every member must understand the basic problem with which the group is confronted.

4. Are feelings being discussed as well as information and opinions? Are participants discussing their feelings as openly as they discuss their opinions?

5. Is there adequate differentiation? Exploring points of disagreement, trying to get at basic assumptions, divulging information, clarifying lines of reasoning, and seeking out differences of opinion are all examples of differentiation.

6. Is there adequate integration? Are ways being sought to combine different information, opinions, and positions into one new position that every member can support?

Stranded in the Desert Exercise: Observation Sheet

Statement	*Frequency of Member Participation*							
	1	2	3	4	5	6	7	8
My position is								
What is your position?								
I am right, you are wrong.								
We have a mutual problem we need to solve.								
The reasons I think the way I do are . . . . ;								
The information I have is								
The basic situation is								
I don't understand your position; would you clarify it?								
I don't understand your position; you are wrong.								
Our differences may be summarized as								
Here is a way to combine or integrate our information and opinions:								
My feelings are								
Other:								
Other:								
Other:								
Other:								
Other:								

Stranded in the Desert Briefing Sheet 1

Study the following briefing carefully, keeping it to yourself. Do not let other group members read it. Try to think up new arguments for your position. Although you should argue your position strongly, you can change your mind if someone else has convincing evidence.

Your position is that the group should stay at the scene of the wreck and not hunt for food. You believe it is vitally important for everyone to remain calm and inactive, as movement and excitement will increase dehydration. You think the mirror is the most important item the group has, as it will help signal for help when search planes come into sight. A mirror can reflect enough light to be seen even beyond the horizon. The water, although it may help somewhat in easing the effects of dehydration, will not, in your opinion, significantly prolong life. There are cacti around, but at this time of year a person would use up more body water cutting them apart than he would gain from sucking their inner fibers. Thus it seems to you that keeping still and signalling from where you are is the best thing to do.

Stranded in the Desert Briefing Sheet 2

Study the following briefing carefully, keeping it to yourself. Do not let other group members read it. Try to think up new arguments for your position. Although you should argue your position strongly, you can change your mind if someone else has convincing evidence.

Your position is that the group should try to walk out to the nearest ranch and hunt for food along the way. It is your opinion that the salt tablets and the water will be sufficient for the trip; you have often taken long hikes, and forty-five miles does not seem an unreasonable distance to you. You know there are barrel cacti along the route the minibus took coming in, and you think that additional water can be got from them. Because you are an expert marksman with a rifle, you think hunting animals for food will be easy. The water, salt tablets, and pistol are all highly important to you. From your point of view the situation is not terribly serious unless you wait too long before starting to walk out and obtain food for energy.

Stranded in the Desert Briefing Sheet 3

Study the following briefing carefully, keeping it to yourself. Do not let other group members read it. Try to think up new arguments for your position. Although you should argue your position strongly, you can change your mind if someone else has convincing evidence.

Your position is that the group should walk out to the nearest ranch, but not do any hunting along the way. The group has lots of water (one quart per person), and a compass and map so that you cannot possibly get lost. The canvas can be rigged for a sunshade during the day, and the group can walk during the night. In your opinion the water, the compass, the map, and the canvas are all vital to the group's survival. Thus it seems to you that resting in the shade during the day and walking out during the night without wasting any time or energy for hunting would be the thing to do.

Stranded in the Desert Briefing Sheet 4

Study the following briefing carefully, keeping it to yourself. Do not let other group members read it. Try to think up new arguments for your position. Although you should argue your position strongly, you can change your mind if someone else has convincing evidence.

Your position is that the group should stay where it is and hunt for food to keep alive while waiting to be rescued. You believe that there is not enough water to last the group on the forty-five-mile walk to the nearest ranch. The salt tablets are highly dangerous and should be destroyed; without a lot of water to dilute them, you would get the same effects as drinking sea water. You also believe that the group may be hard to find and that you may have to stay where you are for several days; hunting would be something to occupy everyone's mind and be a healthy diversion as well as providing food. The two most important items in your opinion are the mirror and the flashlight, as they can be used to signal search planes during the day and night. The water is also important. Thus it seems to you that the group's chance for survival rests in staying where you are and hunting for the food needed to keep you alive.

Stranded in the Desert Briefing Sheet 5

Study the following briefing carefully, keeping it to yourself. Do not let other group members read it. Try to think up new arguments for your position. Although you should argue your position strongly, you can change your mind if someone else has convincing evidence.

Your position is that the group should stay where it is and no one should hunt for food. Your view is that the canvas and the jackets are highly important; the canvas will work nicely as a sunshade, and each person should wear his jacket to help conserve his body water. The hot sun and the dry air circulating next to a person's body cause dehydration, which is the main hazard in the situation. The mirror is an important signaling device. Because you believe that a search party will be able to estimate your approximate location, you expect to be rescued soon—providing the group does not leave the wreckage. Your point of view is that the hope for survival depends upon staying where you are so that search planes can find you and not hunting because the effort will speed dehydration.

Stranded in the Desert Briefing Sheet 6

Study the following briefing carefully, keeping it to yourself. Do not let other group members read it. Try to think up new arguments for your position. Although you should argue your position strongly, you can change your mind if someone else has convincing evidence.

Your position is that the group should walk out but not do any hunting. The water and the salt tablets are important to you—the water to prevent dehydration and the salt to help your bodies retain fluids. Inasmuch as the main objective is to reach the ranch as soon as possible, the group should not waste any time and energy by hunting; a person can live quite a while without food, and hunting is a stupid waste of energy. The protein in the meat of any animal you were lucky enough to kill would require increased amounts of water to digest and there is no water to spare. The compass and map are highly important as they will keep you from getting lost. The survival of the group, from your perspective, depends entirely upon walking out to safety without wasting time and energy on hunting.

Stranded in the Desert Briefing Sheet 7

Study the following briefing carefully, keeping it to yourself. Do not let other group members read it. Try to think up new arguments for your position. Although you should argue your position strongly, you can change your mind if someone else has convincing evidence.

Your position is that the group should stay where it is and hunt for food while it waits to be rescued. The distance to the nearest ranch is too far to walk in the desert and, besides, several members of the group have never walked that far in their lives even under the best conditions. The shock of being in a wreck decreases their strength even further. You have the gun and book to help get food; the book will tell you which animals are edible, and the gun can be used to kill them. A search party is bound to be sent out early tomorrow morning so all the group has to worry about is getting food and waiting. The book and the gun are crucial items for the group's survival. Thus the group's only chance for survival seems to you to be to stay where you are and hunt for food to provide energy to signal to search parties.

Stranded in the Desert Briefing Sheet 8

Study the following briefing carefully, keeping it to yourself. Do not let other group members read it. Try to think up new arguments for your position. Although you should argue your position strongly, you can change your mind if someone else has convincing evidence.

Your position is that the group should walk out and hunt along the way. You think the group should not sit around and bake; it should get to the ranch fast! You can get as much water as you want from the cacti that seem to grow everywhere, so water is not a problem. The hunting is going to be easy because you have the book to tell you what to kill and the pistol to kill with. You have heard of many people disappearing in the desert and never being found; you think if the group is to survive it has to walk out on its own. The book and the gun are important to you. You know that the nights get cold in the desert, so you also think the jackets are highly important. Because the group can follow the tire marks of the minibus, you see no need for the map or compass. The survival of the group, from your perspective, depends entirely upon starting to walk out immediately, while hunting for food to ensure adequate strength along the way.

ROLE DESCRIPTIONS

You are a biology teacher, very much in favor of teaching machines. You have researched the area and presented a twenty-page report to the board, recommending that they be purchased. All of a sudden—everyone is upset! You can't see why. You can't even see why this meeting's been scheduled. The facts are the facts. You can't see emotions and feelings, just facts and logic.

———

You are the school psychologist and you consider yourself better educated than most of these teachers. You feel that they have consistently dehumanized their classrooms, which is why *you* have such a heavy load of counseling. You are against the machines because they're even more dehumanizing. You state your position arrogantly—as the "professional" in the group—then discount all arguments *against* your position by "psychologizing" them away, saying, for example, "What you're *really* saying is that you feel threatened in a live, teacher-student confrontation." You do this even when it's wildly inappropriate. You had a tough time in high school; you feel very hostile toward teachers.

———

You're a gym teacher, and *you* can't see what all the fuss is about. Some subjects *should* be machine taught; some shouldn't. You get very bored at these meetings and show it. "They love to make mountains out of molehills!"

———

You're twenty-two, an art teacher. This is your first year teaching and you feel everyone is against you because you look "hippie." You're against the machines. They're part of an Establishment plot to brainwash the young, to make them all think the same way. You are uncomfortable, though, because the older teachers— the *real* squares—are on *your* side. You try to keep your position while disassociating yourself from them. You despise the school psychologist and will put him down whenever you can, even if it hurts your position.

———

You are a math teacher and head of the salary-negotiation committee. You like the machines, but you think they'll hurt your bargaining position. You argue with *everyone*. "Yes, they're great, but they'll hurt us financially, but they *are* the coming thing." You feel you're the only realistic one in the crowd. No one else can see both sides at once.

———

You are a history teacher who is older than most of the other teachers and single. You are very precise in your diction. You are the most idealistic about teaching; you feel passionately that personal involvement is crucial in a teacher, and you believe that the biology teacher is lazy. You believe that a *good* teacher would not want the teaching machines.

———

You are a Latin teacher; fewer and fewer kids are signing up for your classes. You are older than anyone else, and will retire next year. You are against the machines. You are in sympathy with the history teacher, but you've given up on this "younger generation" of teachers and students. You think the psychologist is a pretentious idiot. You try to make a long, hostile speech about "Education Today."

———

You're an English teacher, just out of school and very keen on new teaching methods of all sorts. This has brought you into conflict with the history teacher, which makes you unhappy because you admire her as almost the ideal teacher—though a bit old-fashioned. You believe the machines may be useful in some classes, but you try to support the history teacher at the same time.

WHAT I VALUE

The following is a list of aspirations, some of which you may value and some of which you may not. Read the list carefully and pick the three most important to you. Then write your rationale for your choices. You have ten minutes to complete this activity.

1. To rid the world of prejudice.
2. To serve the sick and needy.
3. To become a famous figure (movie star, baseball hero, and so on).
4. To have a year of daily massages and the world's finest food from the world's best chef.
5. To know the meaning of life.
6. To set your own working conditions.
7. To be the richest person in the world.
8. To have the perfect love affair.
9. To be the President of the United States.
10. To be the most attractive person in the world.
11. To have a house overlooking the most beautiful view in the world, in which you may keep for one year forty of your favorite works of art.
12. To live to be 100 years old, with no illness.
13. To master the profession of your choice.
14. To have a vaccine to make all persons incapable of lying or graft.
15. To control the destinies of 500,000 people.
16. To have the love and admiration of the whole world.
17. To have an anti-hangup pill.
18. To have your own all-knowing computer, for any and all facts you might need.
19. To spend six months with the greatest religious figure of your faith, past or present.
20. Other:

Post-Decision Reaction Form

1. What did your group decide?

2. How understood and listened to did you feel in the group?
    Not at all 1 : 2 : 3 : 4 : 5 : 6 : 7 : 8 : 9 Completely
3. How much influence do you feel you had on the group's decision?
    None at all 1 : 2 : 3 : 4 : 5 : 6 : 7 : 8 : 9 Complete
4. How responsible and committed do you feel to the decisions that were made?
    Not at all 1 : 2 : 3 : 4 : 5 : 6 : 7 : 8 : 9 Completely
5. How satisfied are you with your group's performance?
Very dissatisfied 1 : 2 : 3 : 4 : 5 : 6 : 7 : 8 : 9 Very satisfied
6. I would assess my learning about the issue under discussion to be:
    None at all 1 : 2 : 3 : 4 : 5 : 6 : 7 : 8 : 9 Complete
7. Write two adjectives describing the way you now feel:

FALLOUT SHELTER EXERCISE

Another situation to use with the identical procedure as that used with the Things I Value Exercise is the Fallout Shelter Exercise. In this exercise the following situation is explained to the participants:

Those in your group are members of a federal department in Washington, D.C., that is in charge of experimental stations in the far outposts of civilization. The Third World War has suddenly broken out and bombs are beginning to drop. Places all across the world are being destroyed. People are heading for whatever fallout shelters are available. You receive a desperate call from one of your experimental stations, asking for help. At the station are ten people, but there is only room in the nearby fallout shelter for six. They have decided to abide by your decision as to which six persons can go into the fallout shelter.

You have only superficial information on the ten people. After your group has made its decision it will try to reach its own fallout shelter. You realize that the six people you choose to go to the shelter may be the only six people left to start the human species over again. The choice, therefore, is crucial. You have half an hour to make your decision. If you do not make the decision within the thirty minutes allowed, all ten will die.

Here is what you know about the ten people:

1. Bookeeper, thirty-one years old
2. His wife, six months pregnant
3. Black militant, second-year medical student
4. Famous historian-author, forty-two years old
5. Hollywood starlet, a singer and dancer
6. Biochemist
7. Rabbi, fifty-four years old
8. Olympic athlete, all sports
9. College coed
10. Policeman with gun (they cannot be separated)

Post-Decision Reaction Form

1. What did your group decide?

2. How understood and listened to did you feel in the group?

     Not at all 1 : 2 : 3 : 4 : 5 : 6 : 7 : 8 : 9 Completely

3. How much influence do you feel you had on the group's decision?

     None at all 1 : 2 : 3 : 4 : 5 : 6 : 7 : 8 : 9 Complete

4. How responsible and committed do you feel to the decisions that were made?

     Not at all 1 : 2 : 3 : 4 : 5 : 6 7 : 8 : 9 Completely

5. How satisfied are you with your group's performance?

Very dissatisfied 1 : 2 : 3 : 4 : 5 : 6 : 7 : 8 : 9 Very satisfied

6. I would assess my learning about the issue under discussion to be:

     None at all 1 : 2 : 3 : 4 : 5 : 6 : 7 : 8 : 9 Complete

7. Write two adjectives describing the way you now feel:

GROUP MEMBERSHIP EXCELLENCE EXERCISE

Instruction Sheet

Systems for evaluating the performance of group members have many shortcomings. Different members behave in different ways to accomplish their objectives. These variations make most comparisons difficult and unfair. To overcome this problem, we have developed a simulation that all members participate in. From your behavior in this exercise we will be able to tell if you are a poor, average, good, or excellent group member. The exercise provides an impartial and equal measure of a participant's performance.

Here is how the exercise works: You are being issued a bag containing ten marbles of four different colors: red, green, blue, and rainbow. Different members have different proportions of the colors, but each person has ten marbles. Your objective is to collect fifteen marbles of the same color and turn them in to the coordinator of the exercise. You will have fifteen minutes to do so. Bonus points will be awarded for more than fifteen marbles; you will receive a 10 percent increase for each marble over the fifteen that you collect. Thus, if you turn in eighteen green marbles, you will receive the regular award for fifteen marbles *plus* 30 percent more.

Observer Instructions

As an observer, your task is to obtain as much information about what is taking place as possible. There are three areas on which you should concentrate most heavily: what strategies of negotiation are being used in the group, how are members reacting to each other's strategies, and how successful are the strategies. Any other aspect of negotiating behavior you can observe will be helpful. Write down your observations and make as many as possible.

Win-Lose Negotiation Instructions

In this exercise your group is to adopt a win-lose negotiation strategy in which each member will try to obtain more marbles of the same color than anyone else. Obviously, some of the members of your group are going to win and some are going to lose. You want to be a winner. The use of deceit, threats, and force may be helpful in negotiating with your group members. In negotiations, try to achieve the best outcome for yourself, and use your power and skill in any way that helps you do so. Remember, if you keep the other group members from winning, you will increase your chances of winning.

GROUP MEMBERSHIP EXCELLENCE EXERCISE

Instruction Sheet

Systems for evaluating the performance of group members have many shortcomings. Different members behave in different ways to accomplish their objectives. These variations make most comparisons difficult and unfair. To overcome this problem, we have developed a simulation that all members participate in. From your behavior in this exercise we will be able to tell if you are a poor, average, good, or excellent group member. The exercise provides an impartial and equal measure of a participant's performance.

Here is how the exercise works: You are being issued a bag containing ten marbles of four different colors: red, green, blue, and rainbow. Different members have different proportions of the colors, but each person has ten marbles. Your objective is to collect fifteen marbles of the same color and turn them in to the coordinator of the exercise. You will have fifteen minutes to do so. Bonus points will be awarded for more than fifteen marbles; you will receive a 10 percent increase for each marble over the fifteen that you collect. Thus, if you turn in eighteen green marbles, you will receive the regular award for fifteen marbles *plus* 30 percent more.

Observer Instructions

As an observer, your task is to obtain as much information about what is taking place as possible. There are three areas on which you should concentrate most heavily: what strategies of negotiation are being used in the group, how are members reacting to each other's strategies, and how successful are the strategies. Any other aspect of negotiating behavior you can observe will be helpful. Write down your observations and make as many as possible.

Problem-solving Negotiation Instructions

In this exercise your group is to adopt a problem-solving negotiation strategy in which members try to define the task and find creative solutions to it that are satisfying to as many members as possible. In negotiating with other group members, try to make the problem solving as creative as possible. Communicate openly and honestly about your needs and try to find ways in which to help both your own and the other group members' success. Avoid all threats and deception that might destroy trust among group members. The problem is to figure out how as many group members as possible can complete the task.

NEGOTIATION EXERCISE: CASE STUDY 1

Background

Jim and Chris (a woman) both work for a research firm but in different divisions. Chris has been assigned as project leader of a study, and Jim has been assigned from the other division to work on it. This does not necessarily imply that Chris is Jim's boss. This arrangement has been in effect for about a year and it is relatively unsatisfactory to Chris, who would like to have Jim taken off the project.

Meetings of the project team often are dominated by arguments between Chris and Jim. As a result Chris has often held meetings without notifying Jim.

Jim and Chris are meeting to see if the conflict between them can be resolved.

Chris

Jim is a know-it-all who is always trying to tell you how to run your project. You do not agree with his approach. What he wants to study is not the subject of the research.

You cannot stand Jim's voice. He has an extremely grating voice that he uses with imperious overtones. He is generally obnoxious.

He comes into meetings, slumps down in a chair, and demands that everyone pay attention to him, even if he is late and they have already started.

He doesn't give other people a chance to talk and always interrupts if they do get a chance.

He does not care about the project. If he finds something else to do that he likes better, he simply ignores his responsibilities for completing work on the project. The group had to miss one deadline because he chose to do something else, and in the report before, you had to rewrite one whole section because what he turned in was not adequate. He was busy working on something for the director of the organization just to make a name for himself. Meanwhile, he sacrificed your reputation by causing your project to be late and your group to produce inferior work.

Jim

Chris thinks she is better than anyone else around here. She thinks she is some kind of prima donna and that only the research she is doing is any good. She thinks all the other work in the organization is "trash" except for hers.

You feel that what you were working on for the director was more important for the organization. But she is not willing to accept the fact that anyone can do anything well except herself.

You do not agree with her approach to the project. What she is putting the main emphasis on is not relevant to the problem. We need answers in order to make decisions today, not five years from now.

You do not really feel involved in the project. Chris accepts what everyone else on the project is doing, but she picks on your area to criticize.

NEGOTIATION EXERCISE: CASE STUDY 2

Background

Pat (a woman) and Rich both work for a research organization. Originally the director of the organization was leader of a project. Rich was interviewed to work on that project and hired by the present director. Pat had also interviewed Rich and strongly opposed his being hired for the project. Pat thought Rich wasn't competent to do the job.

Five or six months after work on the project began, the director wanted to be relieved and proposed that Rich and Pat conduct it jointly. Pat agreed only reluctantly—with the stipulation that it be made clear she was not working for Rich. The director consented. They were to have a shared directorship.

After about a month, Pat was angry because Rich was acting toward others as though he were the director of the entire project and she was working for him.

Pat and Rich are meeting to see if the conflict between them can be resolved.

Pat

Right after the joint-leadership arrangement was reached with the director, Rich called a meeting of the project team without even consulting you about the time or content. He just told you when it was being held and said you should be there.

At the meeting Rich reviewed everyone's paper line-by-line—including yours, thus treating you as just another team member working for him.

He sends out letters and signs himself as project director, which obviously implies to others that you are working for him.

Rich

You think Pat is all hung up with feelings of power and titles. Just because you are project director, or sign yourself that way, doesn't mean that she is working for you. You do not see anything to get excited about. What difference does it make?

She is too sensitive about everything. You call a meeting and right away she thinks you are trying to run everything.

Pat has other things to do—other projects to run—so she does not pay too much attention to this one. She mostly lets things slide. Then when you take the initiative to set up a meeting, she starts jumping up and down about how you are trying to make her work for you.

NEGOTIATION EXERCISE CASE STUDY 3

Background

Samuels Senior High School is in the throes of conflict. Budget cuts have to be made, and the students are in considerable disagreement as to which programs should be cut back or improved. Two students and the principal are meeting to discuss the issue. The purpose of the meeting is to negotiate an agreement on the amount of emphasis to be placed on the athletic and academic programs of the high school.

Academic Student

You are an elected representative of the academically oriented students of Samuels High School. You are actively involved in extracurricular clubs and organizations, such as the Physics Club, French Club, and Future Teachers of America, and you want to get the best education possible because you (and your friends) are concerned about getting into college.

In recent years many graduates have *not* gotten into good colleges. You believe that this is due to the inadequate educational facilities and poorly trained teachers in the school. At your school, athletics is "god" and no real appreciation of intellectual, aesthetic, scientific, or political interests exists. Most of the school's budget goes for new athletic equipment, cheerleader's uniforms, and so on. You have consistently proposed new academic programs, but have seen no results. You have heard that almost the total budget of the school for next year is going to the athletic department. You believe that the board of education and your principal are more interested in state athletic championships than in education.

You are frustrated and upset. Your parents have complained, but to no avail. You are made fun of, ridiculed, and ignored by the sports-centered few who don't have the brains to do well in school.

You are meeting with the principal and another student to discuss the situation. You hope to be able to obtain a commitment from them that much of next year's budget will be spent on improving the academic programs of the school.

Athletic Student

You are an elected representative of the athletically-oriented students of Samuels High School. You are actively involved in athletics, and the school has always had an extremely successful athletic program. Being involved in sports has been important to you and all your friends socially, at home, and with the local businessmen. You value sports and believe sports are as necessary and as educational as any courses taught in the school.

Rumors have been rife that the athletic programs are going to be dropped in order to develop the academic reputation of the school. You have heard that sports are now considered useless by school officials—especially the principal—and because a small group of parents and students interested only in grades and colleges have been making a fuss, it is quite likely that all sports programs will be eliminated (except on a small-time, intramural level).

You are angry and believe that your interests—and those of your friends—are being ignored. You are a good student and most of the athletes have above-average grades. Yet one small clique of students who see no value in sports because they can't make the teams is determined to get rid of all athletic programs. They think there is only one way to get to college and that athletic scholarships are for students with all brawn and no brains.

You are meeting with the principal and another student to discuss the situation. You hope to obtain a commitment from them to use most of next year's budget for badly needed sports equipment and for support of the athletic programs.

Principal

You are the principal of Samuels High School. The superintendent has informed you that the school's budget must be cut drastically in the coming year. You have been considering several possible cutbacks, but as yet you have made no decisions.

Your athletic program has been highly successful—football, baseball, swimming, tennis, gymnastics. Alumni have been supportive and active financially. Athletic events have drawn large crowds from surrounding areas, thereby aiding local businesses.

In the last two years, the academic standards of Samuels High seem to have fallen. Only 10 percent of your recent graduates have been accepted into college programs. As a result, a group of parents and students have been campaigning vigorously for increased emphasis on academic programs—that is, more advanced college-preparatory courses, more laboratory equipment, more innovative teachers. They are not opposed to the athletic programs, but they do feel that competitive sports has been overemphasized and that academic programs have suffered as a consequence.

Rumors have been rampant. Students are angry. Tension is high. You are meeting with two students this afternoon.

Negotiation Exercise: Bargaining Instructions

Bargaining is a process by which a person attempts to reach an agreement as favorable to herself as possible. It is aimed at producing an agreement with another person that settles what each is to give and receive in a transaction between them. Usually in a bargaining situation one person "wins" and the other person "loses." A variety of strategies can be used to influence the other bargainer to reach an agreement as favorable to oneself as possible. They are:

1. Presenting an opening offer very favorable to oneself and refusing to modify one's position.
2. Gathering information about what the other considers a "reasonable" agreement from the other's opening offer and proposals.
3. Continually pointing out the validity of one's own position and the incorrectness of the other person's.
4. Using a combination of threats and promises to convince the other person that he has to accept your offer.
5. Committing oneself to a position in such a way that if an agreement is to be reached, the other person has to agree to one's terms.

In this exercise you are to bargain as toughly as you can to arrive at the best settlement possible for yourself.

Negotiation Exercise: Role Reversal Instructions

Role reversal is defined as a negotiating action in which one person accurately and completely paraphrases, in a warm and involved way, the feelings and position of another. It is the expression of a sincere interest in understanding the other person's position and feelings. The basic rule for role reversal is: each person speaks up for himself only after he has first restated the ideas and feelings of the other person accurately and to the other's satisfaction. In other words, before one person presents her point of view, it is necessary for her to achieve the other person's perspective or frame of reference and to understand the other's position and feelings so well that she can paraphrase them accurately and completely. General guidelines for role reversal are:

1. Restating the other person's expressed ideas and feelings in one's own words rather than mimicking or parroting the exact words of the other person.
2. Prefacing reflected remarks with: "You think . . . ," "Your position is . . . ," "You feel . . . ," "It seems to you that . . . ," and so on.
3. Avoiding any indication of approval or disapproval in paraphrasing the other person's statements. It is important to refrain from interpreting, blaming, persuading, or giving advice.
4. Making one's nonverbal messages congruent with one's verbal paraphrasing. One should look attentive, be interested in and open to the other's ideas and feelings, and appear to be concentrating upon what the other person is trying to communicate.

In this exercise you are to engage in role reversal during the entire negotiating session and use it to arrive at the solution to the problems you and the other person(s) are facing.

FEELINGS OF REJECTION EXERCISE: INSTRUCTIONS

Person No. 1

You are to try to get the person sitting opposite you in your circle (Person 3) rejected from your group. Use any reason you can think of—he has big feet; she's the only person with glasses; he's got chapped hands, anything you think of. Stick to this, and try to convince the other members of your group that this is the person who should be rejected. You can listen to the arguments of the other members in the group, but don't give in. Be sure to talk about the person and not about rules for rejecting.

Person No. 2

You are to try to get the person sitting opposite you in your circle (Person 4) rejected from your group. Use any reason you can think of—he has big hands, she's the only person in a dress, he's got chapped lips, anything you can think of. Stick to this, and try to convince the other members in your group that this is the person who should be rejected. Be sure to talk about the person and not about the rules for rejecting. You can listen to the arguments of other group members, but don't give in.

Person No. 3

You are to try to get the person sitting at your left (Person 2) rejected from your group. Use any reason you can think of—he has large ears, she has freckles, he has dandruff, anything you can think of. Stick to this, and try to convince the other members that this is the person who should be rejected. You can listen to the arguments of other members, but don't give in.

Person No. 4

You are to try to get the person sitting on your right (Person 1) rejected from the group. Use any reason you can think of—he misses too many meetings, she's the only one in the group wearing a sweater, she's the shortest person, anything you can think of. Stick to this, and try to convince the other group members that this is the person who should be rejected. You can listen to the arguments of other people in the group, but don't give in. Be sure you talk about the person and not about rules for rejecting.

FEELINGS OF DISTRUST EXERCISE

Instructions A

Do not share these instructions with the other person in your pair. Your task for the next five minutes is to talk as positively and warmly as you can to the other person. Say only positive and friendly things, especially showing that you want to cooperate and work effectively with him in the future. Your conversation is to concentrate on him, about your impression of him, and the need for cooperation between the two of you. Don't talk about yourself. No matter what happens you say only positive things. Keep the conversation moving along quickly. You are to speak *first*.

Instructions B

Do not share these instructions with the other person in your pair. The other person will speak first. Your task for the next five minutes is to talk with the other person in a way that shows distrust of him. Whatever he says, say something in return that communicates suspicion, distrust, disinterest, defiance, disbelief, or contradiction. Talk only about the things the other person talks about, and avoid starting conversation or bringing up new topics. Try not to help the other person out in any way. As an example, should your partner comment "Say, I like the shirt you're wearing," you might respond "What do you say that for? It's ugly. I don't like it at all. What are you trying to accomplish by complimenting my shirt?"

INTERGROUP CONFLICT EXERCISE: INSTRUCTIONS

Teachers Group

You are residents of a medium-sized but quickly growing suburban community that is within commuting distance of a large city. Your town, Engleston, has recently been torn by a number of civil-rights demonstrations centering on the issue of school integration. Two of the public schools in Engleston contain approximately 90 percent of the underprivileged, culturally different white and Negro children in the community. Moreover, the high-school dropout rate (60 percent) has shown the inadequacy of the educational program for these youngsters. Acts of vandalism and other forms of juvenile delinquency have been pronounced and costly to the town and those responsible are most often among the school dropouts.

Four opposing groups in the community, yours among them, have made various suggestions with respect to finding solutions for some of these problems. The school board has asked the four groups to get together and settle on a single set of four to six proposals, which it will then implement.

As a member of the teachers group, you are essentially opposed to breaking up the schools in any way. You are interested in creating better schools and are generally in favor of creating an expanded educational program.

You are to submit four to six recommendations for dealing with these problems at a meeting at which your spokesman, and one from each of the other three groups, will be present. You may prepare a simple chart as a visual aid to impress the *main* points you wish to emphasize.

Try to make your recommendations original and creative, because it will be to your advantage if the other groups accept your proposals. After the representatives have presented their group's proposals, they will negotiate a *composite proposal* of four to six points to be presented to the school board.

INTERGROUP CONFLICT EXERCISE: REACTION FORM

Group: _____

1. How satisfied are you with your own group's proposals?

Very Dissatisfied 1 : 2 : 3 : 4 : 5 : 6 : 7 : 8 : 9 Very Satisfied

2. How satisfied are you with the negotiator your group has selected?

Very Dissatisfied 1 : 2 : 3 : 4 : 5 : 6 : 7 : 8 : 9 Very Satisfied

3. How satisfied are you with the proposals of the other groups?

Very Dissatisfied 1 : 2 : 3 : 4 : 5 : 6 : 7 : 8 : 9 Very Satisfied

4. How do you think the final composite proposals will compare to your group's proposals?

Very Inferior 1 : 2 : 3 : 4 : 5 : 6 : 7 : 8 : 9 Very Superior

5. Write one adjective describing the way you now feel about what is taking place:

Parents Group

You are residents of a medium-sized but quickly growing suburban community that is within commuting distance of a large city. Your town, Engleston, has recently been torn by a number of civil-rights demonstrations centering on the issue of school integration. Two of the public schools in Engleston contain approximately 90 percent of the underprivileged, culturally different white and Negro children in the community. Moreover, the high-school dropout rate (60 percent) has increasingly shown the inadequacy of the educational program for these youngsters. Acts of vandalism and other forms of juvenile delinquency have become pronounced and costly to the town and those responsible are most often among the school dropouts.

Four opposing groups in the community, yours among them, have made various suggestions with respect to finding solutions for some of these problems. The school board has asked the four groups to get together and settle on a single set of four to six proposals, which it will then implement.

You are a member of the parents group. Because the tax rate is already one of the highest in the state, you favor solutions that will *not* increase your taxes. Generally, you feel that teachers and administrators have been lax, and what is needed is more efficient and immediate use of the present resources. You are absolutely against any busing of students and want all students to attend the school closest to their home.

You are to submit four to six recommendations for dealing with these problems at a meeting at which your spokesman, and one from each of the other three groups, will be present. You may prepare a simple chart as a visual aid to impress the *main* points you wish to emphasize.

Try to make your recommendations original and creative, because it will be to your advantage if the other groups accept your proposals. After the representatives have presented their group's proposals, they will negotiate a composite proposal of four to six points to be presented to the school board.

INTERGROUP CONFLICT EXERCISE: REACTION FORM

Group: _____

1. How satisfied are you with your own group's proposals?

Very Dissatisfied 1 : 2 : 3 : 4 : 5 : 6 : 7 : 8 : 9 Very Satisfied

2. How satisfied are you with the negotiator your group has selected?

Very Dissatisfied 1 : 2 : 3 : 4 : 5 : 6 : 7 : 8 : 9 Very Satisfied

3. How satisfied are you with the proposals of the other groups?

Very Dissatisfied 1 : 2 : 3 : 4 : 5 : 6 : 7 : 8 : 9 Very Satisfied

4. How do you think the final composite proposals will compare to your group's proposals?

Very Inferior 1 : 2 : 3 : 4 : 5 : 6 : 7 : 8 : 9 Very Superior

5. Write one adjective describing the way you now feel about what is taking place:

Civil-Rights Group

You are residents of a medium-sized but quickly growing suburban community that is within commuting distance of a large city. Your town, Engleston, has recently been torn by a number of civil-rights demonstrations centering on the issue of school integration. Two of the public schools in Engleston contain approximately 90 percent of the underprivileged, culturally different white and Negro children in the community. Moreover, the high-school dropout rate (60 percent) has increasingly shown the inadequacy of the education program for these youngsters. Acts of vandalism and other forms of juvenile delinquency have become pronounced and costly to the town and those responsible are most often among the school dropouts.

Four opposing groups in the community, yours among them, have made various suggestions with respect to finding solutions for some of these problems. The school board has asked the four groups to get together and settle on a single set of four to six proposals, which it will then implement.

As a member of the civil-rights group, you are totally committed to immediate integration. You believe the schools have to be integrated through immediate busing of students. You feel that things generally go along too slowly, and you are extremely dissatisfied with the present situation.

You are to submit four to six recommendations for dealing with these problems at a meeting at which your spokesman, and one from each of the other three groups, will be present. You may prepare a simple chart as a visual aid to impress the *main* points you wish to emphasize.

Try to make your recommendations original and creative, because it will be to your advantage if the other groups accept your proposals. After the representatives have presented their group's proposals, they will negotiate a *composite proposal* of four to six points to be presented to the school board.

INTERGROUP CONFLICT EXERCISE: REACTION FORM

Group: _____

1. How satisfied are you with your own group's proposals?

Very Dissatisfied 1 : 2 : 3 : 4 : 5 : 6 : 7 : 8 : 9 Very Satisfied

2. How satisfied are you with the negotiator your group has selected?

Very Dissatisfied 1 : 2 : 3 : 4 : 5 : 6 : 7 : 8 : 9 Very Satisfied

3. How satisfied are you with the proposals of the other groups?

Very Dissatisfied 1 : 2 : 3 : 4 : 5 : 6 : 7 : 8 : 9 Very Satisfied

4. How do you think the final composite proposals will compare to your group's proposals?

Very Inferior 1 : 2 : 3 : 4 : 5 : 6 : 7 : 8 : 9 Very Superior

5. Write one adjective describing the way you now feel about what is taking place:

School Administrators Group

You are residents of a medium-sized but quickly growing suburban community that is within commuting distance of a large city. Your town, Engleston, has recently been torn by a number of civil-rights demonstrations centering on the issue of school integration. Two of the public schools in Engleston contain approximately 90 percent of the underprivileged, culturally deprived white and Negro children in the community. Moreover, the high-school dropout rate (60 percent) has increasingly shown the inadequacy of the educational program for these youngsters. Acts of vandalism and other forms of juvenile delinquency have become pronounced and costly to the town and those responsible are most often among the school dropouts.

Four opposing groups in the community, yours among them, have made various suggestions with respect to finding solutions for some of these problems. The school board has asked the four groups to get together and settle on a single set of four to six proposals, which it will then implement.

As a member of the school administrators group, you are generally satisfied with the way things are and believe that anything but gradual and carefully planned change would lead to chaos. Moreover, you believe that the complaining has been done chiefly by extremist groups at work in the community. In your opinion all school-policy decisions should be made by your group—and parents, teachers, and community groups should not butt in.

You are to submit four to six recommendations for dealing with these problems at a meeting at which your spokesman, and one from each of the other three groups, will be present. You may prepare a simple chart as a visual aid to emphasize the *main* points you wish to present.

Try to make your recommendations original and creative, because it will be to your advantage if the other groups accept your proposals. After the representatives have presented their group's proposals, they will negotiate a *composite proposal* of four to six points to be presented to the school board.

INTERGROUP CONFLICT EXERCISE: REACTION FORM

Group: _____

1. How satisfied are you with your own group's proposals?

Very Dissatisfied 1 : 2 : 3 : 4 : 5 : 6 : 7 : 8 : 9 Very Satisfied

2. How satisfied are you with the negotiator your group has selected?

Very Dissatisfied 1 : 2 : 3 : 4 : 5 : 6 : 7 : 8 : 9 Very Satisfied

3. How satisfied are you with the proposals of the other groups?

Very Dissatisfied 1 : 2 : 3 : 4 : 5 : 6 : 7 : 8 : 9 Very Satisfied

4. How do you think the final composite proposals will compare to your group's proposals?

Very Inferior 1 : 2 : 3 : 4 : 5 : 6 : 7 : 8 : 9 Very Superior

5. Write one adjective describing the way you now feel about what is taking place:

BATTLESHIP EXERCISE

Instructions

1. The object of the exercise is to get the highest possible score from shooting sixteen shots at a target.

2. The shots have to be fired in four salvos of four shots each. Any salvo may be fired at any time prior to the expiration of the time limit. If any salvos are not fired before the time limit expires, the coordinator will automatically give a score of zero for unfired shots.

3. On the ten-by-ten-square grid, there is a target mass consisting of between six and fifteen adjacent squares. "Adjacent" means horizontally or vertically, not diagonally.

4. The squares in which the target is located differ in point value; some are one point, some are three points, and some are five.

5. A salvo is "fired" by being announced to the coordinator in terms of its coordinates (that is, A3, E5, C10, F2). The coordinator will then announce the *total* score obtained by the group on that salvo. He will *not* report the individual point value of a shot, only the *total* salvo score.

6. Shots may continue to be fired at the same squares. For example, if a group fires a four-shot salvo and gets a score of six points, it may continue to fire its remaining salvos at these same squares and obtain a score of six points on each salvo.

7. Your group must select a spokesman who will announce the coordinates of all salvos to the coordinator. Only the spokesman's "shots" will be accepted. If the spokesman announces a shot not on the grid, for example, P5, the coordinator will automatically give it a score of zero.

8. Your group may mark its Grid Sheet up in any way it chooses.

9. Your group may not ask any questions of the coordinator. All the necessary instructions are contained on this sheet.

10. Remember, the thirty-minute period began with the distribution of these instructions.

BATTLESHIP EXERCISE: GRID SHEET

	A	B	C	D	E	F	G	H	I	J
1										
2										
3										
4										
5										
6										
7										
8										
9										
10										

UNEQUAL RESOURCES EXERCISE: TASKS SHEET

Each group is to complete the following tasks:

1. Make a three-by-three-inch square of white paper.
2. Make a four-by-two-inch rectangle of gold paper.
3. Make a T-shaped piece three-by-five-inches in green and white paper.
4. Make a four-link paper chain, each link in a different color.
5. Make a four-by-four-inch flag, in any three colors.

The first group to complete all tasks is the winner. Groups may negotiate with other groups for the use of materials and tools to complete the tasks on any mutually agreeable basis.

POWER POLITICS EXERCISE: INSTRUCTION SHEET

This is a game of power politics. Your group is to become the governing body of a political party and your task is to select a general chairman. This is a crucial decision for the party. The person you elect will have extensive power and control over who gets how much patronage from the party. He will have 100 units of patronage to distribute among deserving members of the group. Members of your group may negotiate for votes and the distribution of the patronage. Each of you controls a different number of votes. One member controls 100 votes, a second controls 200, a third controls 300, and so on, with one member controlling 1,200 votes. The number of votes you have is on a slip of paper given to you by the coordinator of the exercise. Keep this slip. *Do not show it to any other group member.* You may commit your votes to any member you wish; you may also split your votes among several members if you so desire. A member must receive 4,000 votes to become chairman.

POWER TO THE ANIMALS EXERCISE

General Instructions

This exercise involves a group in which there are three levels of power in the form of marbles. Group members have the chance to progress from one level of power to another by obtaining marbles through negotiation. The three members who get the most power will be declared the winners when the exercise ends. You will be given six marbles each. The scoring system for the marbles is given below. Additional points are given if a member is able to get several marbles of the same color:

Color	Points		Number of a kind	Points
Green	50		6	50
Yellow	25		5	30
Red	15		4	20
White	10		3	10
Blue	5			

For example, a person's total score if she had 6 green marbles would be 300 (6 x 50) plus 50 (for 6 of a kind) or 350 points.

The rules for negotiation are as follows:

1. You have five minutes to improve your scores.
2. You improve your scores by negotiating with other group members.
3. People must be holding hands to have an agreement.
4. Only one-for-one trades are legal. Two for one or any other combination is illegal.
5. Once members touch the hand of another member, a marble of unequal value (or color) must be traded. If two members cannot make an agreement they may have to hold hands for the entire negotiating round.
6. There is no talking unless hands are touching. This rule must be strictly followed.
7. People with folded arms do not have to negotiate with other people.
8. All marbles must be hidden. This rule must be strictly followed.

Strategies for Influencing High-power Group

1. Build your own organizations and resources to make the low-power group less exposed to being taken advantage of.
2. Form coalitions.
3. Change the attitudes of high-power group members through education or moral persuasion.
4. Use existing legal procedures to bring pressures for change.
5. Search for ways in which to make high-power group members dependent upon the low-power group.
6. Use harassment techniques to increase the high-power group's costs of sticking with the status quo.

CAMPUS DEVELOPMENT EXERCISE

rate best 0-5 worst

Observer Note Form

For each of the following questions related to group problem solving, please describe briefly the performance of the group you observed. This report will not be turned in; you will use your notes later as a guide in discussion. Feel free, therefore, to abbreviate your notes in whatever way suits you. When possible, illustrate your comments with specific examples of what the group did.

1. How well did the group clarify its problems?
2. How well did the group determine alternative approaches toward a solution? *1*
3. How well did the group get and analyze the facts? *1*
4. How well did the group decide on action? *0*
5. How did the group organize itself? *very well*
6. How was leadership handled within the group?
7. How effectively did the group work with other groups? Was it cooperative or competitive?
8. How effective were communications within the group and with other groups?
9. Was communication guarded or open within the group? among groups?
10. How well did the group utilize its total resources, including its total membership? *2*
11. Other comments. *motivation*

City Council

You are a member of the City Council. The city owns Plots B3, B4, and D4.

	A1	A2	A3	A4
	B1	B2	B3	B4
	C1	C2	C3	C4
	D1	D2	D3	D4

N ↗

The council desires to own Plots A4 and C4 because a strip down the center of A4, B4, C4, and D4 is to be purchased for a new federal highway site. This will make the land on either side of the highway very valuable. If the city owned this property, it could later sell it at a high price and obtain some much needed funds. In addition, it could control more readily how this property is eventually used.

The news of the highway is not common knowledge and if word gets out, it may be difficult to get the land at a good price. Normally, plots would sell for $5,000 each. Your available cash amounts to $15,000.

You have heard rumors that BIG Fraternity wishes to expand by obtaining land adjacent to their present house on Plot A3.

Other organizations involved are:

College Faculty Club
BIG Fraternity
College Housing Office
Investments, Inc.

Starting materials:

Deeds to B3, B4, D4
Two $5,000 bills, five $1,000 bills
Option form

Investments, Inc.

You are a member of Investments, Inc., a private investment company. In addition to other assets, your group owns Plots A2, A4, and C2.

N

A1	A2	A3	A4
B1	B2	B3	B4
C1	C2	C3	C4
D1	D2	D3	D4

The board of directors of your company has decided to sell all land holdings as soon as possible at the best possible price.

Plots normally sell for $5,000, but this price will go up if two groups begin competing for a plot or if some other impending event would make the property more valuable.

Other organizations involved are:

City Council
College Faculty Club
College Housing Office
BIG Fraternity

Starting materials:

Deeds to A2, A4, and C2
Option form

BIG Fraternity

You are a member of **BIG** Fraternity. Thanks to alumni gifts, your group now owns Plots A3, B1, and C1.

N

A1	A2	A3	A4
B1	B2	B3	B4
C1	C2	C3	C4
D1	D2	D3	D4

Your present fraternity house is located on Plot A3. You desire to own any two plots adjoining your present house site, for ease of expansion of the present house and new facilities for members. Cash available for this expansion is $8,000, but this amount would be very useful in your future building plans. Plots normally sell for $5,000 each.

Other organizations involved are:

College Faculty Club
City Council
College Housing Office
Investments, Inc.

Starting materials:

Deeds to A3, B1, C1
One $5,000 bill, three $1,000 bills
Option form

College Housing Office

You are a member of the College Housing Office. Your group now owns Plots A1, C4, D1, and D2.

	A1	A2	A3	A4
	B1	B2	B3	B4
	C1	C2	C3	C4
	D1	D2	D3	D4

N ↑

Your group desires to own any four adjacent plots on which to build housing facilities for married students.

Your group has no available cash for this investment, since all your budgeted funds will be needed for construction. You have hopes of raising some money by selling one of your plots of land. Those plots normally sell for $5,000, but perhaps you can get more.

Other organizations involved are:

College Faculty Club
City Council
BIG Fraternity
Investments, Inc.

Starting Materials:

Deeds to A1, C4, D1, and D2
Option form

463

College Faculty Club

You are a member of the planning committee of the College Faculty Club. Your group owns Plots B2, C3 and D3.

	A1	A2	A3	A4
N	B1	B2	B3	B4
	C1	C2	C3	C4
	D1	D2	D3	D4

Your group, which receives no financial support from the college, desires to own Plots B3 and C2. All of your present designs for a large faculty club facility are based on a square plot of land with a modern building in the center and ample parking all around the building.

You have heard rumors of a highway going in somewhere in the neighborhood, but are not sure where it is going.

Thanks to recent gifts, you have $10,000 available for this investment. Plots are normally priced at $5,000.

Other organizations involved are:

City Council
BIG Fraternity
College Housing Office
Investments, Inc.

Starting materials:

Deeds to B2, C3, D3
One $5,000 bill, five $1,000 bills
Option form

References

Allport, G. W., and L. J. Postman. The basic psychology of rumor. *Transactions of the New York Academy of Sciences*, series II, 1945, *8*, 61–81.

Bales, R. F. *Interaction Process Analysis*. Reading, Mass.: Addison-Wesley, 1950.

———. Some uniformities of behavior in small social systems. In G. E. Swanson, T. M. Newcomb, and E. L. Hartley (eds.), *Readings in Social Psychology*. New York: Holt, 1952, 146–59.

———, and E. F. Borgatta. Size of group as a factor in the interaction profile. In A. P. Hare, E. F. Borgatta, and R. F. Bales (eds.), *Small Groups*. New York: Knopf, 1955, 396–413.

Bandura, A. *Principles of Behavior Modification*. New York: Holt, Rinehart, and Winston, 1969.

Bartlett, F. C. *Remembering*. Cambridge: Cambridge University Press, 1932.

Beckhard, R. *Organizational Development*. Reading, Mass.: Addison-Wesley, 1969.

———, and D. G. Lake. Short and long-range effects of a team development effort. In H. A. Hornstein, B. A. Benedict, W. W. Burke, R. Lewicki, and M. G. Gindes, *Strategies of Social Intervention: A Behavioral Science Analysis*. New York: Free Press, 1971, 421–39.

Bierman, R. Dimensions for interpersonal facilitation in psychotherapy in child development. *Psychological Bulletin*, 1969, *72*, 338–52.

Blake, R. R., and J. S. Mouton. The intergroup dynamics of win-lose conflict and problem-solving collaboration in union-management relations. In Muzafer Sherif (ed). *Intergroup Relations and Leadership*. New York: John Wiley and Sons, Inc., 1962, 94–142.

Cartwright, D. The nature of group cohesiveness. In D. Cartwright and D. A. Zandler, *Group Dynamics: Research and Theory*, 3rd ed. New York: Harper and Row, 1968, 91–109.

———, and A. Zander. (eds.) *Group Dynamics*. New York: Harper and Row, 1968.

Coch, L. and J. R. P. French, Jr. Overcoming resistance to change. *Human Relations*, 1948, *1*, 512–33.

Dance, F. E. X. The "concept" of communication. *Journal of Communication*, 1970, *20*, 201–10.

David, G. A. and S. E. Houtman. *Thinking Creatively: A Guide to Training Imagination*. Madison, Wisc.: Wisconsin Research and Development Center for Cognitive Learning, 1968.

Deutsch, M. A theory of cooperation and competition. *Human Relations*, 1949, *2*, 129–52.

_____.Trust and suspicion. *Journal of Conflict Resolution*, 1958, *2*, 265–79.

_____.The effect of motivational orientation upon trust and suspicion. *Human Relations, 13*, 123–39, 1960.

_____.Cooperation and trust: some theoretical notes. In M. R. Jones (ed.), *Nebraska Symposium on Motivation*. Lincoln, Neb.: University of Nebraska Press, 1962, 275–320.

_____.Conflicts: productive and destructive. *Journal of Social Issues*, 1969, *25*, 7–43.

Fiedler, F. E. A contingency model of leadership effectiveness. In L. Berkowitz (ed.), *Advances in Experimental Social Psychology* Vol. 1. New York: Academic Press, 1964, 149–90.

_____.*A Theory of Leadership Effectiveness*. New York: McGraw-Hill, 1967.

_____.Style or circumstance: the leadership enigma. *Psychology Today*, 1969, *2*, 38–46.

French, J. R. P., and B. H. Raven. The basis of social power. In D. Cartwright (ed.), *Studies in Social Power*. Ann Arbor: University of Michigan, 1959, 150–67.

Friedlander, F. The impact of organizational training laboratories upon the effectiveness and interaction of ongoing groups. *Personnel Psychology*, 1967, *20*, 289–308.

_____. A comparative study of consulting processes and group development. *Journal of Applied Behavioral Science*, 1968, *4*, 377–99.

Gibb, J. R. Defensive communication. *Journal of Communication*, 1961, *11*, 141–48.

Glidewell, J. C. Group emotionality and productivity. Unpublished doctoral dissertation, Department of Psychology, University of Chicago, 1953.

Hall, J. Systems maintenance: gatekeeping and the involvement process. Monroe, Texas: Teleometrics International, 1969.

_____,and M. S. Williams. A comparison of decision-making performances in established and ad hoc groups. *Journal of Personality and Social Psychology*, 1966, *3*, 214–22.

Halle, L. J. Overestimating the power of power. *The New Republic*, June 10, 1967, 15–17.

Harrison, R. Impact of the laboratory on perceptions of others by the experimental group. In C. Argyris, *Interpersonal Competence and Organizational Effectiveness*. Homewood, Ill.: Irwin, 1962.

Hill, W. F. *Learning Through Discussion*. Los Angeles: University of Southern California Press, Youth Studies Center, 1962.

Hoffman, L. R., E. Harburg, and N. R. F. Maier. Differences and disagreement as factors in creative problem solving. *Journal of Abnormal and Social Psychology*, 1962, *64*, 206–14.

Janis, I. L. Group think. *Psychology Today*, 1971, *5*(6) 43–46, 74–76.

Johnson, D. W. *The Social Psychology of Education*. New York: Holt, Rinehart, and Winston, 1970.

_____.Role reversal: a summary and review of the research. *International Journal of Group Tensions*, 1971, *1*, 318–34.

_____. *Reaching Out: Interpersonal Effectiveness and Self-Actualization*. Englewood Cliffs, N. J.: Prentice-Hall, 1972.

_____. *Contemporary Social Psychology*. Philadelphia: J. B. Lippincott, 1973.

_____. Communication and the inducement of cooperative behavior in conflicts: a critical review. *Speech Monographs*, 1974a, *41*, 64—78.

_____. Cooperativeness and social perspective taking. *Journal of Personality and Social Psychology*, 1974, in press.

_____, and R. T. Johnson. Instructional goal structure: cooperative, competitive, or individualistic. *Review of Educational Research*, 1974, *44*.

_____. Learning Together and Alone. Englewood Cliffs, N. J.: Prentice-Hall, 1975.

Johnson, R. T., Jr., Personal communication on inquiry procedures in discovery learning. 1972.

Jones, E. E., and H. B. Gerard. *Foundations of Social Psychology*. New York: John Wiley and Sons, 1967.

Kelly, H. H., and A. J. Stahelski. Social interaction basis of cooperators' and competitors' beliefs about others. *Journal of Personality and Social Psychology*, 1970, *16*, 66—91.

Lakin, M. *Interpersonal Encounter: Theory and Practice in Sensitivity Training*. New York: McGraw-Hill, 1972.

Leiberman, M. A., I. D. Yalom, and M. B. Miles. *Encounter Groups: First Facts*. New York: Basic Books, 1973.

Lewin, K. A Dynamic Theory of Personality. New York: McGraw-Hill, 1935.

_____, T. Dembo, L. Festinger, and P. Sears. Level of aspiration. In J. M. V. Hunt (ed.), *Personality and the Behavior Disorders*. New York: Ronald Press, 1944, 333—78.

_____, Group decisions and social change. In T. M. Newcomb and E. L. Hartly (eds.), *Readings in Social Psychology*. New York: Holt, Rinehart and Winston, 1947.

_____, R. Lippitt, and R. K. White. Patterns of aggressive behavior in experimentally created social climates. *Journal of Social Psychology*, 1939, *10*, 271—99.

Maier, N. R. F. Reasoning in humans. I. on direction. *Journal of Comparative Psychology*, 1930, *10*, 115—43.

_____, and A. R. Solem. The contribution of a discussion leader to the quality of group thinking: the effective use of minority opinions. *Human Relations,* 1952, *5*, 277—88.

Maslow, A. H. *Motivation and Personality*. New York: Harper and Row, 1954.

_____. *Toward a Psychology of Being*. Princeton, N. J.: Van Nostrand, 1962.

McGregor, D. *The Human Side of Enterprise*. New York: McGraw-Hill, 1960.

_____. *The Professional Manager*. New York: McGraw-Hill, 1967.

Morton, R. B. and A. Wright. A critical incidents evaluation of an organizational training laboratory. Working paper, Aerojet General Corporation, 1964.

Nesbitt, P., A. Pond, and W. Allen. *The Survival Book*. New York: Funk and Wagnall, 1959.

Pepitone, A., and G. Reichling. Group cohesiveness and the expression of hostility. *Human Relations*, 1955, *8*, 327—39.

Peters, D. R. Identification and personal change in laboratory training. Unpublished doctoral dissertation, Massachusetts Institute of Technology, 1966.

Report of the National Advisory Commission on Civil Disorders. New York: Bantam, 1968.

Rogers, C. R., and F. J. Roethlisberger. Barriers and gateways to communication. *Harvard Business Review*, July-August, 1952, 28–35.

Rokeach, M. *The Open and Closed Mind*. New York: Basic Books, 1960.

Rutstrum, C. *The New Way of the Wilderness*. New York: Collier, 1973.

Schein, E. H. *Process Consultation*. Reading, Mass.: Addison-Wesley, 1969.

Schutz, W. C. *Firo: A Three Dimensional Theory of Interpersonal Behavior*. New York: Holt, Rinehart and Winston, 1958.

Sherif, M. *In Common Predicament*. Boston: Houghton Mifflin, 1966.

Stein, M. I. *The Creative Individual*. In manuscript, 1968.

Thibaut, J. W., and H. H. Kelly. *The Social Psychology of Groups*. New York: Wiley, 1959.

Torrance, E. P. Group decision-making and disagreement. *Social Forces*, 1957, *35*, 314–18.

Walton, R. *Interpersonal Peacemaking*. Reading, Mass.: Addison-Wesley, 1969.

Watson, G., and D. W. Johnson. *Social Psychology: Issues and Insights*, 2nd ed. Philadelphia: Lippincott, 1972.

Wright, M. E. The influence of frustration upon social relations of young children. *Character and Personality*, 1943, *12*, 111–22.

Zenger, J. P. As cited in D. G. Lake, M. R. Ritvo, and G. M. St. L. O'Brien, Applying behavioral science: current projects. *Journal of Applied Behavioral Science*, 1969, *5*, 385–85.